Shojo Beat

OTOMEN

STORY AND ART BY AYA KANNO

VAMPIRE KNIGHT

STORY AND ART BY MATSURI HINO

Natsume's BOOK of FRIENDS

STORY AND ART BY YUKI MIDORIKAWA

Want to see more of what you're looking for?

Let your voice be heard!

shojobeat.com/mangasurvey

Help us give you more manga from the heart!

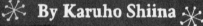

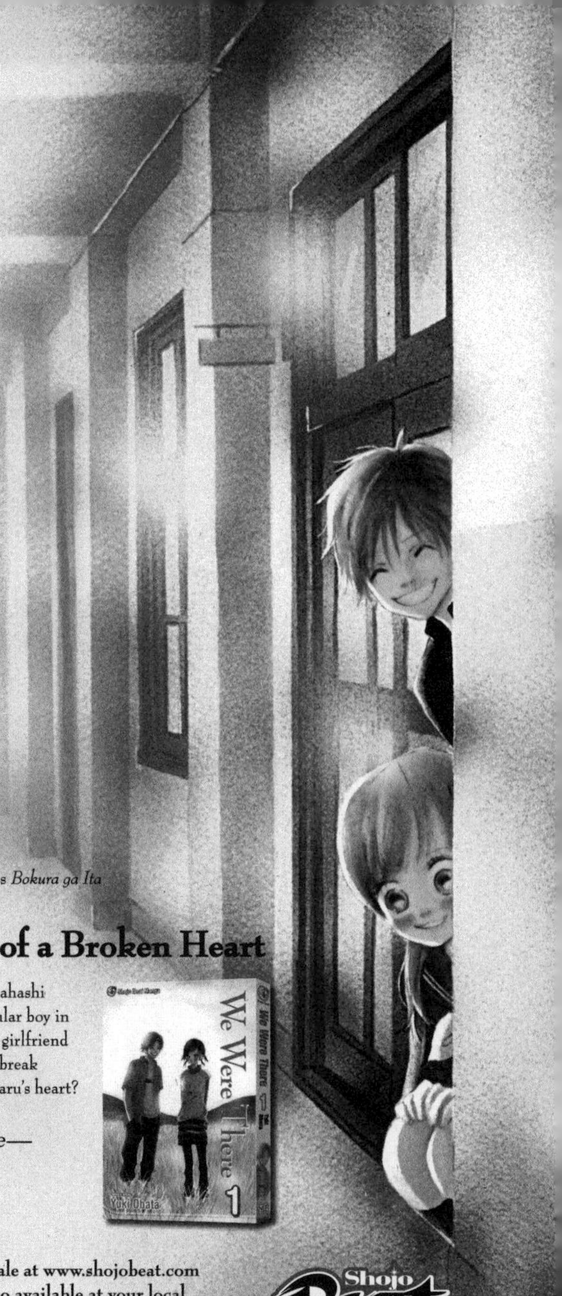

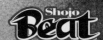

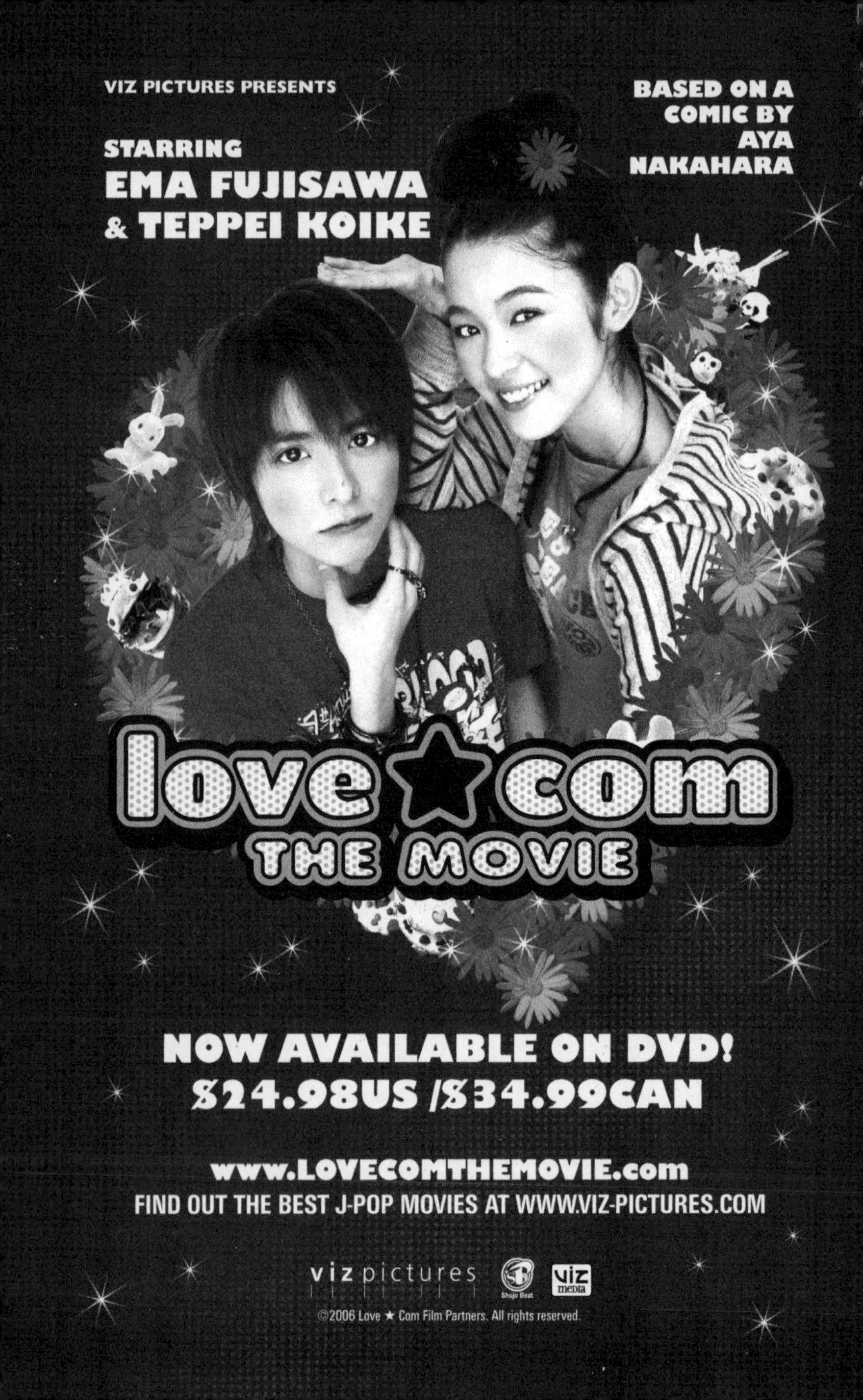
VIZ PICTURES PRESENTS
STARRING
EMA FUJISAWA
& TEPPEI KOIKE
BASED ON A
COMIC BY
AYA
NAKAHARA
love★com
THE MOVIE
NOW AVAILABLE ON DVD!
$24.98US /$34.99CAN
www.LOVECOMTHEMOVIE.com
FIND OUT THE BEST J-POP MOVIES AT WWW.VIZ-PICTURES.COM
viz pictures
Shojo Beat
viz media
©2006 Love ★ Com Film Partners. All rights reserved.

Shojo Beat

honey and clover

Vol. 10

Story & Art by

Chica Umino

honey and clover

Volume 10
CONTENTS

Chapter 61 -- 3

Chapter 62 -------------------------------------- 27

Chapter 63 ------------------------------------- 48

Chapter 64 ------------------------------------- 76

Umino and Her Fun Friends ------ 109

Birds in the Sky --------------------------- 115

Mini Bonus Episode:
Valentine's Day Memory ----------- 137

Bonus Episode ------------------------------ 147

Opera of the Stars --------------------- 163

A Little Extra --------------------------- 181

Study Guide ---------------------------- 184

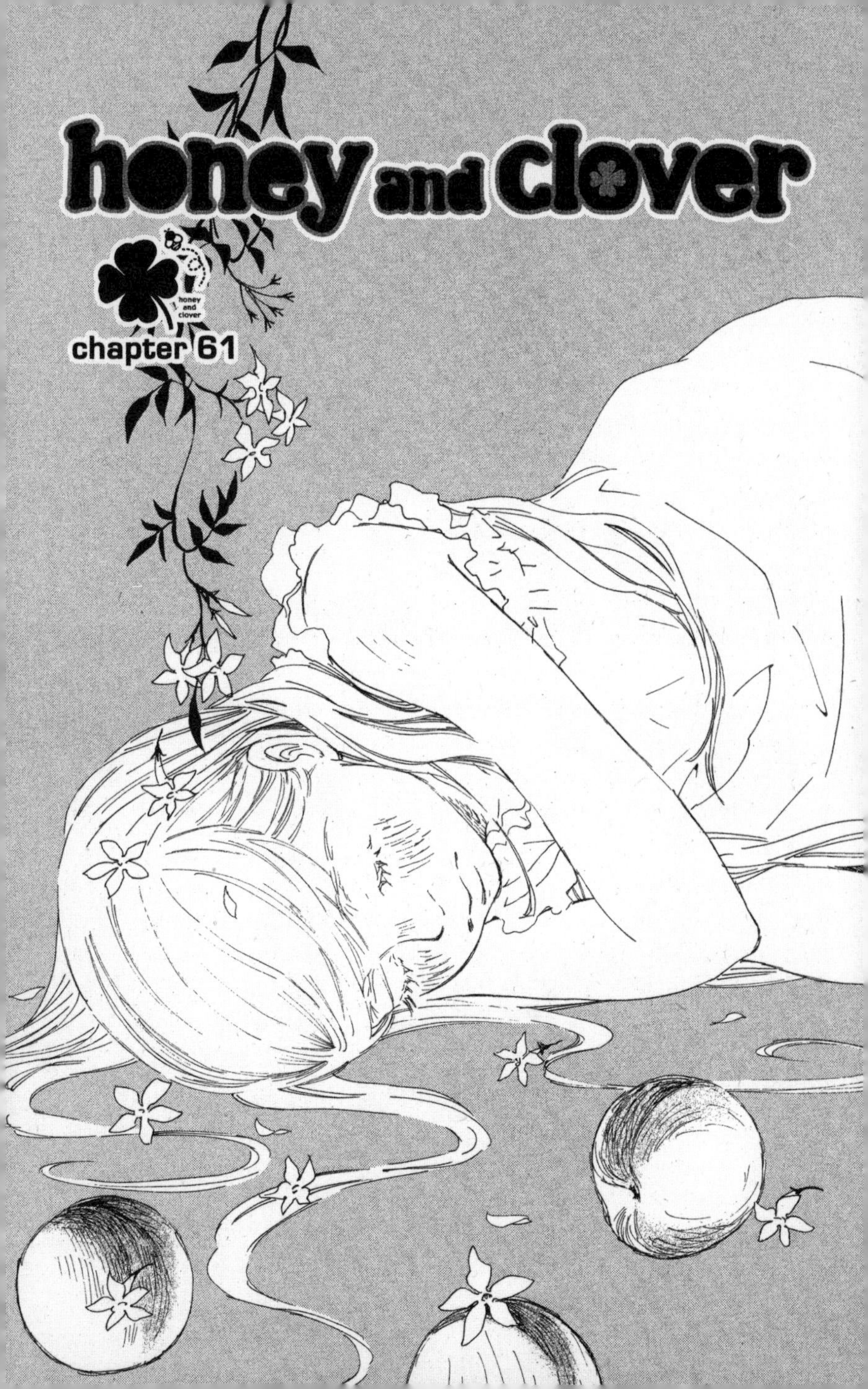
honey and clover
honey and clover
chapter 61

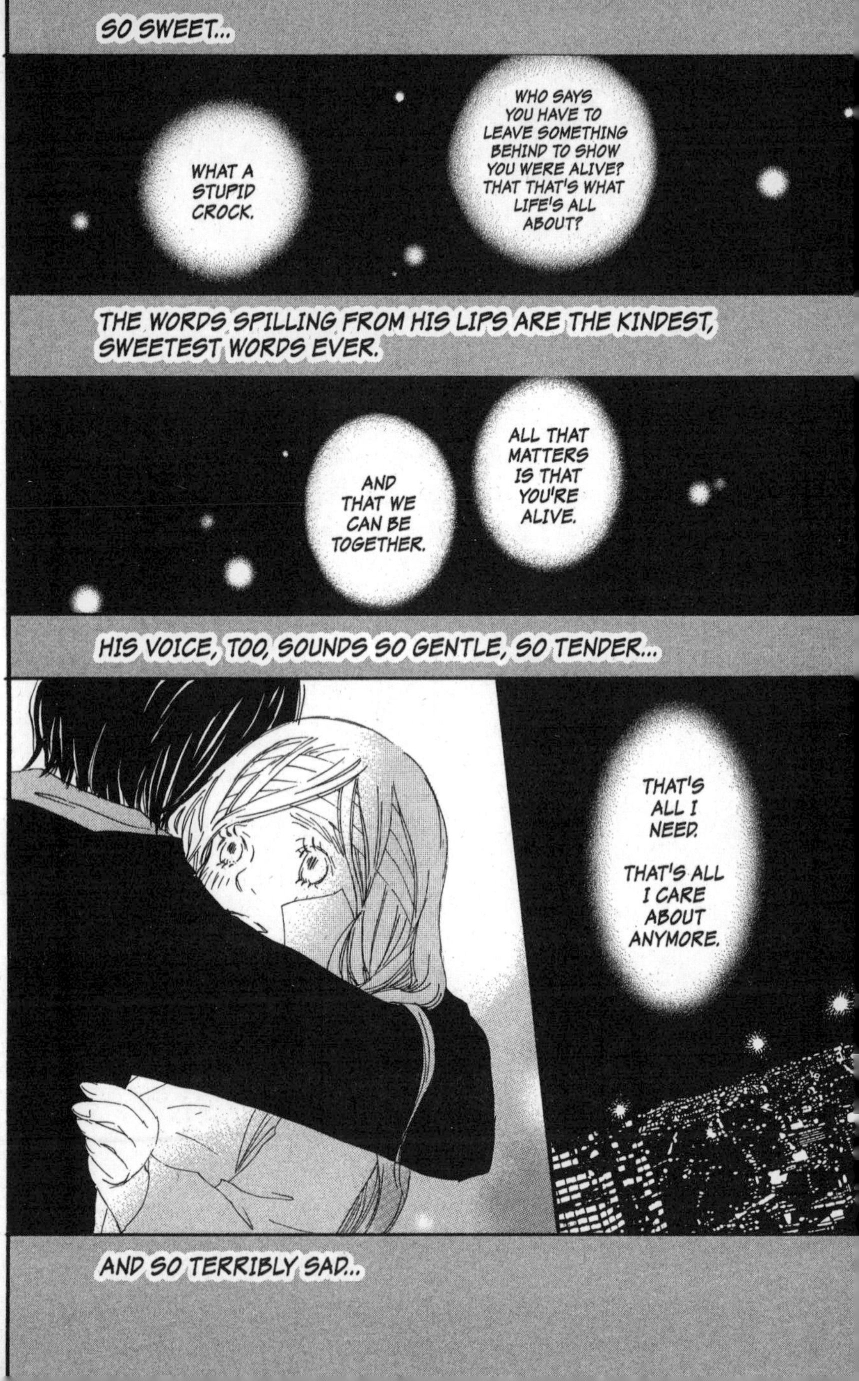
SO SWEET...
WHO SAYS YOU HAVE TO LEAVE SOMETHING BEHIND TO SHOW YOU WERE ALIVE? THAT THAT'S WHAT LIFE'S ALL ABOUT?
WHAT A STUPID CROCK.
THE WORDS SPILLING FROM HIS LIPS ARE THE KINDEST, SWEETEST WORDS EVER.
ALL THAT MATTERS IS THAT YOU'RE ALIVE.
AND THAT WE CAN BE TOGETHER.
HIS VOICE, TOO, SOUNDS SO GENTLE, SO TENDER...
THAT'S ALL I NEED.
THAT'S ALL I CARE ABOUT ANYMORE.
AND SO TERRIBLY SAD...

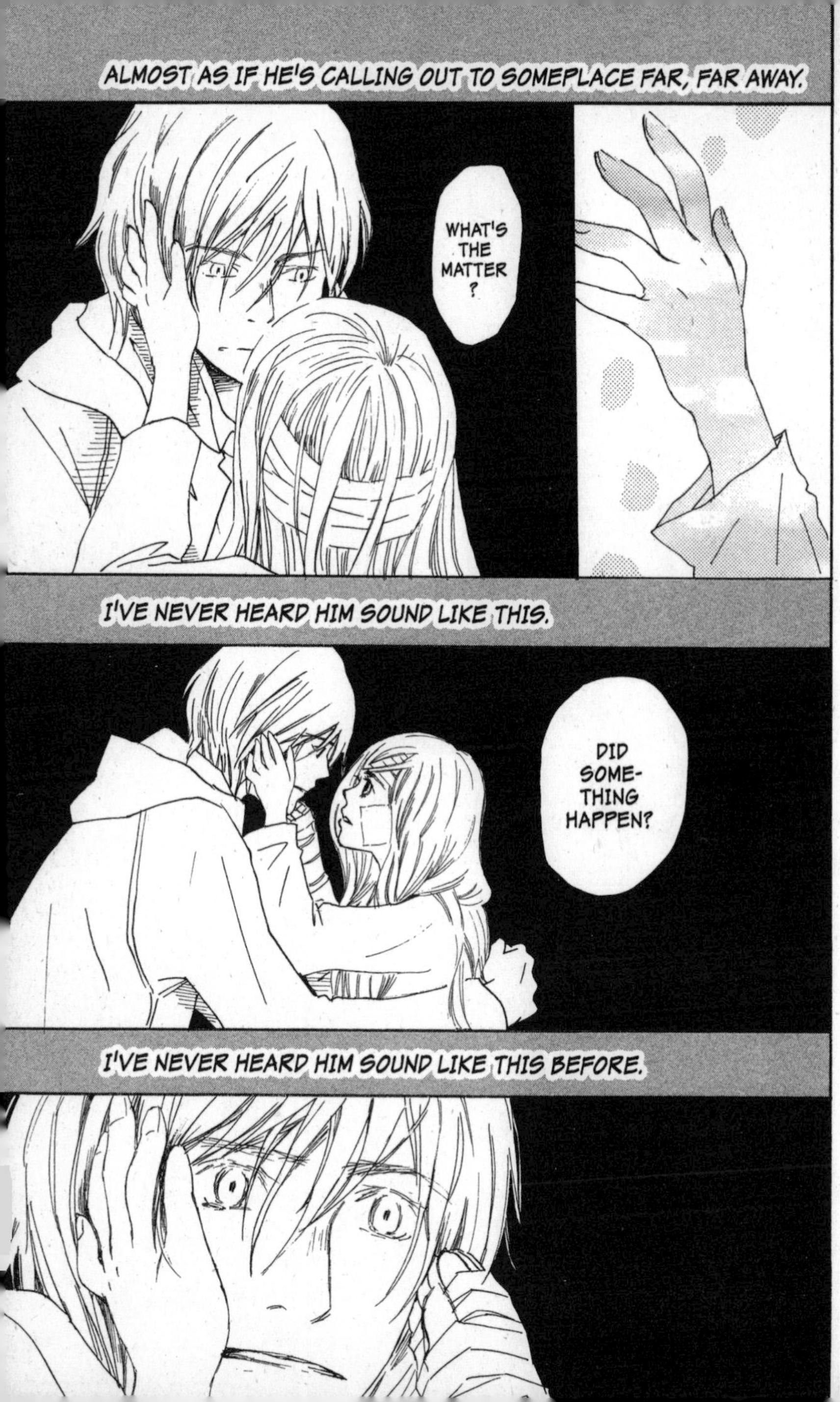
ALMOST AS IF HE'S CALLING OUT TO SOMEPLACE FAR, FAR AWAY.
WHAT'S THE MATTER?
I'VE NEVER HEARD HIM SOUND LIKE THIS.
DID SOMETHING HAPPEN?
I'VE NEVER HEARD HIM SOUND LIKE THIS BEFORE.

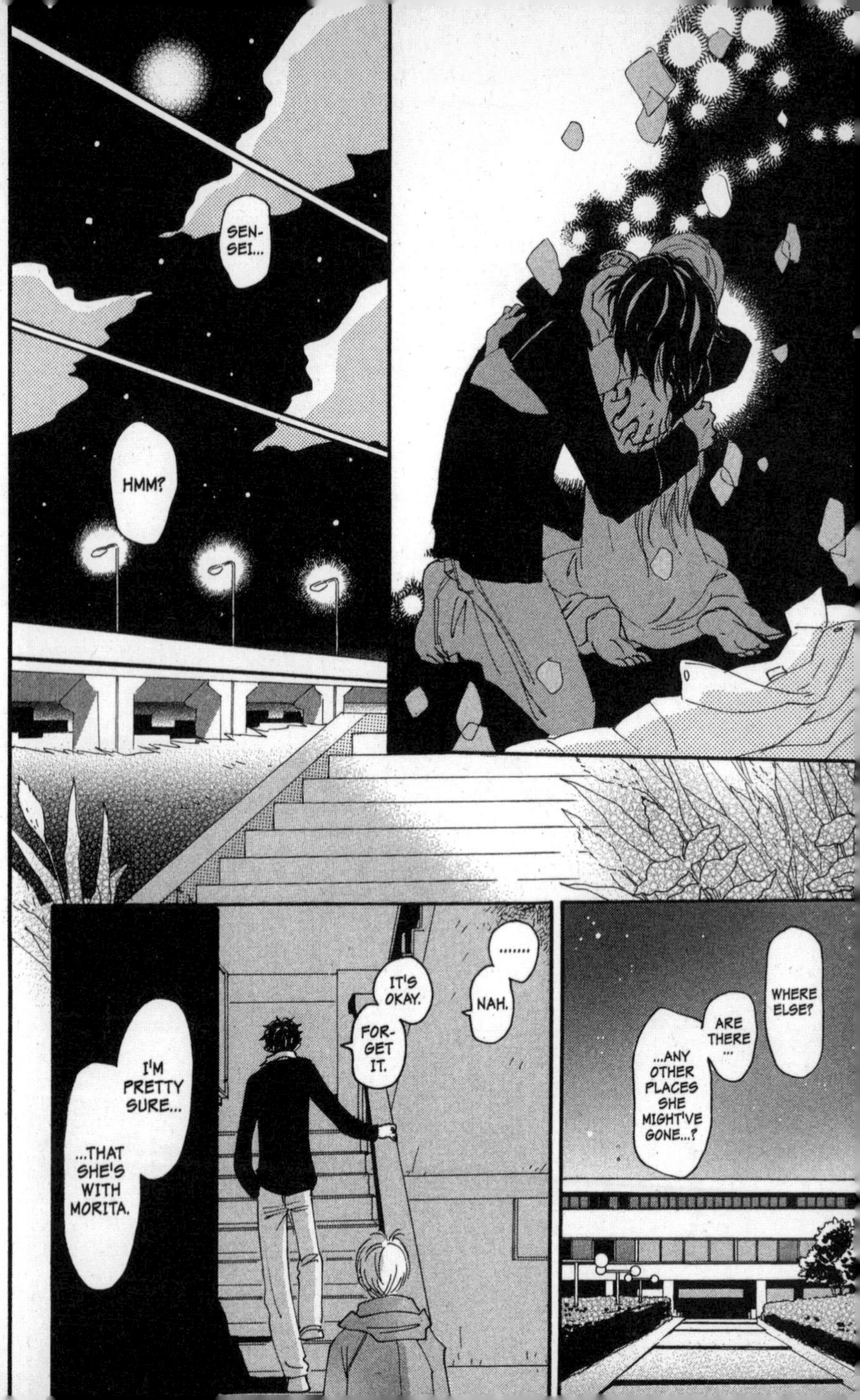
SEN-SEI...
HMM?
WHERE ELSE?
ARE THERE ...
...ANY OTHER PLACES SHE MIGHT'VE GONE...?
....
NAH.
IT'S OKAY.
FOR-GET IT.
I'M PRETTY SURE...
...THAT SHE'S WITH MORITA.

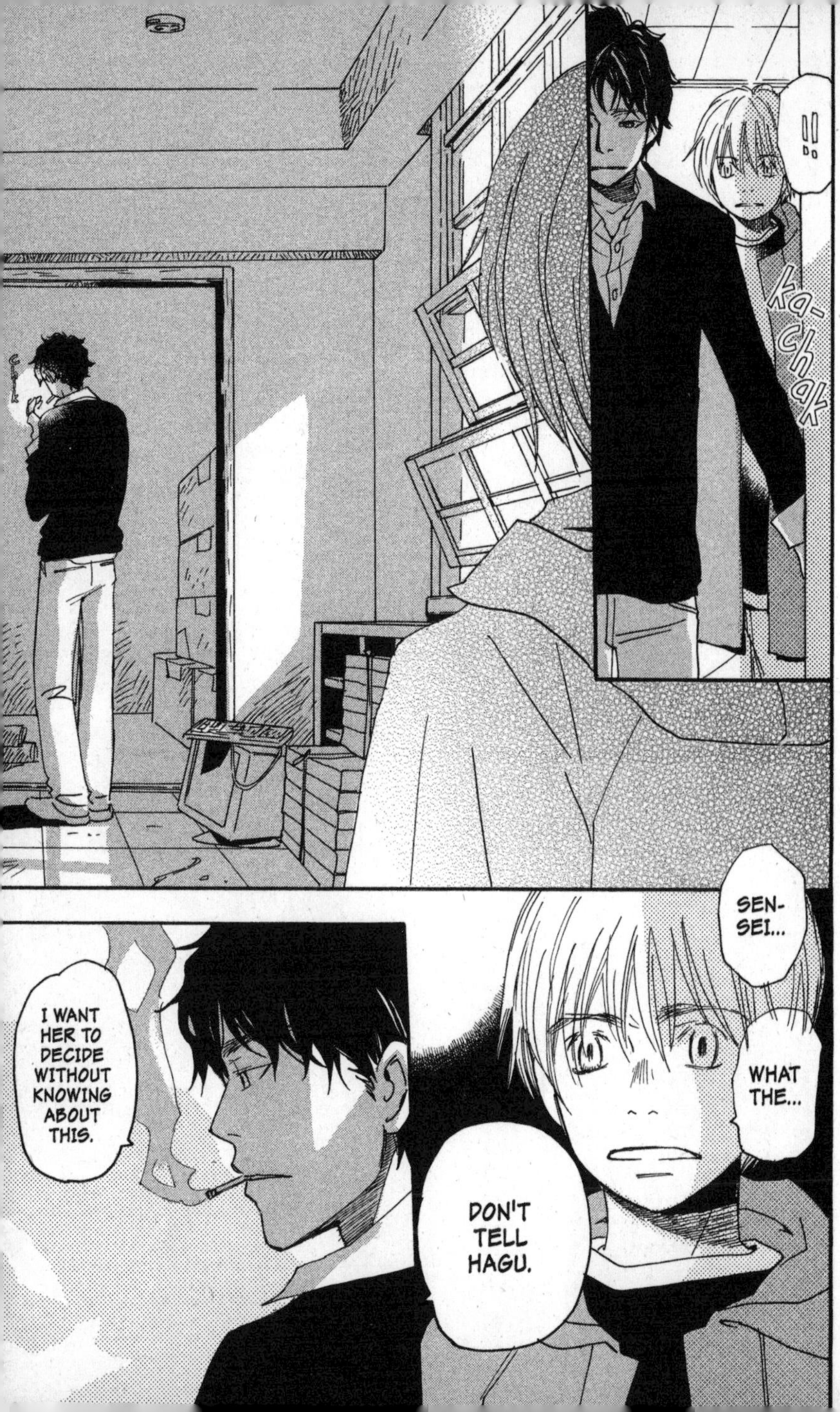
!!
ka-chak
SEN-SEI...
WHAT THE...
DON'T TELL HAGU.
I WANT HER TO DECIDE WITHOUT KNOWING ABOUT THIS.

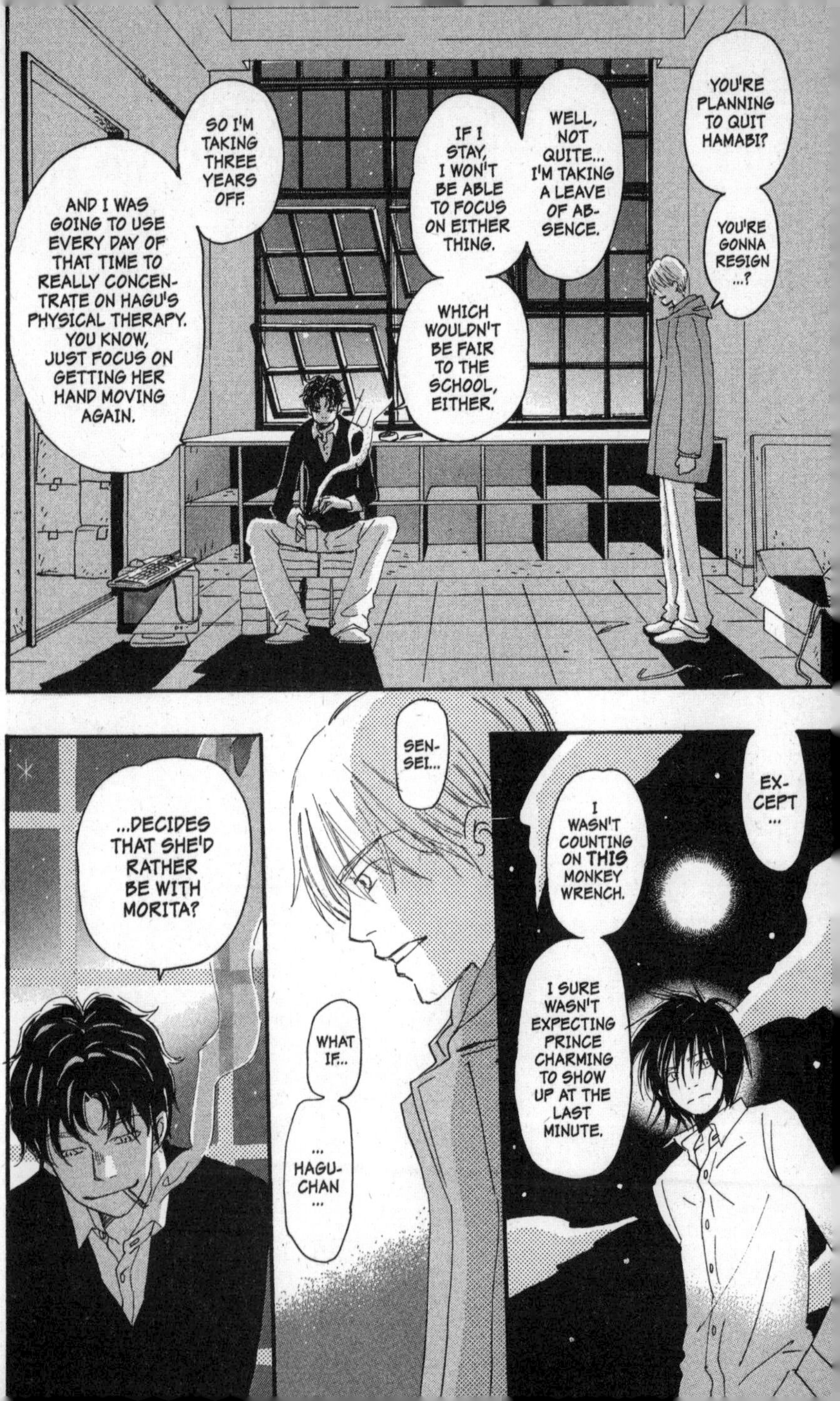
YOU'RE PLANNING TO QUIT HAMABI?
YOU'RE GONNA RESIGN ...?
WELL, NOT QUITE... I'M TAKING A LEAVE OF ABSENCE.
IF I STAY, I WON'T BE ABLE TO FOCUS ON EITHER THING.
WHICH WOULDN'T BE FAIR TO THE SCHOOL, EITHER.
SO I'M TAKING THREE YEARS OFF.
AND I WAS GOING TO USE EVERY DAY OF THAT TIME TO REALLY CONCENTRATE ON HAGU'S PHYSICAL THERAPY. YOU KNOW, JUST FOCUS ON GETTING HER HAND MOVING AGAIN.
EX-CEPT ...
I WASN'T COUNTING ON THIS MONKEY WRENCH.
I SURE WASN'T EXPECTING PRINCE CHARMING TO SHOW UP AT THE LAST MINUTE.
SEN-SEI...
WHAT IF...
... HAGU-CHAN ...
...DECIDES THAT SHE'D RATHER BE WITH MORITA?

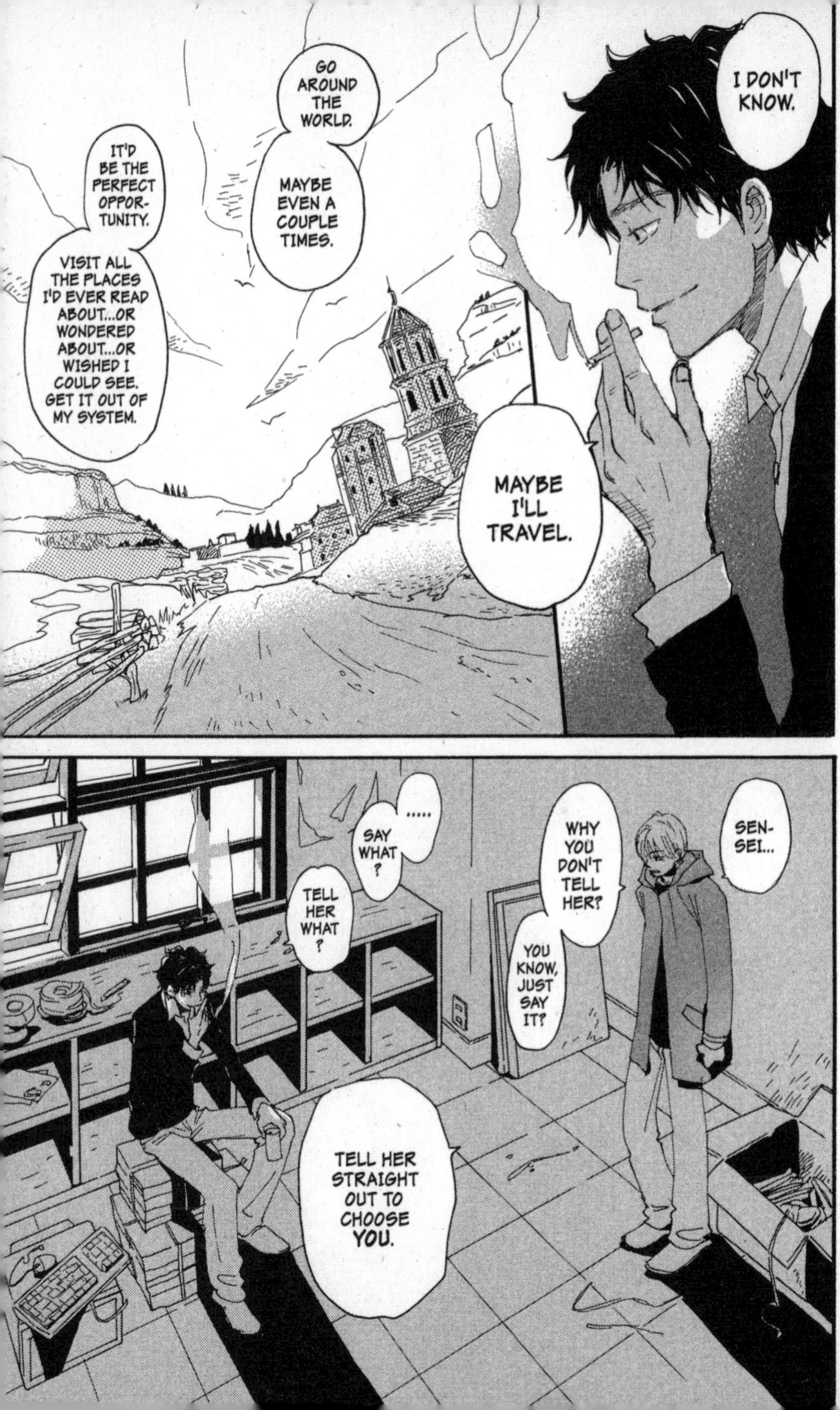
I DON'T KNOW.
MAYBE I'LL TRAVEL.
GO AROUND THE WORLD.
MAYBE EVEN A COUPLE TIMES.
IT'D BE THE PERFECT OPPORTUNITY.
VISIT ALL THE PLACES I'D EVER READ ABOUT...OR WONDERED ABOUT...OR WISHED I COULD SEE. GET IT OUT OF MY SYSTEM.
SEN-SEI...
WHY YOU DON'T TELL HER?
YOU KNOW, JUST SAY IT?
.....
SAY WHAT?
TELL HER WHAT?
TELL HER STRAIGHT OUT TO CHOOSE YOU.

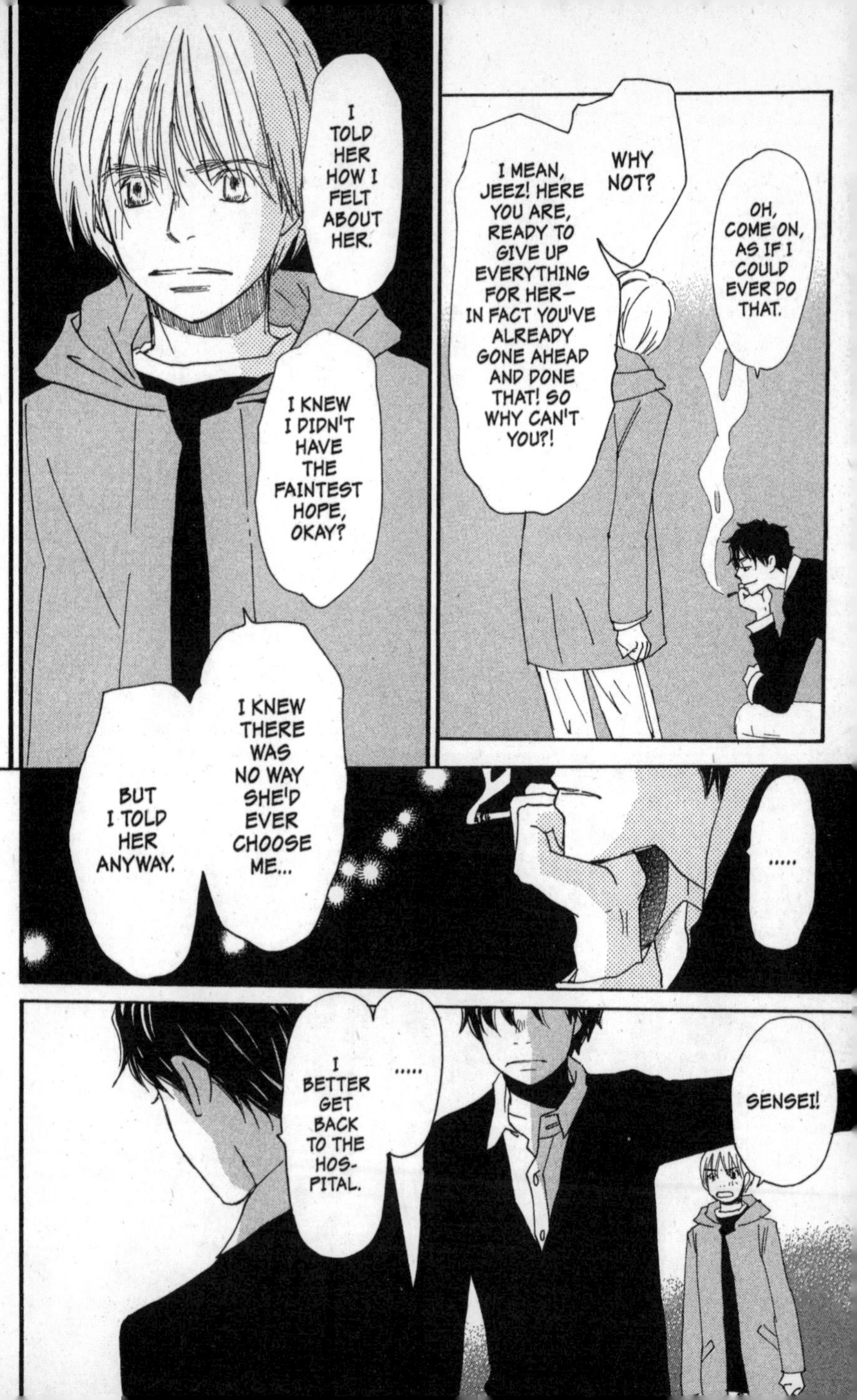

OH, COME ON, AS IF I COULD EVER DO THAT.
WHY NOT?
I MEAN, JEEZ! HERE YOU ARE, READY TO GIVE UP EVERYTHING FOR HER— IN FACT YOU'VE ALREADY GONE AHEAD AND DONE THAT! SO WHY CAN'T YOU?!
I TOLD HER HOW I FELT ABOUT HER.
I KNEW I DIDN'T HAVE THE FAINTEST HOPE, OKAY?
.....
I KNEW THERE WAS NO WAY SHE'D EVER CHOOSE ME...
BUT I TOLD HER ANYWAY.
SENSEI!
.....
I BETTER GET BACK TO THE HOS-PITAL.

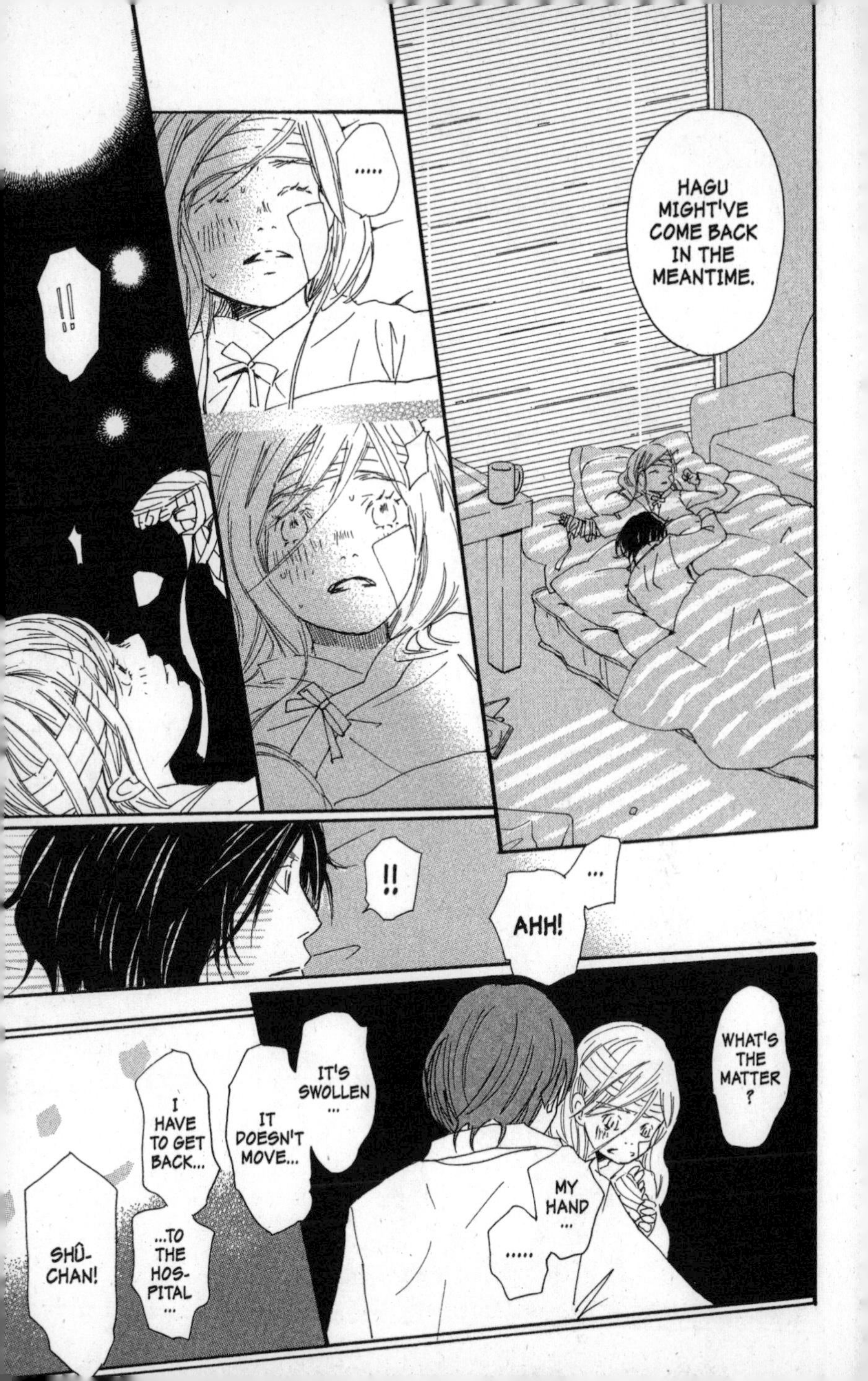
HAGU MIGHT'VE COME BACK IN THE MEANTIME.
.....
!!
...
AHH!
!!
WHAT'S THE MATTER?
MY HAND...
.....
IT'S SWOLLEN...
IT DOESN'T MOVE...
I HAVE TO GET BACK...
...TO THE HOSPITAL...
SHÛ-CHAN!

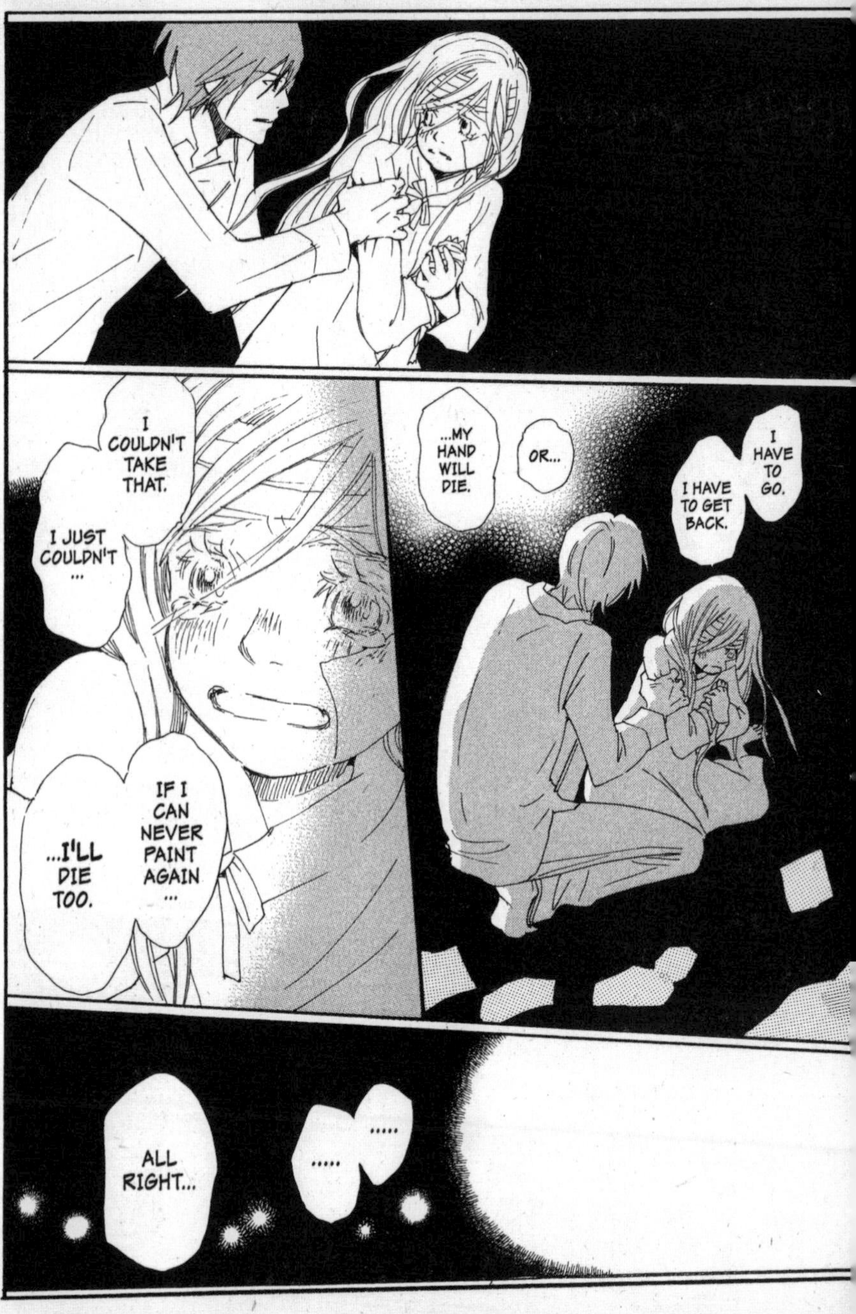
I HAVE TO GO.
I HAVE TO GET BACK.
OR...
...MY HAND WILL DIE.
I COULDN'T TAKE THAT.
I JUST COULDN'T...
IF I CAN NEVER PAINT AGAIN...
...I'LL DIE TOO.
.....
.....
ALL RIGHT...

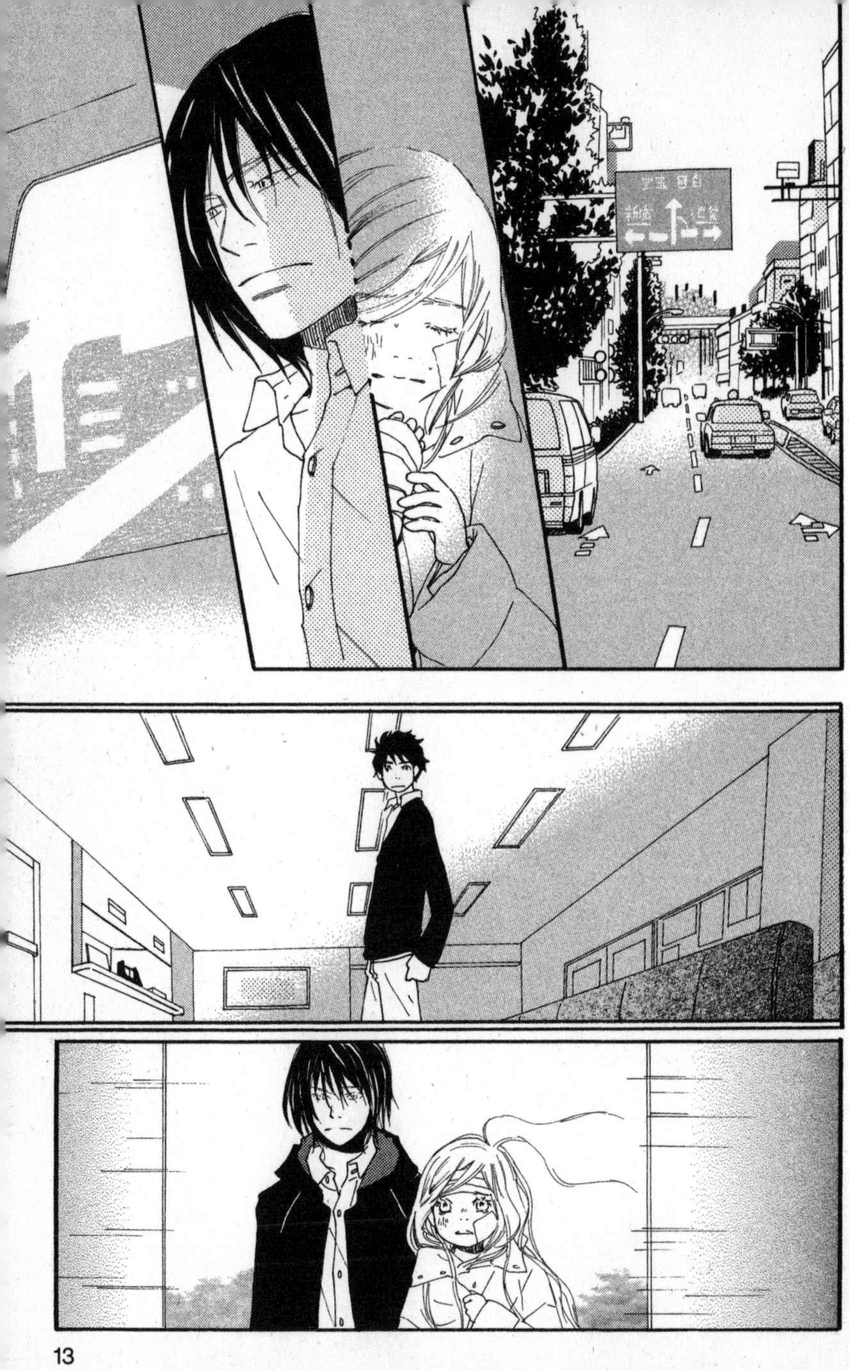

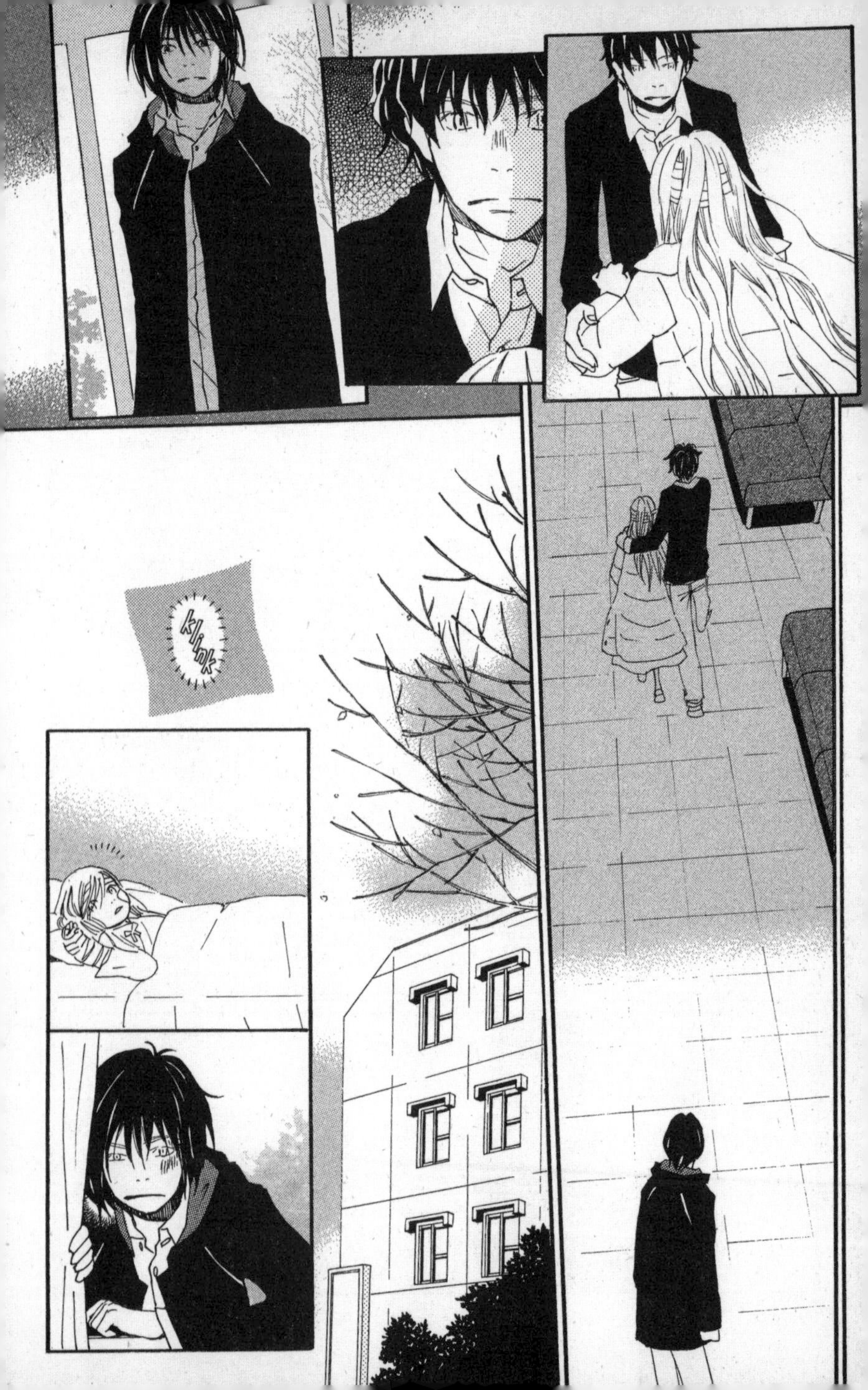
klink

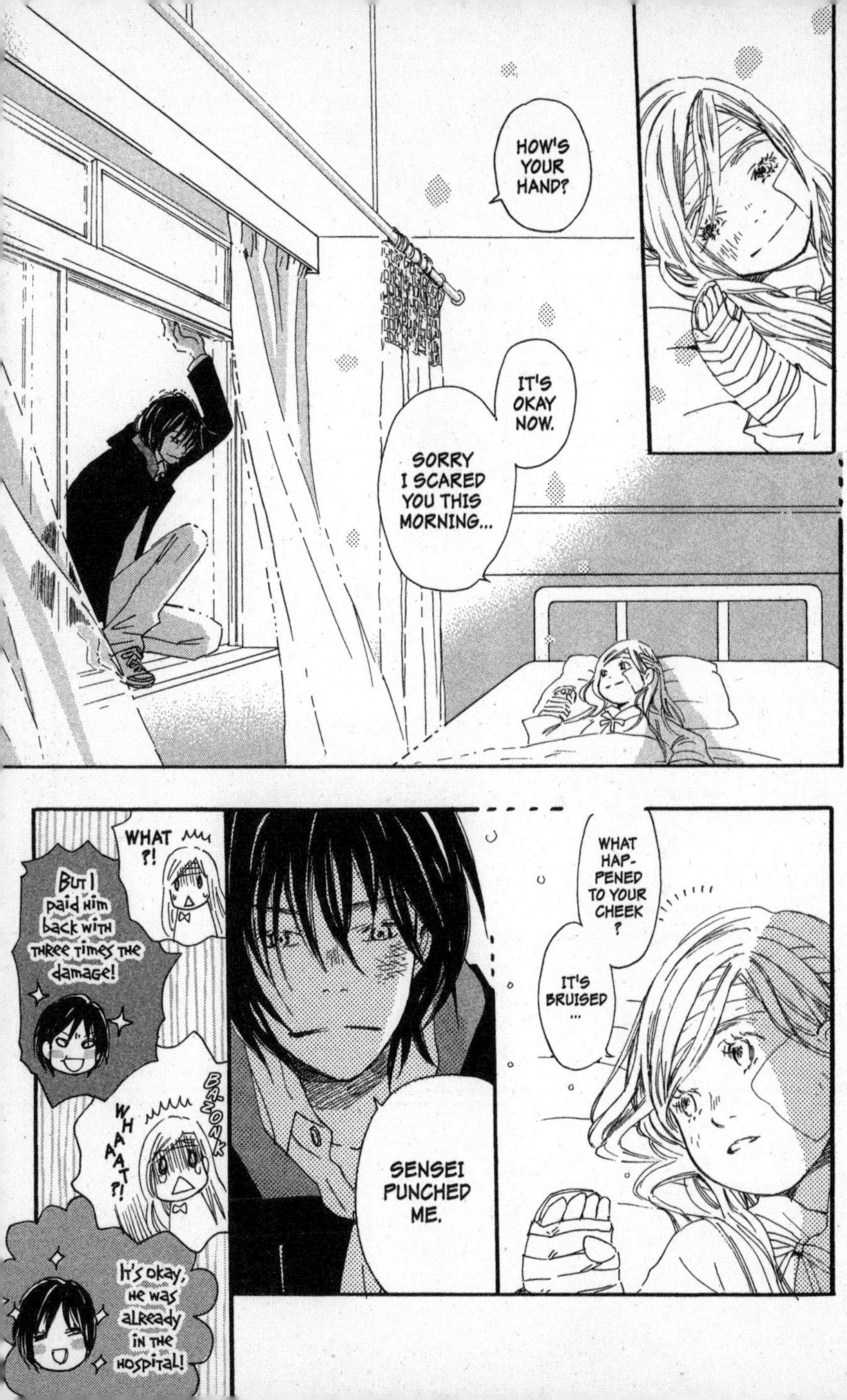
HOW'S YOUR HAND?
IT'S OKAY NOW.
SORRY I SCARED YOU THIS MORNING...
WHAT HAP-PENED TO YOUR CHEEK ?
IT'S BRUISED ...
SENSEI PUNCHED ME.
WHAT ?!
But I paid him back with three times the damage!
BA-ZONK
WHAAAT ?!
It's okay, he was already in the hospital!

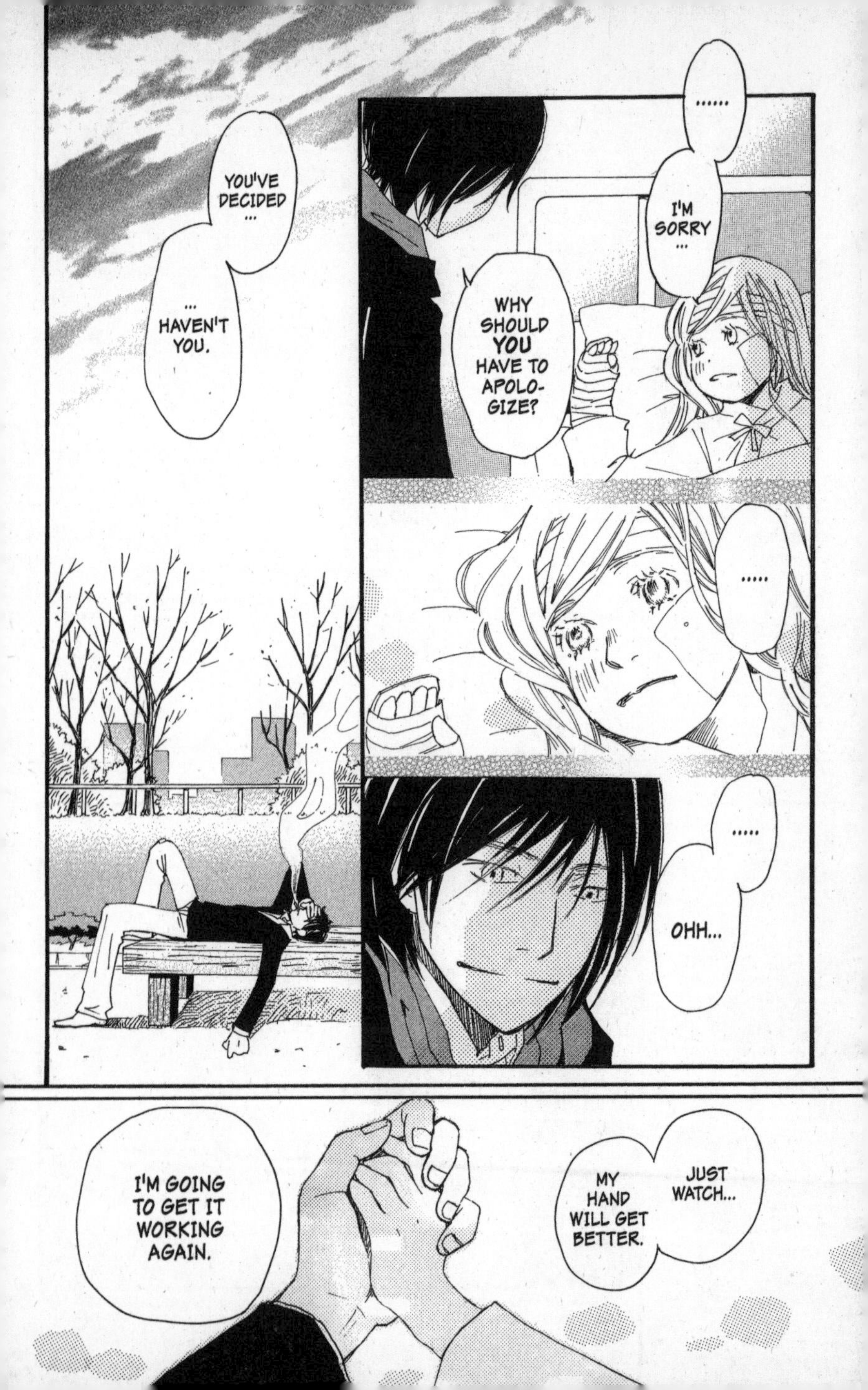
......
I'M SORRY ...
WHY SHOULD YOU HAVE TO APOLOGIZE?
......
......
OHH...
YOU'VE DECIDED ...
... HAVEN'T YOU.
JUST WATCH... MY HAND WILL GET BETTER.
I'M GOING TO GET IT WORKING AGAIN.

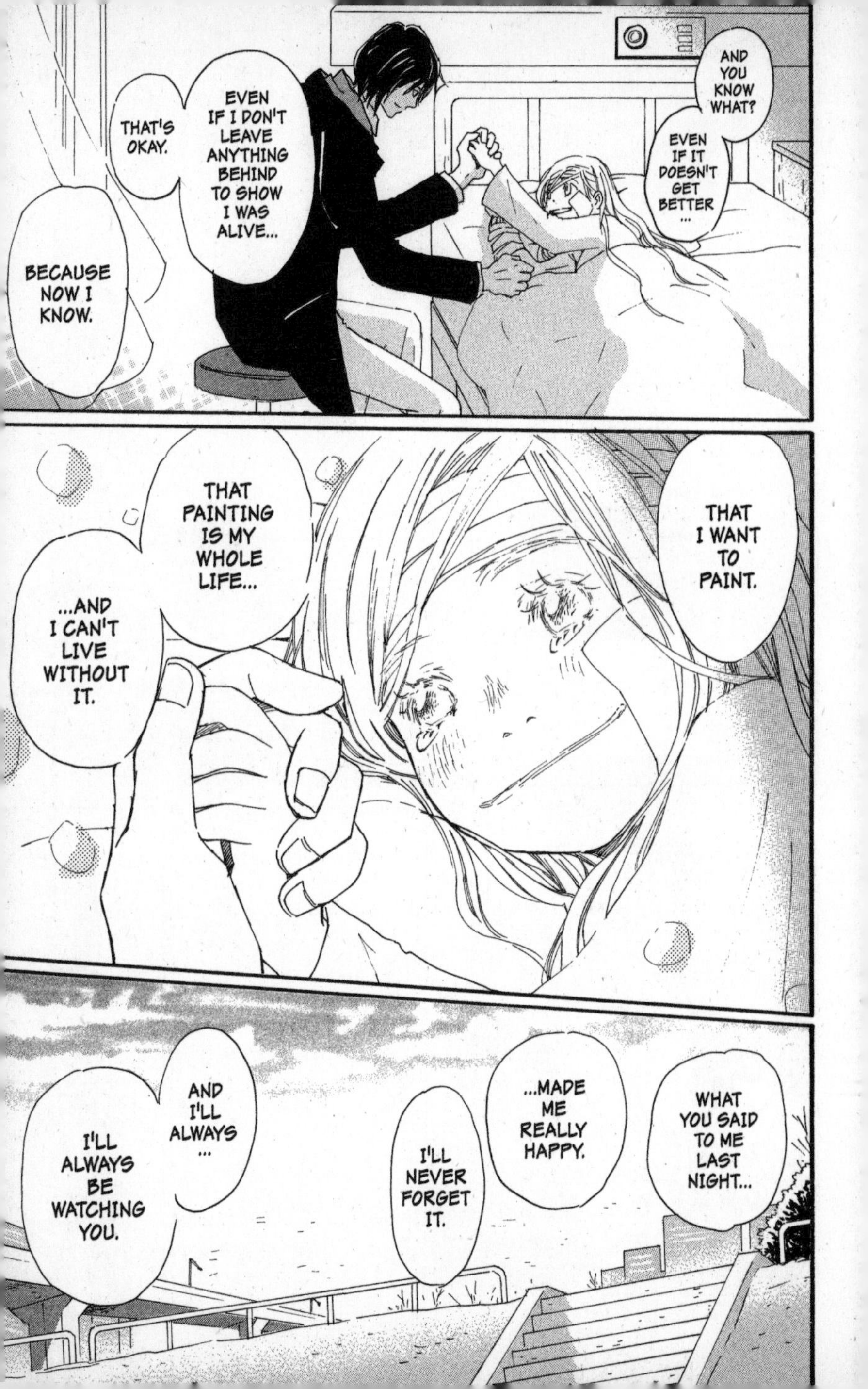
AND YOU KNOW WHAT?
EVEN IF IT DOESN'T GET BETTER ...
EVEN IF I DON'T LEAVE ANYTHING BEHIND TO SHOW I WAS ALIVE...
THAT'S OKAY.
BECAUSE NOW I KNOW.
THAT I WANT TO PAINT.
THAT PAINTING IS MY WHOLE LIFE...
...AND I CAN'T LIVE WITHOUT IT.
WHAT YOU SAID TO ME LAST NIGHT...
...MADE ME REALLY HAPPY.
I'LL NEVER FORGET IT.
AND I'LL ALWAYS ...
I'LL ALWAYS BE WATCHING YOU.

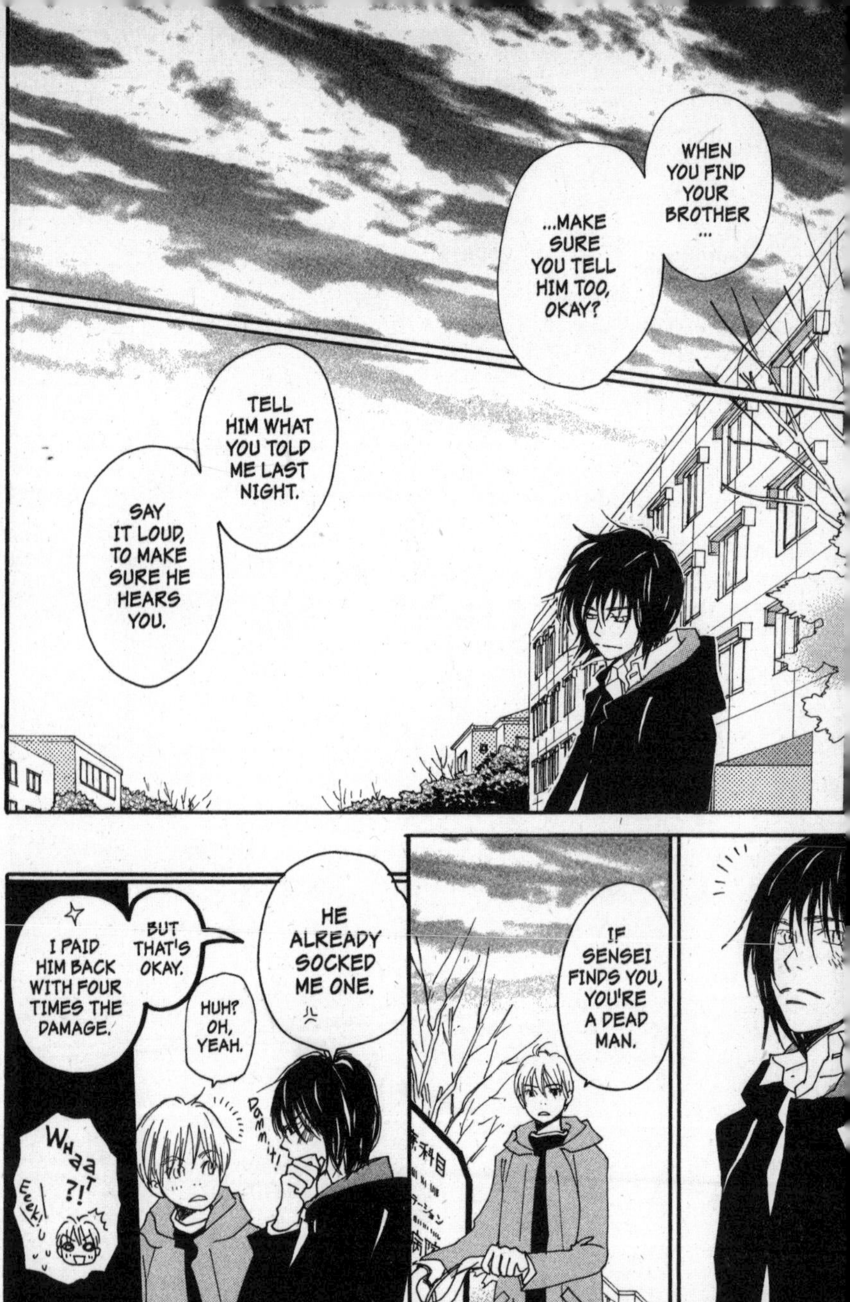
WHEN YOU FIND YOUR BROTHER ...
...MAKE SURE YOU TELL HIM TOO, OKAY?
TELL HIM WHAT YOU TOLD ME LAST NIGHT.
SAY IT LOUD, TO MAKE SURE HE HEARS YOU.
IF SENSEI FINDS YOU, YOU'RE A DEAD MAN.
HE ALREADY SOCKED ME ONE.
Dammit!
HUH? OH, YEAH.
BUT THAT'S OKAY.
I PAID HIM BACK WITH FOUR TIMES THE DAMAGE.
Whaaat?!
Eeek!

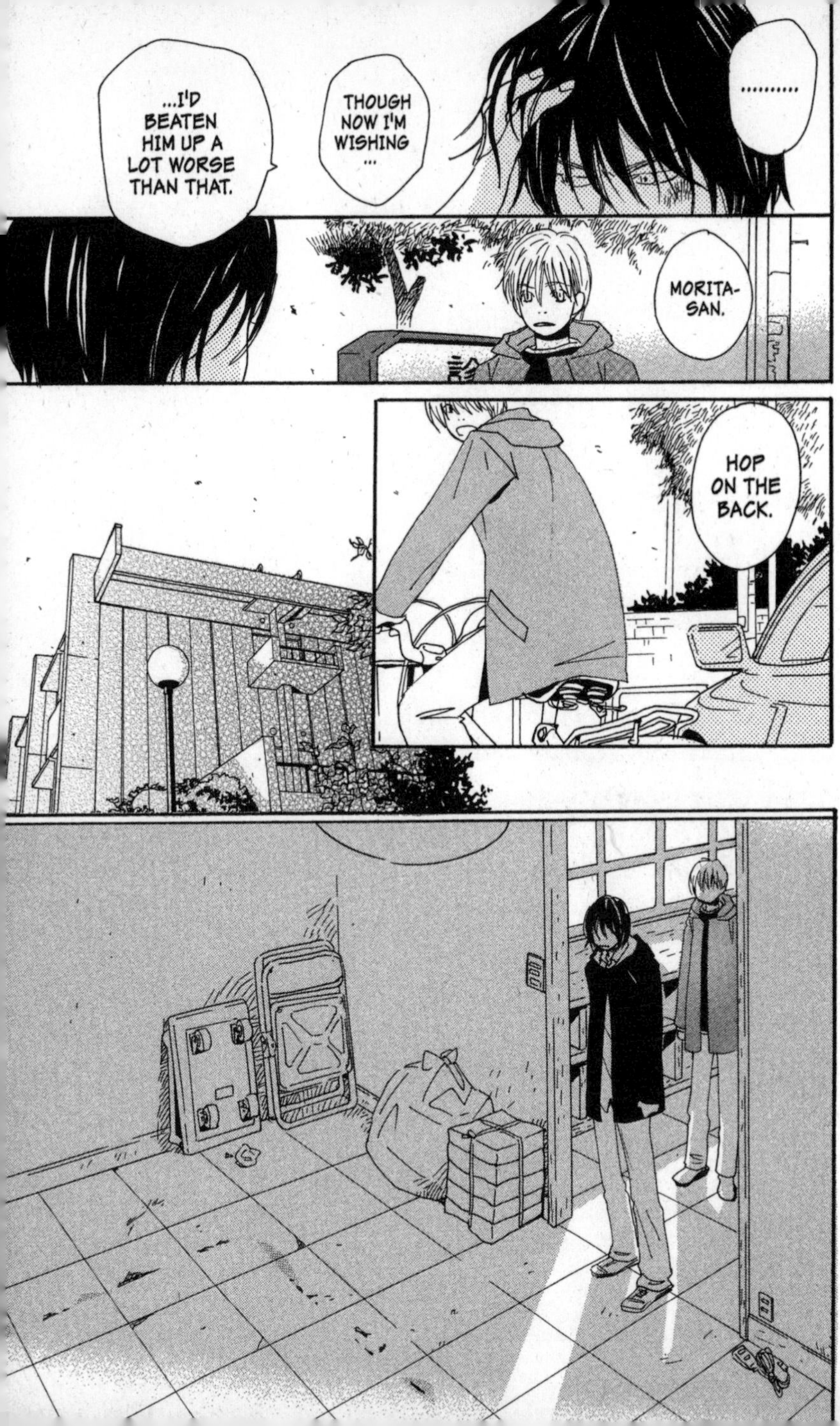
....
THOUGH NOW I'M WISHING ...
...I'D BEATEN HIM UP A LOT WORSE THAN THAT.
MORITA-SAN.
HOP ON THE BACK.

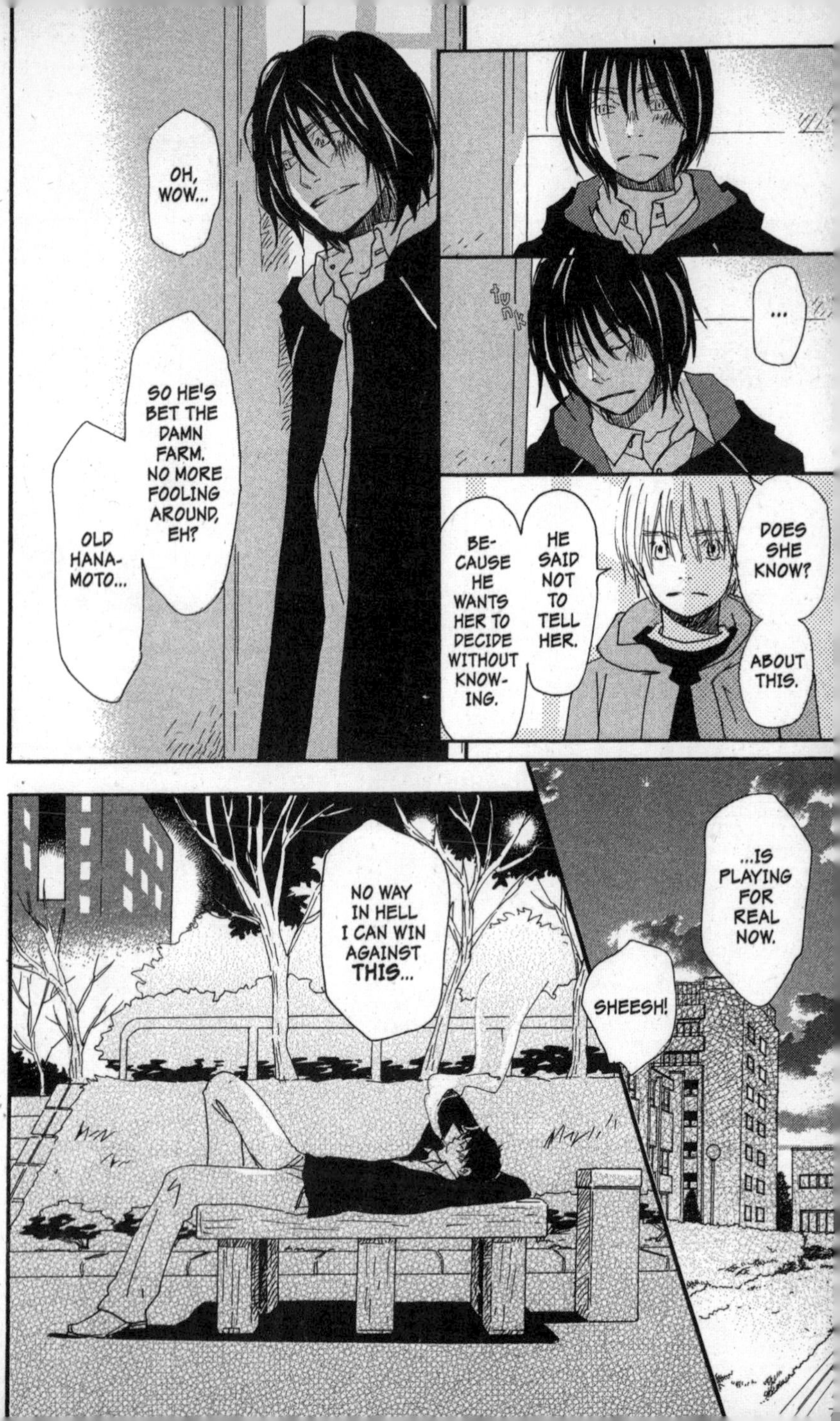
...
tunk
DOES SHE KNOW?
ABOUT THIS.
HE SAID NOT TO TELL HER.
BE-CAUSE HE WANTS HER TO DECIDE WITHOUT KNOW-ING.
OH, WOW...
SO HE'S BET THE DAMN FARM. NO MORE FOOLING AROUND, EH?
OLD HANA-MOTO...
...IS PLAYING FOR REAL NOW.
SHEESH!
NO WAY IN HELL I CAN WIN AGAINST THIS...

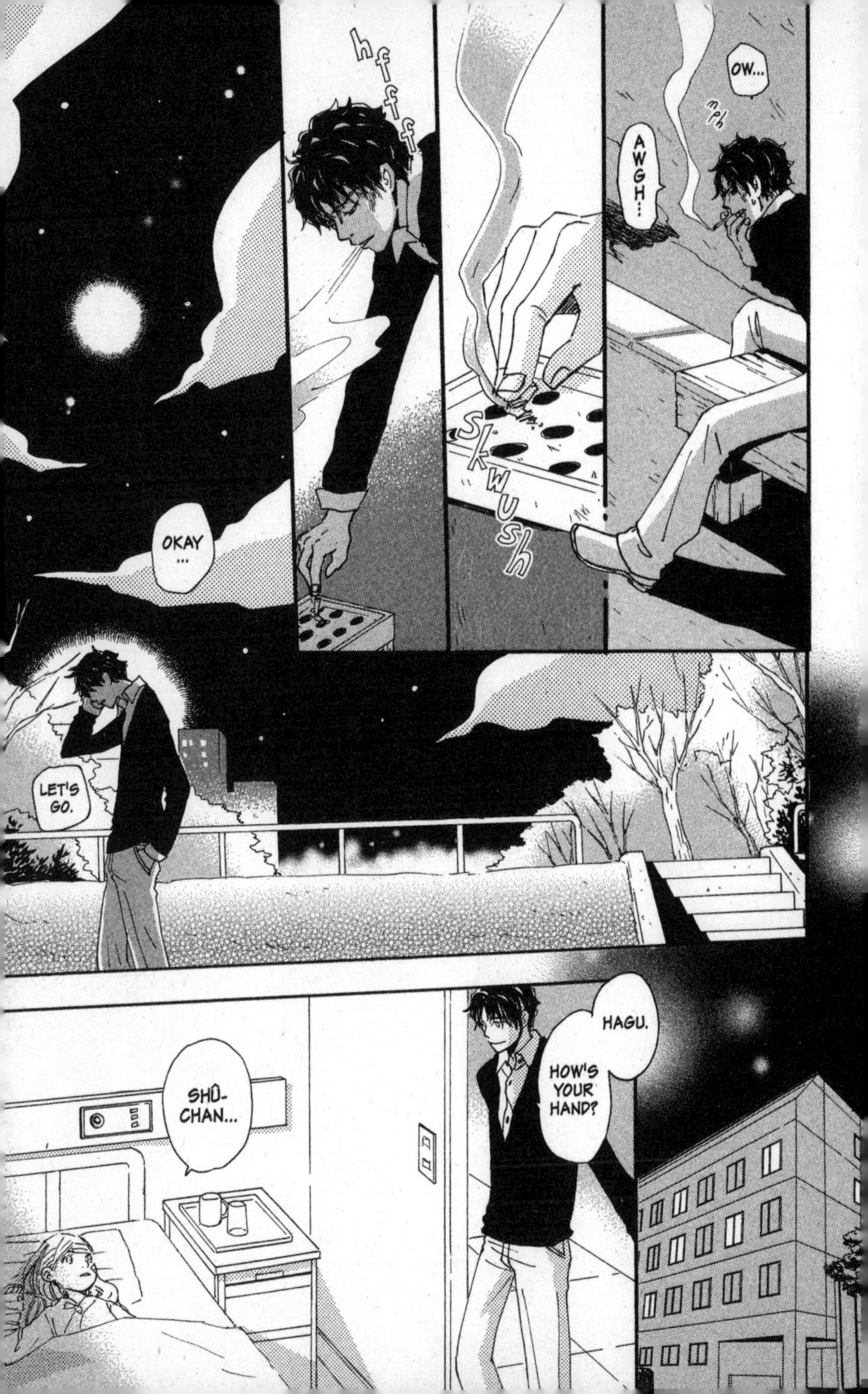
OW...
mph
AWGH...
skwush
hffff
OKAY...
LET'S GO.
HAGU.
HOW'S YOUR HAND?
SHÛ-CHAN...

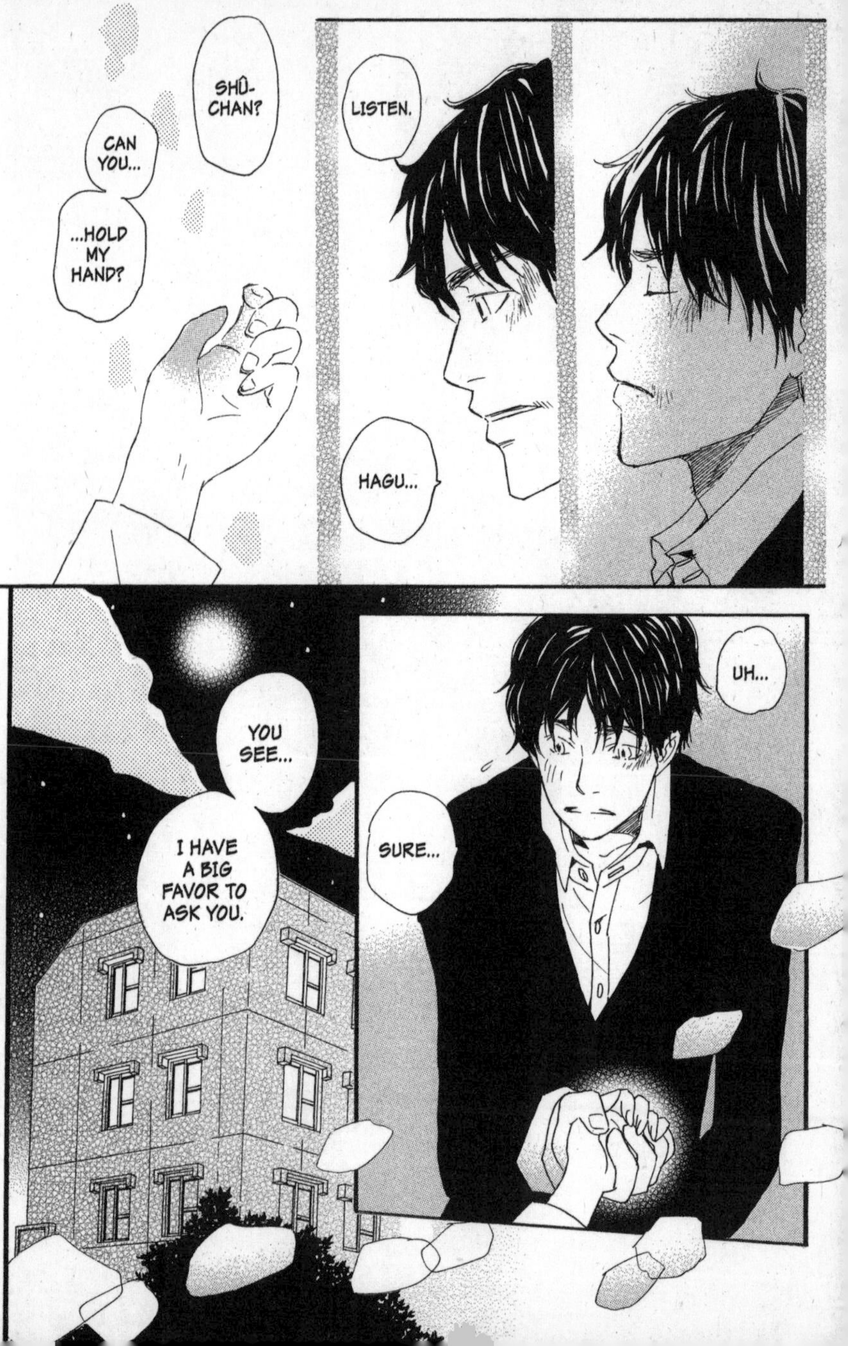
LISTEN.
HAGU...
SHÛ-CHAN?
CAN YOU...
...HOLD MY HAND?
UH...
SURE...
YOU SEE...
I HAVE A BIG FAVOR TO ASK YOU.

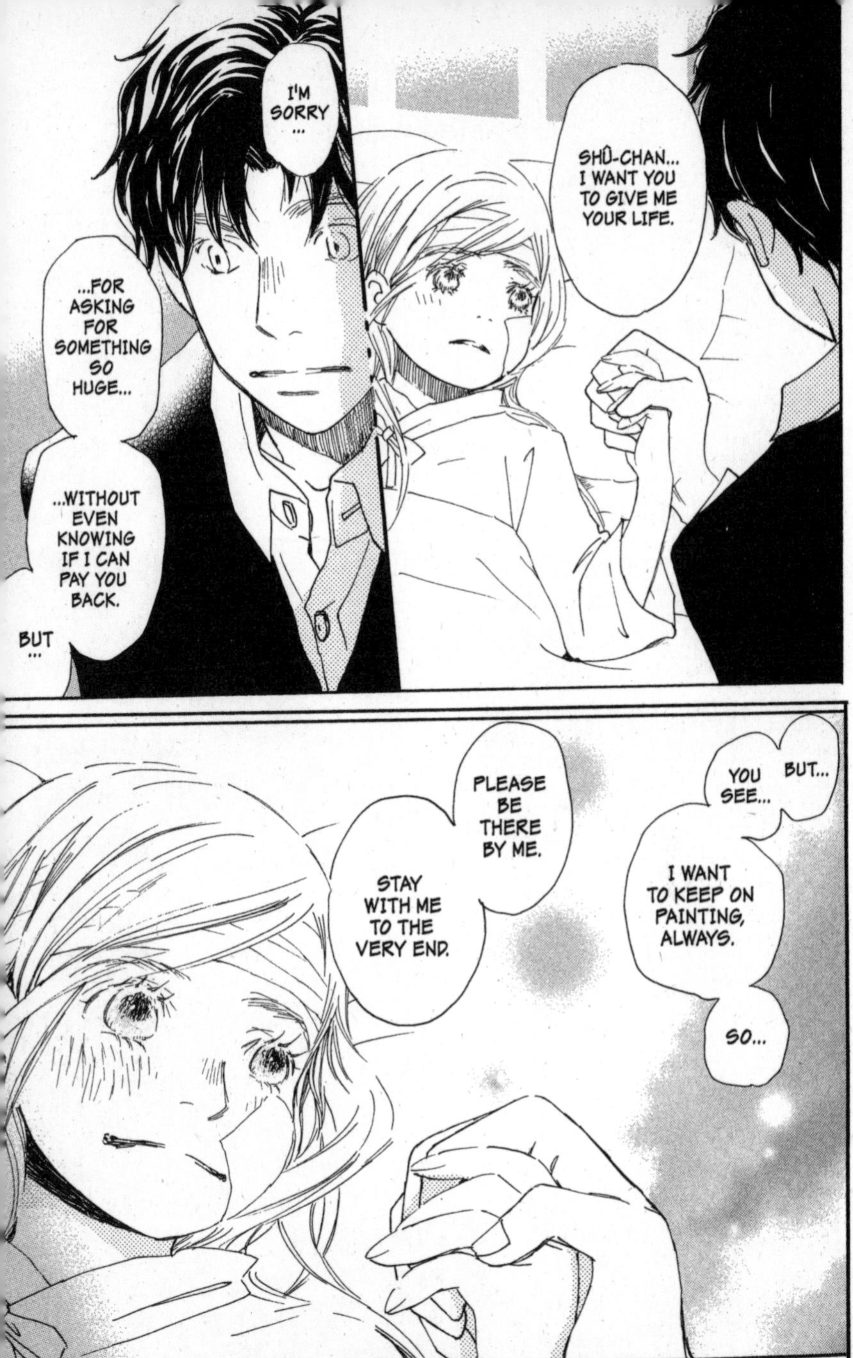
SHÔ-CHAN... I WANT YOU TO GIVE ME YOUR LIFE.
I'M SORRY ...
...FOR ASKING FOR SOMETHING SO HUGE...
...WITHOUT EVEN KNOWING IF I CAN PAY YOU BACK.
BUT ...
BUT...
YOU SEE...
I WANT TO KEEP ON PAINTING, ALWAYS.
SO...
PLEASE BE THERE BY ME.
STAY WITH ME TO THE VERY END.

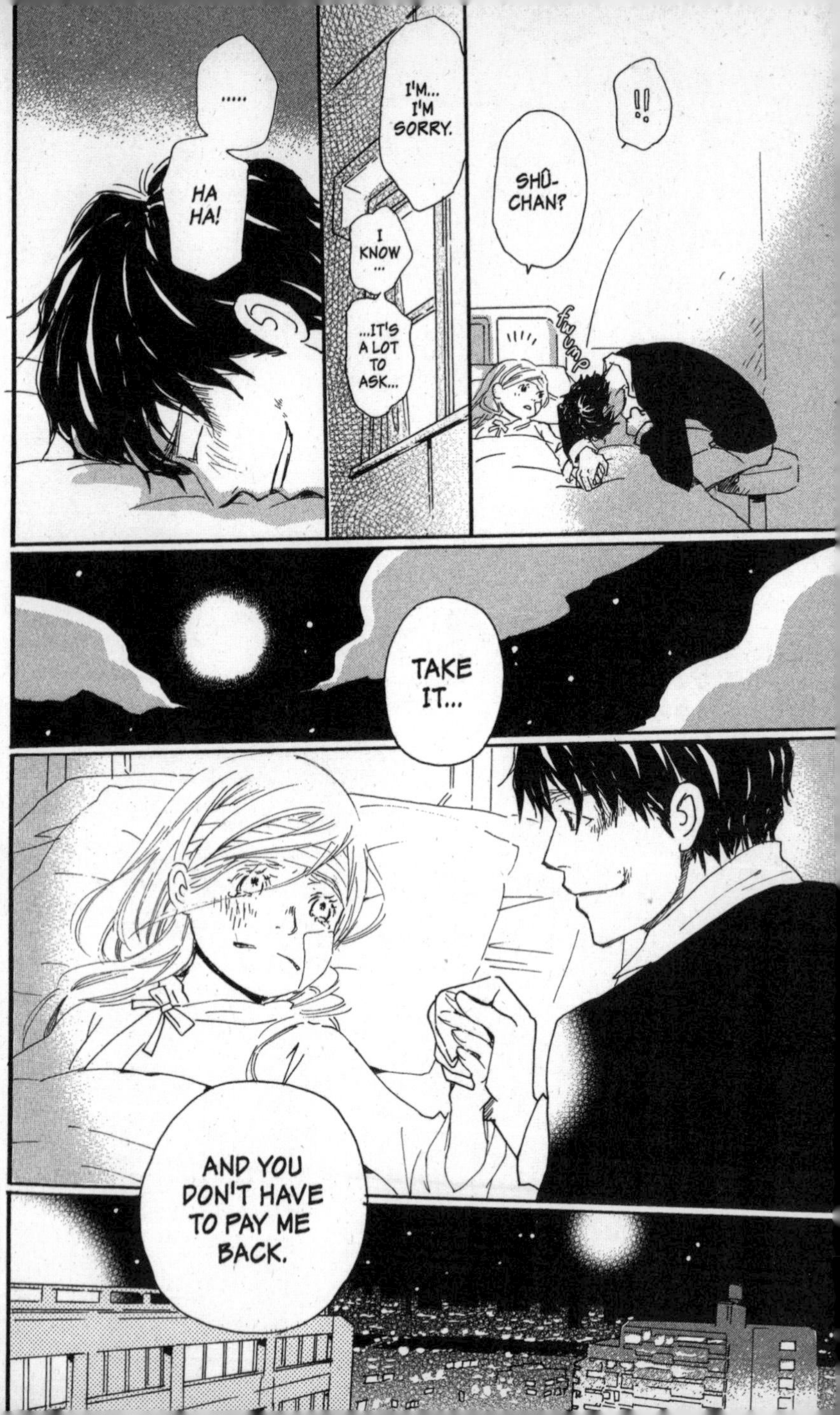
!!
SHŌ-CHAN?
fwump
I'M... I'M SORRY.
I KNOW...
...IT'S A LOT TO ASK...
.....
HA HA!
TAKE IT...
AND YOU DON'T HAVE TO PAY ME BACK.

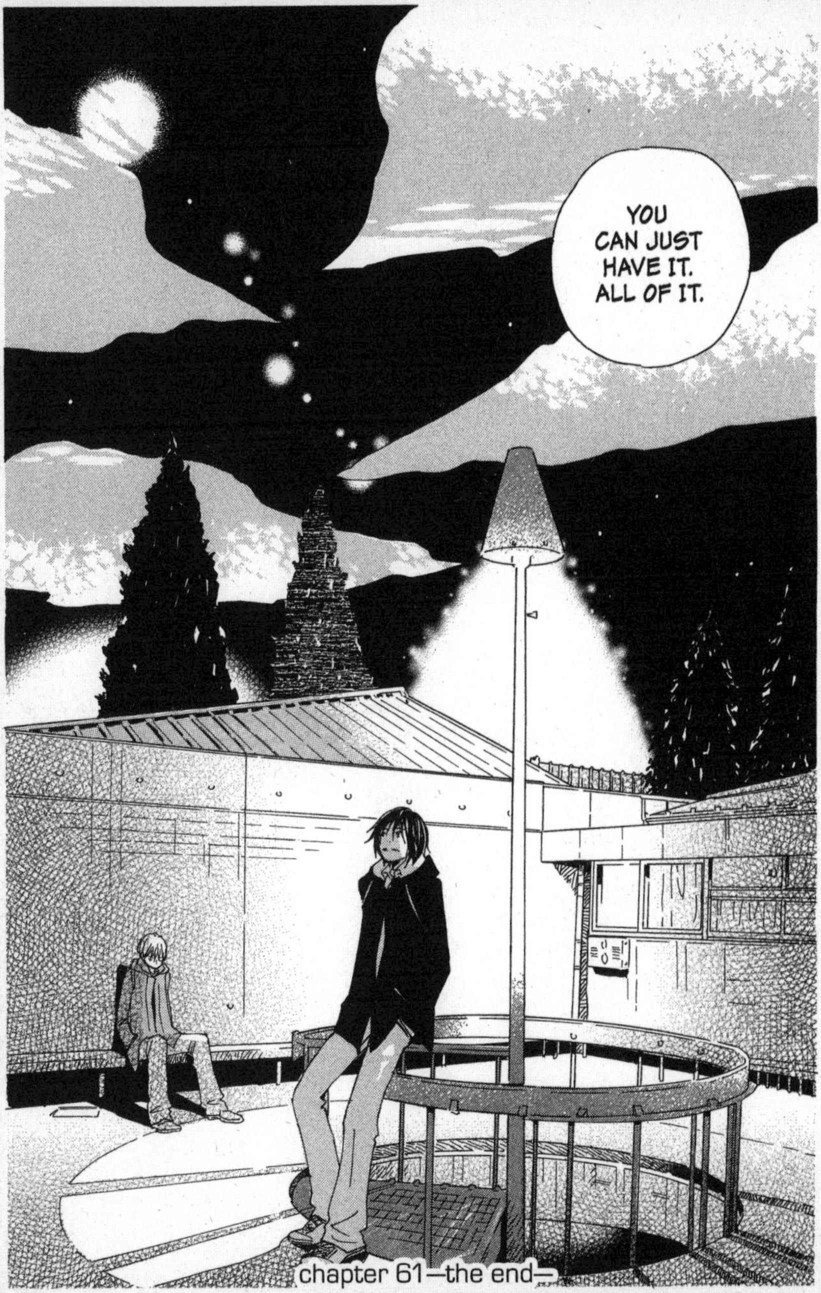
YOU CAN JUST HAVE IT. ALL OF IT.
chapter 61—the end—

Squirrel &
Rabbit ☆

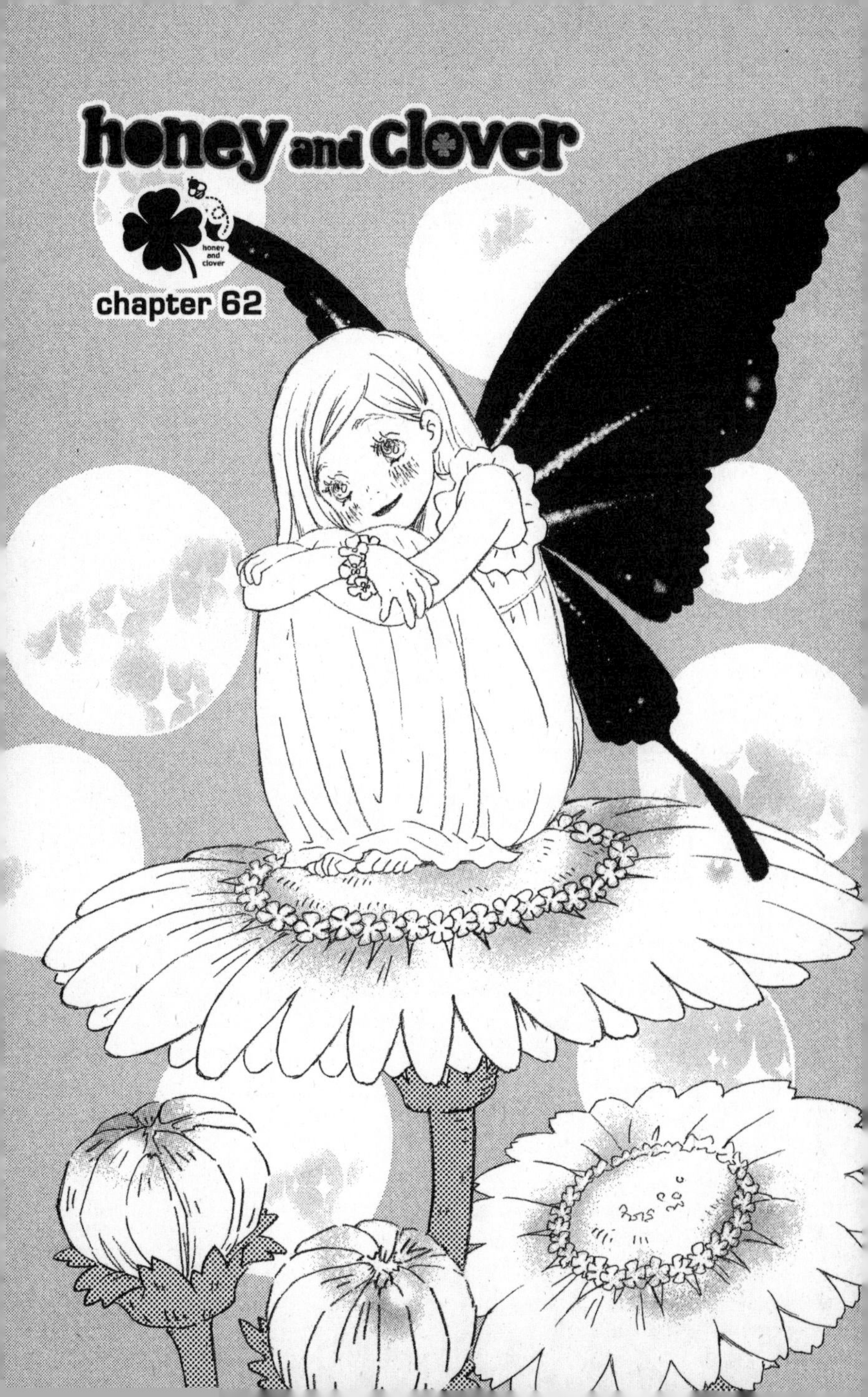
honey and clover
honey and clover
chapter 62

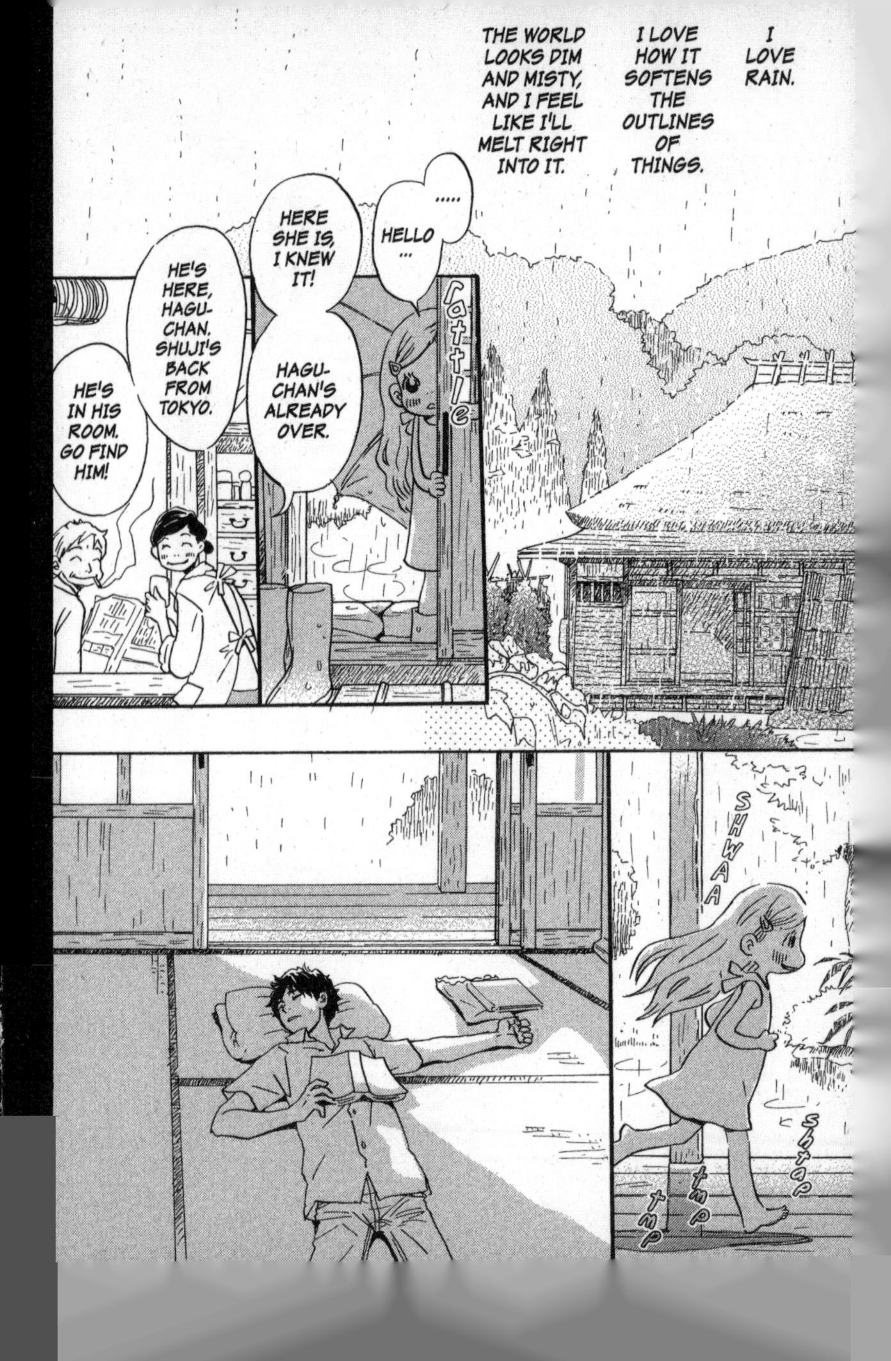
I LOVE RAIN.
I LOVE HOW IT SOFTENS THE OUTLINES OF THINGS.
THE WORLD LOOKS DIM AND MISTY, AND I FEEL LIKE I'LL MELT RIGHT INTO IT.
rattle
..... HELLO ...
HERE SHE IS, I KNEW IT!
HAGU-CHAN'S ALREADY OVER.
HE'S HERE, HAGU-CHAN. SHUJI'S BACK FROM TOKYO.
HE'S IN HIS ROOM. GO FIND HIM!
SHWAA
shtap
tmp
tmp

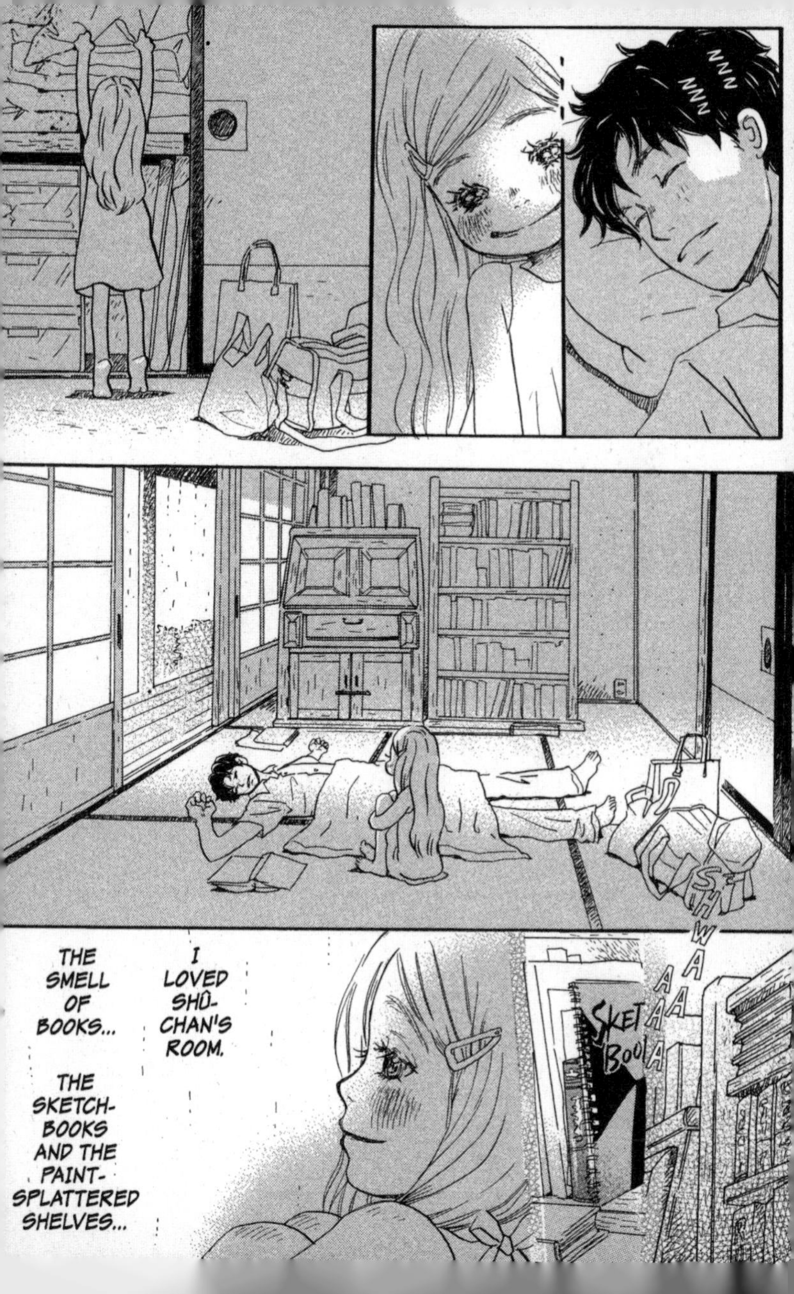
NNN NNN
SHWAAAAAA
SKET BOO
I LOVED SHÛ-CHAN'S ROOM.
THE SMELL OF BOOKS...
THE SKETCHBOOKS AND THE PAINT-SPLATTERED SHELVES...

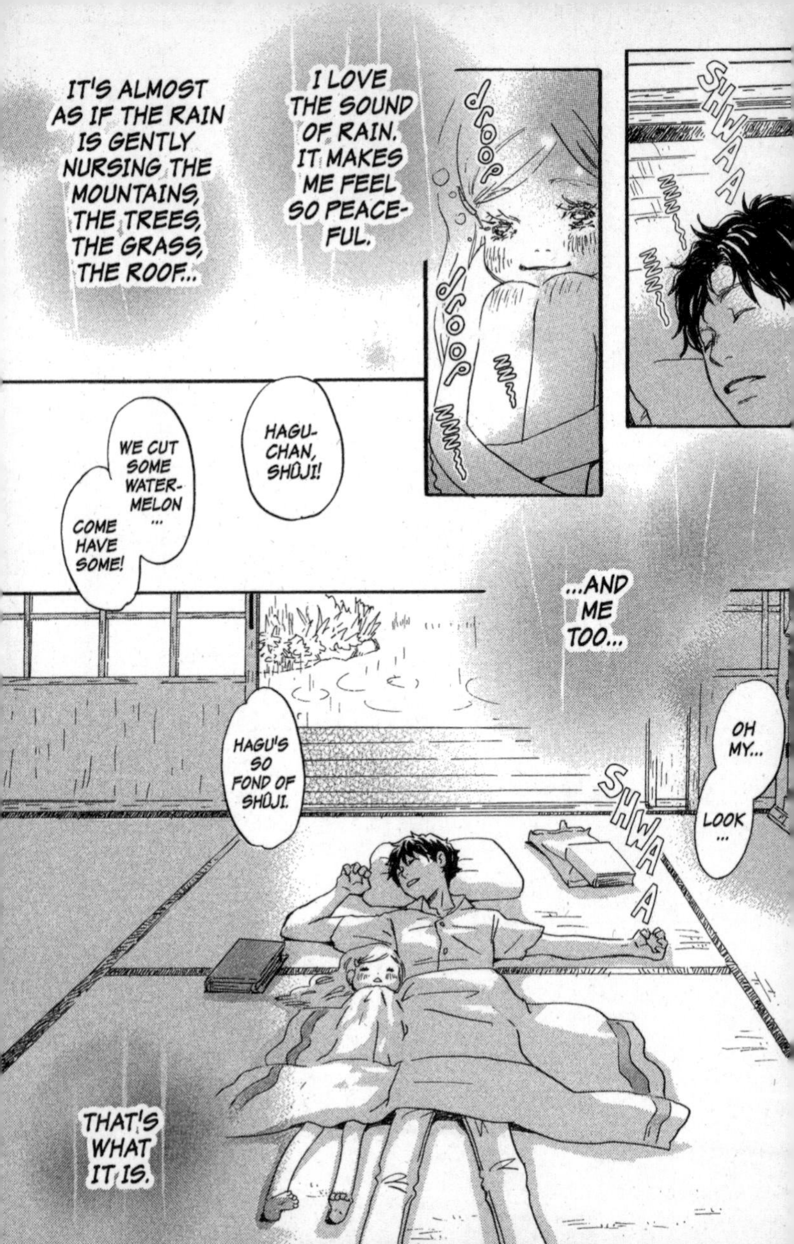
SHWAAA
MMM~
MMM~
droop droop
droop droop
MMM~
MMM~
I LOVE THE SOUND OF RAIN. IT MAKES ME FEEL SO PEACEFUL.
IT'S ALMOST AS IF THE RAIN IS GENTLY NURSING THE MOUNTAINS, THE TREES, THE GRASS, THE ROOF...
HAGU-CHAN, SHŪJI!
WE CUT SOME WATER-MELON ...
COME HAVE SOME!
...AND ME TOO...
OH MY...
LOOK ...
SHWAAA
HAGU'S SO FOND OF SHŪJI.
THAT'S WHAT IT IS.

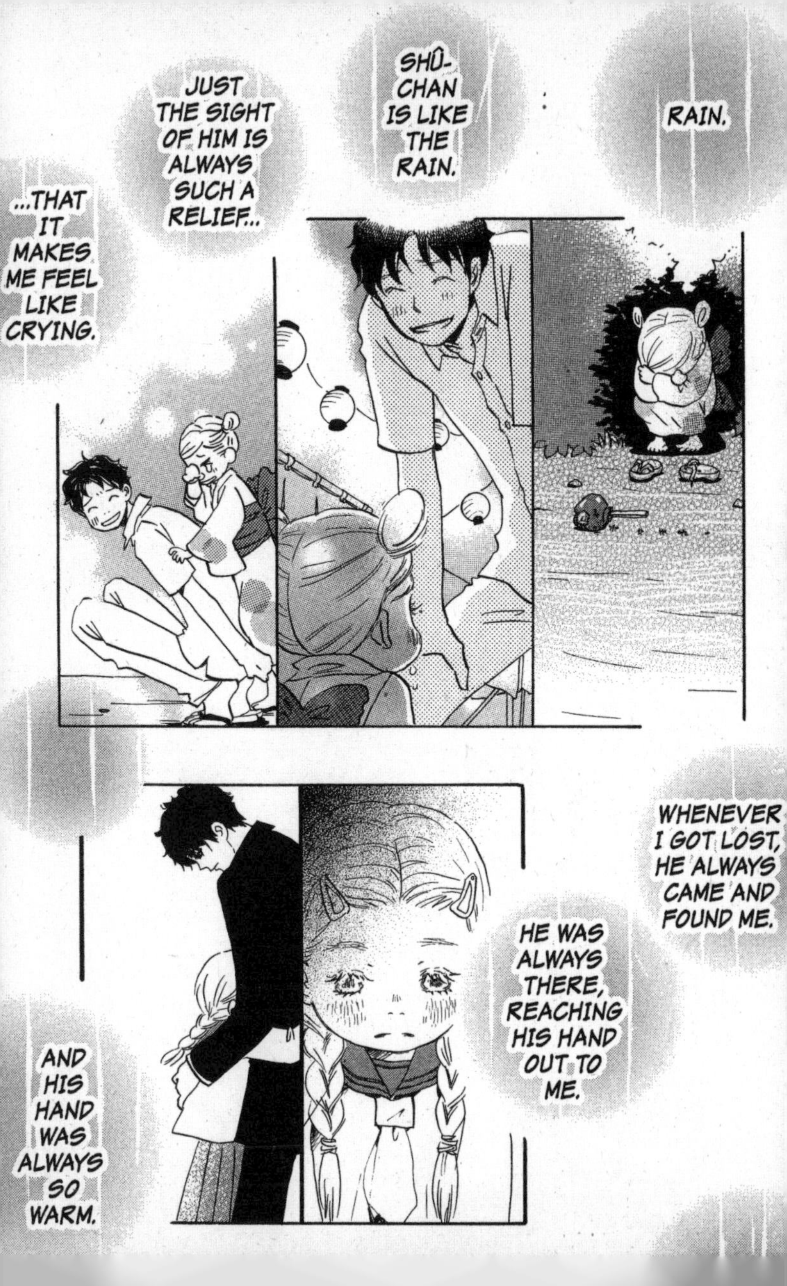
RAIN.
SHÛ-CHAN IS LIKE THE RAIN.
JUST THE SIGHT OF HIM IS ALWAYS SUCH A RELIEF...
...THAT IT MAKES ME FEEL LIKE CRYING.
WHENEVER I GOT LOST, HE ALWAYS CAME AND FOUND ME.
HE WAS ALWAYS THERE, REACHING HIS HAND OUT TO ME.
AND HIS HAND WAS ALWAYS SO WARM.

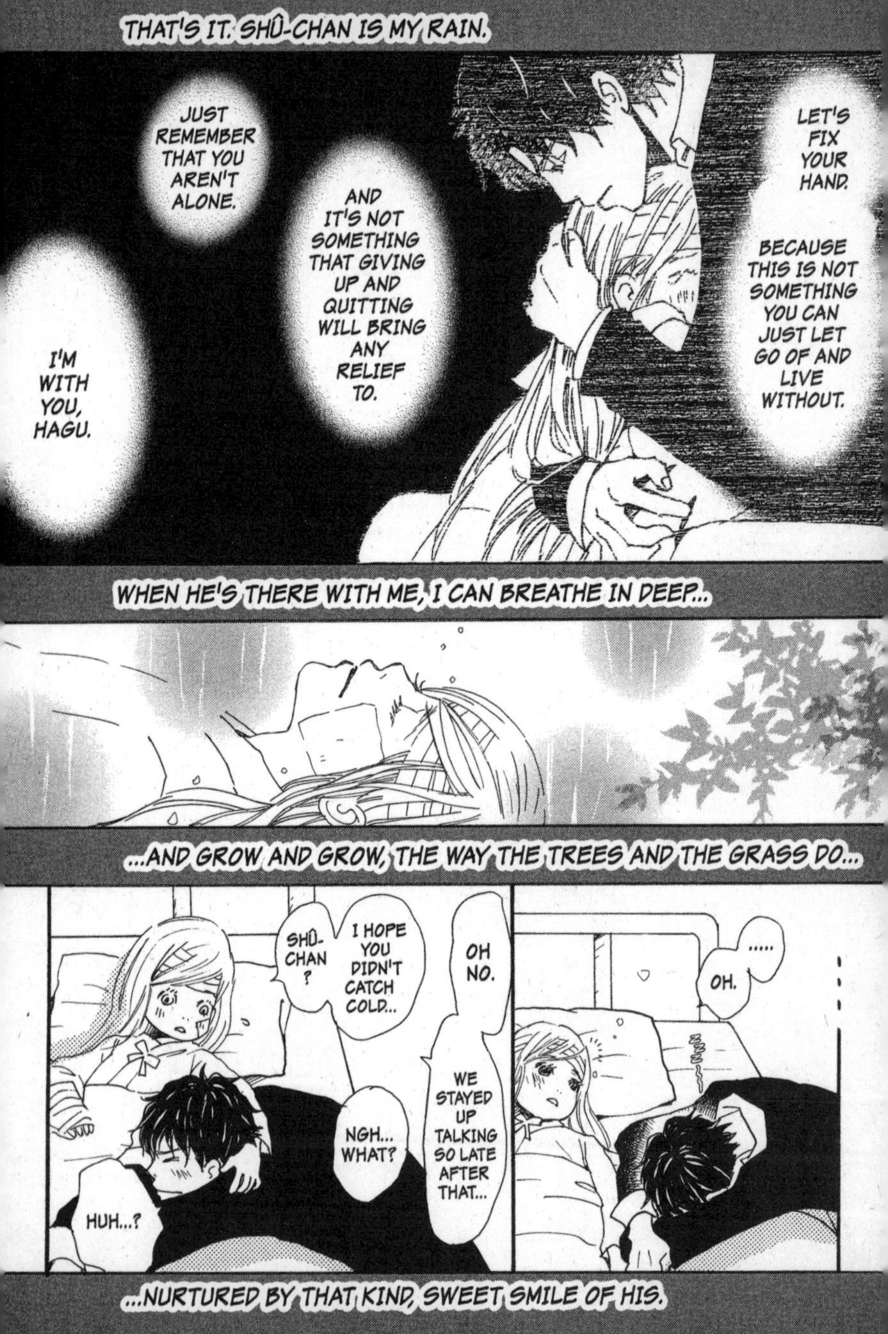
THAT'S IT. SHÛ-CHAN IS MY RAIN.
LET'S FIX YOUR HAND.
BECAUSE THIS IS NOT SOMETHING YOU CAN JUST LET GO OF AND LIVE WITHOUT.
AND IT'S NOT SOMETHING THAT GIVING UP AND QUITTING WILL BRING ANY RELIEF TO.
JUST REMEMBER THAT YOU AREN'T ALONE.
I'M WITH YOU, HAGU.
WHEN HE'S THERE WITH ME, I CAN BREATHE IN DEEP...
...AND GROW AND GROW, THE WAY THE TREES AND THE GRASS DO...
.....
OH.
OH NO.
I HOPE YOU DIDN'T CATCH COLD...
SHÛ-CHAN?
WE STAYED UP TALKING SO LATE AFTER THAT...
NGH... WHAT?
HUH...?
...NURTURED BY THAT KIND, SWEET SMILE OF HIS.

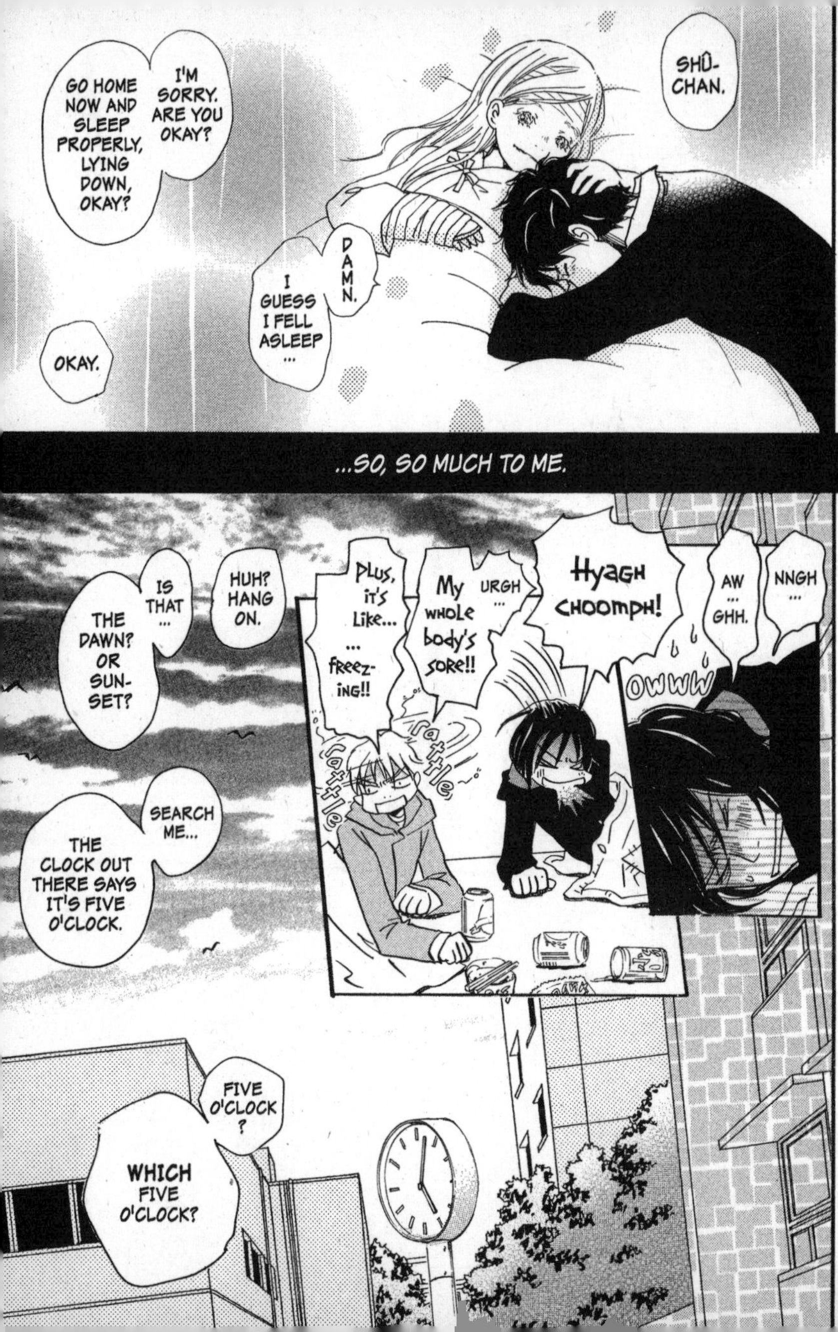
SHÛ-CHAN.
DAMN.
I GUESS I FELL ASLEEP...
I'M SORRY. ARE YOU OKAY?
GO HOME NOW AND SLEEP PROPERLY, LYING DOWN, OKAY?
OKAY.
...SO, SO MUCH TO ME.
NNGH...
AW... GHH.
OWWW
Hyagh CHOOMPH!
URGH...
My whole body's sore!!
Plus, it's like... ...freezing!!
rattle
rattle
HUH? HANG ON.
IS THAT...
THE DAWN? OR SUNSET?
SEARCH ME...
THE CLOCK OUT THERE SAYS IT'S FIVE O'CLOCK.
FIVE O'CLOCK?
WHICH FIVE O'CLOCK?

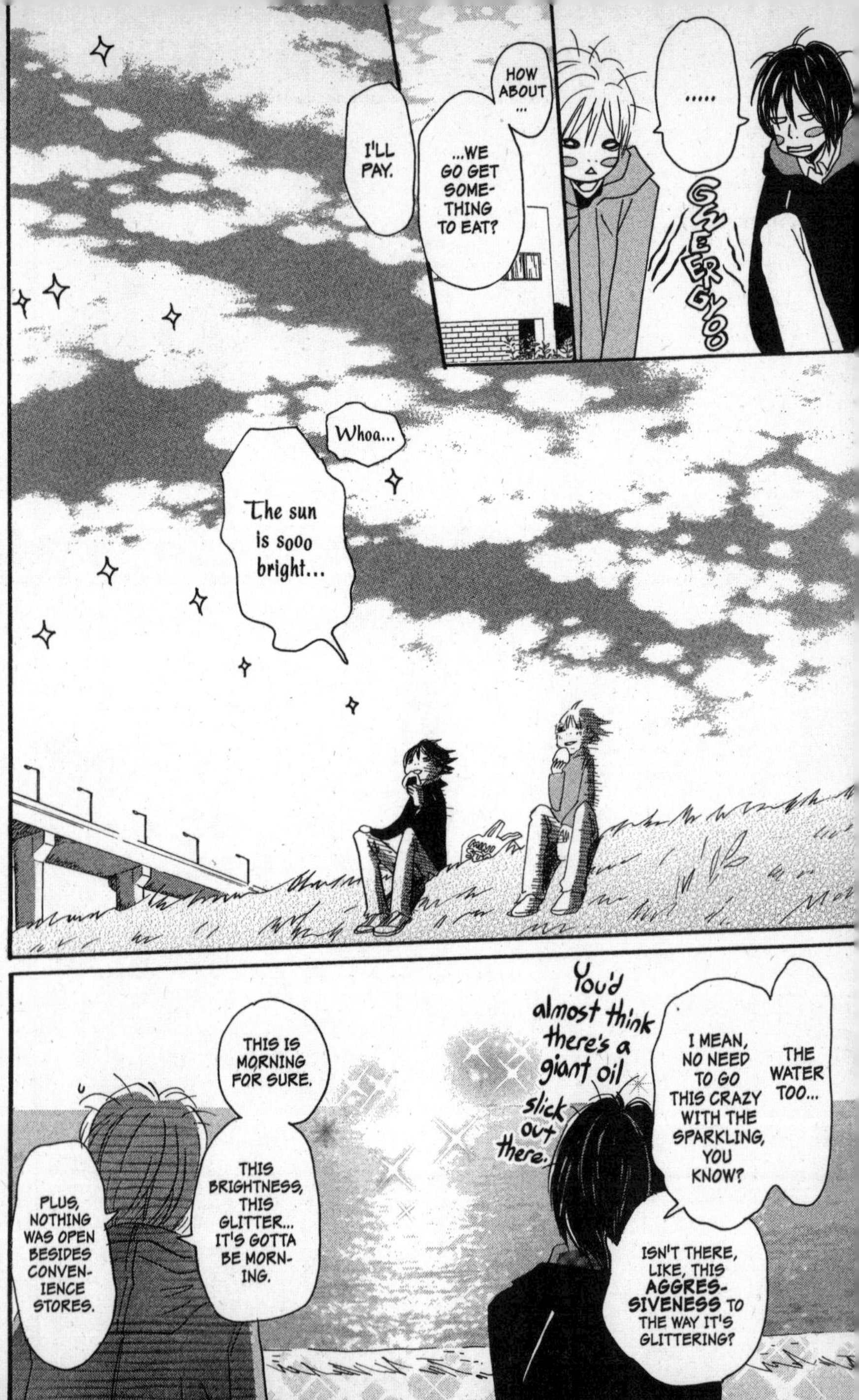
.....
GWERGYOO
HOW ABOUT ...
...WE GO GET SOME-THING TO EAT?
I'LL PAY.
Whoa...
The sun is sooo bright...
THE WATER TOO...
I MEAN, NO NEED TO GO THIS CRAZY WITH THE SPARKLING, YOU KNOW?
You'd almost think there's a giant oil slick out there.
ISN'T THERE, LIKE, THIS **AGGRES-SIVENESS** TO THE WAY IT'S GLITTERING?
THIS IS MORNING FOR SURE.
THIS BRIGHTNESS, THIS GLITTER... IT'S GOTTA BE MORN-ING.
PLUS, NOTHING WAS OPEN BESIDES CONVEN-IENCE STORES.

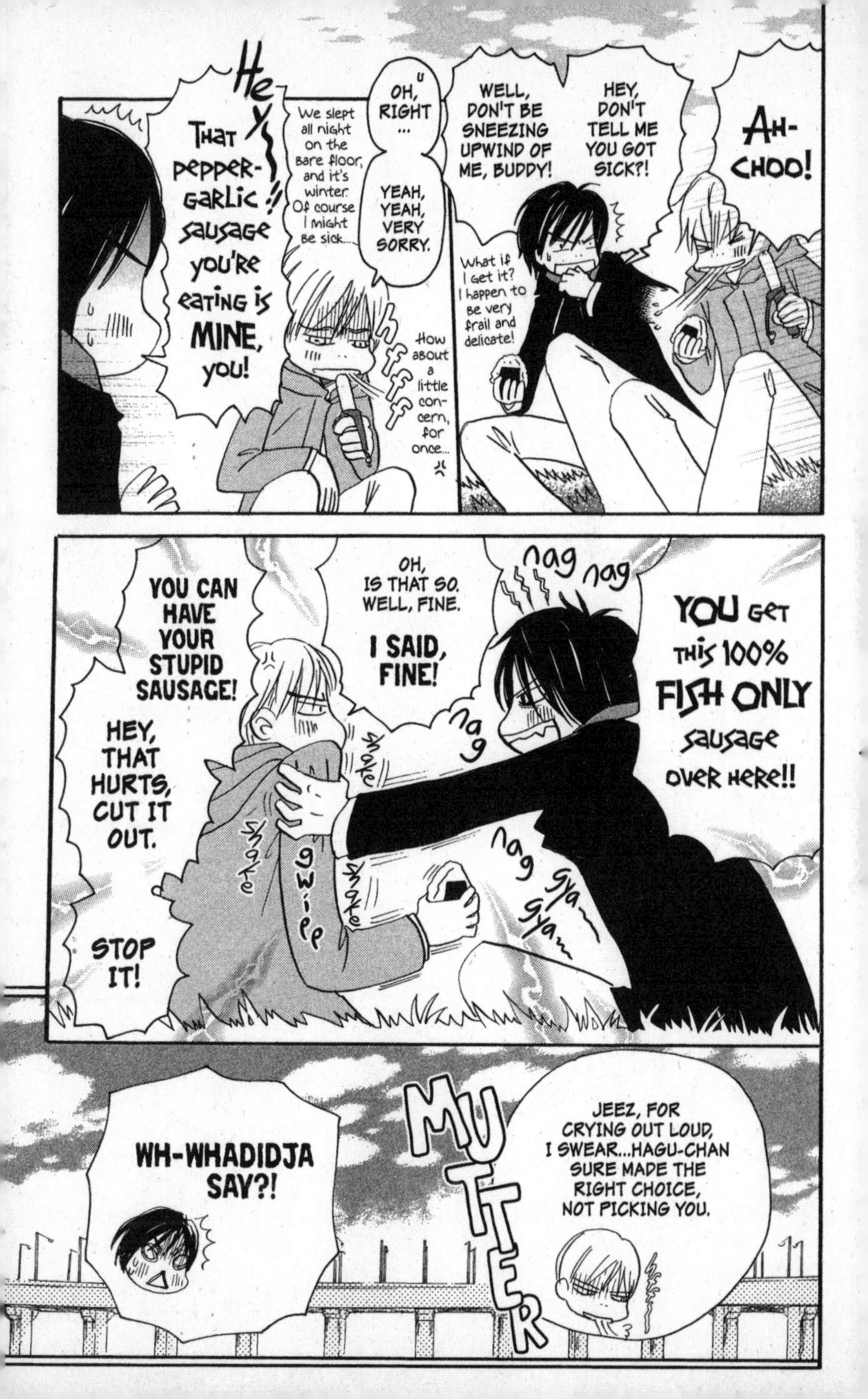
AH-CHOO!
HEY, DON'T TELL ME YOU GOT SICK?!
WELL, DON'T BE SNEEZING UPWIND OF ME, BUDDY!
What if I get it? I happen to be very frail and delicate!
OH, RIGHT...
YEAH, YEAH, VERY SORRY.
We slept all night on the bare floor, and it's winter. Of course I might be sick...
How about a little concern, for once...
hffff
Hey
That pepper-garlic sausage you're eating is MINE, you!
YOU get this 100% FISH ONLY sausage over here!!
nag nag
OH, IS THAT SO. WELL, FINE.
I SAID, FINE!
YOU CAN HAVE YOUR STUPID SAUSAGE!
nag
shake
nag gya gya
HEY, THAT HURTS, CUT IT OUT.
shake
gwiee
shake
STOP IT!
JEEZ, FOR CRYING OUT LOUD, I SWEAR...HAGU-CHAN SURE MADE THE RIGHT CHOICE, NOT PICKING YOU.
MUTTER
WH-WHADIDJA SAY?!

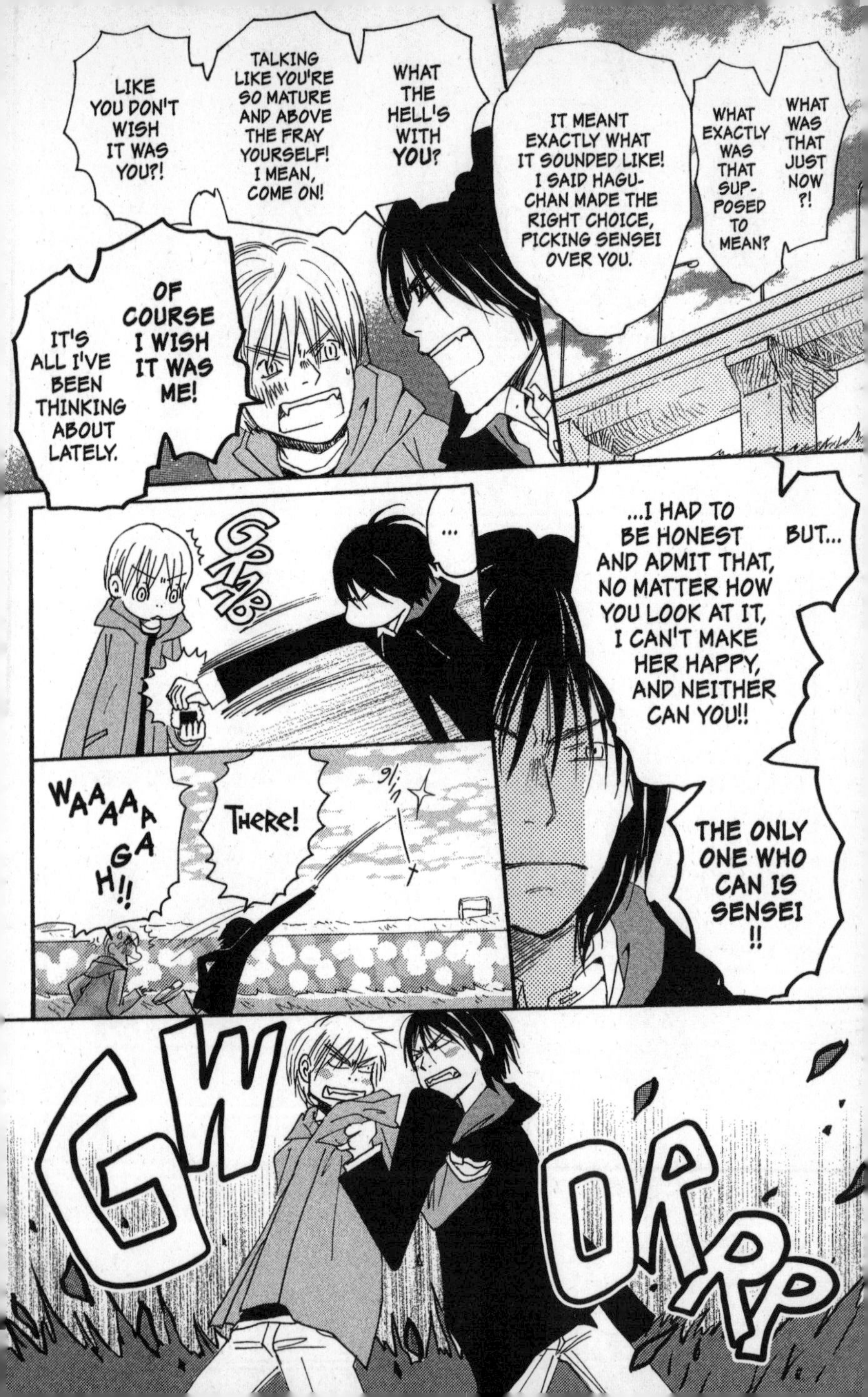
WHAT WAS THAT JUST NOW?!
WHAT EXACTLY WAS THAT SUPPOSED TO MEAN?
IT MEANT EXACTLY WHAT IT SOUNDED LIKE! I SAID HAGU-CHAN MADE THE RIGHT CHOICE, PICKING SENSEI OVER YOU.
WHAT THE HELL'S WITH YOU?
TALKING LIKE YOU'RE SO MATURE AND ABOVE THE FRAY YOURSELF! I MEAN, COME ON!
LIKE YOU DON'T WISH IT WAS YOU?!
OF COURSE I WISH IT WAS ME!
IT'S ALL I'VE BEEN THINKING ABOUT LATELY.
BUT...
...I HAD TO BE HONEST AND ADMIT THAT, NO MATTER HOW YOU LOOK AT IT, I CAN'T MAKE HER HAPPY, AND NEITHER CAN YOU!!
THE ONLY ONE WHO CAN IS SENSEI!!
...
GRAB
There!
WAAAAAGAH!!
GWORRP

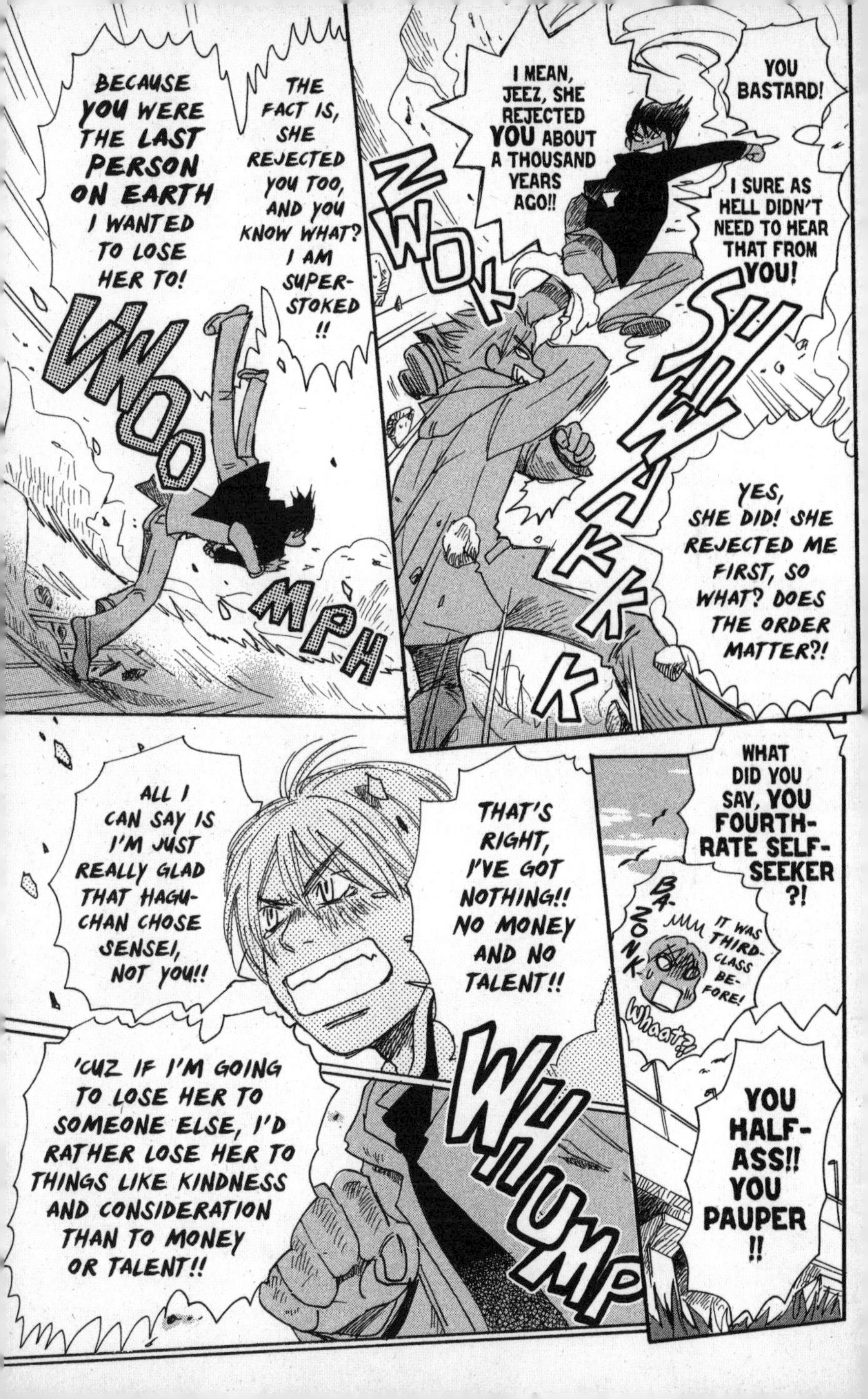
YOU BASTARD!
I MEAN, JEEZ, SHE REJECTED YOU ABOUT A THOUSAND YEARS AGO!!
I SURE AS HELL DIDN'T NEED TO HEAR THAT FROM YOU!
NWOK
SHWAKKKK
YES, SHE DID! SHE REJECTED ME FIRST, SO WHAT? DOES THE ORDER MATTER?!
THE FACT IS, SHE REJECTED YOU TOO, AND YOU KNOW WHAT? I AM SUPER-STOKED!!
BECAUSE YOU WERE THE LAST PERSON ON EARTH I WANTED TO LOSE HER TO!
WOOMPH
WHAT DID YOU SAY, YOU FOURTH-RATE SELF-SEEKER?!
BA-ZONK
IT WAS THIRD-CLASS BEFORE!
Whaat?!
YOU HALF-ASS!! YOU PAUPER!!
THAT'S RIGHT, I'VE GOT NOTHING!! NO MONEY AND NO TALENT!!
ALL I CAN SAY IS I'M JUST REALLY GLAD THAT HAGU-CHAN CHOSE SENSEI, NOT YOU!!
'CUZ IF I'M GOING TO LOSE HER TO SOMEONE ELSE, I'D RATHER LOSE HER TO THINGS LIKE KINDNESS AND CONSIDERATION THAN TO MONEY OR TALENT!!
WHUMP

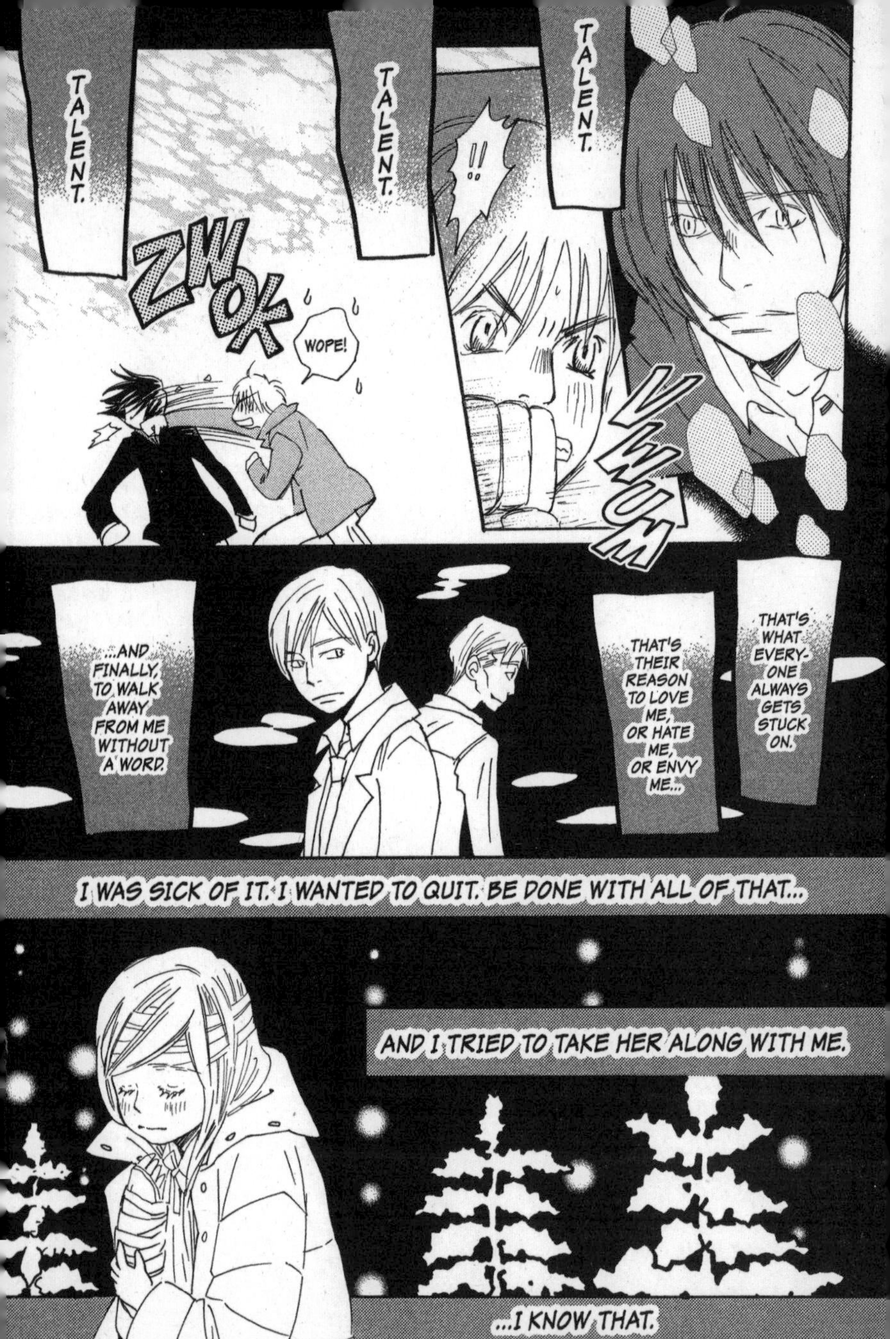
TALENT.
!!
VWUM
TALENT.
TALENT.
ZWOK
WOPE!
THAT'S WHAT EVERY-ONE ALWAYS GETS STUCK ON.
THAT'S THEIR REASON TO LOVE ME, OR HATE ME, OR ENVY ME...
...AND FINALLY, TO WALK AWAY FROM ME WITHOUT A WORD.
I WAS SICK OF IT. I WANTED TO QUIT. BE DONE WITH ALL OF THAT...
AND I TRIED TO TAKE HER ALONG WITH ME.
...I KNOW THAT.

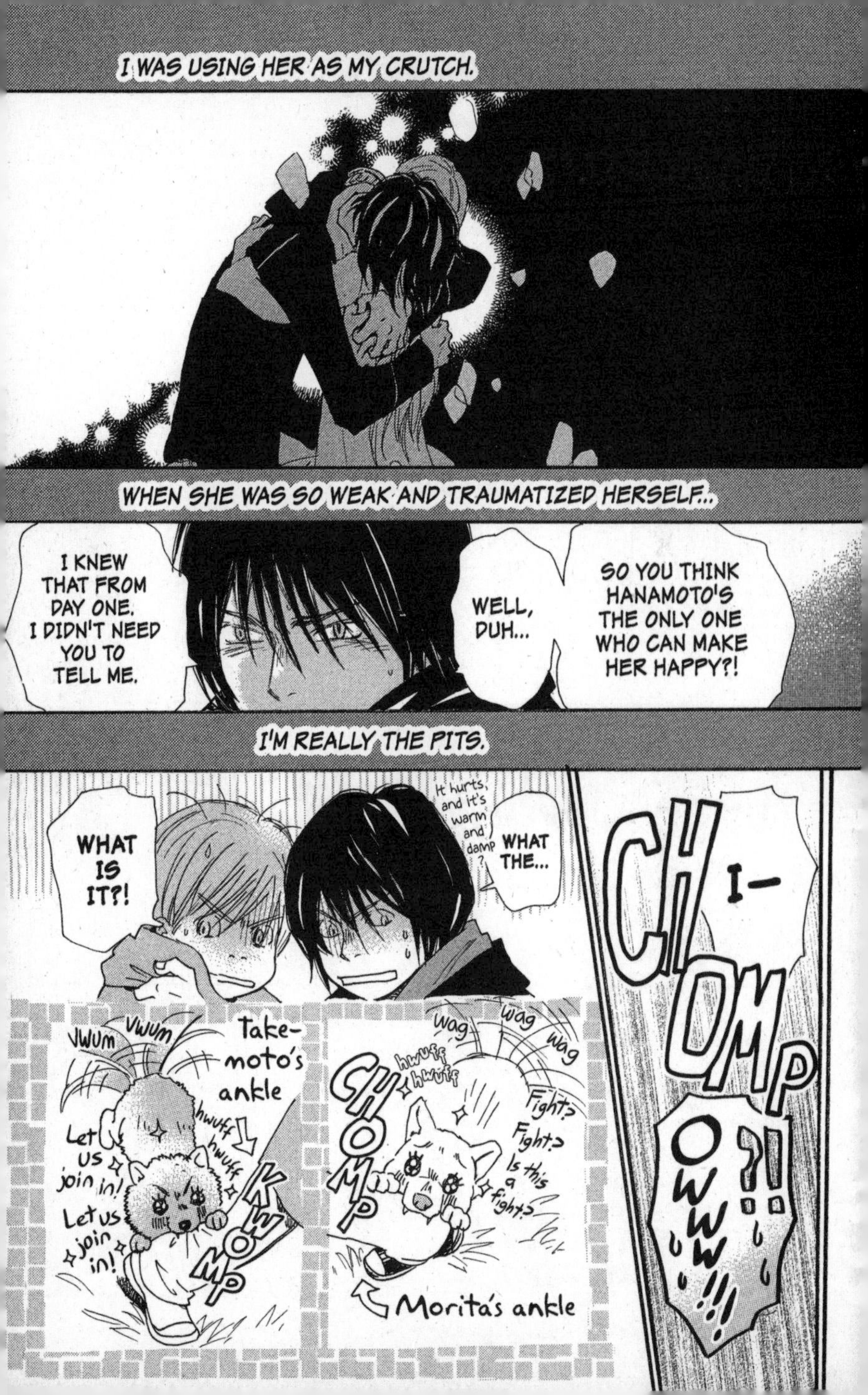
I WAS USING HER AS MY CRUTCH.
WHEN SHE WAS SO WEAK AND TRAUMATIZED HERSELF...
SO YOU THINK HANAMOTO'S THE ONLY ONE WHO CAN MAKE HER HAPPY?!
WELL, DUH...
I KNEW THAT FROM DAY ONE. I DIDN'T NEED YOU TO TELL ME.
I'M REALLY THE PITS.
I—
CHOMP
OWWW!!!
?!
It hurts, and it's warm and damp?
WHAT THE...
WHAT IS IT?!
wag wag wag
hwuff hwuff
CHOMP
Fight? Fight? Is this a fight?
Morita's ankle
VWUM VWUM
Take-moto's ankle
hwuff hwuff
KWOMP
Let us join in!
Let us join in!

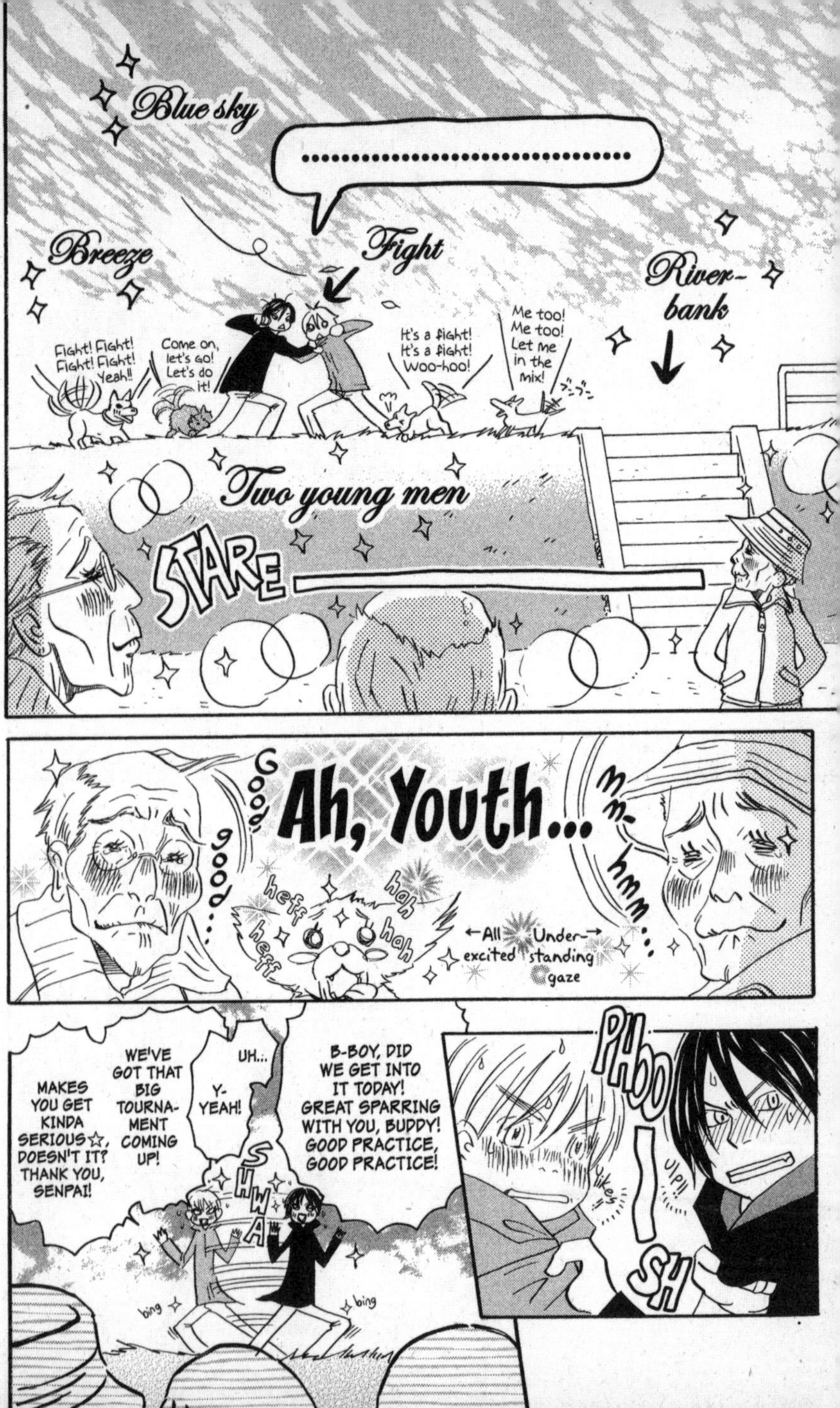
River-bank
Me too! Me too! Let me in the mix!
Fight
It's a fight! It's a fight! Woo-hoo!
....
Blue sky
Breeze
Come on, let's go! Let's do it!
Fight! Fight! Fight! Fight! Yeah!!
Two young men
STARE
Mm-hmm...
Under-standing gaze
Ah, Youth...
hah hah
heff heff
All excited
Good, good...
PHBOOSH
ulp!!
yikes
B-BOY, DID WE GET INTO IT TODAY! GREAT SPARRING WITH YOU, BUDDY! GOOD PRACTICE, GOOD PRACTICE!
UH...
Y-YEAH!
WE'VE GOT THAT BIG TOURNAMENT COMING UP!
MAKES YOU GET KINDA SERIOUS☆, DOESN'T IT? THANK YOU, SENPAI!
SHWA
bing
bing

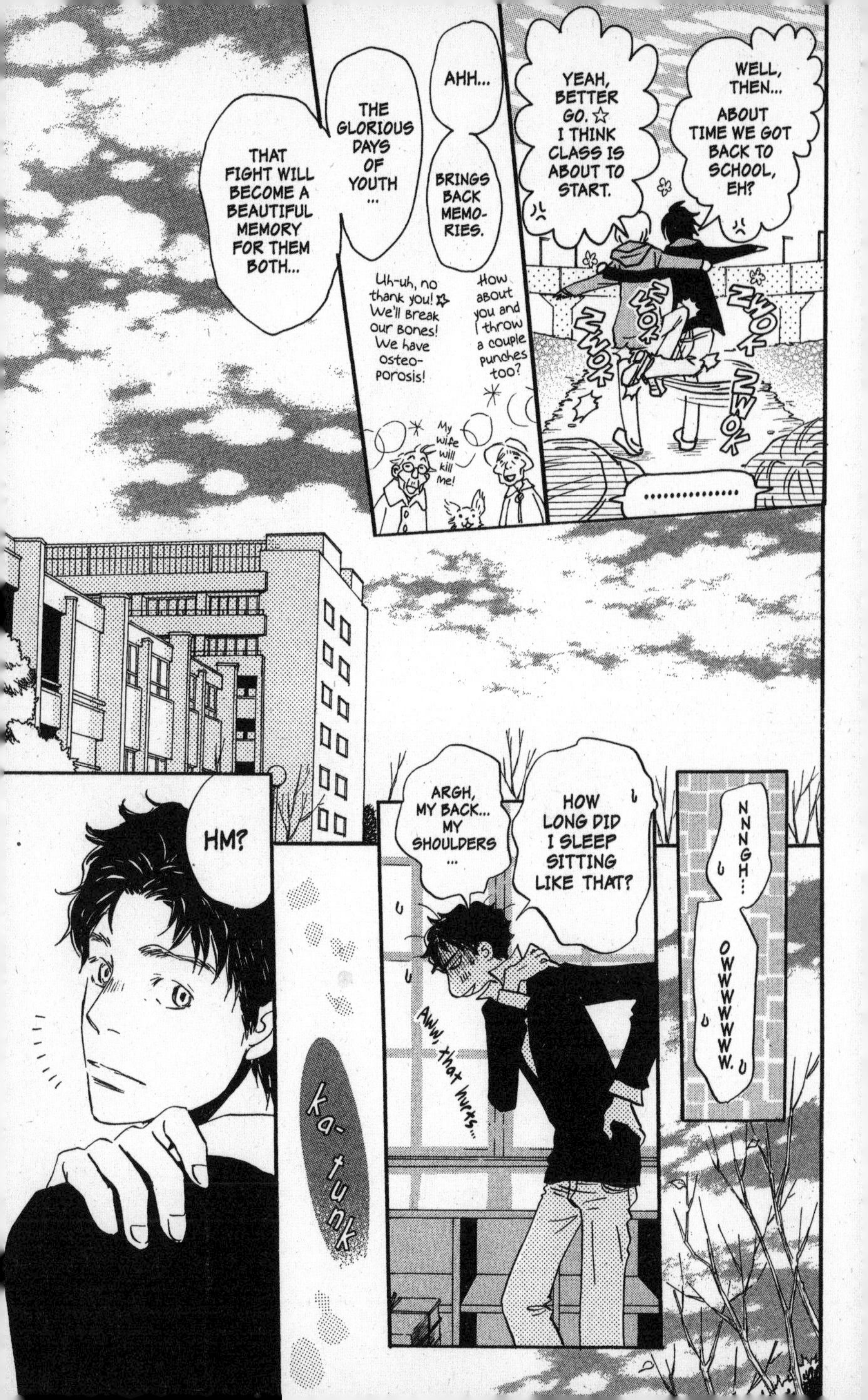
WELL, THEN... ABOUT TIME WE GOT BACK TO SCHOOL, EH?
YEAH, BETTER GO. ☆ I THINK CLASS IS ABOUT TO START.
ZWOK
ZWOK
ZWOK
ZWOK
....
AHH... BRINGS BACK MEMORIES.
How about you and I throw a couple punches too?
Uh-uh, no thank you! ☆ We'll break our bones! We have osteoporosis!
My wife will kill me!
THE GLORIOUS DAYS OF YOUTH...
THAT FIGHT WILL BECOME A BEAUTIFUL MEMORY FOR THEM BOTH...
NNNGH...
OWWWWWWW.
HOW LONG DID I SLEEP SITTING LIKE THAT?
ARGH, MY BACK... MY SHOULDERS...
Aww, that hurts...
ka-tunk
HM?

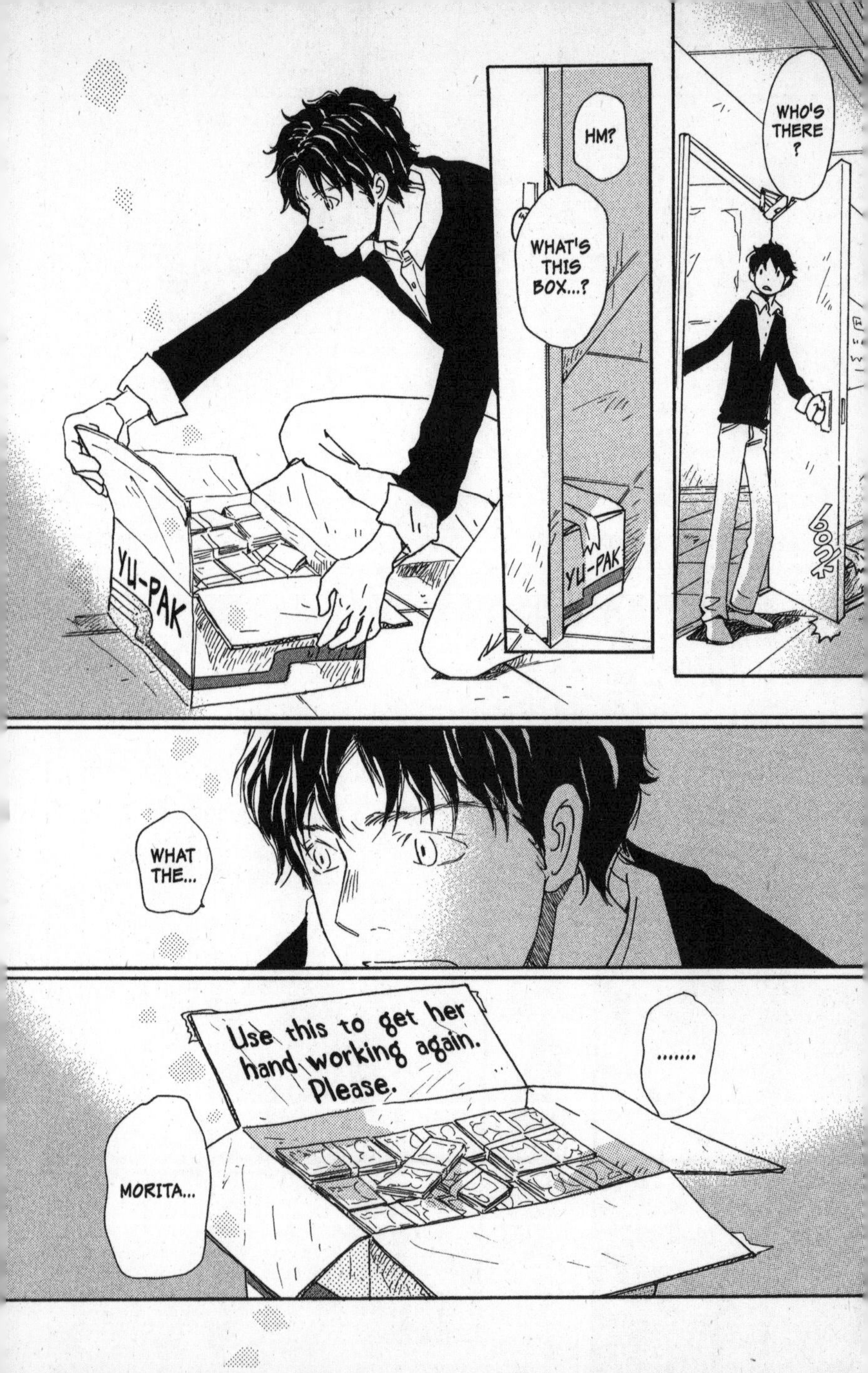
WHO'S THERE ?
bonk
HM?
WHAT'S THIS BOX...?
YU-PAK
YU-PAK
WHAT THE...
....
Use this to get her hand working again. Please.
MORITA...

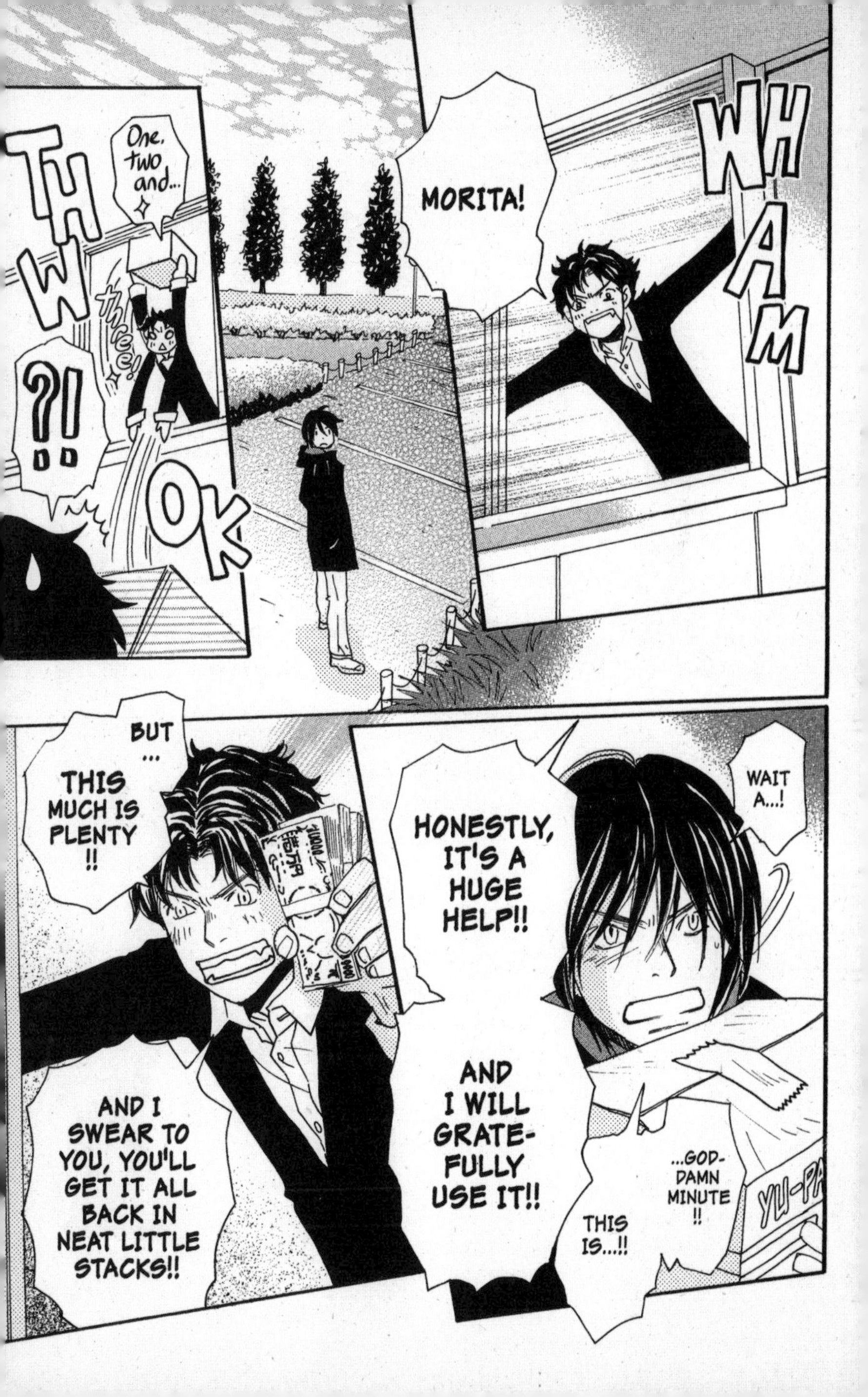
MORITA!
WHAM
One, two and...
three!
THW
OK
?!
WAIT A...!
...GOD-DAMN MINUTE!!
THIS IS...!!
YU-PA
HONESTLY, IT'S A HUGE HELP!!
AND I WILL GRATE-FULLY USE IT!!
BUT ...
THIS MUCH IS PLENTY!!
AND I SWEAR TO YOU, YOU'LL GET IT ALL BACK IN NEAT LITTLE STACKS!!

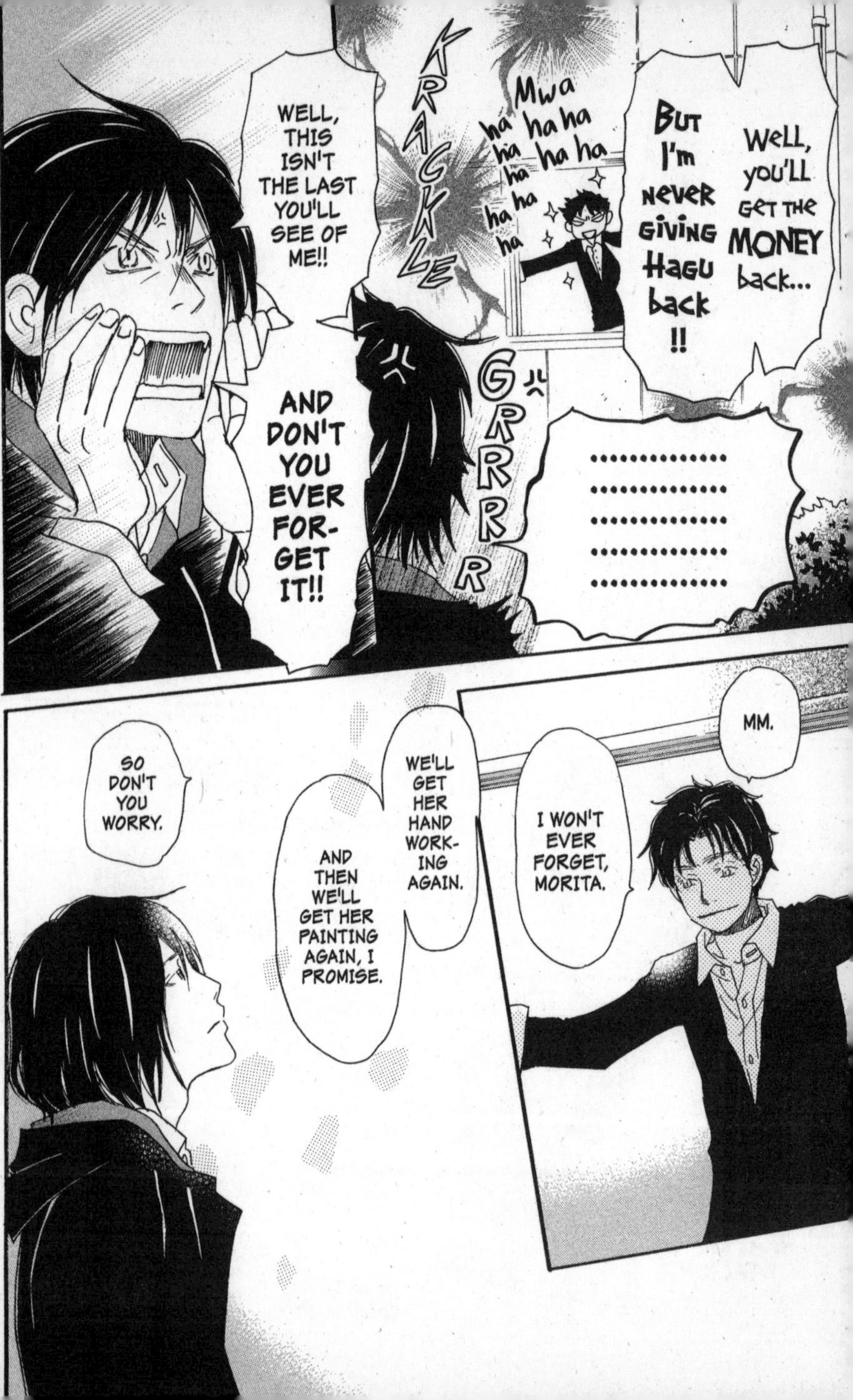

Well, you'll get the MONEY back...
But I'm never giving Hagu back!!
Mwa ha ha ha ha ha ha ha ha ha ha
KRACKLE
WELL, THIS ISN'T THE LAST YOU'LL SEE OF ME!!
....
GRRRRR
AND DON'T YOU EVER FOR-GET IT!!
MM.
I WON'T EVER FORGET, MORITA.
WE'LL GET HER HAND WORK-ING AGAIN.
AND THEN WE'LL GET HER PAINTING AGAIN, I PROMISE.
SO DON'T YOU WORRY.

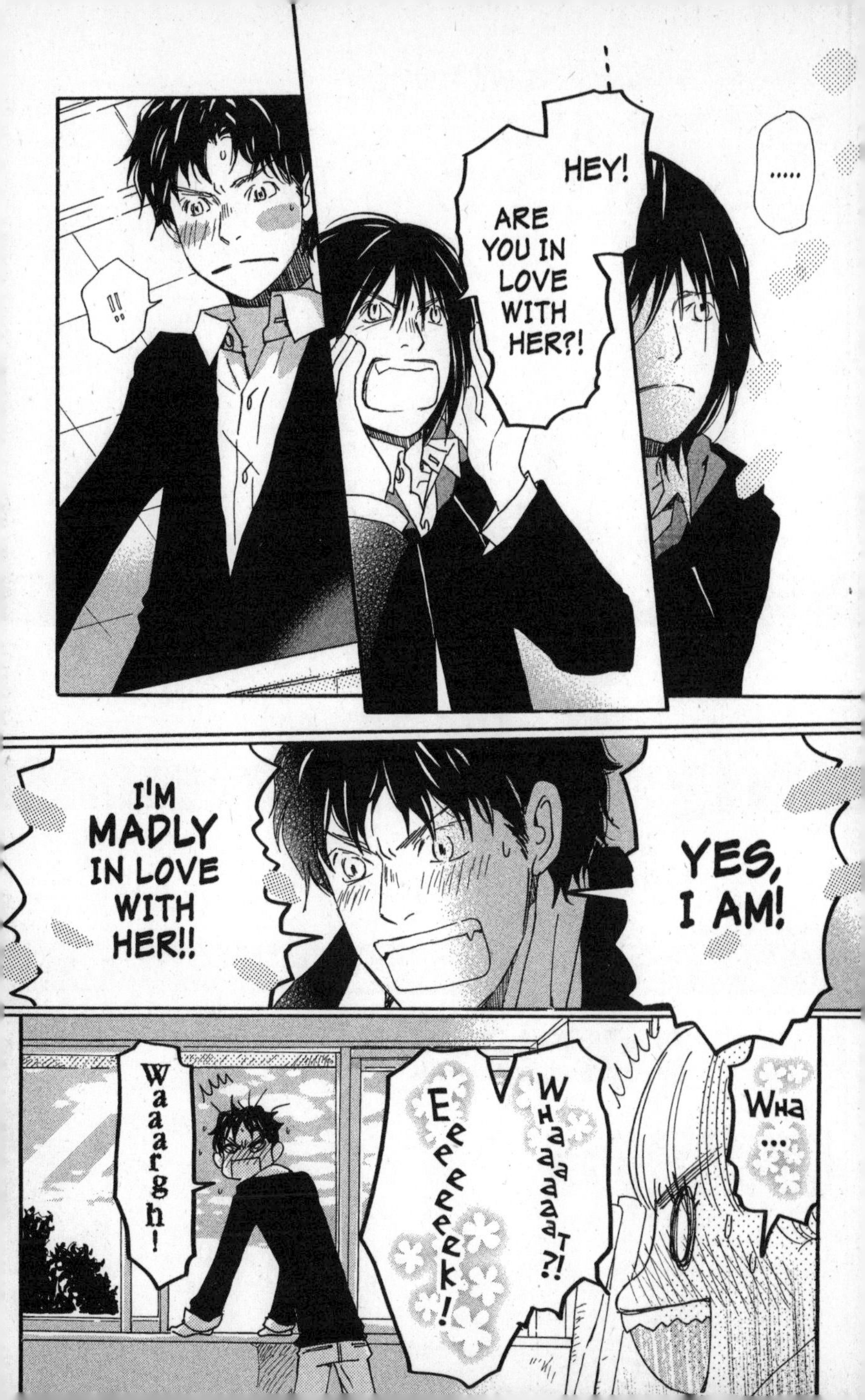
.....
HEY! ARE YOU IN LOVE WITH HER?!
!!
YES, I AM!
I'M MADLY IN LOVE WITH HER!!
Wha...
Whaaaaaat?!
Eeeeeeek!
Waaaargh!

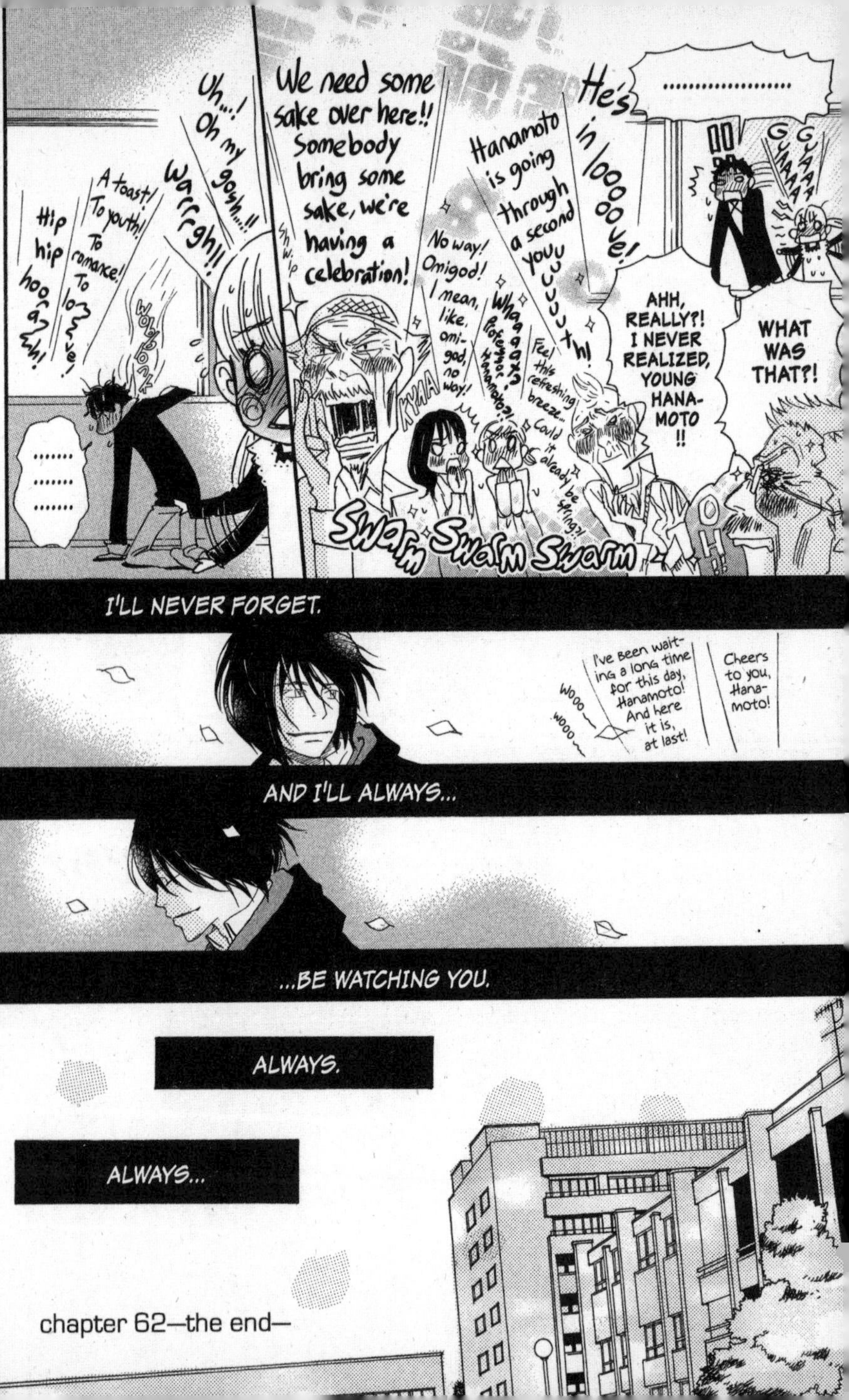
....
GUAAAA GUAAAA
WHAT WAS THAT?!
AHH, REALLY?! I NEVER REALIZED, YOUNG HANAMOTO!!
He's in looooove!
Hanamoto is going through a second youuuuuuuth!
Feel this refreshing breeze... Could it already be spring?!
Whaaaaa?! Professor Hanamoto?!
No way! Omigod! I mean, like, omigod, no way!
KYAA
OH
Swarm Swarm Swarm
We need some sake over here!! Somebody bring some sake, we're having a celebration!
Shwip
Uh...! Oh my gosh...!!
Warrgh!!
A toast! To youth! To romance! To lo~ve!
Hip hip hooraaah!
....
I'LL NEVER FORGET.
Cheers to you, Hanamoto!
I've been waiting a long time for this day, Hanamoto! And here it is, at last!
Wooo~ wooo~
AND I'LL ALWAYS...
...BE WATCHING YOU.
ALWAYS.
ALWAYS...
chapter 62—the end—

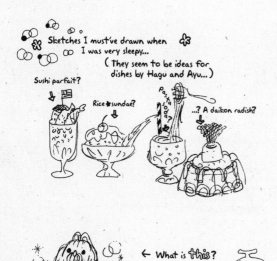

Sketches I must've drawn when I was very sleepy...

(They seem to be ideas for dishes by Hagu and Ayu...)

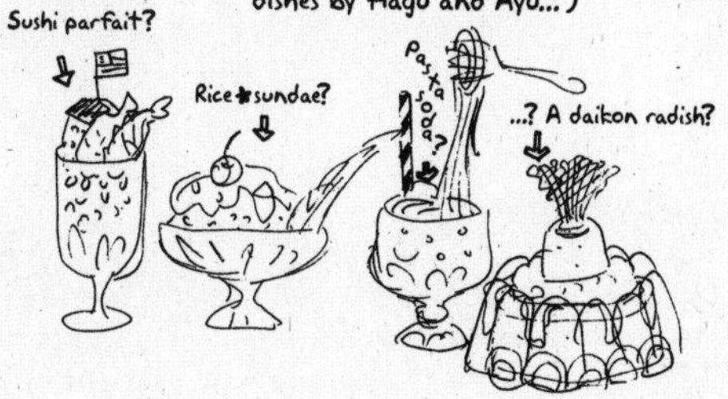
Sushi parfait?
Rice★sundae?
Pasta soda?
...? A daikon radish?

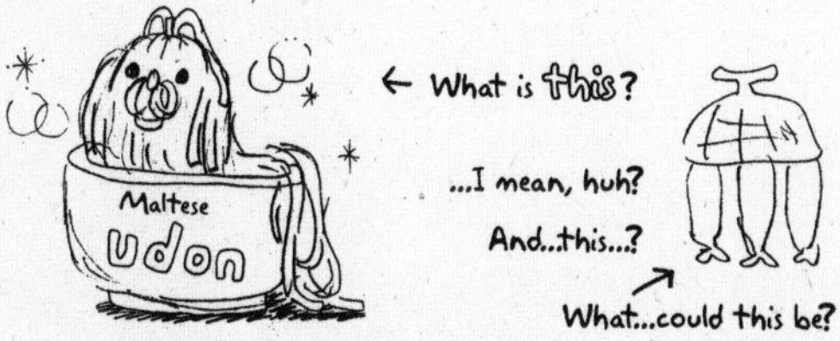
Maltese
udon
← What is this?
...I mean, huh?
And...this...?
What...could this be?

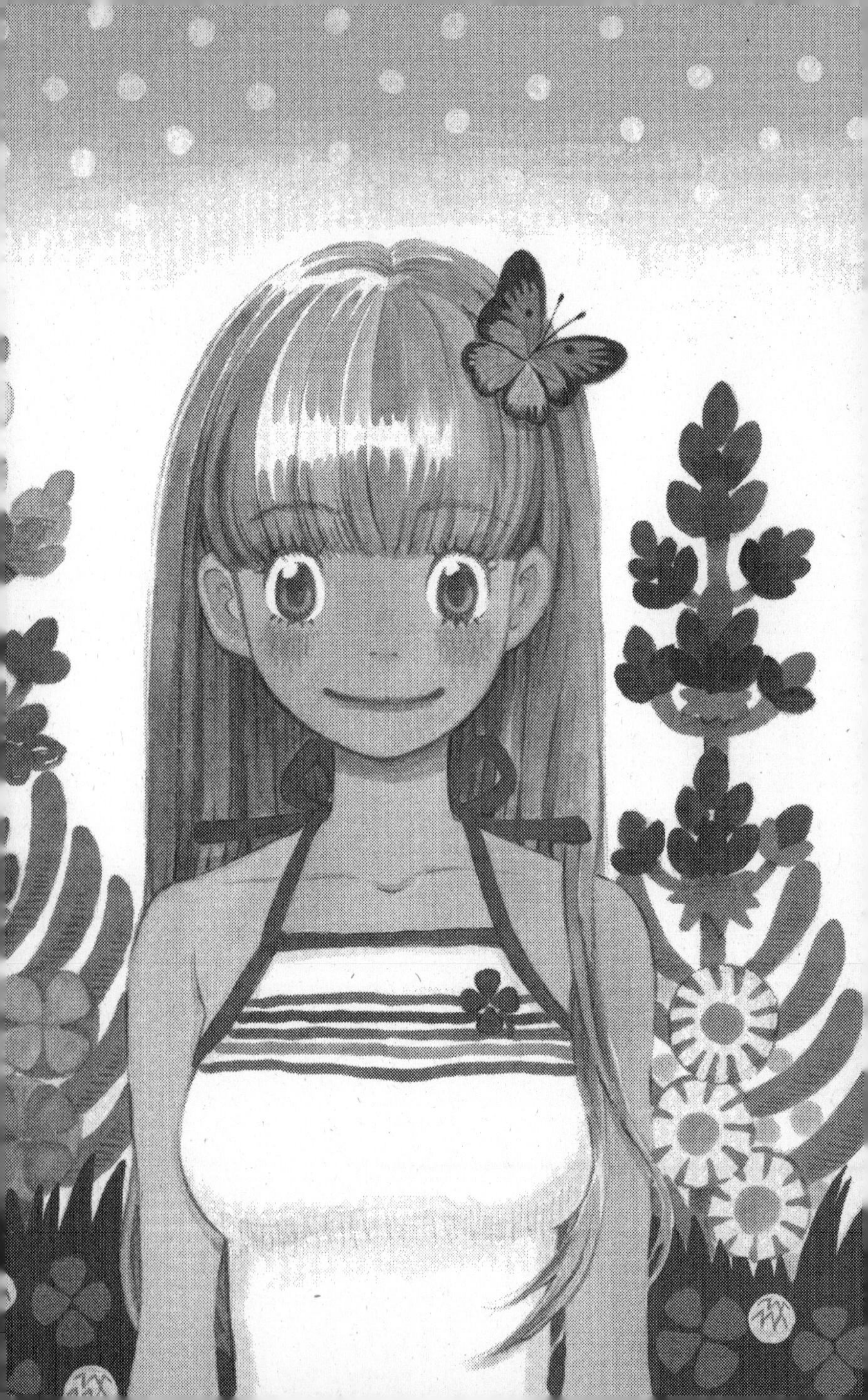

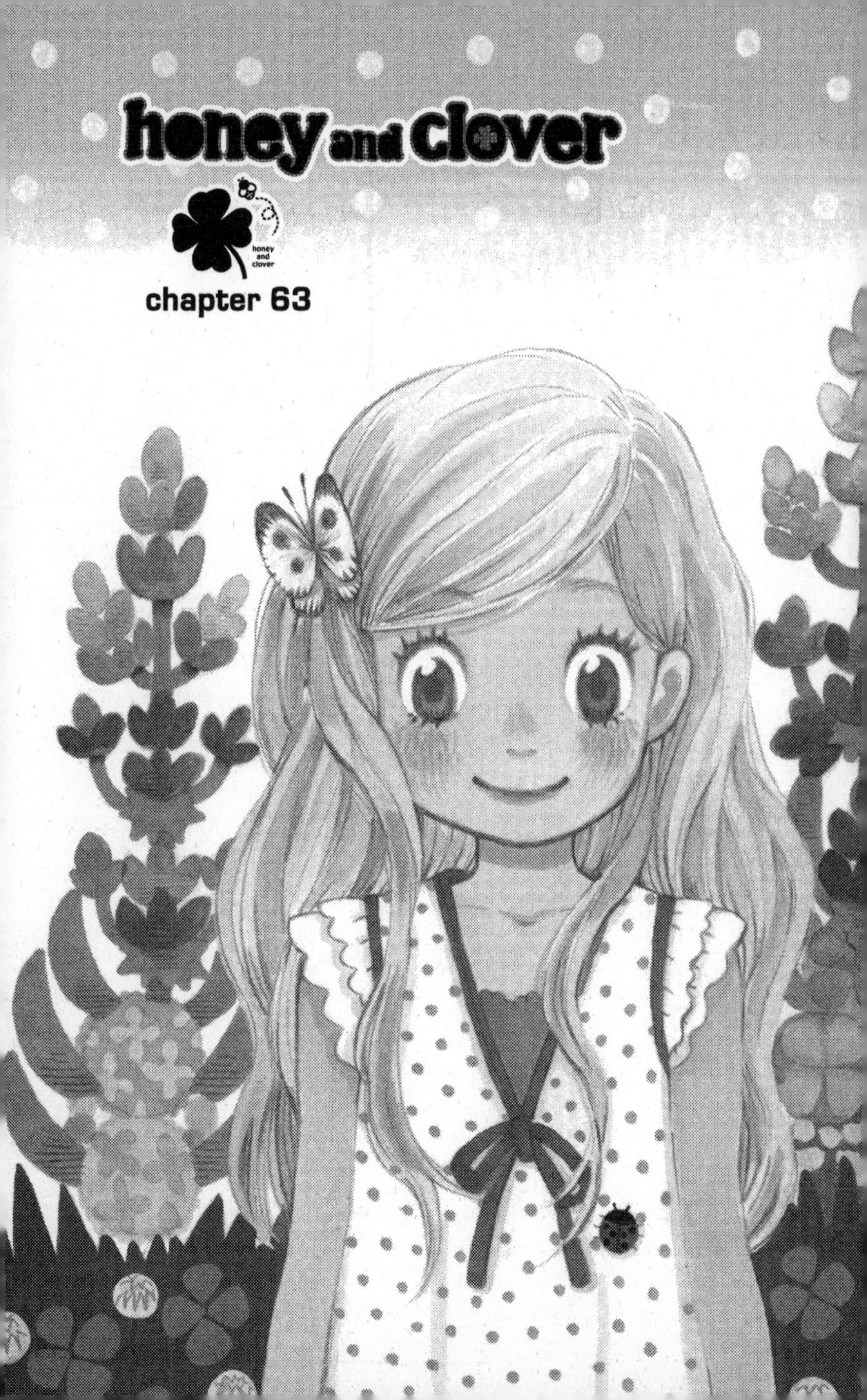
honey and clover
honey and clover
chapter 63

I mean it... He looked great no matter what we made him wear...

hahaha

hee hee hee

Yamazaki had a lot of fans in Umino Village ☆...

Rejected rough sketches for DVD packaging illustrations

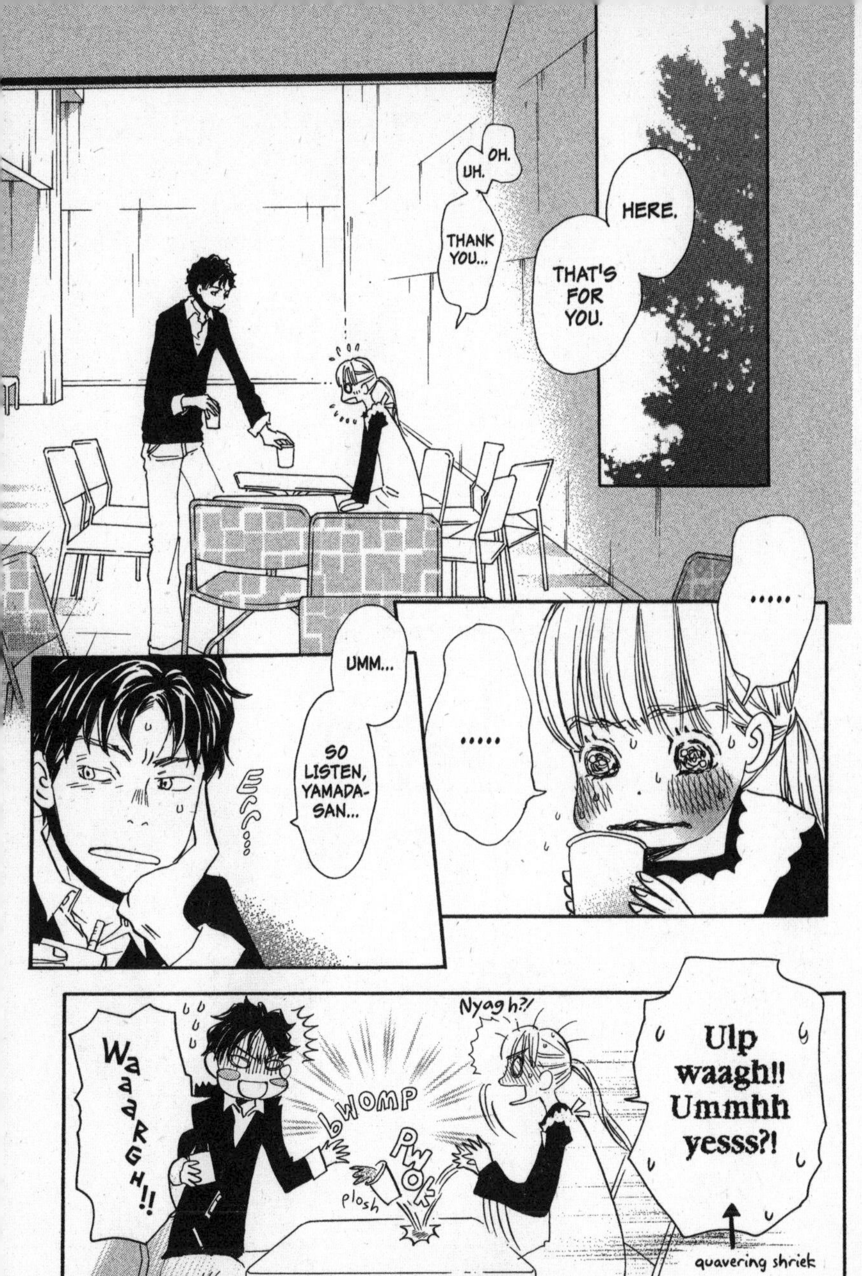
HERE.
THAT'S FOR YOU.
OH.
UH.
THANK YOU...
.....
.....
UMM...
SO LISTEN, YAMADA-SAN...
Errr...
Ulp waagh!! Ummhh yesss?!
quavering shriek
Nyagh?!
PWOK
plosh
bWOMP
WaaaRGH!!

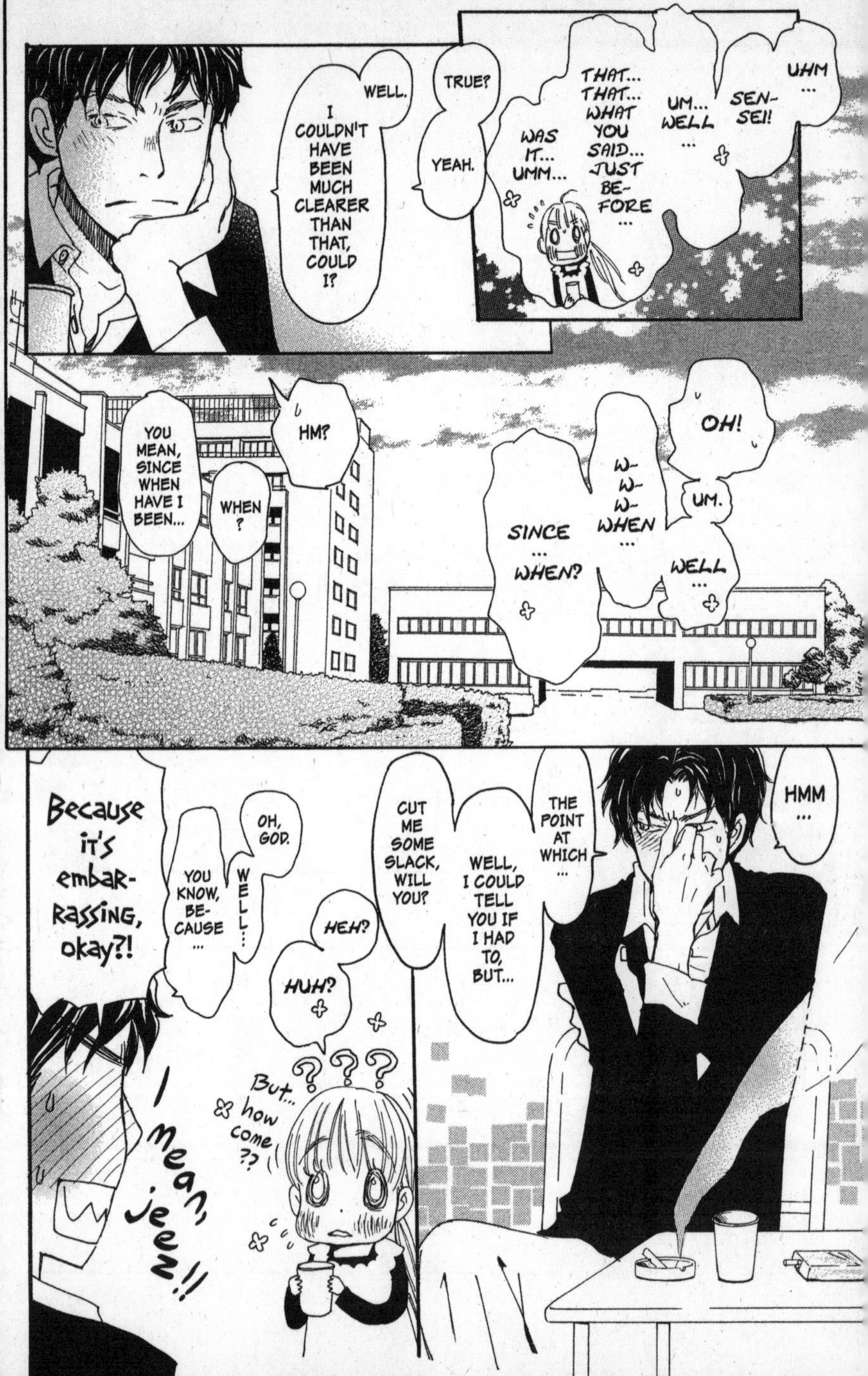
UHM ...
SENSEI!
UM... WELL ...
THAT... THAT... WHAT YOU SAID... JUST BEFORE ...
WAS IT... UMM...
TRUE?
YEAH.
WELL.
I COULDN'T HAVE BEEN MUCH CLEARER THAN THAT, COULD I?
OH!
UM.
WELL ...
W-W-W-WHEN ...
SINCE ... WHEN?
HM?
WHEN ?
YOU MEAN, SINCE WHEN HAVE I BEEN...
HMM ...
THE POINT AT WHICH ...
WELL, I COULD TELL YOU IF I HAD TO, BUT...
CUT ME SOME SLACK, WILL YOU?
HEH?
HUH?
But... how come ??
OH, GOD.
WELL...
YOU KNOW, BECAUSE ...
Because it's embarrassing, okay?!
I mean, jeez!!

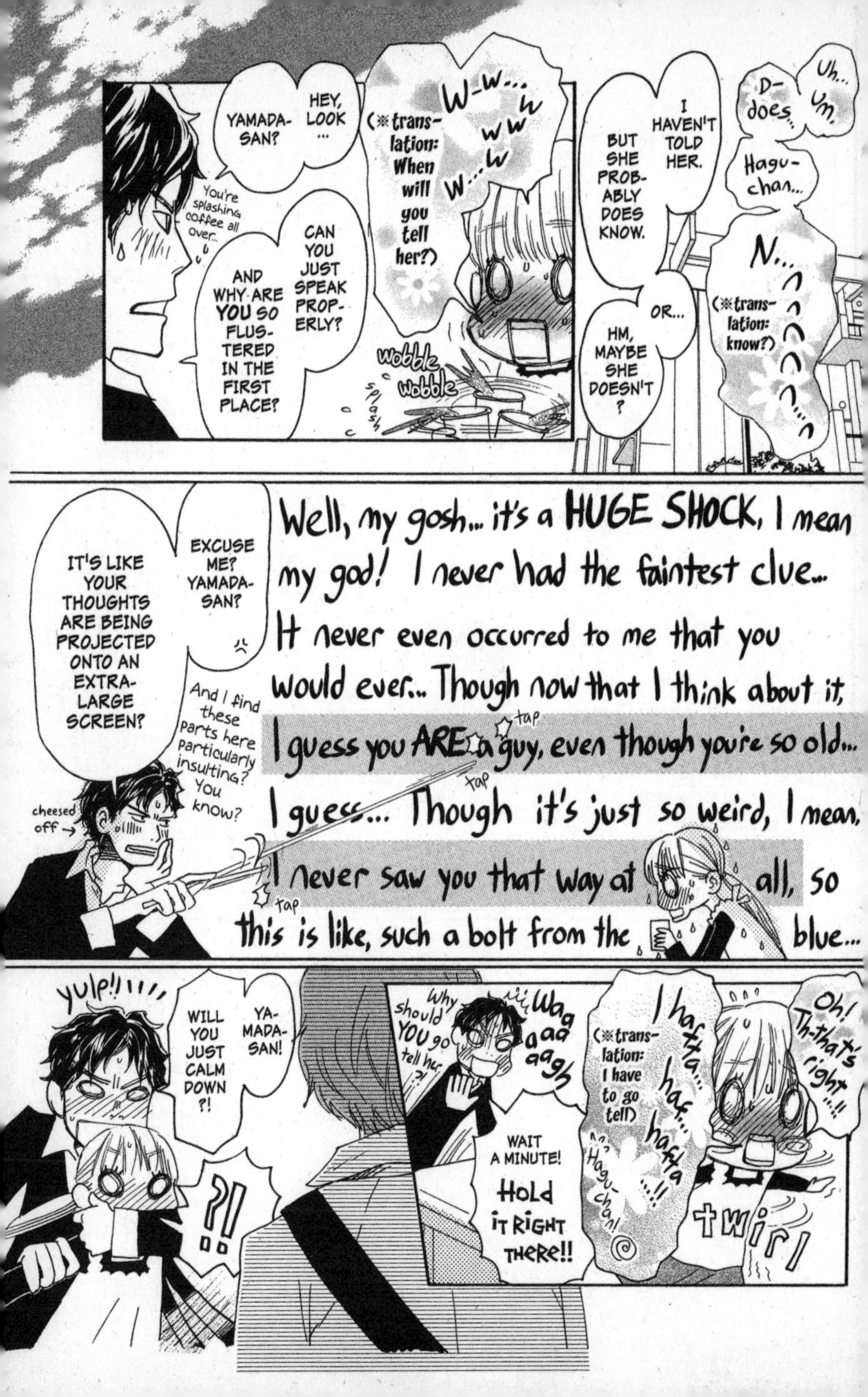
Uh... Um.
D-does...
Hagu-chan...
N... ^^^^^^...^
(※translation: know?)
I HAVEN'T TOLD HER.
BUT SHE PROBABLY DOES KNOW.
OR...
HM, MAYBE SHE DOESN'T?
W-w... w ww w... w
(※translation: When will you tell her?)
wobble wobble
splash
HEY, LOOK...
YAMADA-SAN?
CAN YOU JUST SPEAK PROPERLY?
AND WHY ARE YOU SO FLUSTERED IN THE FIRST PLACE?
You're splashing coffee all over...
Well, my gosh... it's a HUGE SHOCK, I mean my god! I never had the faintest clue... It never even occurred to me that you would ever... Though now that I think about it, I guess you ARE a guy, even though you're so old... I guess... Though it's just so weird, I mean, I never saw you that way at all, so this is like, such a bolt from the blue...
tap
tap
tap
EXCUSE ME? YAMADA-SAN?
IT'S LIKE YOUR THOUGHTS ARE BEING PROJECTED ONTO AN EXTRA-LARGE SCREEN?
And I find these parts here particularly insulting? You know?
cheesed off
Oh! Th-that's right...!!
I hafta... haf... hafta...!!
(※translation: I have to go tell)
twirl
Hagu-chan!
Waaaaagh
Why should YOU go tell her?!
WAIT A MINUTE! HOLD IT RIGHT THERE!!
YA-MADA-SAN!
WILL YOU JUST CALM DOWN?!
yulp!!
?!

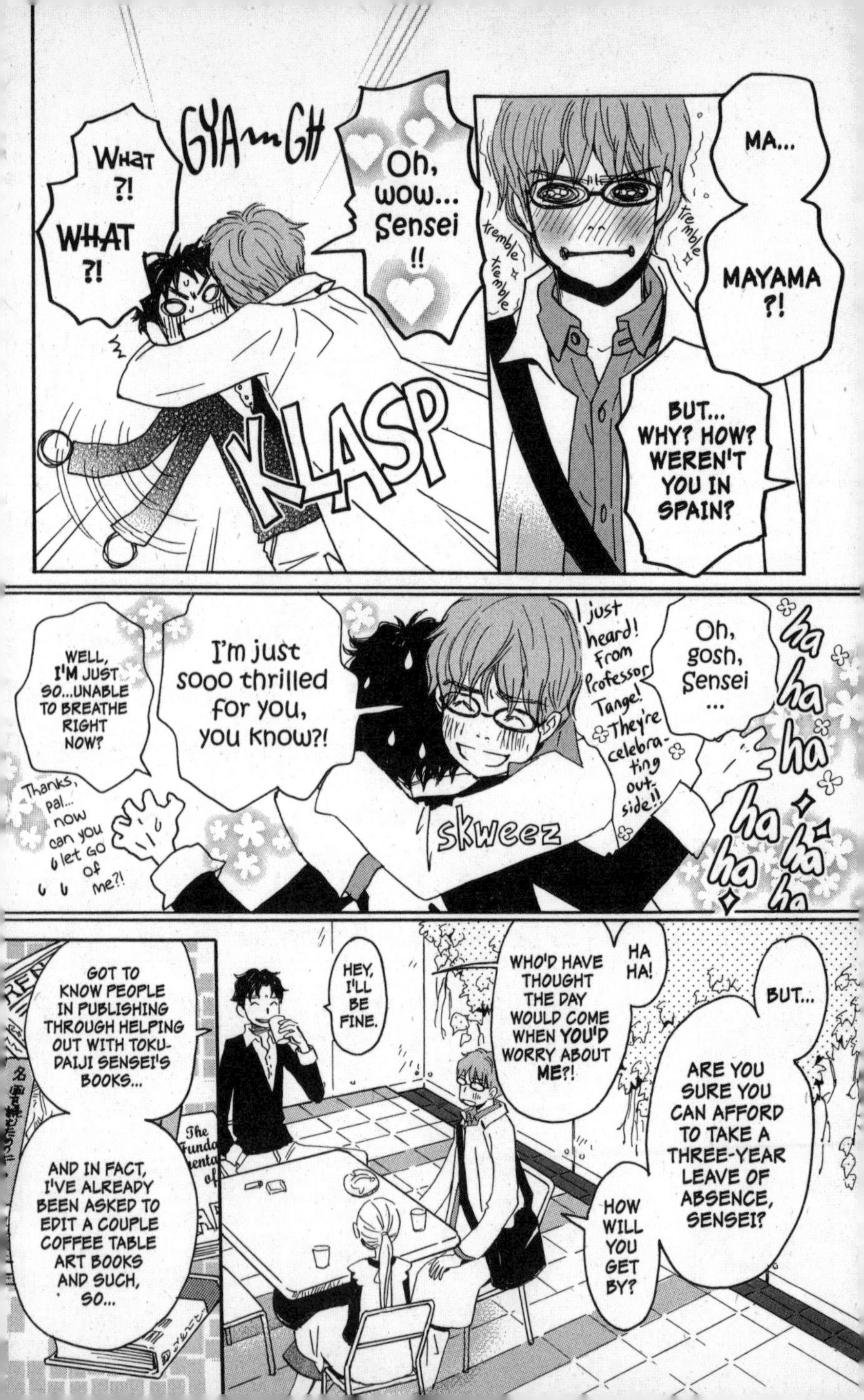
MA...
MAYAMA ?!
tremble tremble tremble tremble
BUT... WHY? HOW? WEREN'T YOU IN SPAIN?
Oh, wow... Sensei !!
GYAmmGH
WHAT ?! WHAT ?!
KLASP
ha ha ha ha ha ha ha ha
Oh, gosh, Sensei ...
I just heard! From Professor Tange! They're celebra-ting out-side!!
I'm just sooo thrilled for you, you know?!
skweez
WELL, I'M JUST SO...UNABLE TO BREATHE RIGHT NOW?
Thanks, pal... now can you let go of me?!
BUT...
ARE YOU SURE YOU CAN AFFORD TO TAKE A THREE-YEAR LEAVE OF ABSENCE, SENSEI?
HOW WILL YOU GET BY?
HA HA!
WHO'D HAVE THOUGHT THE DAY WOULD COME WHEN YOU'D WORRY ABOUT ME?!
HEY, I'LL BE FINE.
GOT TO KNOW PEOPLE IN PUBLISHING THROUGH HELPING OUT WITH TOKU-DAIJI SENSEI'S BOOKS...
AND IN FACT, I'VE ALREADY BEEN ASKED TO EDIT A COUPLE COFFEE TABLE ART BOOKS AND SUCH, SO...

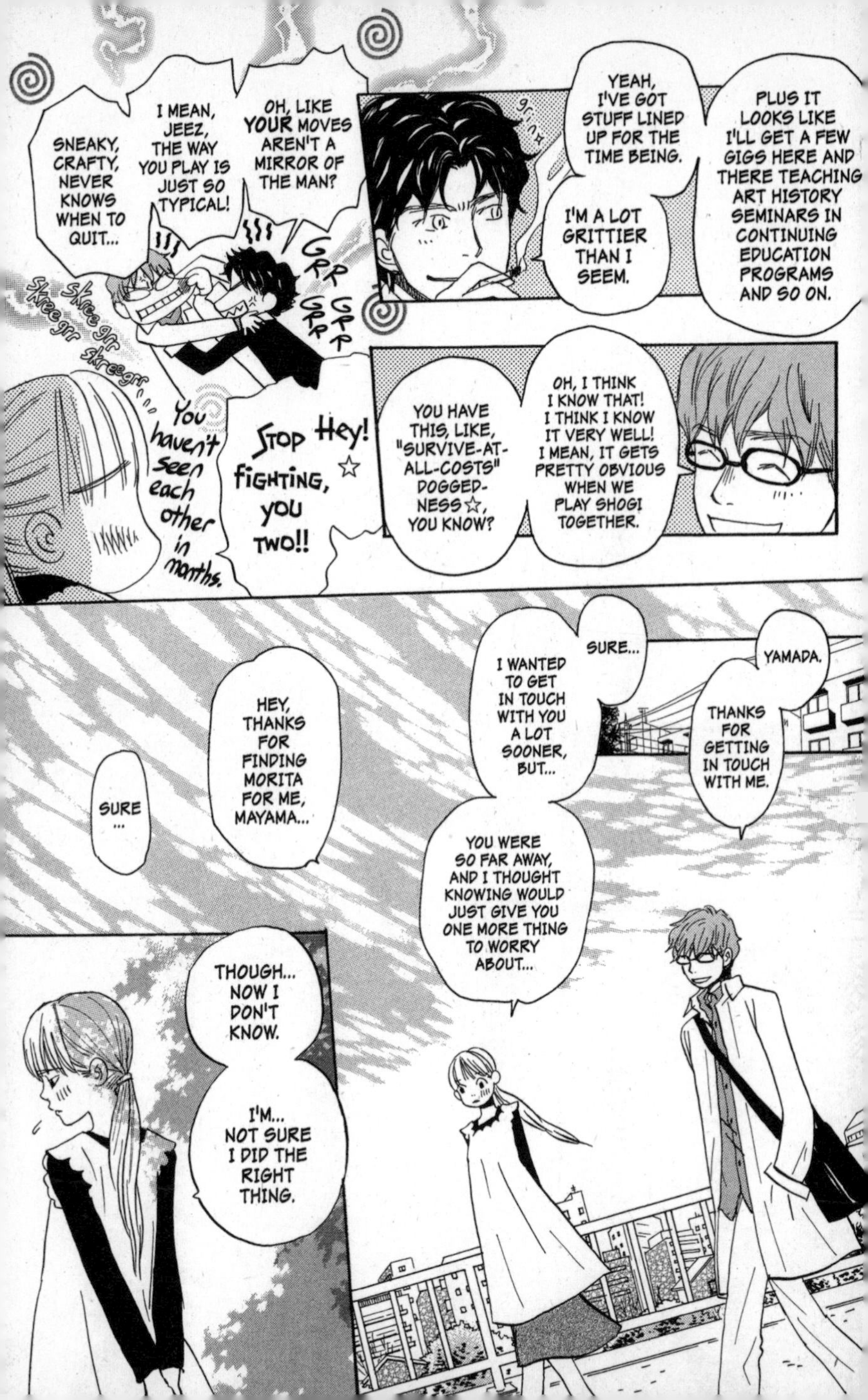
YEAH, I'VE GOT STUFF LINED UP FOR THE TIME BEING.
PLUS IT LOOKS LIKE I'LL GET A FEW GIGS HERE AND THERE TEACHING ART HISTORY SEMINARS IN CONTINUING EDUCATION PROGRAMS AND SO ON.
grr
I'M A LOT GRITTIER THAN I SEEM.
OH, I THINK I KNOW THAT! I THINK I KNOW IT VERY WELL! I MEAN, IT GETS PRETTY OBVIOUS WHEN WE PLAY SHOGI TOGETHER.
YOU HAVE THIS, LIKE, "SURVIVE-AT-ALL-COSTS" DOGGEDNESS☆, YOU KNOW?
SNEAKY, CRAFTY, NEVER KNOWS WHEN TO QUIT...
I MEAN, JEEZ, THE WAY YOU PLAY IS JUST SO TYPICAL!
OH, LIKE **YOUR** MOVES AREN'T A MIRROR OF THE MAN?
GRR GRR GRR
skree grr skree grr skreegrr
Hey! ☆
Stop fighting, you two!!
You haven't seen each other in months.
YAMADA.
THANKS FOR GETTING IN TOUCH WITH ME.
SURE...
I WANTED TO GET IN TOUCH WITH YOU A LOT SOONER, BUT...
YOU WERE SO FAR AWAY, AND I THOUGHT KNOWING WOULD JUST GIVE YOU ONE MORE THING TO WORRY ABOUT...
HEY, THANKS FOR FINDING MORITA FOR ME, MAYAMA...
SURE ...
THOUGH... NOW I DON'T KNOW.
I'M... NOT SURE I DID THE RIGHT THING.

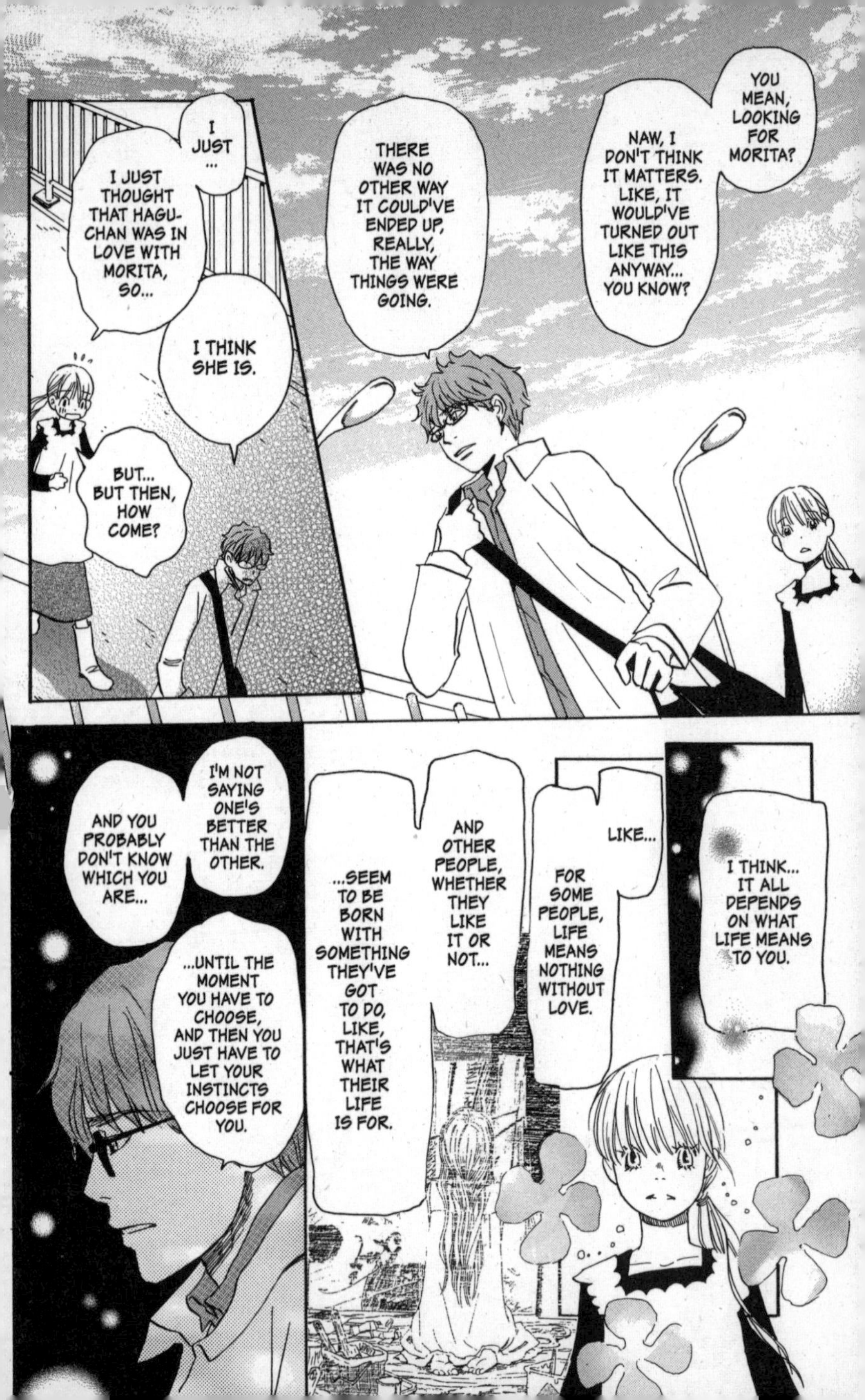
YOU MEAN, LOOKING FOR MORITA?
NAW, I DON'T THINK IT MATTERS. LIKE, IT WOULD'VE TURNED OUT LIKE THIS ANYWAY... YOU KNOW?
THERE WAS NO OTHER WAY IT COULD'VE ENDED UP, REALLY, THE WAY THINGS WERE GOING.
I JUST ...
I JUST THOUGHT THAT HAGU-CHAN WAS IN LOVE WITH MORITA, SO...
I THINK SHE IS.
BUT... BUT THEN, HOW COME?
I THINK... IT ALL DEPENDS ON WHAT LIFE MEANS TO YOU.
LIKE...
FOR SOME PEOPLE, LIFE MEANS NOTHING WITHOUT LOVE.
AND OTHER PEOPLE, WHETHER THEY LIKE IT OR NOT...
...SEEM TO BE BORN WITH SOMETHING THEY'VE GOT TO DO, LIKE, THAT'S WHAT THEIR LIFE IS FOR.
I'M NOT SAYING ONE'S BETTER THAN THE OTHER.
AND YOU PROBABLY DON'T KNOW WHICH YOU ARE...
...UNTIL THE MOMENT YOU HAVE TO CHOOSE, AND THEN YOU JUST HAVE TO LET YOUR INSTINCTS CHOOSE FOR YOU.

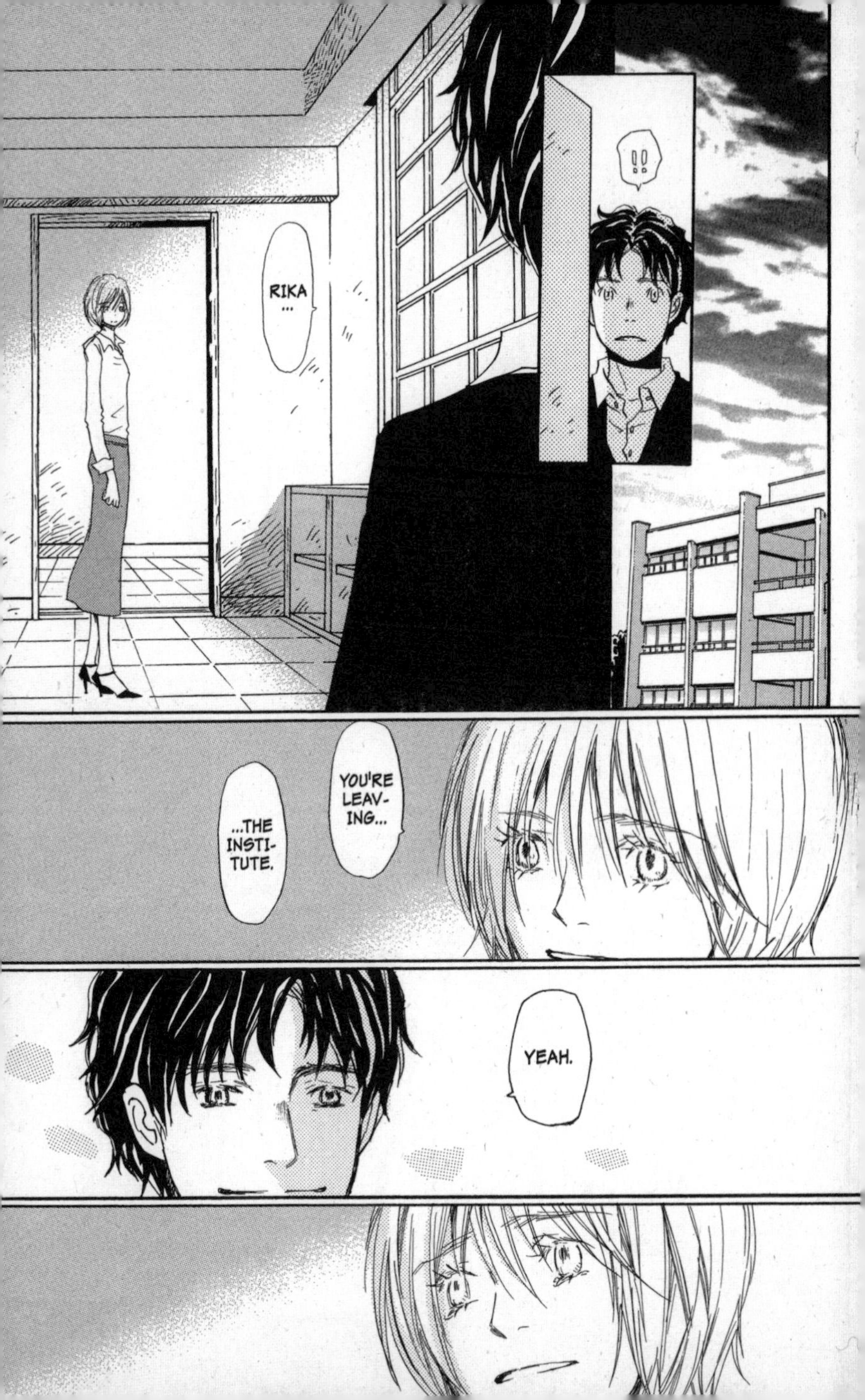
!!
RIKA ...
YOU'RE LEAVING...
...THE INSTITUTE.
YEAH.

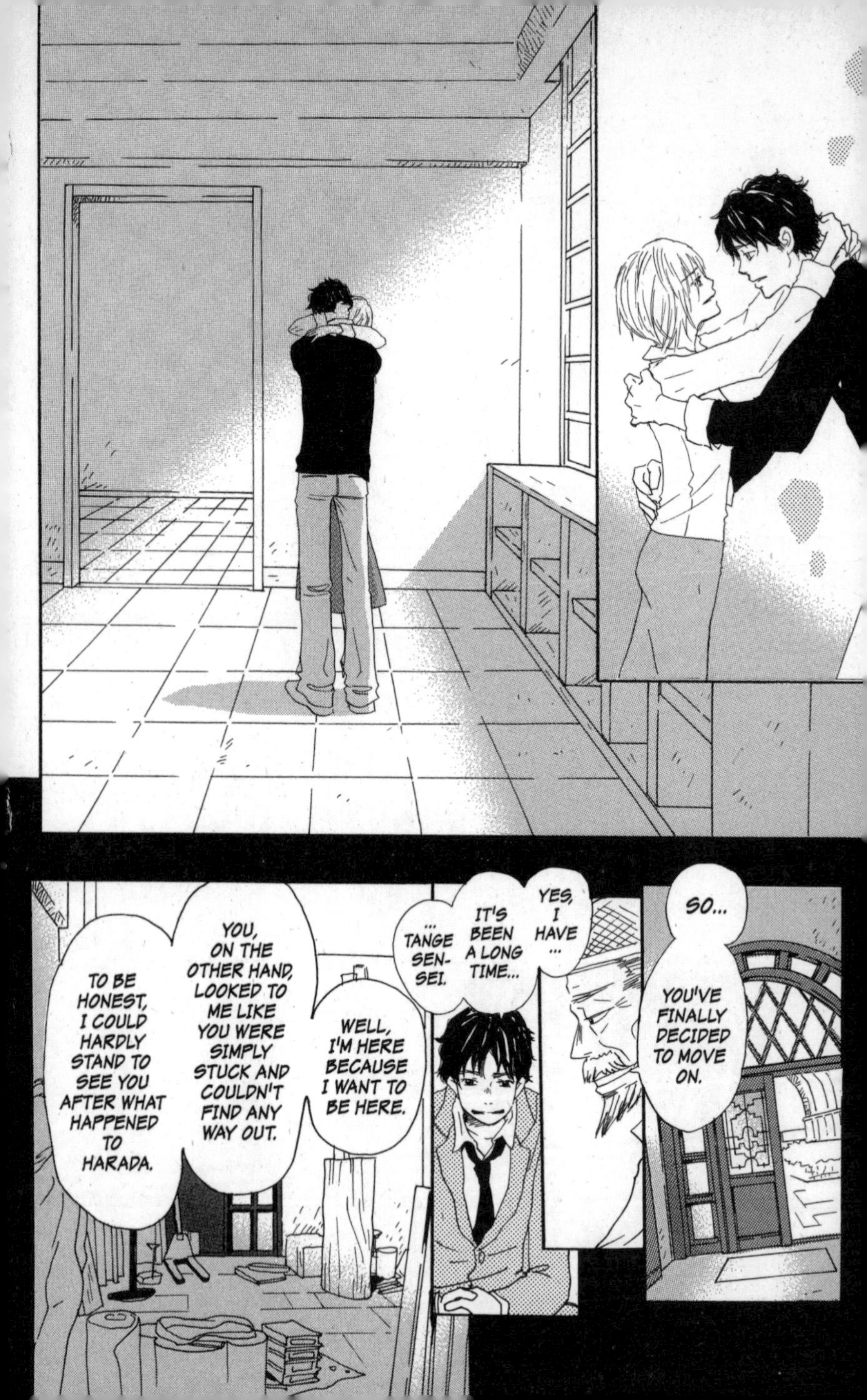
SO...
YOU'VE FINALLY DECIDED TO MOVE ON.
YES, I HAVE...
IT'S BEEN A LONG TIME...
...TANGE SEN-SEI.
WELL, I'M HERE BECAUSE I WANT TO BE HERE.
YOU, ON THE OTHER HAND, LOOKED TO ME LIKE YOU WERE SIMPLY STUCK AND COULDN'T FIND ANY WAY OUT.
TO BE HONEST, I COULD HARDLY STAND TO SEE YOU AFTER WHAT HAPPENED TO HARADA.

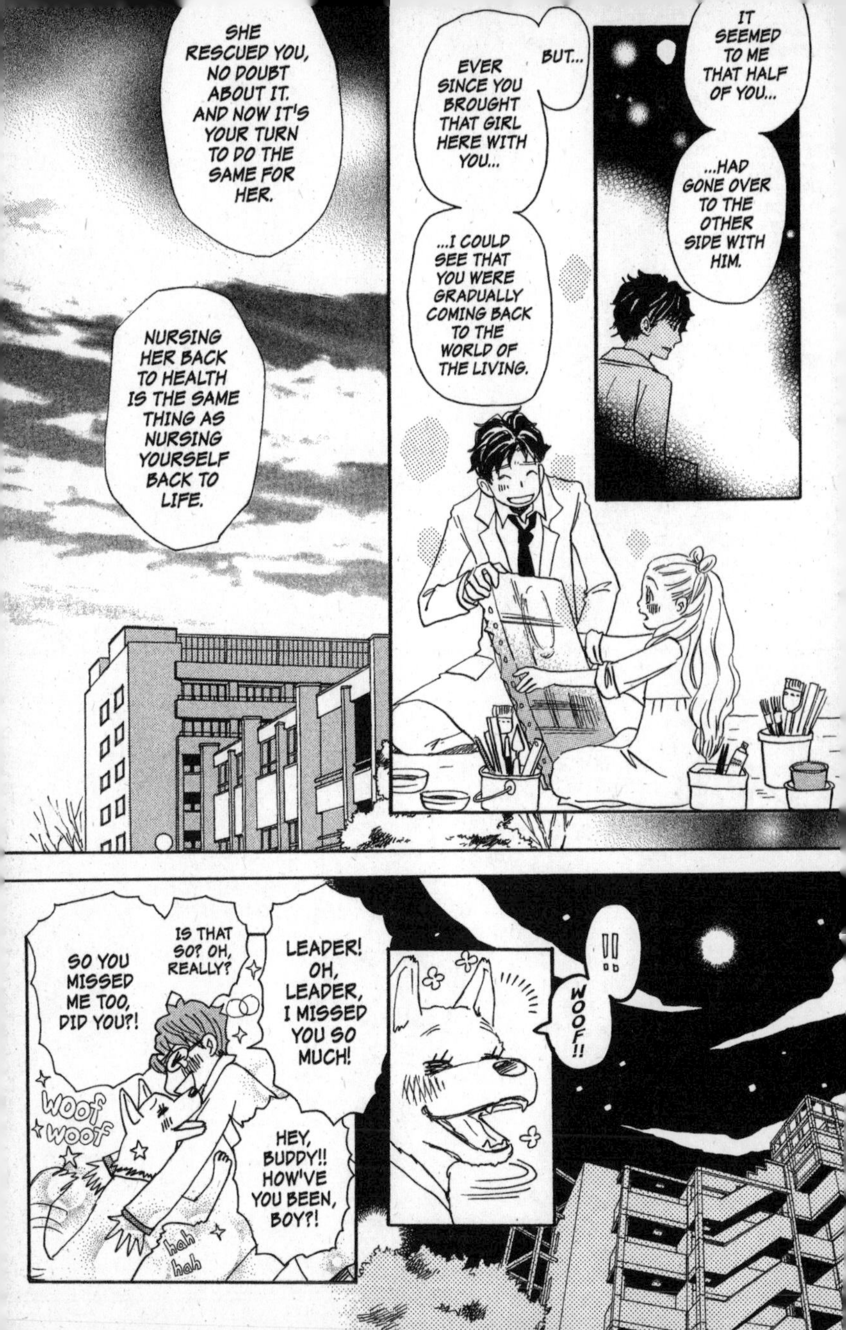
IT SEEMED TO ME THAT HALF OF YOU...
...HAD GONE OVER TO THE OTHER SIDE WITH HIM.
BUT...
EVER SINCE YOU BROUGHT THAT GIRL HERE WITH YOU...
...I COULD SEE THAT YOU WERE GRADUALLY COMING BACK TO THE WORLD OF THE LIVING.
SHE RESCUED YOU, NO DOUBT ABOUT IT. AND NOW IT'S YOUR TURN TO DO THE SAME FOR HER.
NURSING HER BACK TO HEALTH IS THE SAME THING AS NURSING YOURSELF BACK TO LIFE.
!!
WOOF!!
LEADER! OH, LEADER, I MISSED YOU SO MUCH!
IS THAT SO? OH, REALLY?
SO YOU MISSED ME TOO, DID YOU?!
HEY, BUDDY!! HOW'VE YOU BEEN, BOY?!
woof woof
hah hah

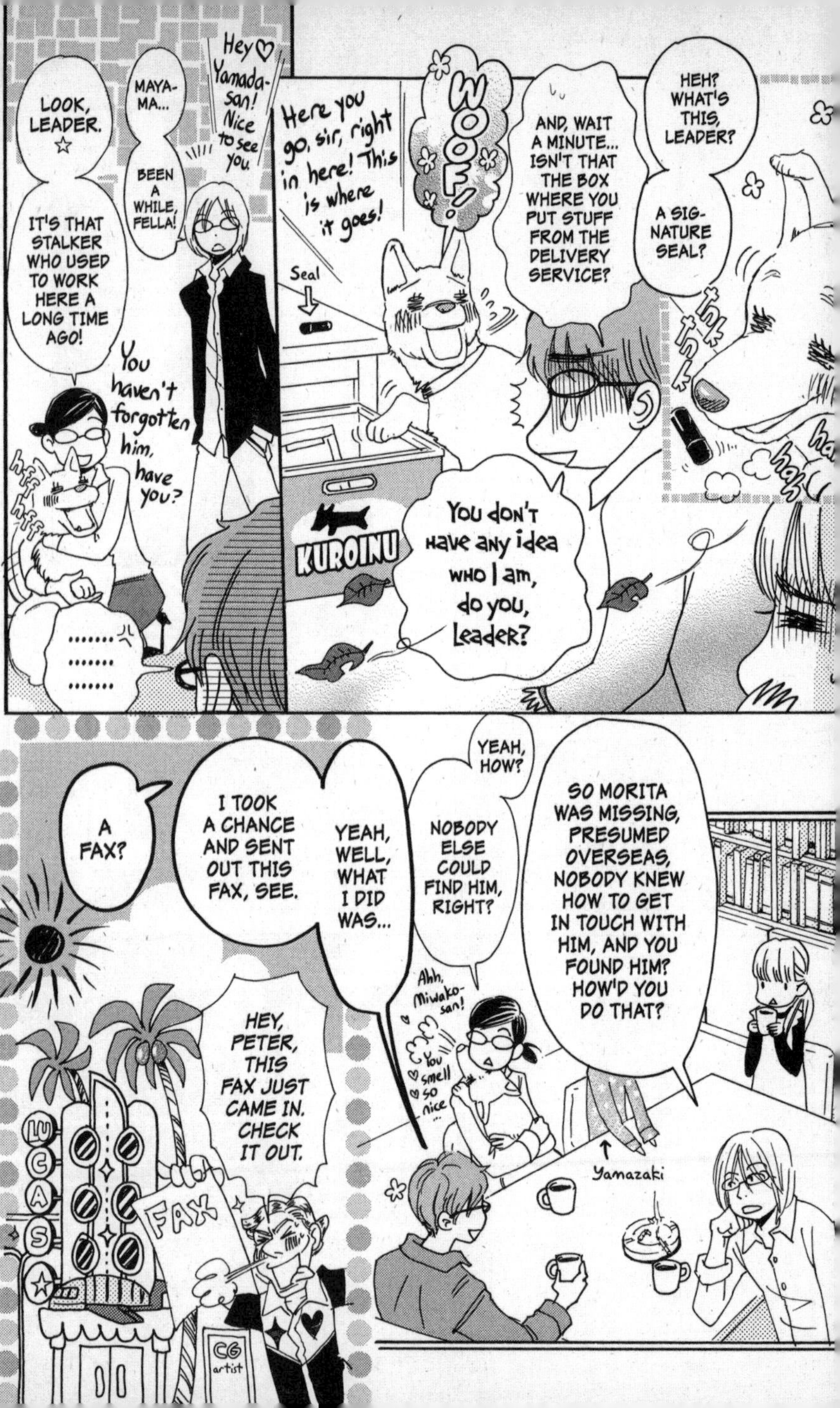
HEH? WHAT'S THIS, LEADER?
A SIGNATURE SEAL?
thk thk
hah hah
AND, WAIT A MINUTE... ISN'T THAT THE BOX WHERE YOU PUT STUFF FROM THE DELIVERY SERVICE?
WOOF!
Here you go, sir, right in here! This is where it goes!
Seal
KUROINU
You don't have any idea who I am, do you, Leader?
Hey♡ Yamada-san! Nice to see you.
MAYAMA...
BEEN A WHILE, FELLA!
LOOK, LEADER. ☆
IT'S THAT STALKER WHO USED TO WORK HERE A LONG TIME AGO!
You haven't forgotten him, have you?
hff hff
....
SO MORITA WAS MISSING, PRESUMED OVERSEAS, NOBODY KNEW HOW TO GET IN TOUCH WITH HIM, AND YOU FOUND HIM? HOW'D YOU DO THAT?
YEAH, HOW?
NOBODY ELSE COULD FIND HIM, RIGHT?
YEAH, WELL, WHAT I DID WAS...
I TOOK A CHANCE AND SENT OUT THIS FAX, SEE.
Ahh, Miwako-san!
♡ You ♡ smell ♡ so nice...
Yamazaki
A FAX?
HEY, PETER, THIS FAX JUST CAME IN. CHECK IT OUT.
LUCAS
FAX
CG artist

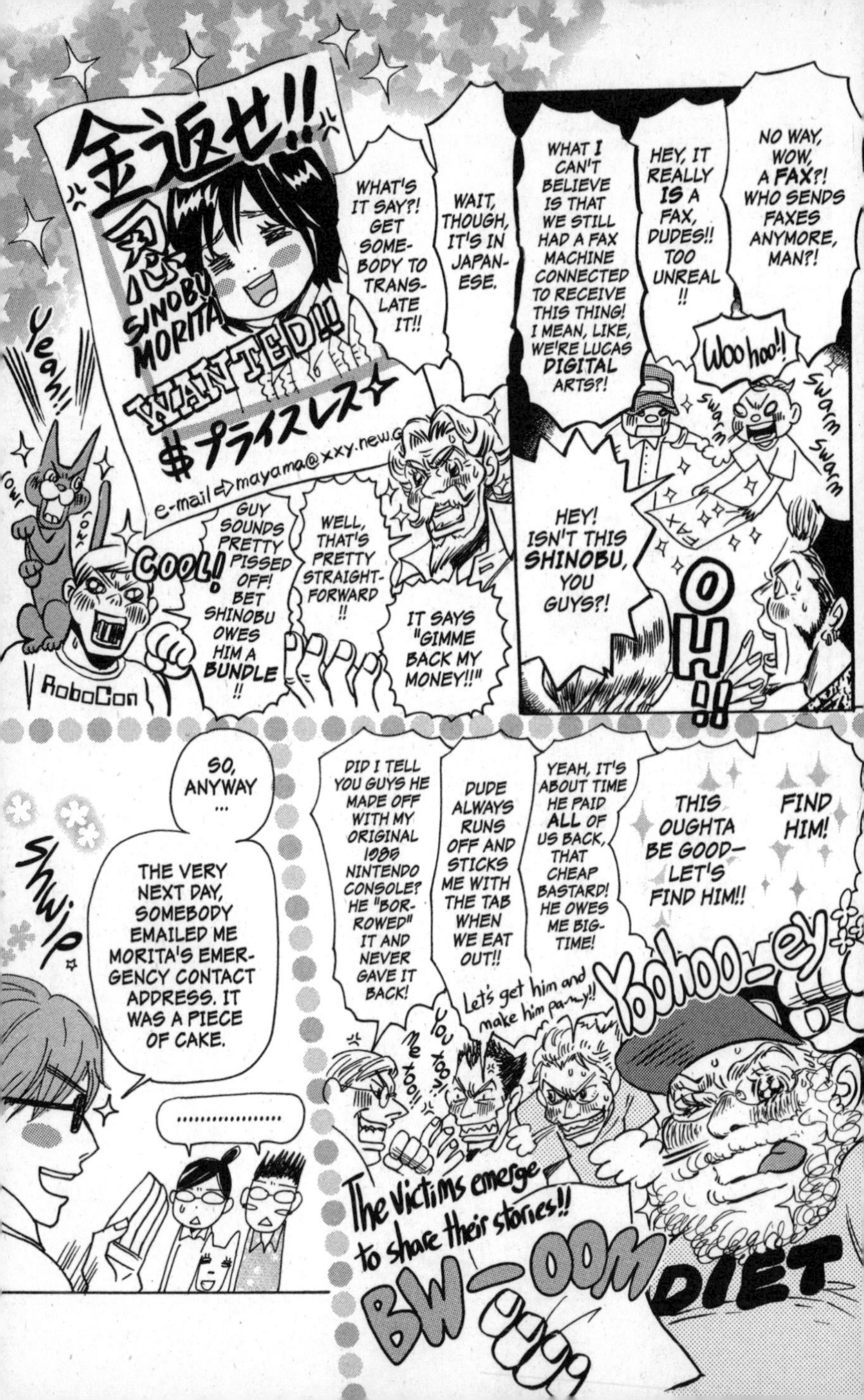
NO WAY, WOW, A FAX?! WHO SENDS FAXES ANYMORE, MAN?!
HEY, IT REALLY IS A FAX, DUDES!! TOO UNREAL!!
WHAT I CAN'T BELIEVE IS THAT WE STILL HAD A FAX MACHINE CONNECTED TO RECEIVE THIS THING! I MEAN, LIKE, WE'RE LUCAS DIGITAL ARTS?!
Woo hoo!!
Swarm swarm swarm swarm
FAX
HEY! ISN'T THIS SHINOBU, YOU GUYS?!
OOH!!
WAIT, THOUGH, IT'S IN JAPANESE.
WHAT'S IT SAY?! GET SOMEBODY TO TRANSLATE IT!!
金返せ!!
忍
SINOBU MORITA
WANTED!!
$プライスレス☆
e-mail ⇨ mayama@xxy.new.G
IT SAYS "GIMME BACK MY MONEY!!!"
WELL, THAT'S PRETTY STRAIGHTFORWARD!!
GUY SOUNDS PRETTY PISSED OFF! BET SHINOBU OWES HIM A BUNDLE!!
COOL!
Yeah!!
Cowr cow
RoboCon
FIND HIM!
THIS OUGHTA BE GOOD—LET'S FIND HIM!!
YEAH, IT'S ABOUT TIME HE PAID ALL OF US BACK, THAT CHEAP BASTARD! HE OWES ME BIG-TIME!
DUDE ALWAYS RUNS OFF AND STICKS ME WITH THE TAB WHEN WE EAT OUT!!
DID I TELL YOU GUYS HE MADE OFF WITH MY ORIGINAL 1985 NINTENDO CONSOLE? HE "BORROWED" IT AND NEVER GAVE IT BACK!
Yoohoo-ey
Let's get him and make him pay!!
You too?!
Me too!!
The victims emerge to share their stories!!
BW—OOM
DIET
SO, ANYWAY...
THE VERY NEXT DAY, SOMEBODY EMAILED ME MORITA'S EMERGENCY CONTACT ADDRESS. IT WAS A PIECE OF CAKE.
Shwip
....

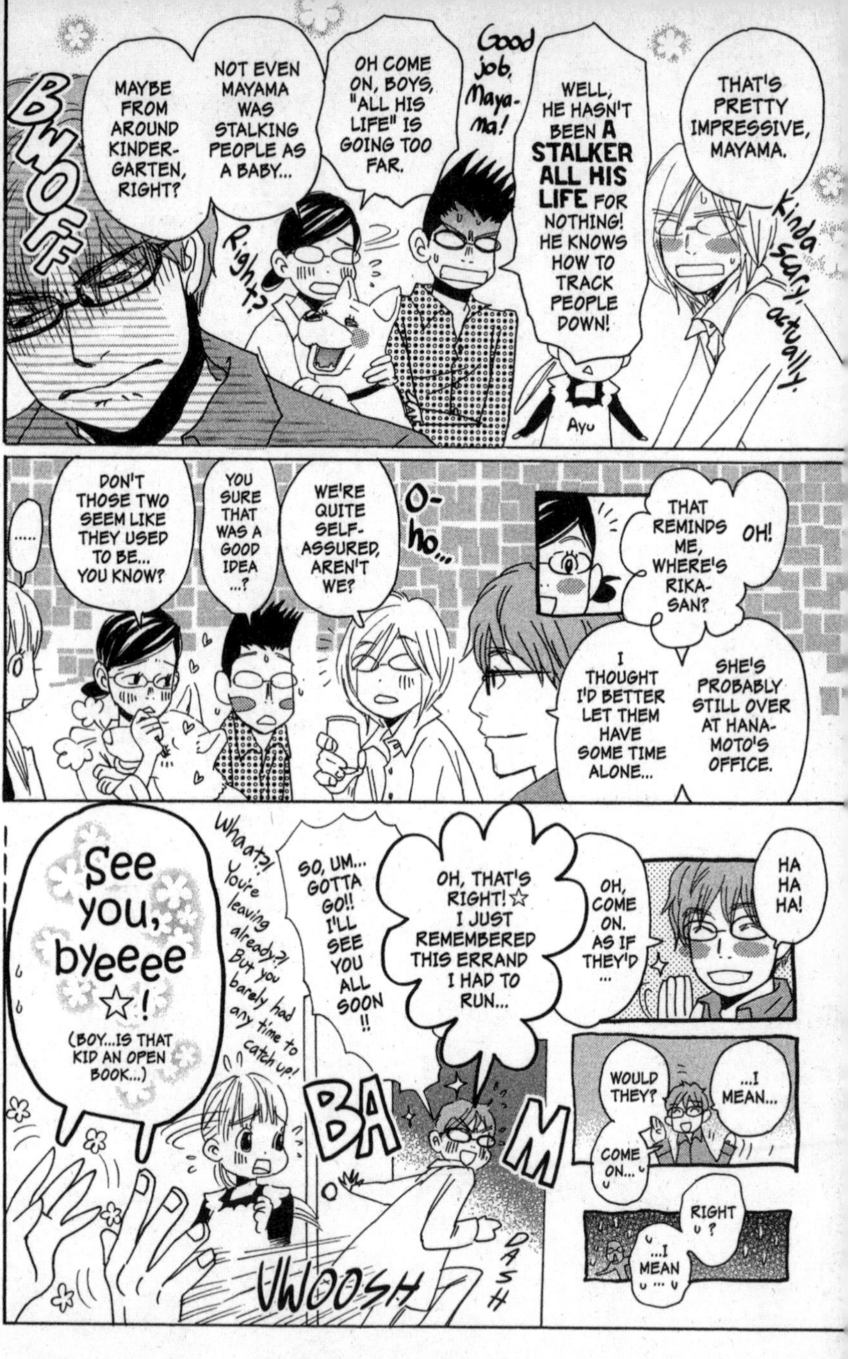
THAT'S PRETTY IMPRESSIVE, MAYAMA.
Kinda scary, actually.
WELL, HE HASN'T BEEN A STALKER ALL HIS LIFE FOR NOTHING! HE KNOWS HOW TO TRACK PEOPLE DOWN!
Good job, Mayama!
Ayu
OH COME ON, BOYS, "ALL HIS LIFE" IS GOING TOO FAR.
NOT EVEN MAYAMA WAS STALKING PEOPLE AS A BABY...
Right?
MAYBE FROM AROUND KINDER-GARTEN, RIGHT?
BWOFF
OH!
THAT REMINDS ME, WHERE'S RIKA-SAN?
SHE'S PROBABLY STILL OVER AT HANA-MOTO'S OFFICE.
I THOUGHT I'D BETTER LET THEM HAVE SOME TIME ALONE...
O-ho...
WE'RE QUITE SELF-ASSURED, AREN'T WE?
YOU SURE THAT WAS A GOOD IDEA ...?
DON'T THOSE TWO SEEM LIKE THEY USED TO BE... YOU KNOW?
.....
HA HA HA!
OH, COME ON. AS IF THEY'D ...
...I MEAN...
WOULD THEY?
COME ON...
RIGHT?
...I MEAN...
OH, THAT'S RIGHT! ☆ I JUST REMEMBERED THIS ERRAND I HAD TO RUN...
BAM
DASH
SO, UM... GOTTA GO!! I'LL SEE YOU ALL SOON!!
Whaat?! You're leaving already?! But you barely had any time to catch up!
WOOSH
See you, byeeee ☆!
(BOY...IS THAT KID AN OPEN BOOK...)

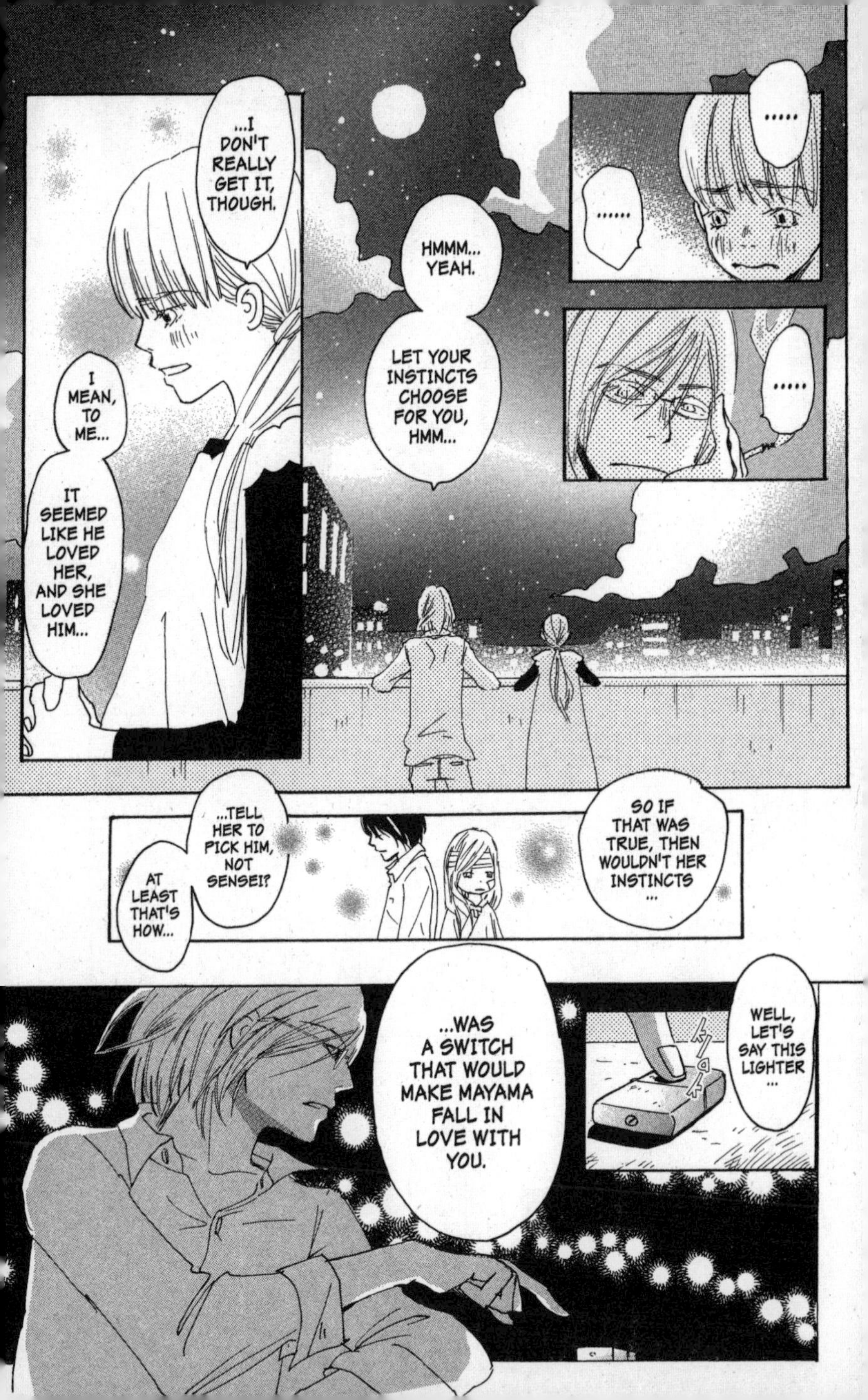
......
......
......
HMMM... YEAH.
LET YOUR INSTINCTS CHOOSE FOR YOU, HMM...
...I DON'T REALLY GET IT, THOUGH.
I MEAN, TO ME...
IT SEEMED LIKE HE LOVED HER, AND SHE LOVED HIM...
SO IF THAT WAS TRUE, THEN WOULDN'T HER INSTINCTS ...
...TELL HER TO PICK HIM, NOT SENSEI?
AT LEAST THAT'S HOW...
WELL, LET'S SAY THIS LIGHTER ...
...WAS A SWITCH THAT WOULD MAKE MAYAMA FALL IN LOVE WITH YOU.

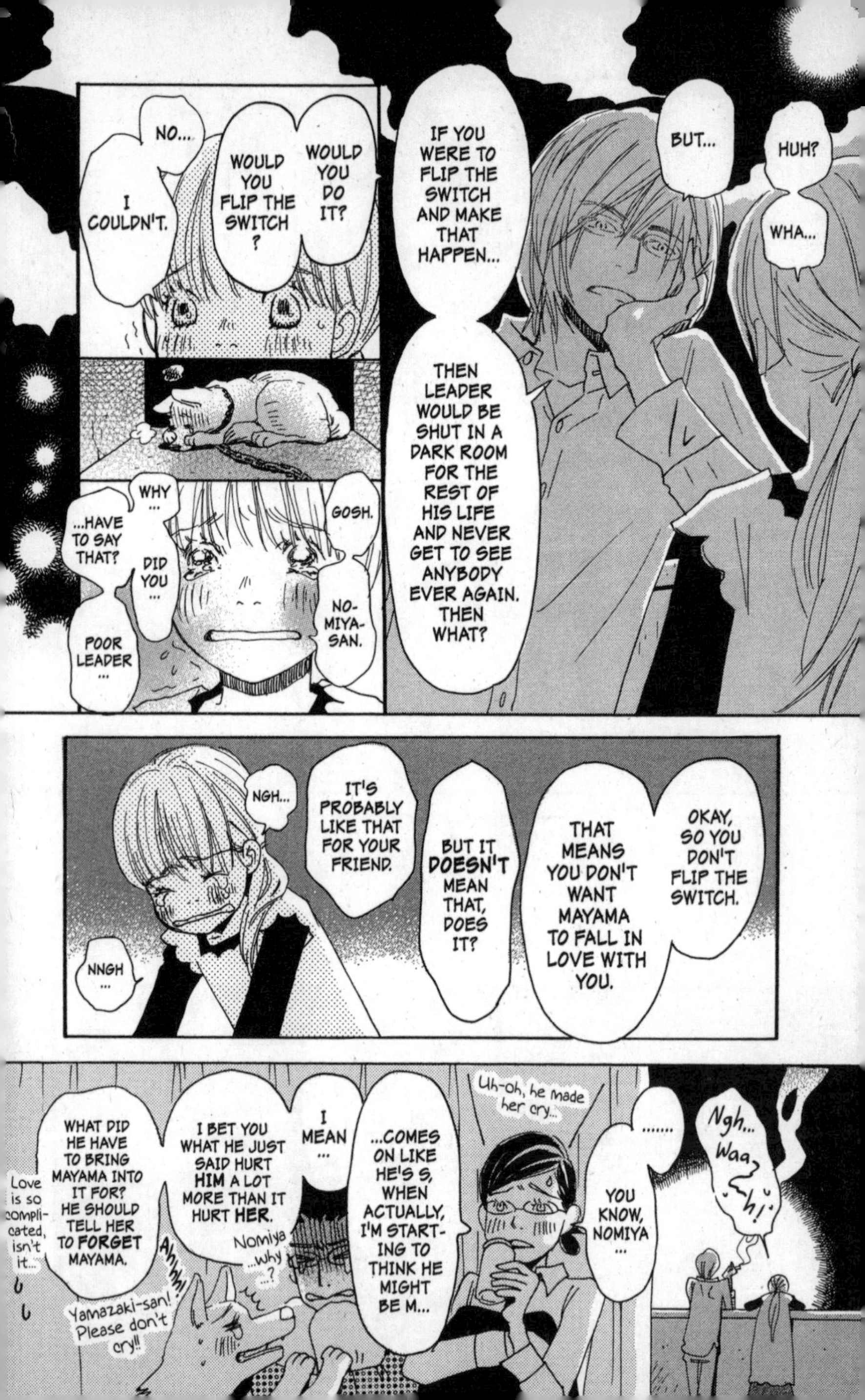
HUH?
WHA...
BUT...
IF YOU WERE TO FLIP THE SWITCH AND MAKE THAT HAPPEN...
THEN LEADER WOULD BE SHUT IN A DARK ROOM FOR THE REST OF HIS LIFE AND NEVER GET TO SEE ANYBODY EVER AGAIN. THEN WHAT?
WOULD YOU DO IT?
WOULD YOU FLIP THE SWITCH?
NO...
I COULDN'T.
GOSH.
NO-MIYA-SAN.
DID YOU...
WHY...
...HAVE TO SAY THAT?
POOR LEADER...
OKAY, SO YOU DON'T FLIP THE SWITCH.
THAT MEANS YOU DON'T WANT MAYAMA TO FALL IN LOVE WITH YOU.
BUT IT **DOESN'T** MEAN THAT, DOES IT?
IT'S PROBABLY LIKE THAT FOR YOUR FRIEND.
NGH...
NNGH...
Ngh... Waaah!
....
Uh-oh, he made her cry...
YOU KNOW, NOMIYA...
...COMES ON LIKE HE'S S, WHEN ACTUALLY, I'M STARTING TO THINK HE MIGHT BE M...
I MEAN...
I BET YOU WHAT HE JUST SAID HURT **HIM** A LOT MORE THAN IT HURT **HER**.
Nomiya ...why...?
WHAT DID HE HAVE TO BRING MAYAMA INTO IT FOR? HE SHOULD TELL HER TO **FORGET** MAYAMA.
Ahhh!
Love is so compli-cated, isn't it...
Yamazaki-san! Please don't cry!!

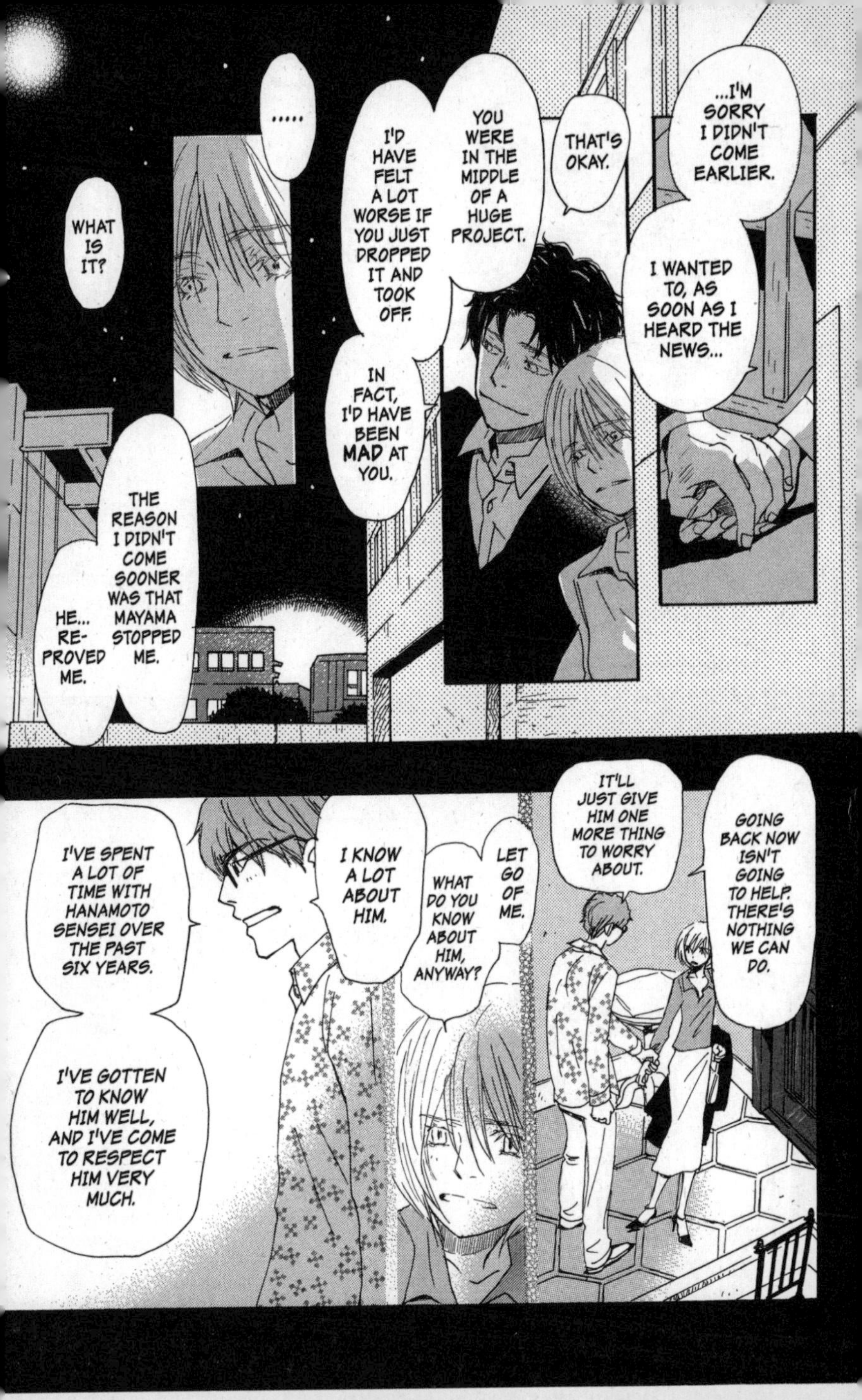
...I'M SORRY I DIDN'T COME EARLIER.
I WANTED TO, AS SOON AS I HEARD THE NEWS...
THAT'S OKAY.
YOU WERE IN THE MIDDLE OF A HUGE PROJECT.
I'D HAVE FELT A LOT WORSE IF YOU JUST DROPPED IT AND TOOK OFF.
IN FACT, I'D HAVE BEEN MAD AT YOU.
......
WHAT IS IT?
THE REASON I DIDN'T COME SOONER WAS THAT MAYAMA STOPPED ME.
HE... RE-PROVED ME.
GOING BACK NOW ISN'T GOING TO HELP. THERE'S NOTHING WE CAN DO.
IT'LL JUST GIVE HIM ONE MORE THING TO WORRY ABOUT.
LET GO OF ME.
WHAT DO YOU KNOW ABOUT HIM, ANYWAY?
I KNOW A LOT ABOUT HIM.
I'VE SPENT A LOT OF TIME WITH HANAMOTO SENSEI OVER THE PAST SIX YEARS.
I'VE GOTTEN TO KNOW HIM WELL, AND I'VE COME TO RESPECT HIM VERY MUCH.

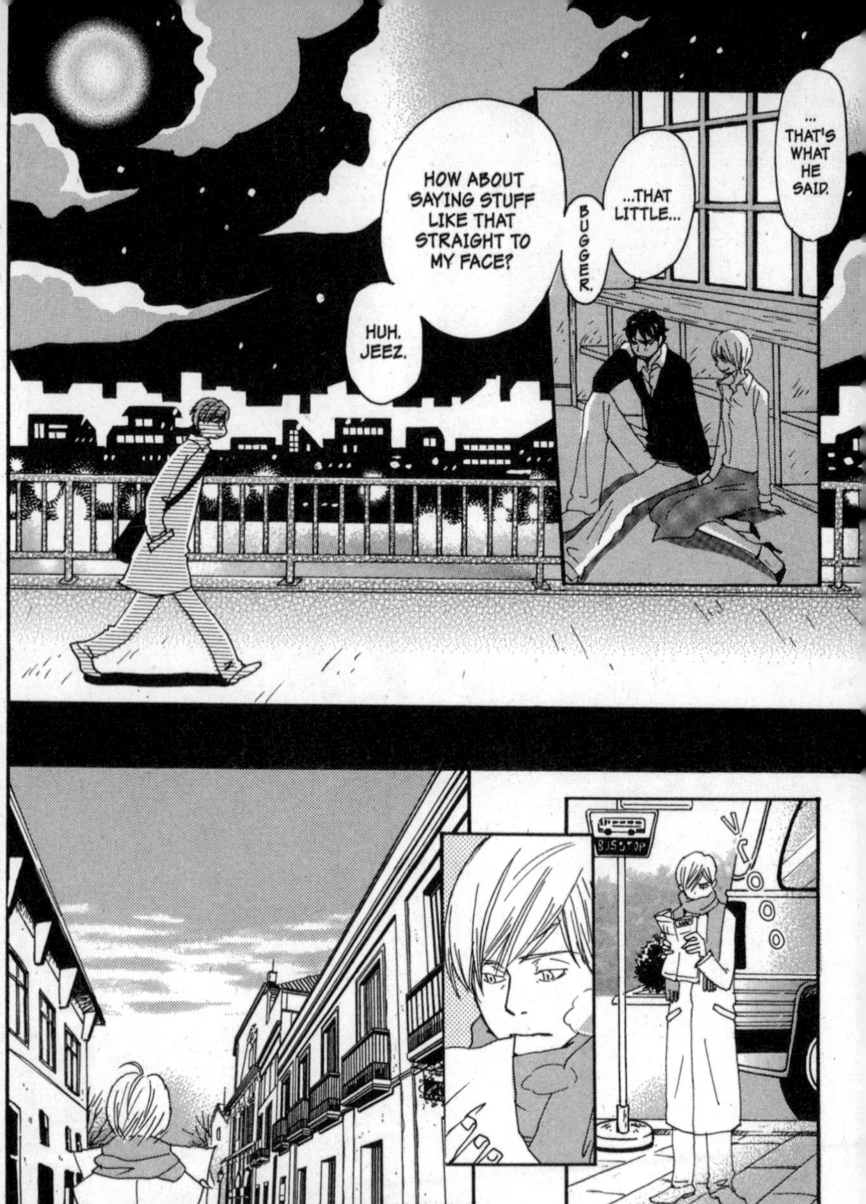
...THAT'S WHAT HE SAID.
...THAT LITTLE...
BUGGER.
HOW ABOUT SAYING STUFF LIKE THAT STRAIGHT TO MY FACE?
HUH. JEEZ.

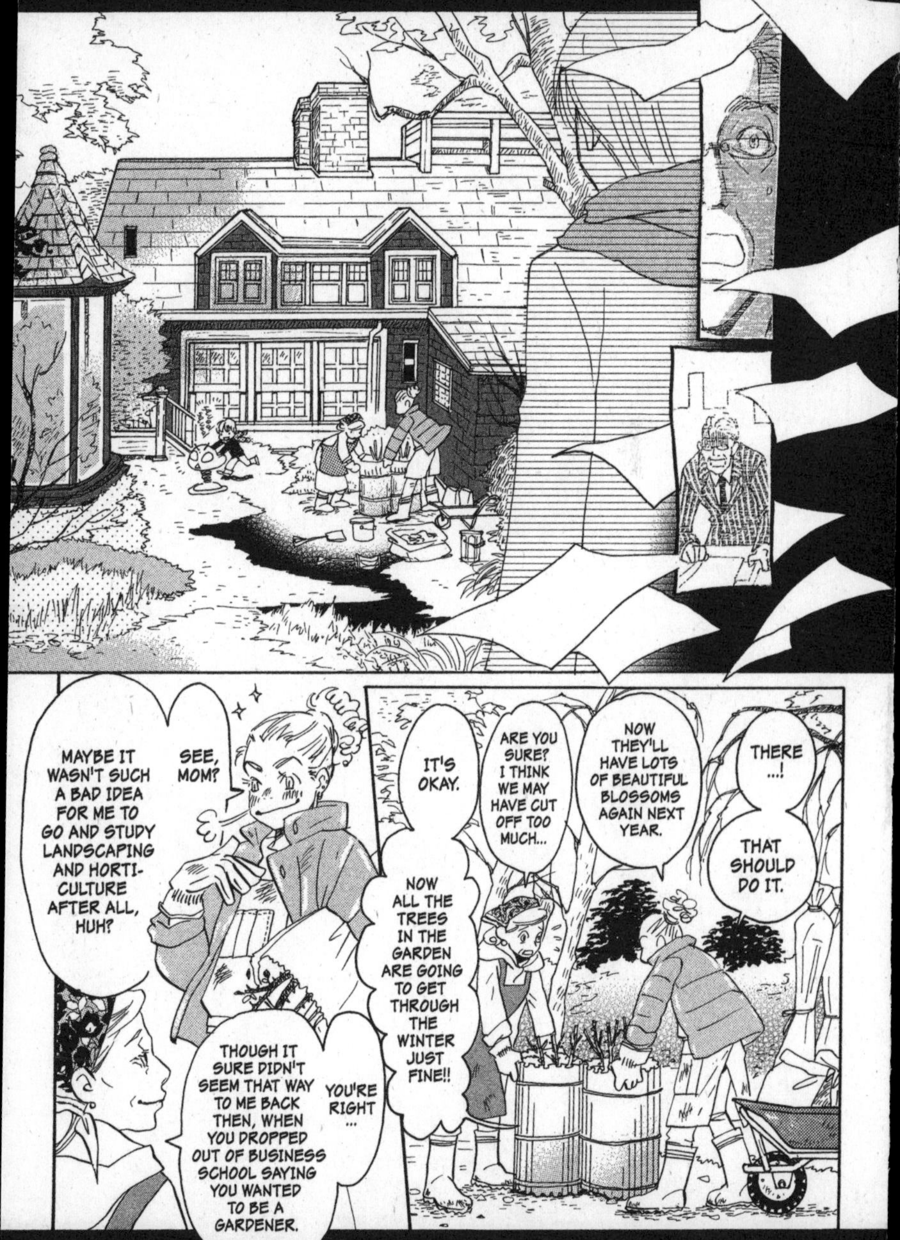
THERE ...!
THAT SHOULD DO IT.
NOW THEY'LL HAVE LOTS OF BEAUTIFUL BLOSSOMS AGAIN NEXT YEAR.
ARE YOU SURE? I THINK WE MAY HAVE CUT OFF TOO MUCH...
IT'S OKAY.
NOW ALL THE TREES IN THE GARDEN ARE GOING TO GET THROUGH THE WINTER JUST FINE!!
SEE, MOM?
MAYBE IT WASN'T SUCH A BAD IDEA FOR ME TO GO AND STUDY LANDSCAPING AND HORTI-CULTURE AFTER ALL, HUH?
YOU'RE RIGHT ...
THOUGH IT SURE DIDN'T SEEM THAT WAY TO ME BACK THEN, WHEN YOU DROPPED OUT OF BUSINESS SCHOOL SAYING YOU WANTED TO BE A GARDENER.

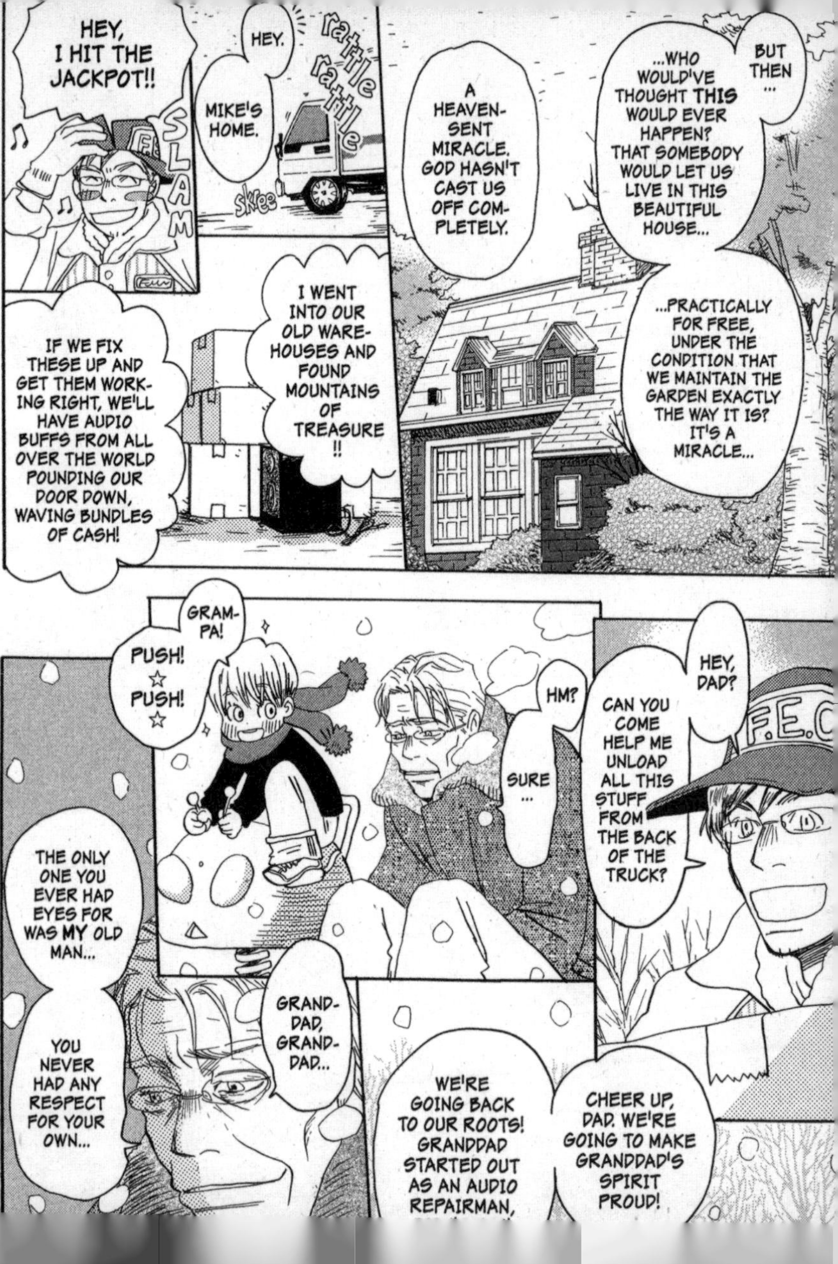
BUT THEN...
...WHO WOULD'VE THOUGHT THIS WOULD EVER HAPPEN? THAT SOMEBODY WOULD LET US LIVE IN THIS BEAUTIFUL HOUSE...
A HEAVEN-SENT MIRACLE. GOD HASN'T CAST US OFF COMPLETELY.
...PRACTICALLY FOR FREE, UNDER THE CONDITION THAT WE MAINTAIN THE GARDEN EXACTLY THE WAY IT IS? IT'S A MIRACLE...
rattle rattle
HEY.
MIKE'S HOME.
skree
HEY, I HIT THE JACKPOT!!
SLAM
I WENT INTO OUR OLD WAREHOUSES AND FOUND MOUNTAINS OF TREASURE!!
IF WE FIX THESE UP AND GET THEM WORKING RIGHT, WE'LL HAVE AUDIO BUFFS FROM ALL OVER THE WORLD POUNDING OUR DOOR DOWN, WAVING BUNDLES OF CASH!
HEY, DAD?
CAN YOU COME HELP ME UNLOAD ALL THIS STUFF FROM THE BACK OF THE TRUCK?
HM?
SURE...
GRAMPA!
PUSH! ☆ PUSH! ☆
CHEER UP, DAD. WE'RE GOING TO MAKE GRANDDAD'S SPIRIT PROUD!
WE'RE GOING BACK TO OUR ROOTS! GRANDDAD STARTED OUT AS AN AUDIO REPAIRMAN,
GRANDDAD, GRANDDAD...
THE ONLY ONE YOU EVER HAD EYES FOR WAS MY OLD MAN...
YOU NEVER HAD ANY RESPECT FOR YOUR OWN...

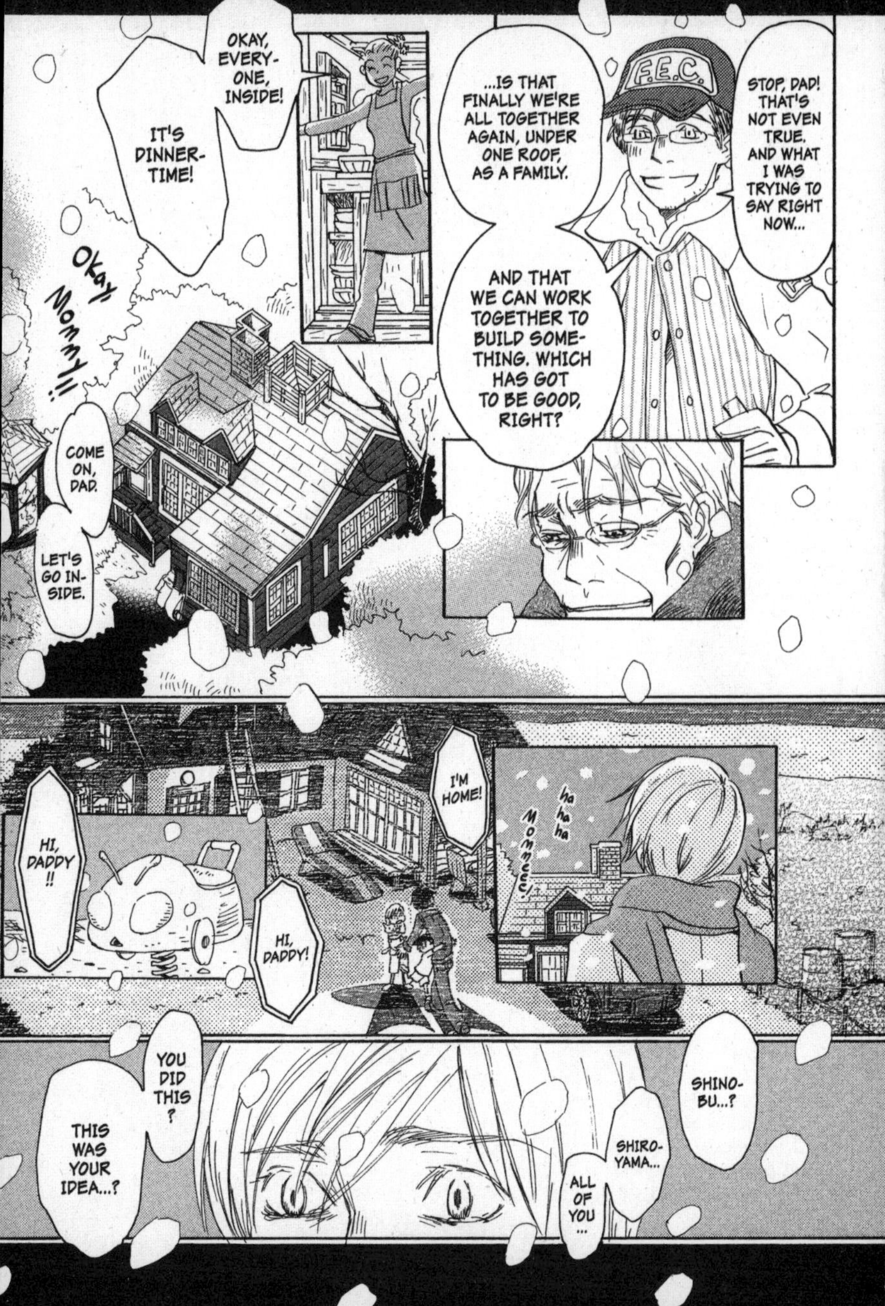
STOP, DAD! THAT'S NOT EVEN TRUE. AND WHAT I WAS TRYING TO SAY RIGHT NOW...
...IS THAT FINALLY WE'RE ALL TOGETHER AGAIN, UNDER ONE ROOF, AS A FAMILY.
AND THAT WE CAN WORK TOGETHER TO BUILD SOMETHING. WHICH HAS GOT TO BE GOOD, RIGHT?
OKAY, EVERYONE, INSIDE!
IT'S DINNERTIME!
Okay Mommy!!!
COME ON, DAD.
LET'S GO INSIDE.
ha ha ha
Mommeee!
I'M HOME!
HI, DADDY!
HI, DADDY!!
SHINOBU...?
SHIROYAMA...
ALL OF YOU...
YOU DID THIS?
THIS WAS YOUR IDEA...?

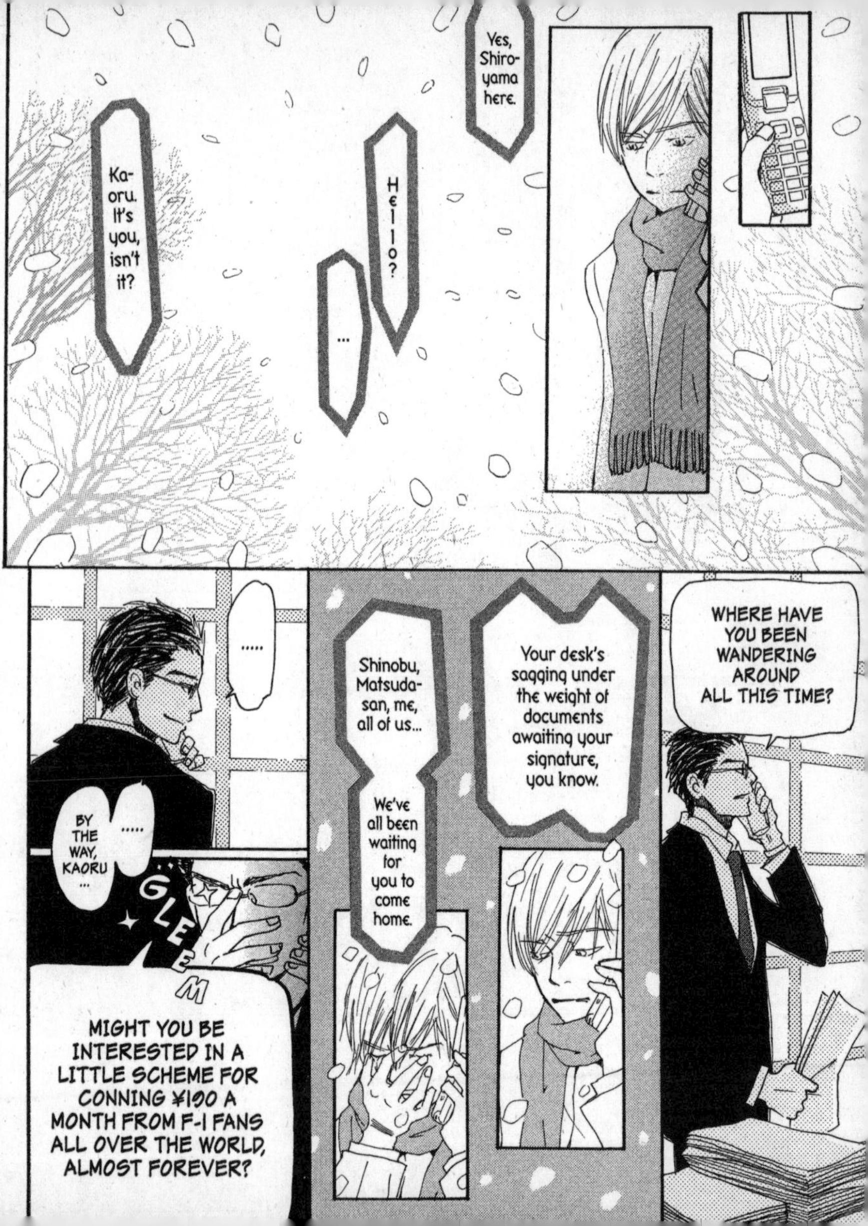

Yes, Shiroyama here.
Hello?
...
Kaoru. It's you, isn't it?
WHERE HAVE YOU BEEN WANDERING AROUND ALL THIS TIME?
Your desk's sagging under the weight of documents awaiting your signature, you know.
Shinobu, Matsuda-san, me, all of us...
We've all been waiting for you to come home.
.....
.....
BY THE WAY, KAORU ...
GLEEM
MIGHT YOU BE INTERESTED IN A LITTLE SCHEME FOR CONNING ¥100 A MONTH FROM F-1 FANS ALL OVER THE WORLD, ALMOST FOREVER?

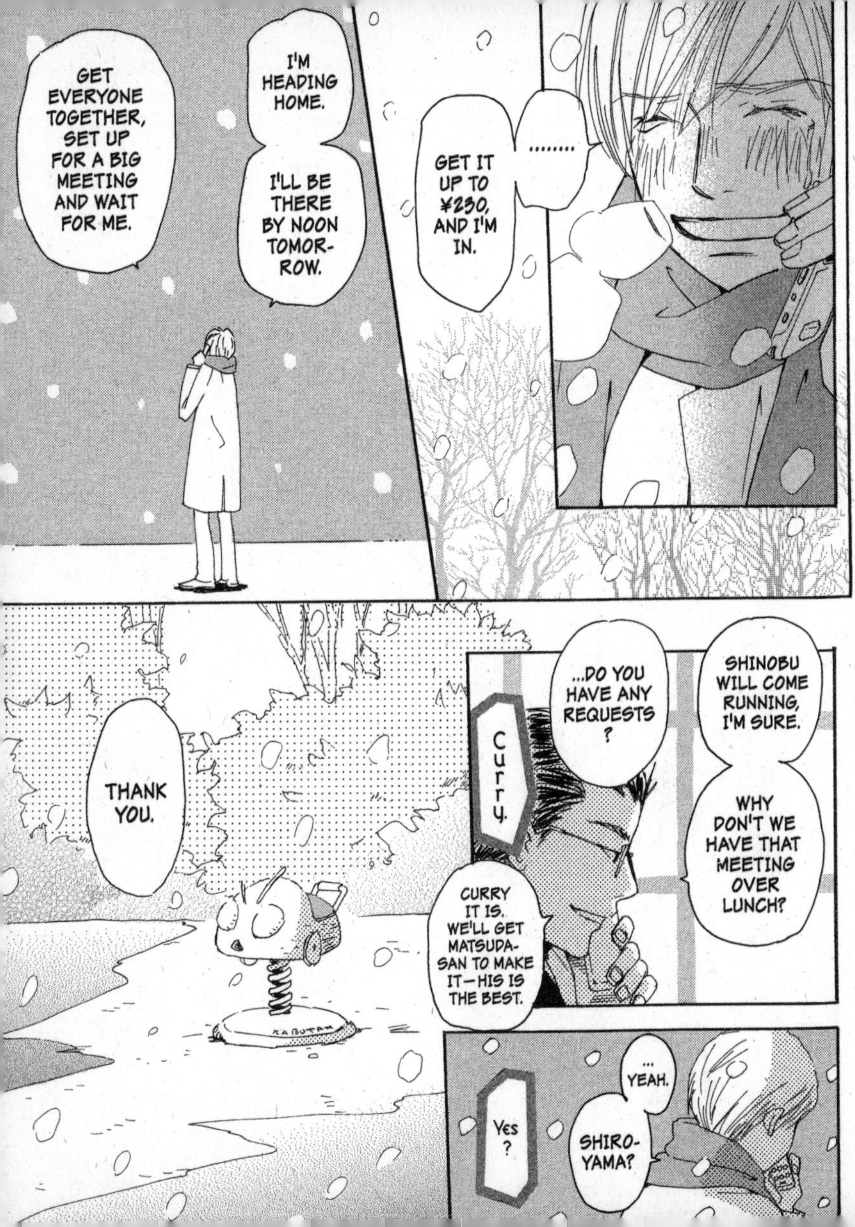
....
GET IT UP TO ¥230, AND I'M IN.
I'M HEADING HOME.
I'LL BE THERE BY NOON TOMORROW.
GET EVERYONE TOGETHER, SET UP FOR A BIG MEETING AND WAIT FOR ME.
SHINOBU WILL COME RUNNING, I'M SURE.
WHY DON'T WE HAVE THAT MEETING OVER LUNCH?
...DO YOU HAVE ANY REQUESTS?
Curry.
CURRY IT IS. WE'LL GET MATSUDA-SAN TO MAKE IT—HIS IS THE BEST.
... YEAH.
SHIROYAMA?
Yes?
THANK YOU.
KABUTAN

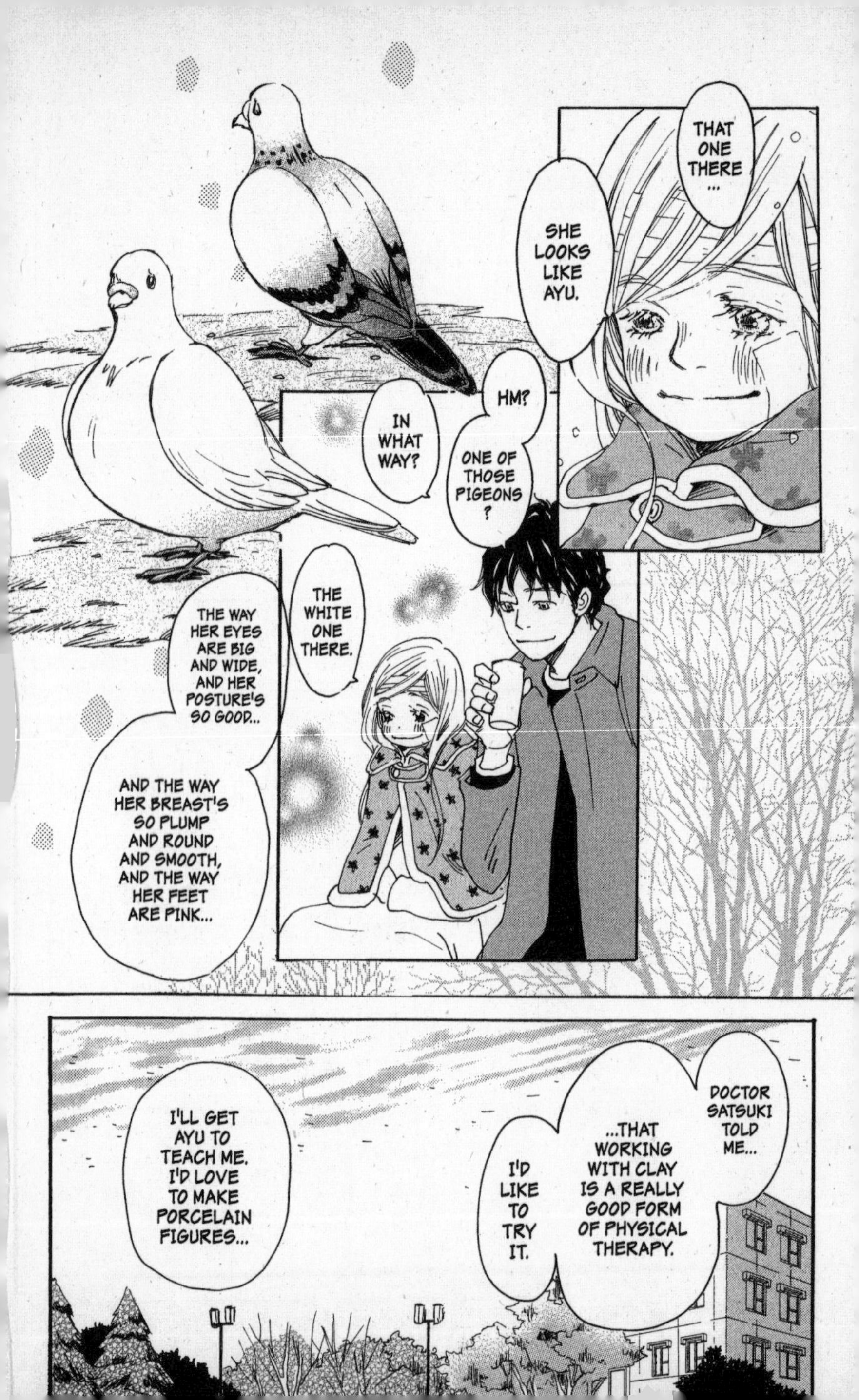
THAT ONE THERE...
SHE LOOKS LIKE AYU.
HM?
ONE OF THOSE PIGEONS?
IN WHAT WAY?
THE WHITE ONE THERE.
THE WAY HER EYES ARE BIG AND WIDE, AND HER POSTURE'S SO GOOD...
AND THE WAY HER BREAST'S SO PLUMP AND ROUND AND SMOOTH, AND THE WAY HER FEET ARE PINK...
DOCTOR SATSUKI TOLD ME...
...THAT WORKING WITH CLAY IS A REALLY GOOD FORM OF PHYSICAL THERAPY.
I'D LIKE TO TRY IT.
I'LL GET AYU TO TEACH ME. I'D LOVE TO MAKE PORCELAIN FIGURES...

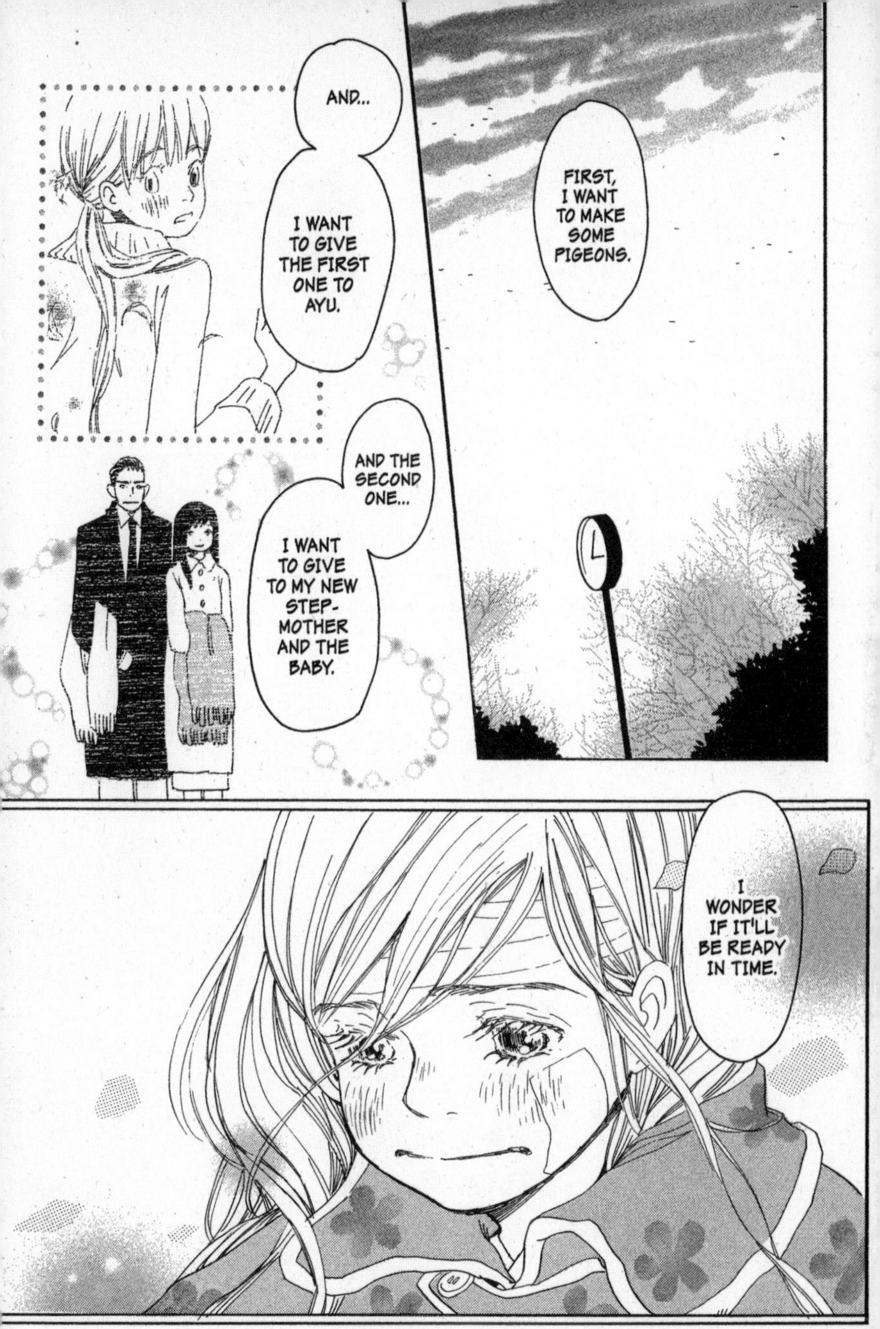
FIRST, I WANT TO MAKE SOME PIGEONS.
AND...
I WANT TO GIVE THE FIRST ONE TO AYU.
AND THE SECOND ONE...
I WANT TO GIVE TO MY NEW STEP-MOTHER AND THE BABY.
I WONDER IF IT'LL BE READY IN TIME.

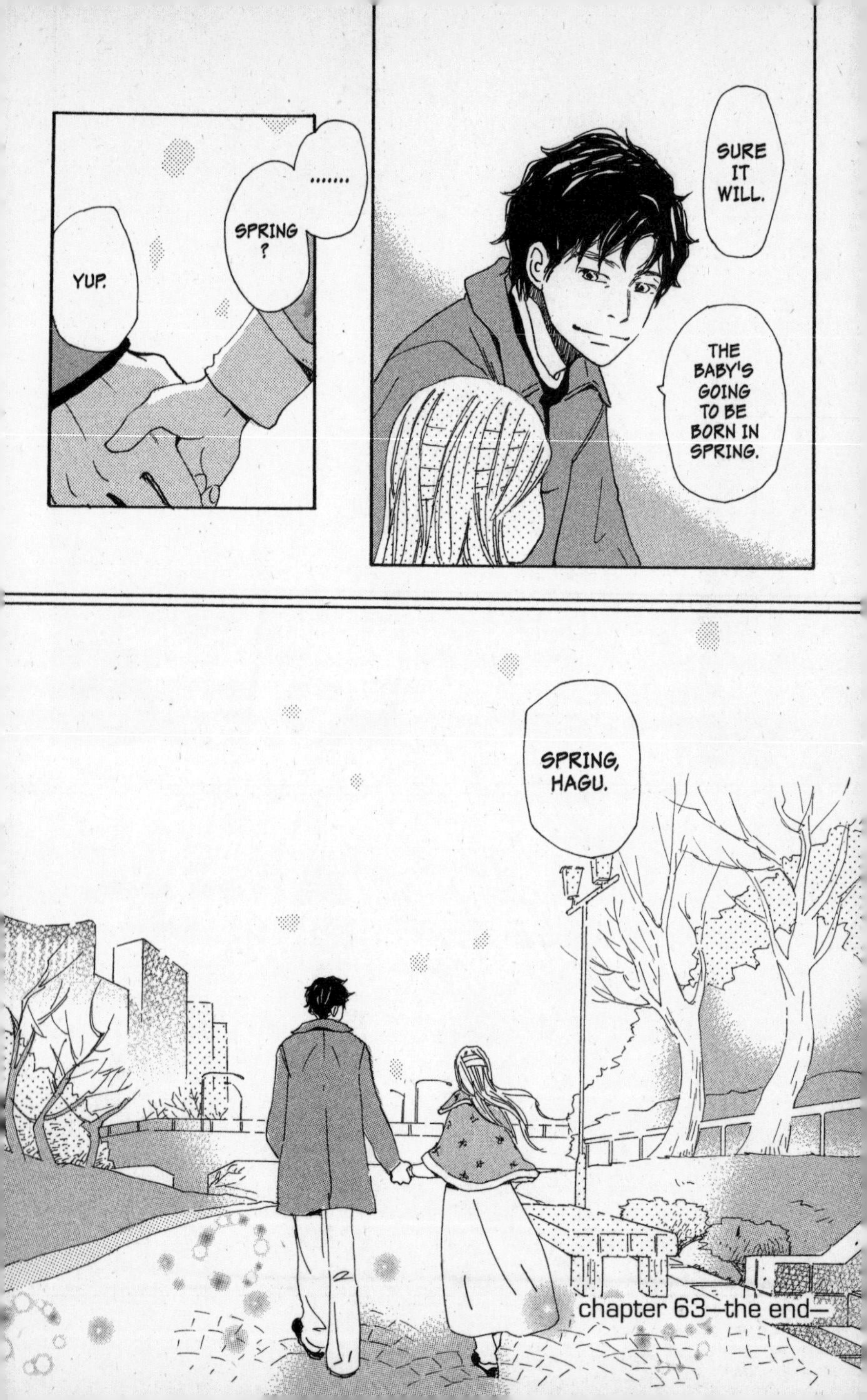
SURE IT WILL.
THE BABY'S GOING TO BE BORN IN SPRING.
....
SPRING ?
YUP.
SPRING, HAGU.
chapter 63—the end—

Rough sketch for a Chorus magazine cover.
Since it was spring, I used a lot of pink—
the color of cherry blossoms.

Pale but colorful balls

Pale branches

Watercolor circles (to be pink)

Pinkish kimono collar
Black-and-white
gingham-checked
kimono

Red or pink
shawl

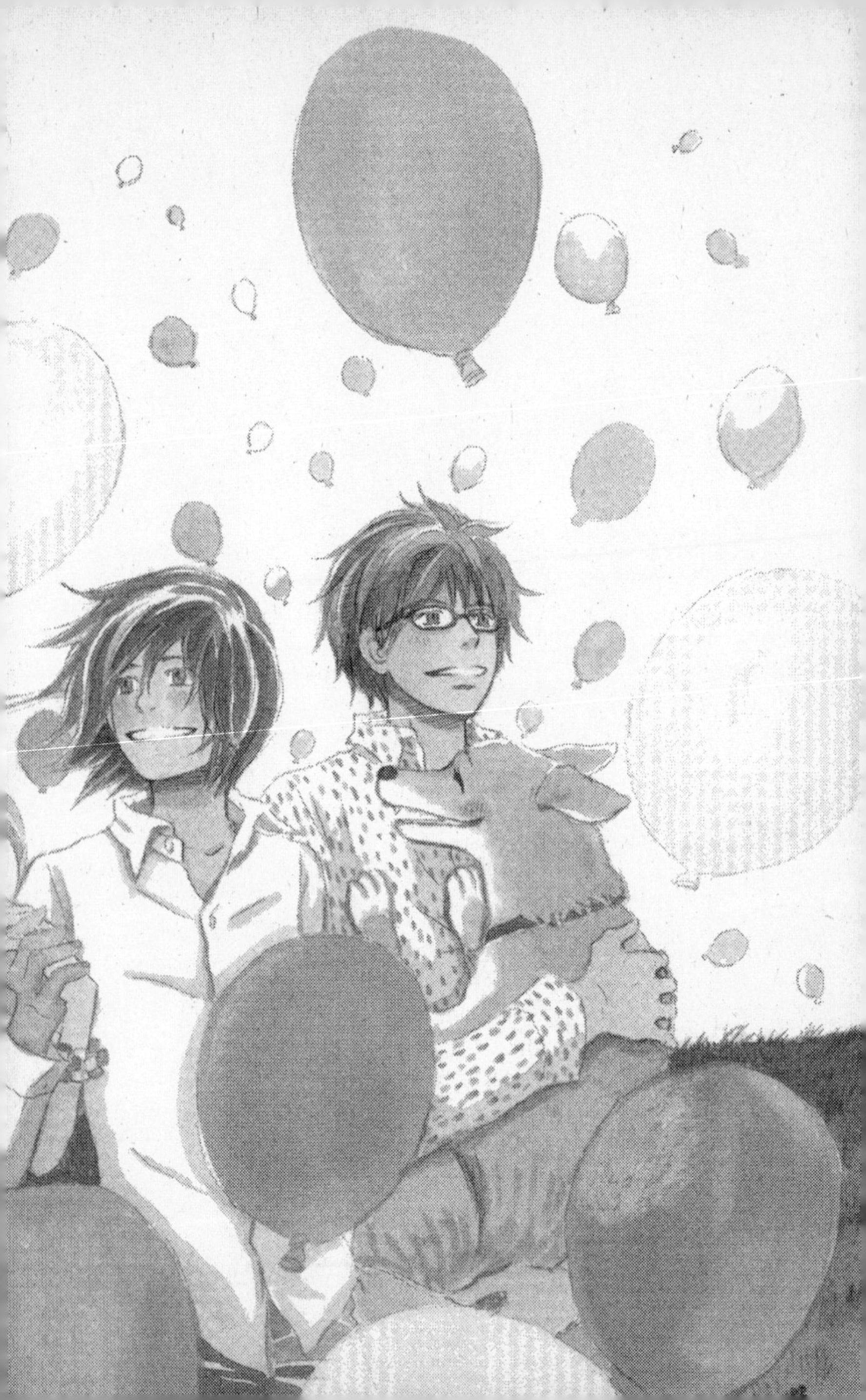

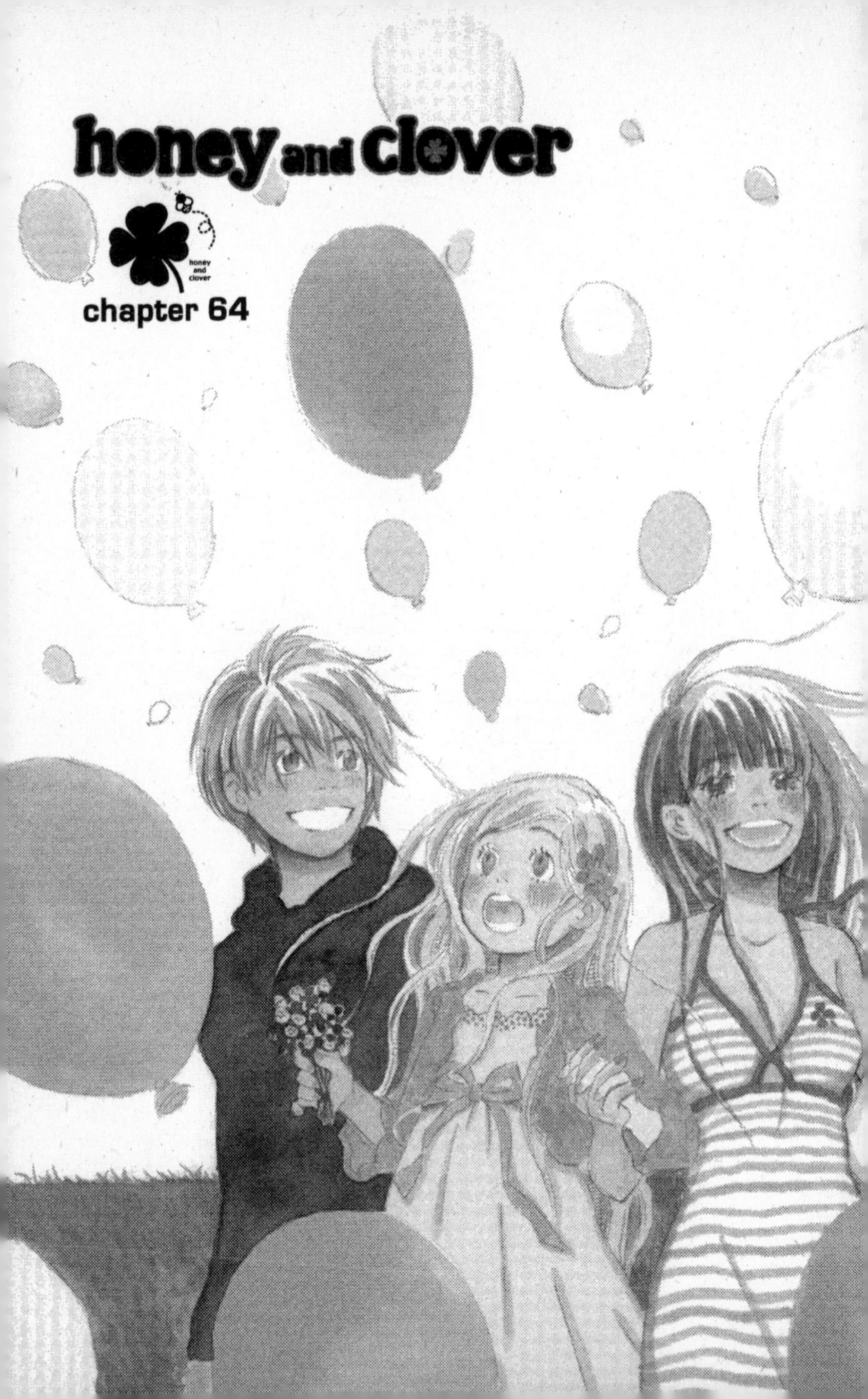
honey and clover
honey and clover
chapter 64

Yokohama appeared in *HoneyClo* several times—
The Ferris wheel in chapter 35 was the one in Minato Mirai.
The place where Mayama took Rika in chapter 29 was Daikoku Wharf.
And the place where Nomiya takes Ayu in chapter 64 is Ōsanbashi Pier.
I really love Yokohama.

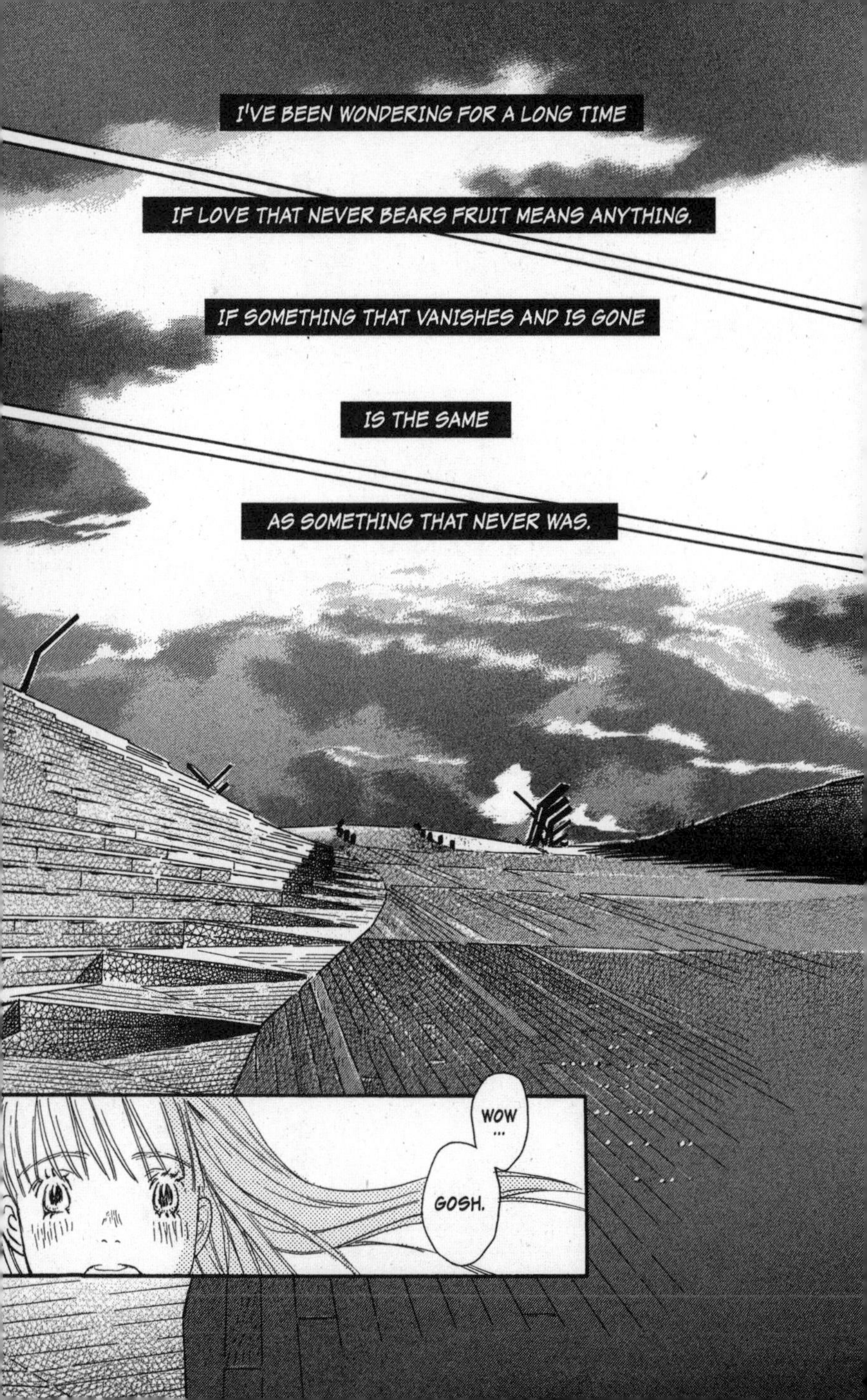
I'VE BEEN WONDERING FOR A LONG TIME
IF LOVE THAT NEVER BEARS FRUIT MEANS ANYTHING.
IF SOMETHING THAT VANISHES AND IS GONE
IS THE SAME
AS SOMETHING THAT NEVER WAS.
WOW...
GOSH.

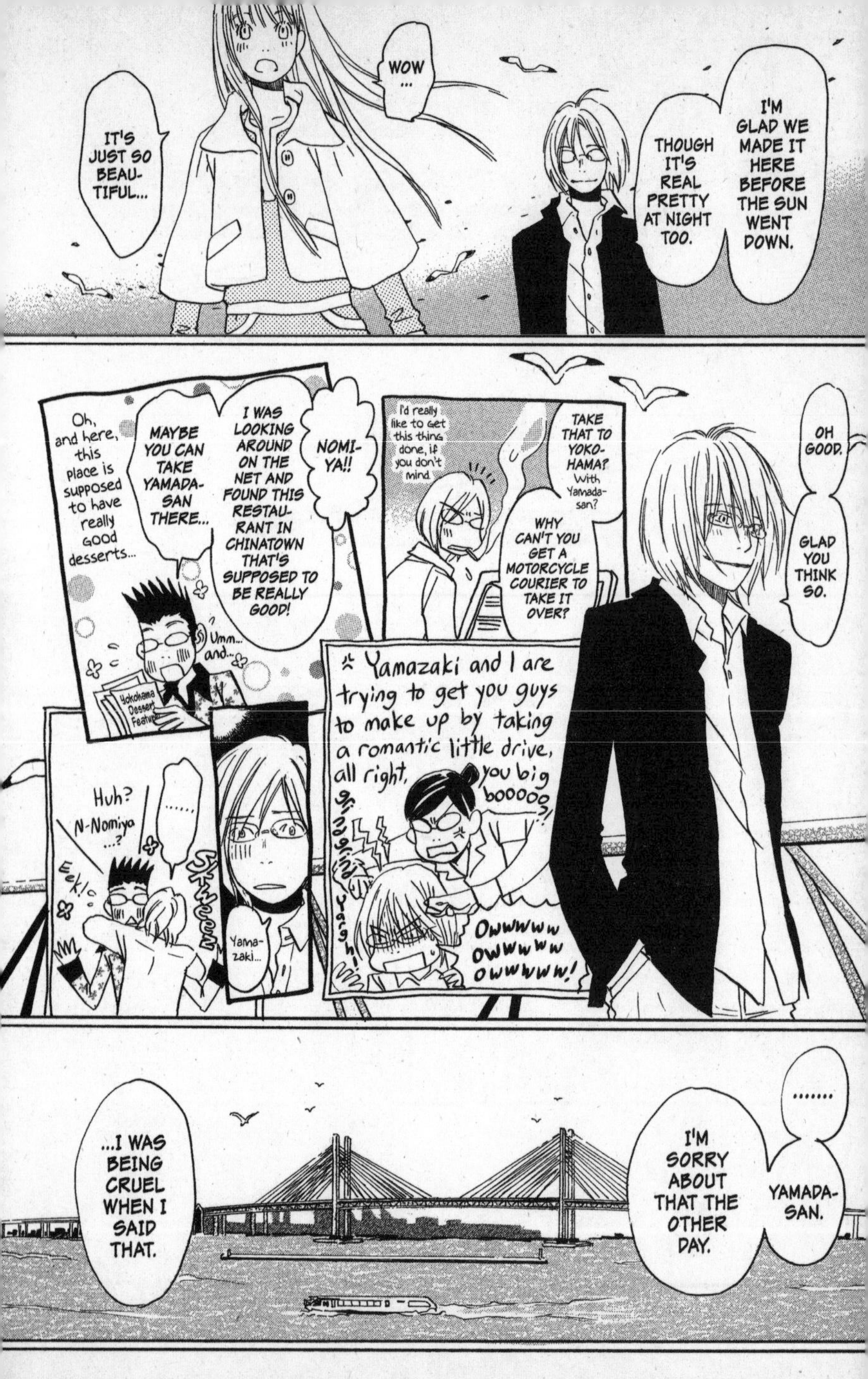
I'M GLAD WE MADE IT HERE BEFORE THE SUN WENT DOWN.
THOUGH IT'S REAL PRETTY AT NIGHT TOO.
WOW...
IT'S JUST SO BEAUTIFUL...
OH GOOD.
GLAD YOU THINK SO.
TAKE THAT TO YOKOHAMA? With Yamada-san?
I'd really like to get this thing done, if you don't mind.
WHY CAN'T YOU GET A MOTORCYCLE COURIER TO TAKE IT OVER?
NOMIYA!!
I WAS LOOKING AROUND ON THE NET AND FOUND THIS RESTAURANT IN CHINATOWN THAT'S SUPPOSED TO BE REALLY GOOD!
MAYBE YOU CAN TAKE YAMADA-SAN THERE...
Oh, and here, this place is supposed to have really good desserts...
Umm... and...
Yokohama Dessert Feature
Yamazaki and I are trying to get you guys to make up by taking a romantic little drive, all right, you big booooo?!
OWWWWW OWWWWW OWWWWW!
......
Yamazaki...
Huh? N-Nomiya...?
Eek!
....
YAMADA-SAN.
I'M SORRY ABOUT THAT THE OTHER DAY.
...I WAS BEING CRUEL WHEN I SAID THAT.

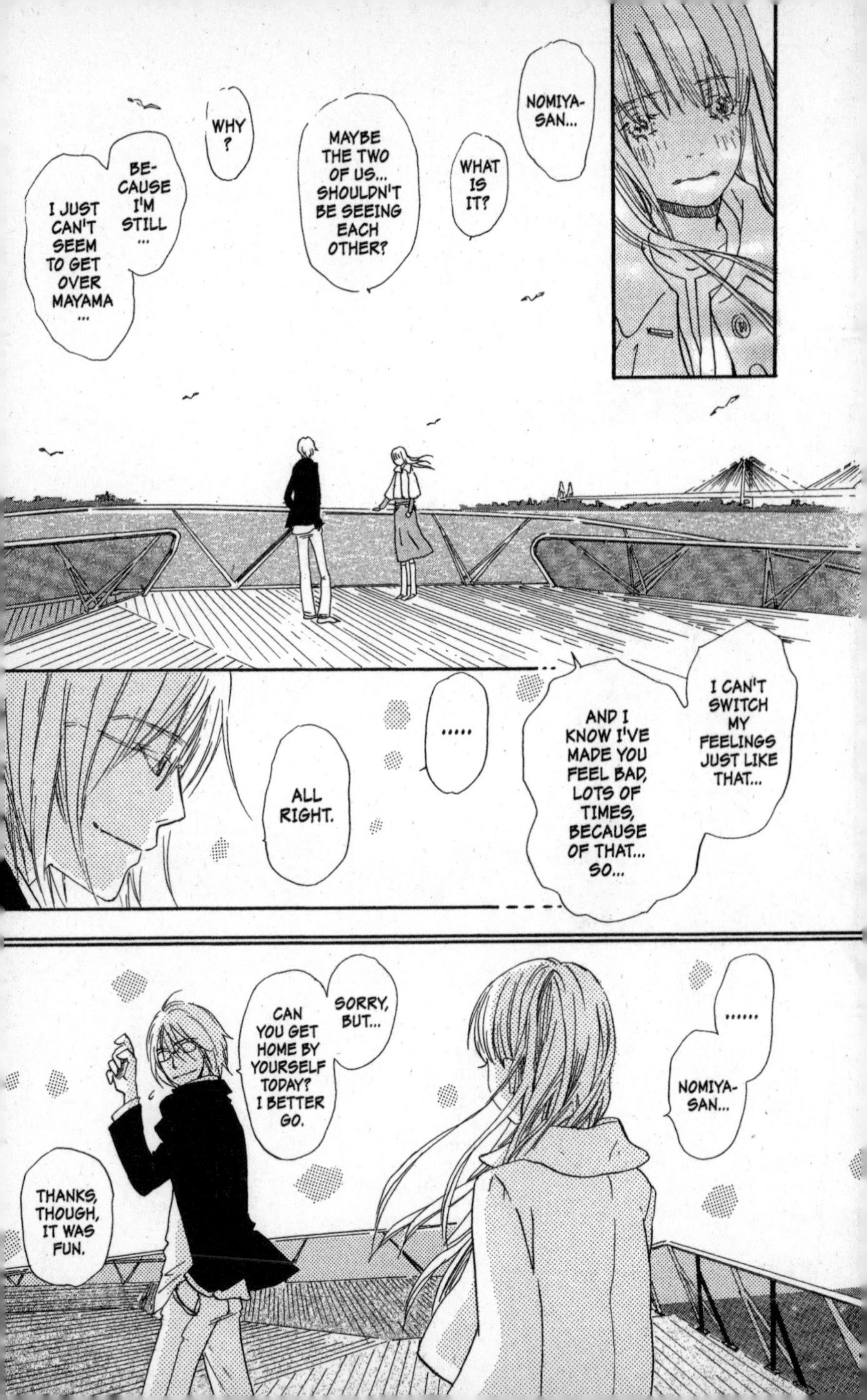
NOMIYA-SAN...
WHAT IS IT?
MAYBE THE TWO OF US... SHOULDN'T BE SEEING EACH OTHER?
WHY?
BE-CAUSE I'M STILL...
I JUST CAN'T SEEM TO GET OVER MAYAMA...
I CAN'T SWITCH MY FEELINGS JUST LIKE THAT...
AND I KNOW I'VE MADE YOU FEEL BAD, LOTS OF TIMES, BECAUSE OF THAT... SO...
......
ALL RIGHT.
......
NOMIYA-SAN...
SORRY, BUT...
CAN YOU GET HOME BY YOURSELF TODAY? I BETTER GO.
THANKS, THOUGH, IT WAS FUN.

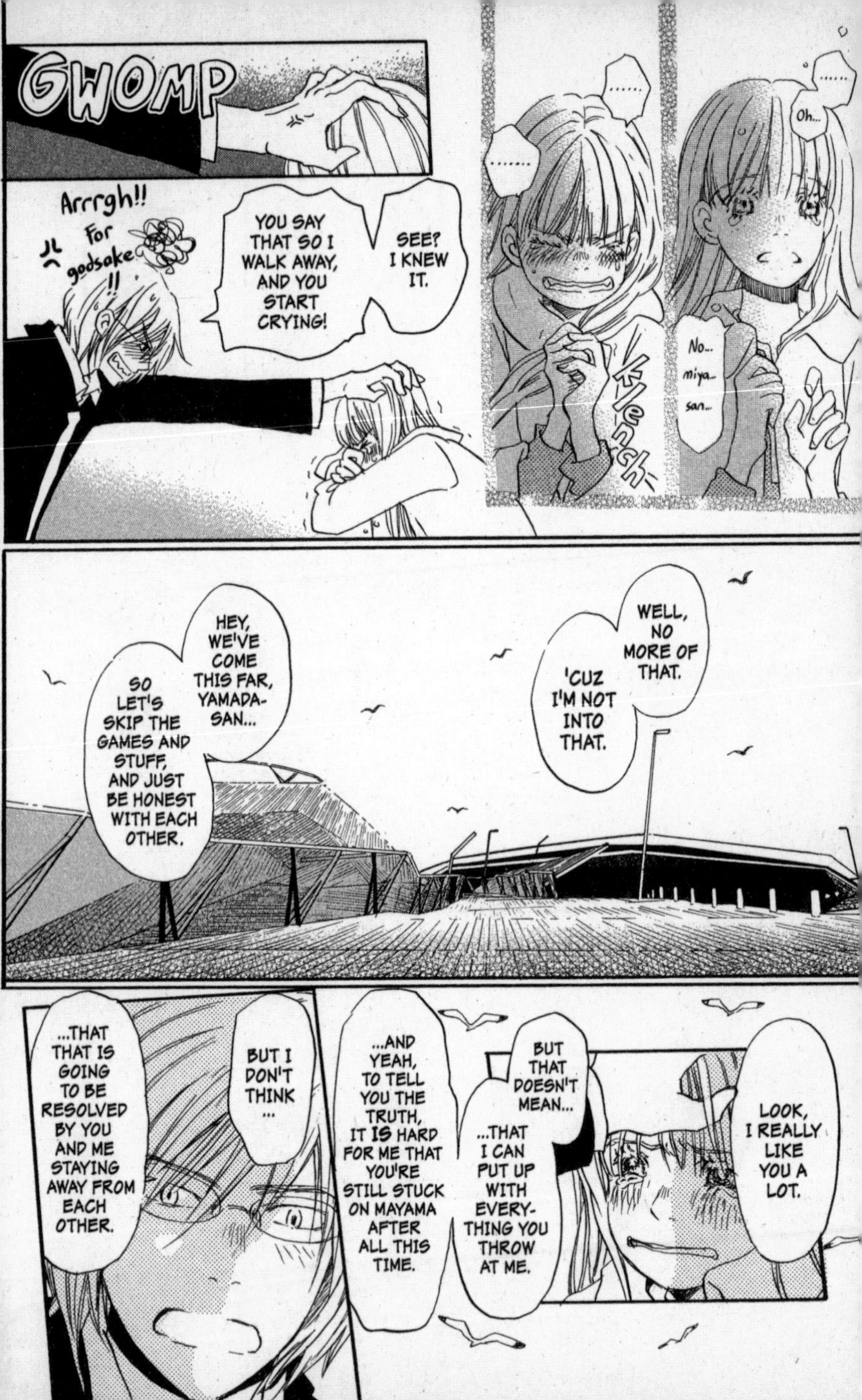
......
Oh...
No... miya... san...
......
......
klench
GWOMP
SEE? I KNEW IT.
YOU SAY THAT SO I WALK AWAY, AND YOU START CRYING!
Arrrgh!! For godsake!!
WELL, NO MORE OF THAT.
'CUZ I'M NOT INTO THAT.
HEY, WE'VE COME THIS FAR, YAMADA-SAN...
SO LET'S SKIP THE GAMES AND STUFF, AND JUST BE HONEST WITH EACH OTHER.
LOOK, I REALLY LIKE YOU A LOT.
BUT THAT DOESN'T MEAN...
...THAT I CAN PUT UP WITH EVERYTHING YOU THROW AT ME.
...AND YEAH, TO TELL YOU THE TRUTH, IT IS HARD FOR ME THAT YOU'RE STILL STUCK ON MAYAMA AFTER ALL THIS TIME.
BUT I DON'T THINK ...
...THAT THAT IS GOING TO BE RESOLVED BY YOU AND ME STAYING AWAY FROM EACH OTHER.

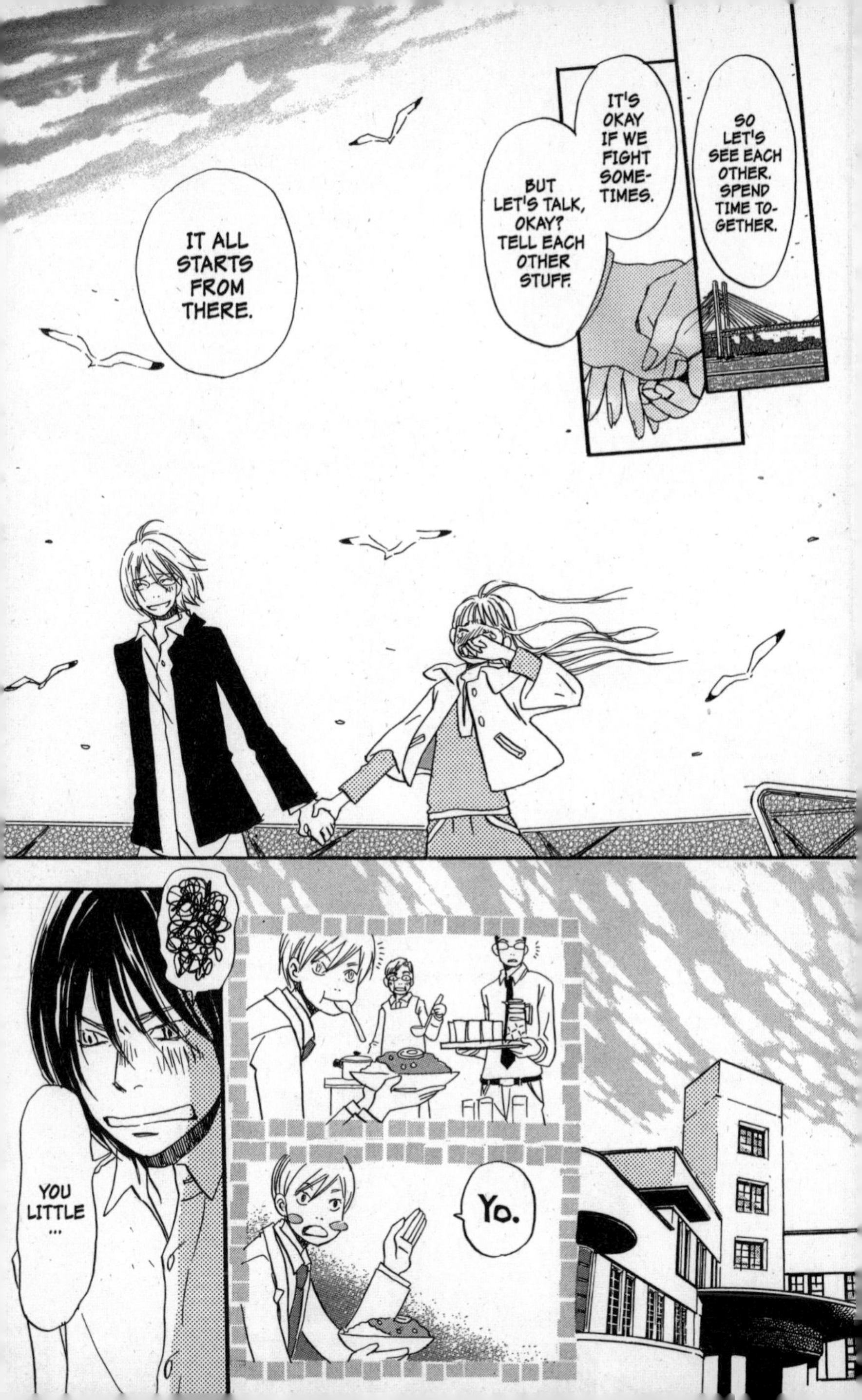
SO LET'S SEE EACH OTHER. SPEND TIME TO-GETHER.
IT'S OKAY IF WE FIGHT SOME-TIMES.
BUT LET'S TALK, OKAY? TELL EACH OTHER STUFF.
IT ALL STARTS FROM THERE.
YO.
YOU LITTLE ...

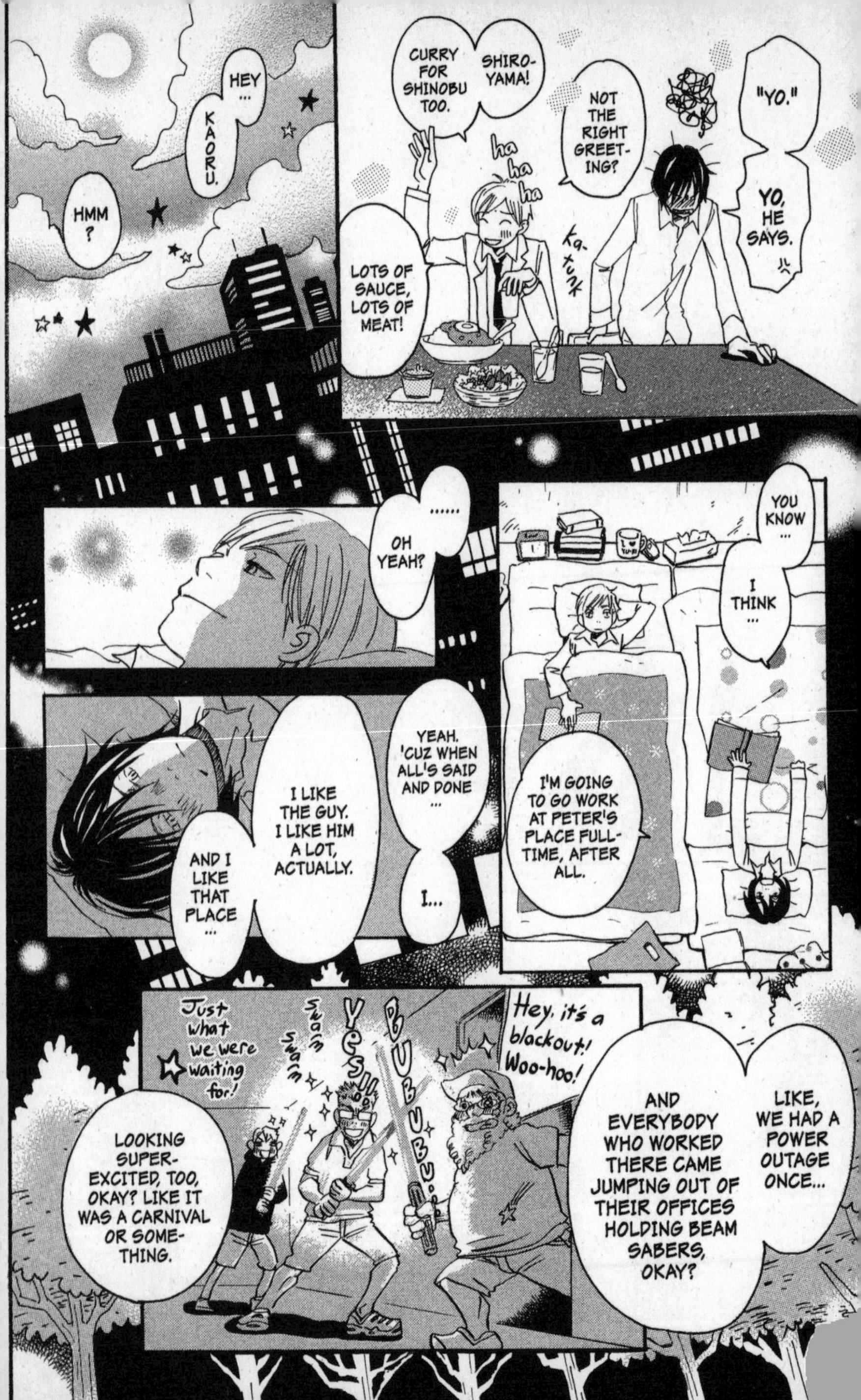
"YO."
YO, HE SAYS.
NOT THE RIGHT GREETING?
SHIRO-YAMA!
CURRY FOR SHINOBU TOO.
ha ha ha
Ka-tunk
LOTS OF SAUCE, LOTS OF MEAT!
HEY... KAORU.
HMM?
YOU KNOW...
I THINK...
I'M GOING TO GO WORK AT PETER'S PLACE FULL-TIME, AFTER ALL.
...... OH YEAH?
YEAH. 'CUZ WHEN ALL'S SAID AND DONE...
I...
I LIKE THE GUY. I LIKE HIM A LOT, ACTUALLY.
AND I LIKE THAT PLACE...
LIKE, WE HAD A POWER OUTAGE ONCE...
AND EVERYBODY WHO WORKED THERE CAME JUMPING OUT OF THEIR OFFICES HOLDING BEAM SABERS, OKAY?
Hey, it's a blackout! Woo-hoo!
BUBUBUBU
YES!!
swarm swarm
Just what we were waiting for!
LOOKING SUPER-EXCITED, TOO, OKAY? LIKE IT WAS A CARNIVAL OR SOME-THING.

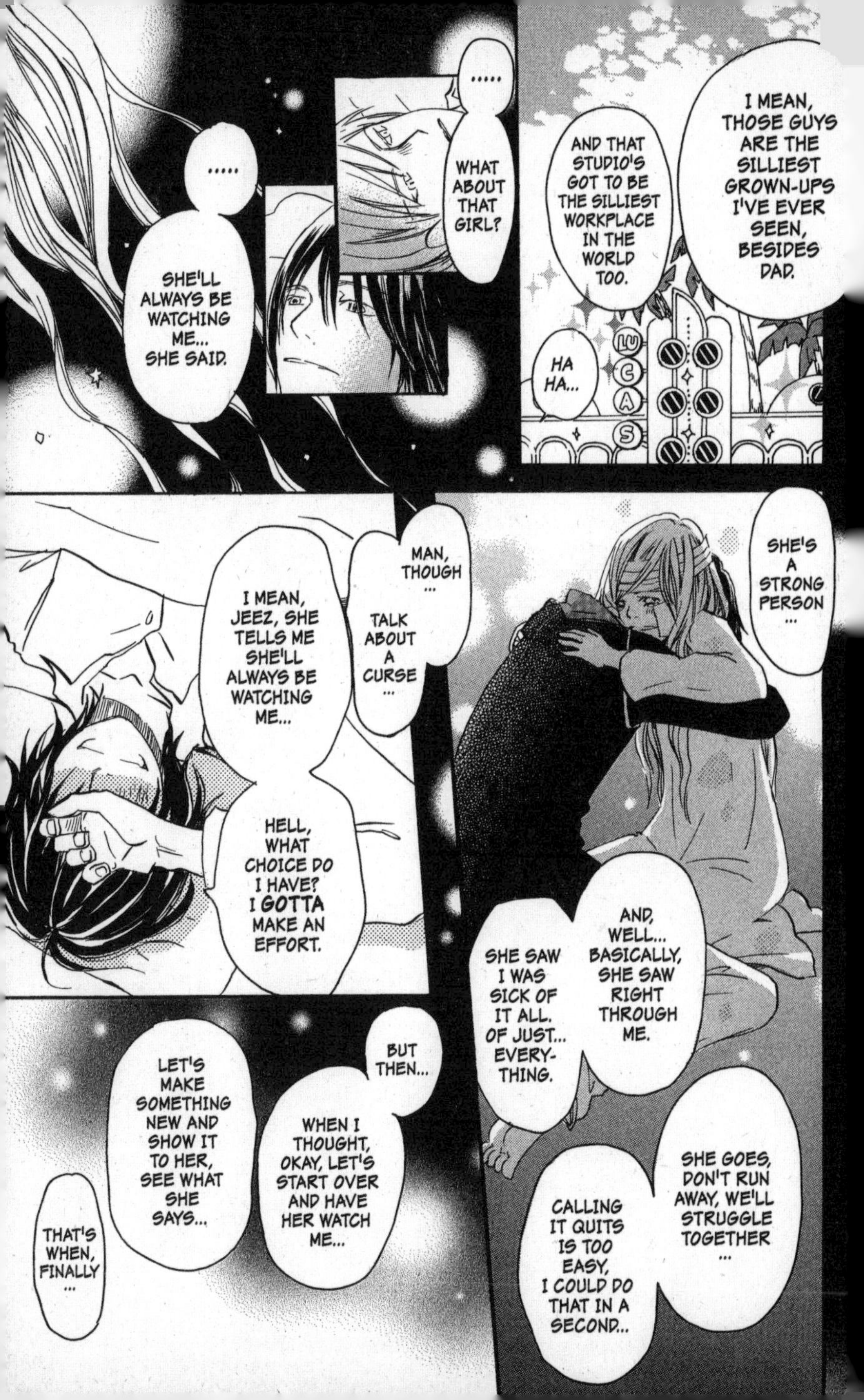
I MEAN, THOSE GUYS ARE THE SILLIEST GROWN-UPS I'VE EVER SEEN, BESIDES DAD.
AND THAT STUDIO'S GOT TO BE THE SILLIEST WORKPLACE IN THE WORLD TOO.
HA HA...
LUCAS
......
WHAT ABOUT THAT GIRL?
......
SHE'LL ALWAYS BE WATCHING ME... SHE SAID.
SHE'S A STRONG PERSON...
AND, WELL... BASICALLY, SHE SAW RIGHT THROUGH ME.
SHE SAW I WAS SICK OF IT ALL. OF JUST... EVERY-THING.
SHE GOES, DON'T RUN AWAY, WE'LL STRUGGLE TOGETHER...
CALLING IT QUITS IS TOO EASY, I COULD DO THAT IN A SECOND...
MAN, THOUGH...
TALK ABOUT A CURSE...
I MEAN, JEEZ, SHE TELLS ME SHE'LL ALWAYS BE WATCHING ME...
HELL, WHAT CHOICE DO I HAVE? I GOTTA MAKE AN EFFORT.
BUT THEN...
WHEN I THOUGHT, OKAY, LET'S START OVER AND HAVE HER WATCH ME...
LET'S MAKE SOMETHING NEW AND SHOW IT TO HER, SEE WHAT SHE SAYS...
THAT'S WHEN, FINALLY...

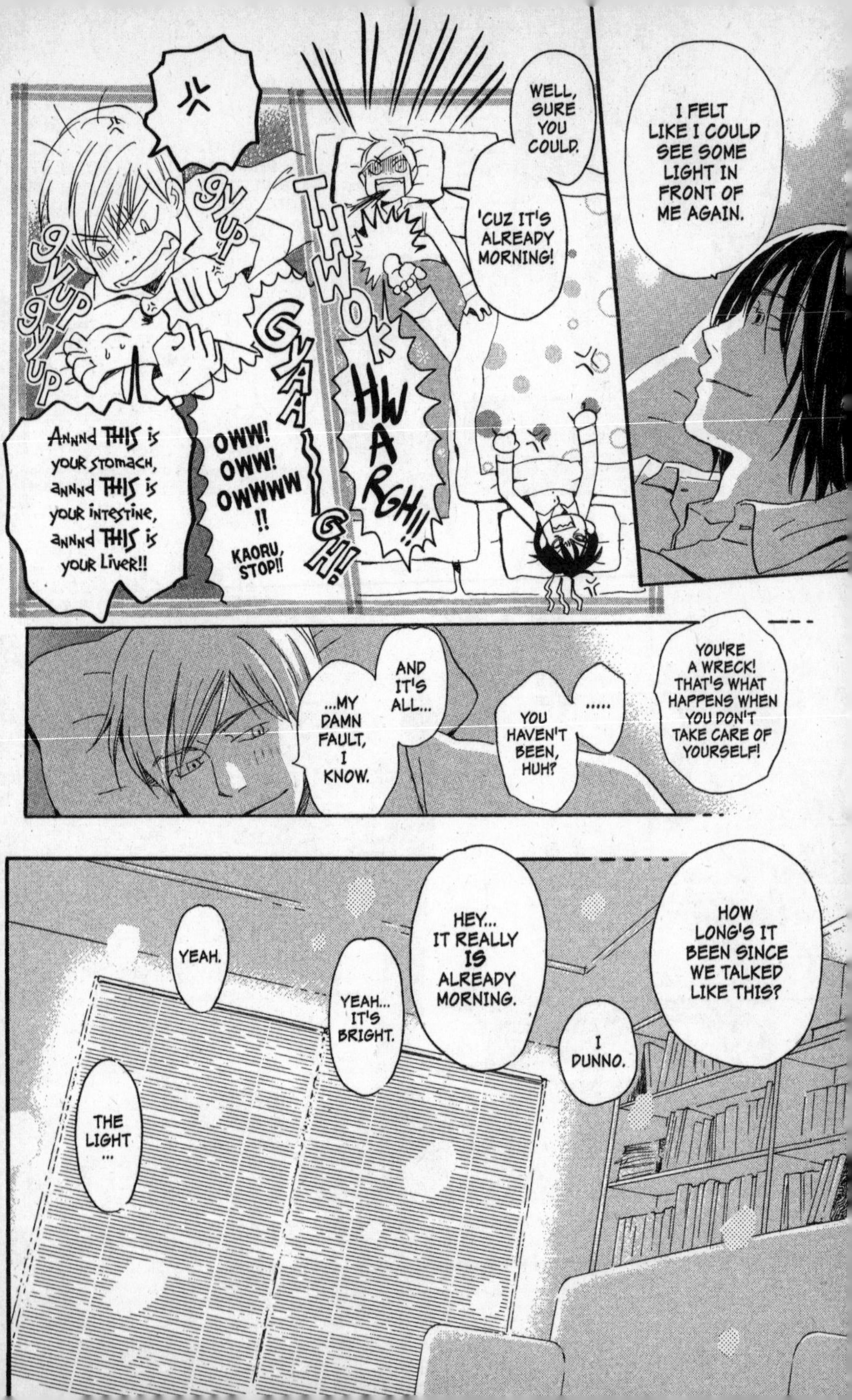
I FELT LIKE I COULD SEE SOME LIGHT IN FRONT OF ME AGAIN.
WELL, SURE YOU COULD.
'CUZ IT'S ALREADY MORNING!
THWOK
HWARGH!!
GYAAA~GH!
gyup gyup
OWW! OWW! OWWWW!!
KAORU, STOP!!
Annnd THIS is your stomach, annnd THIS is your intestine, annnd THIS is your Liver!!
gyup gyup gyup
YOU'RE A WRECK! THAT'S WHAT HAPPENS WHEN YOU DON'T TAKE CARE OF YOURSELF!
.....
YOU HAVEN'T BEEN, HUH?
AND IT'S ALL...
...MY DAMN FAULT, I KNOW.
HOW LONG'S IT BEEN SINCE WE TALKED LIKE THIS?
I DUNNO.
HEY... IT REALLY IS ALREADY MORNING.
YEAH... IT'S BRIGHT.
YEAH.
THE LIGHT...

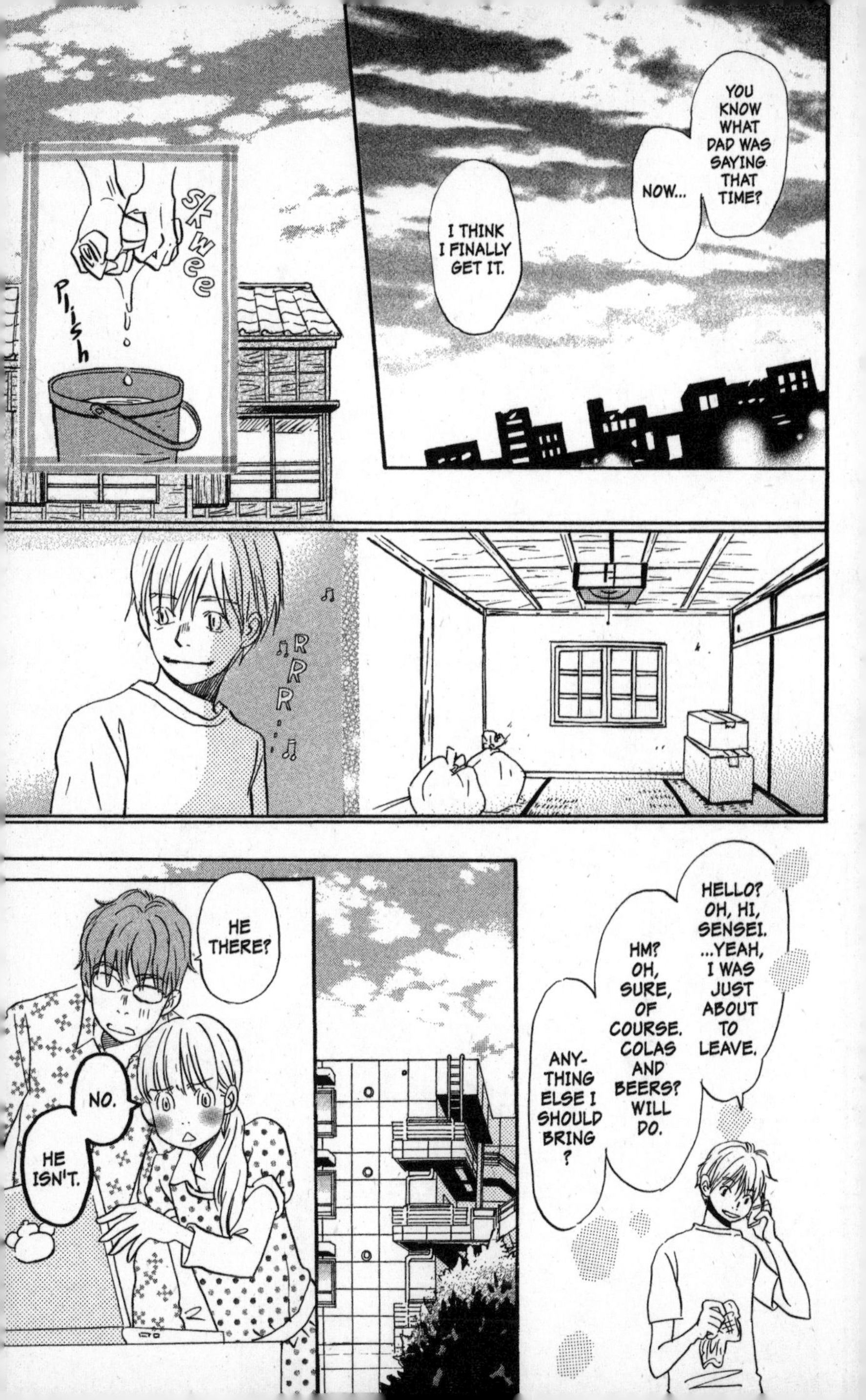
YOU KNOW WHAT DAD WAS SAYING THAT TIME?
NOW...
I THINK I FINALLY GET IT.
SKWEE
PLISH
RRR
HELLO? OH, HI, SENSEI. ...YEAH, I WAS JUST ABOUT TO LEAVE.
HM? OH, SURE, OF COURSE. COLAS AND BEERS? WILL DO.
ANYTHING ELSE I SHOULD BRING?
HE THERE?
NO.
HE ISN'T.

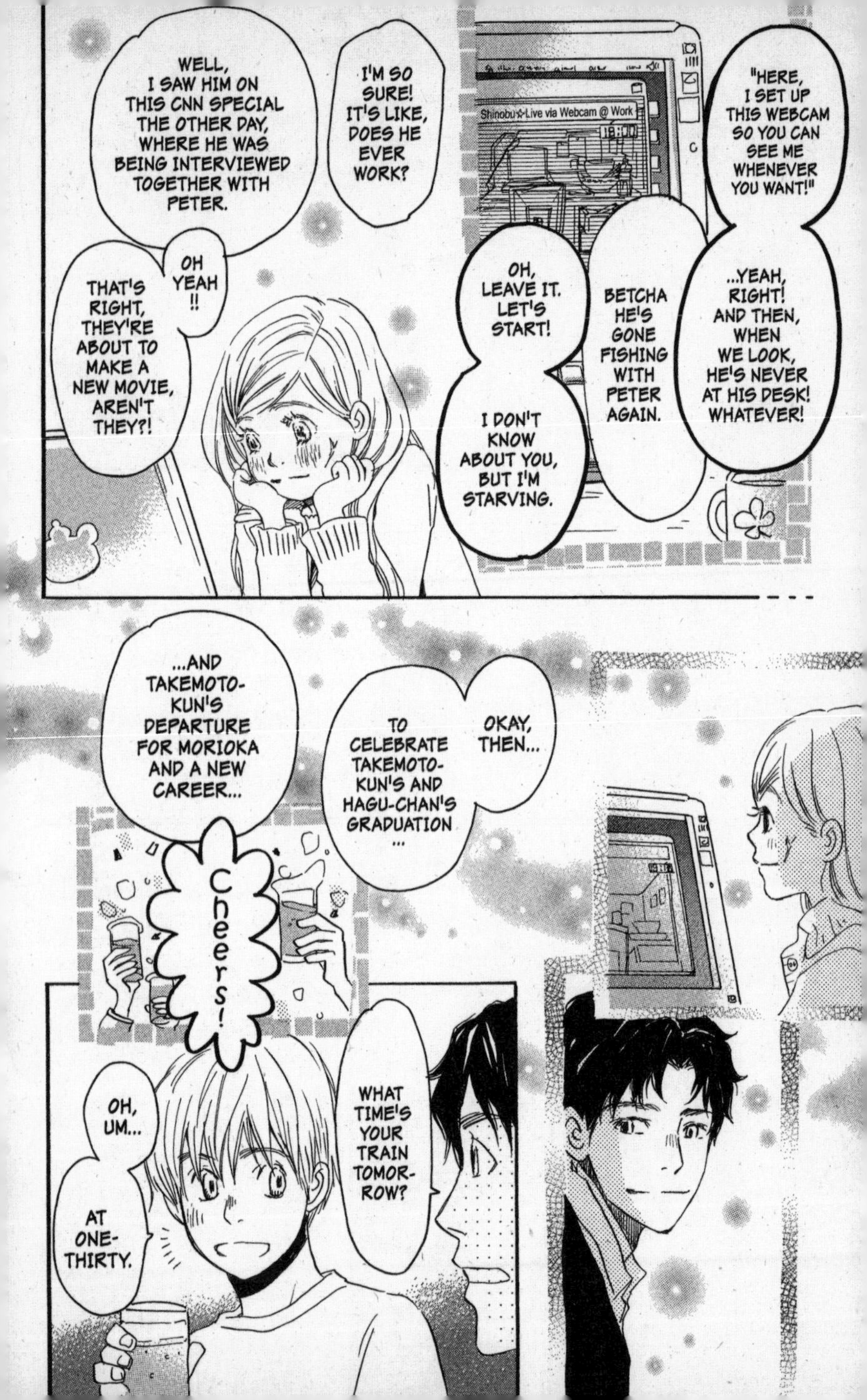
Shinobu☆Live via Webcam @ Work
"HERE, I SET UP THIS WEBCAM SO YOU CAN SEE ME WHENEVER YOU WANT!"
...YEAH, RIGHT! AND THEN, WHEN WE LOOK, HE'S NEVER AT HIS DESK! WHATEVER!
BETCHA HE'S GONE FISHING WITH PETER AGAIN.
OH, LEAVE IT. LET'S START!
I DON'T KNOW ABOUT YOU, BUT I'M STARVING.
I'M SO SURE! IT'S LIKE, DOES HE EVER WORK?
WELL, I SAW HIM ON THIS CNN SPECIAL THE OTHER DAY, WHERE HE WAS BEING INTERVIEWED TOGETHER WITH PETER.
OH YEAH!!
THAT'S RIGHT, THEY'RE ABOUT TO MAKE A NEW MOVIE, AREN'T THEY?!
OKAY, THEN...
TO CELEBRATE TAKEMOTO-KUN'S AND HAGU-CHAN'S GRADUATION...
...AND TAKEMOTO-KUN'S DEPARTURE FOR MORIOKA AND A NEW CAREER...
Cheers!
WHAT TIME'S YOUR TRAIN TOMORROW?
OH, UM...
AT ONE-THIRTY.

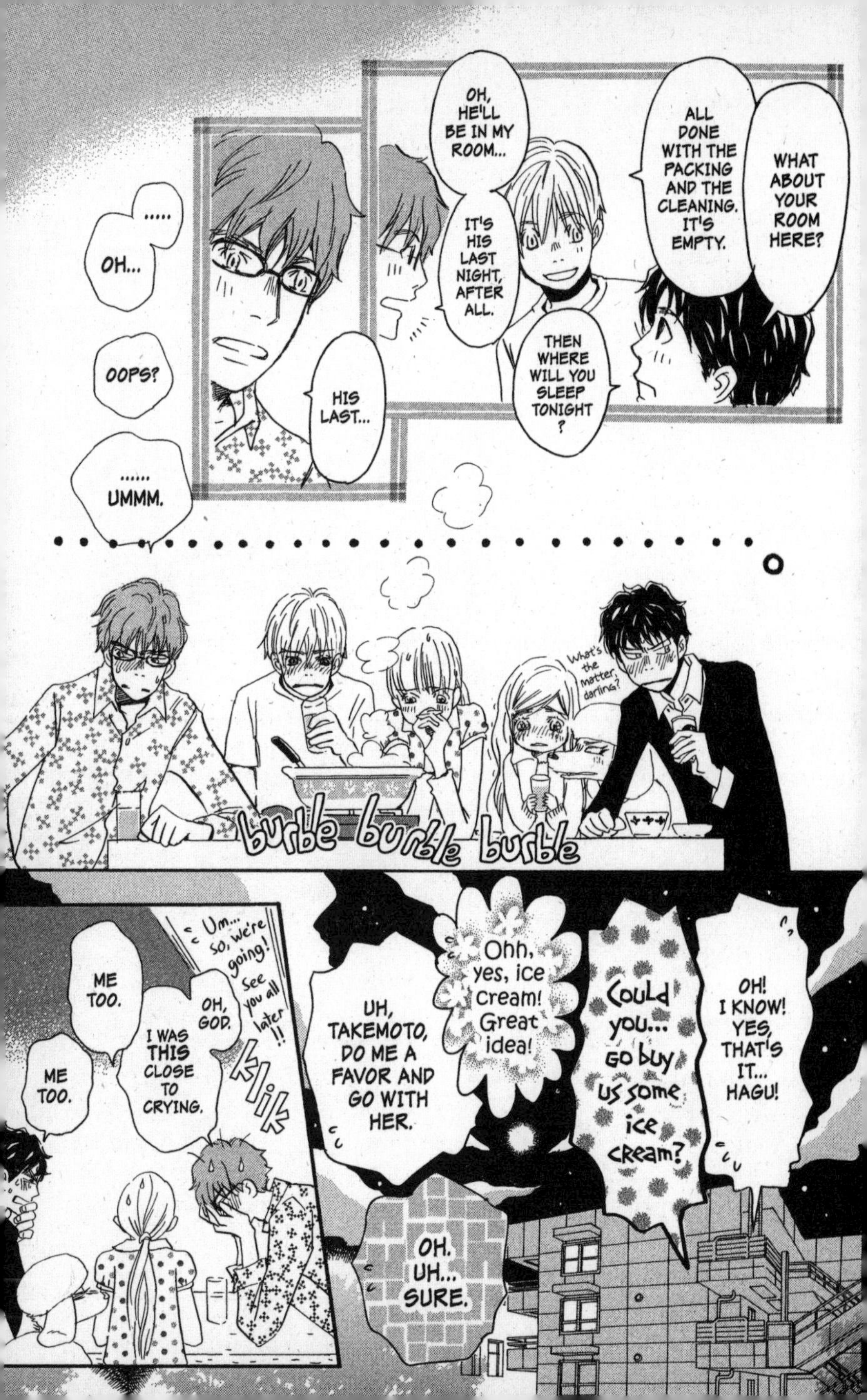
WHAT ABOUT YOUR ROOM HERE?
ALL DONE WITH THE PACKING AND THE CLEANING. IT'S EMPTY.
THEN WHERE WILL YOU SLEEP TONIGHT?
OH, HE'LL BE IN MY ROOM...
IT'S HIS LAST NIGHT, AFTER ALL.
HIS LAST...
......
OH...
OOPS?
...... UMMM.
What's the matter, darling?
burble burble burble
OH! I KNOW! YES, THAT'S IT... HAGU!
Could you... go buy us some ice cream?
Ohh, yes, ice cream! Great idea!
UH, TAKEMOTO, DO ME A FAVOR AND GO WITH HER.
OH. UH... SURE.
Um... so, we're going! See you all later!!
klik
OH, GOD.
I WAS THIS CLOSE TO CRYING.
ME TOO.
ME TOO.

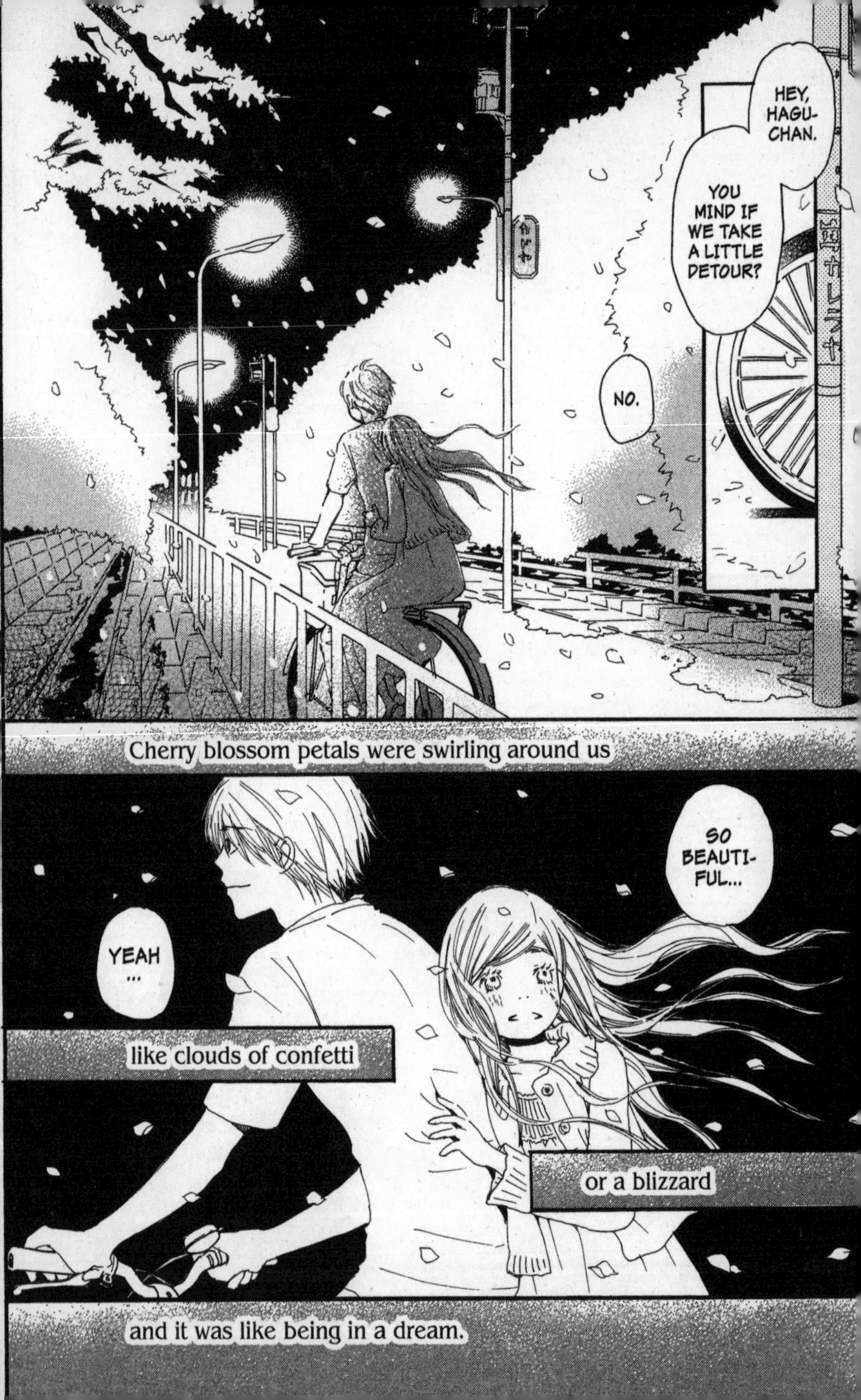
HEY, HAGU-CHAN.
YOU MIND IF WE TAKE A LITTLE DETOUR?
NO.
Cherry blossom petals were swirling around us
SO BEAUTI-FUL...
YEAH ...
like clouds of confetti
or a blizzard
and it was like being in a dream.

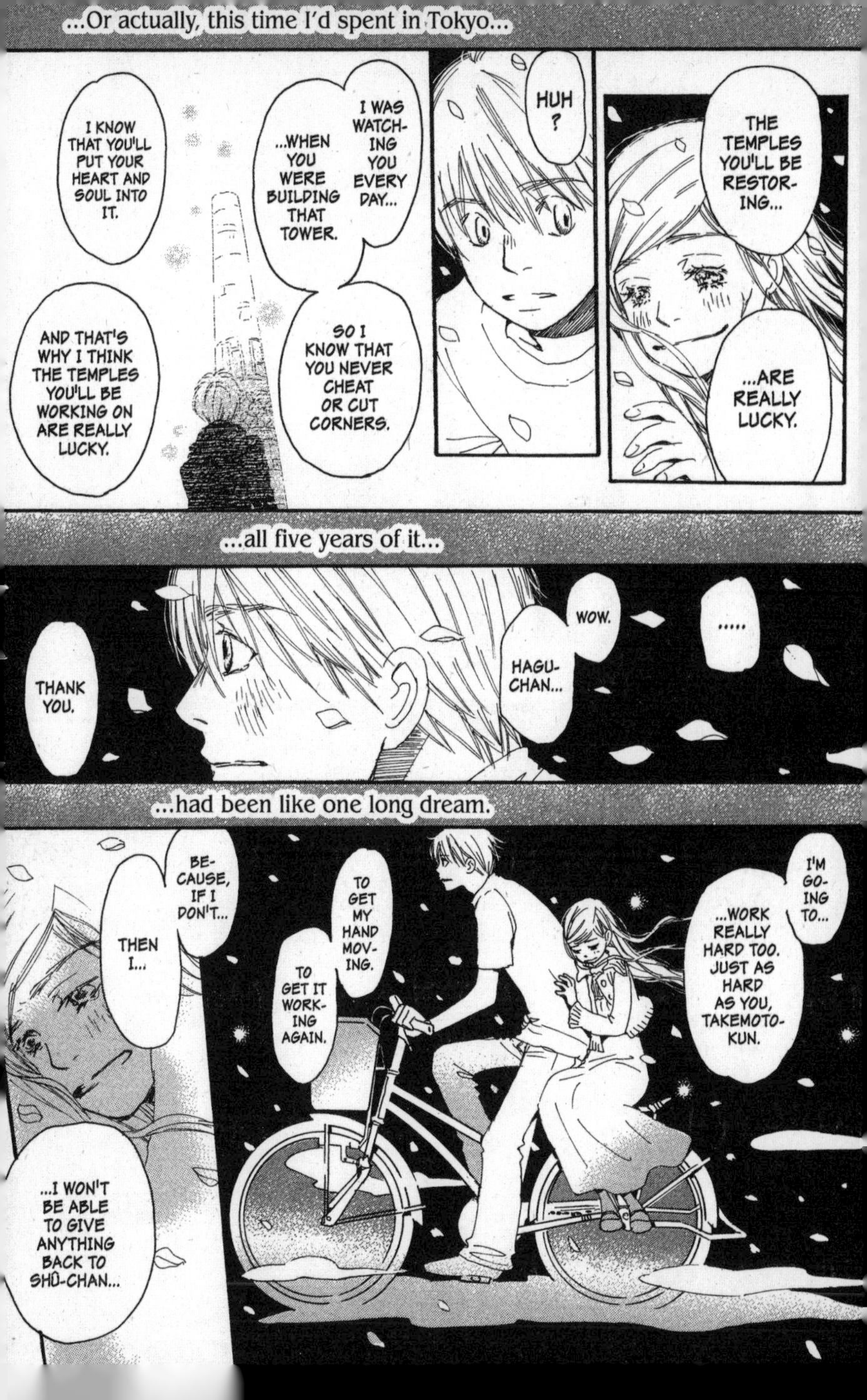
...Or actually, this time I'd spent in Tokyo...
THE TEMPLES YOU'LL BE RESTORING...
...ARE REALLY LUCKY.
HUH?
I WAS WATCHING YOU EVERY DAY...
...WHEN YOU WERE BUILDING THAT TOWER.
SO I KNOW THAT YOU NEVER CHEAT OR CUT CORNERS.
I KNOW THAT YOU'LL PUT YOUR HEART AND SOUL INTO IT.
AND THAT'S WHY I THINK THE TEMPLES YOU'LL BE WORKING ON ARE REALLY LUCKY.
...all five years of it...
.....
WOW.
HAGU-CHAN...
THANK YOU.
...had been like one long dream.
I'M GOING TO...
...WORK REALLY HARD TOO. JUST AS HARD AS YOU, TAKEMOTO-KUN.
TO GET MY HAND MOVING.
TO GET IT WORKING AGAIN.
BECAUSE, IF I DON'T...
THEN I...
...I WON'T BE ABLE TO GIVE ANYTHING BACK TO SHŪ-CHAN...

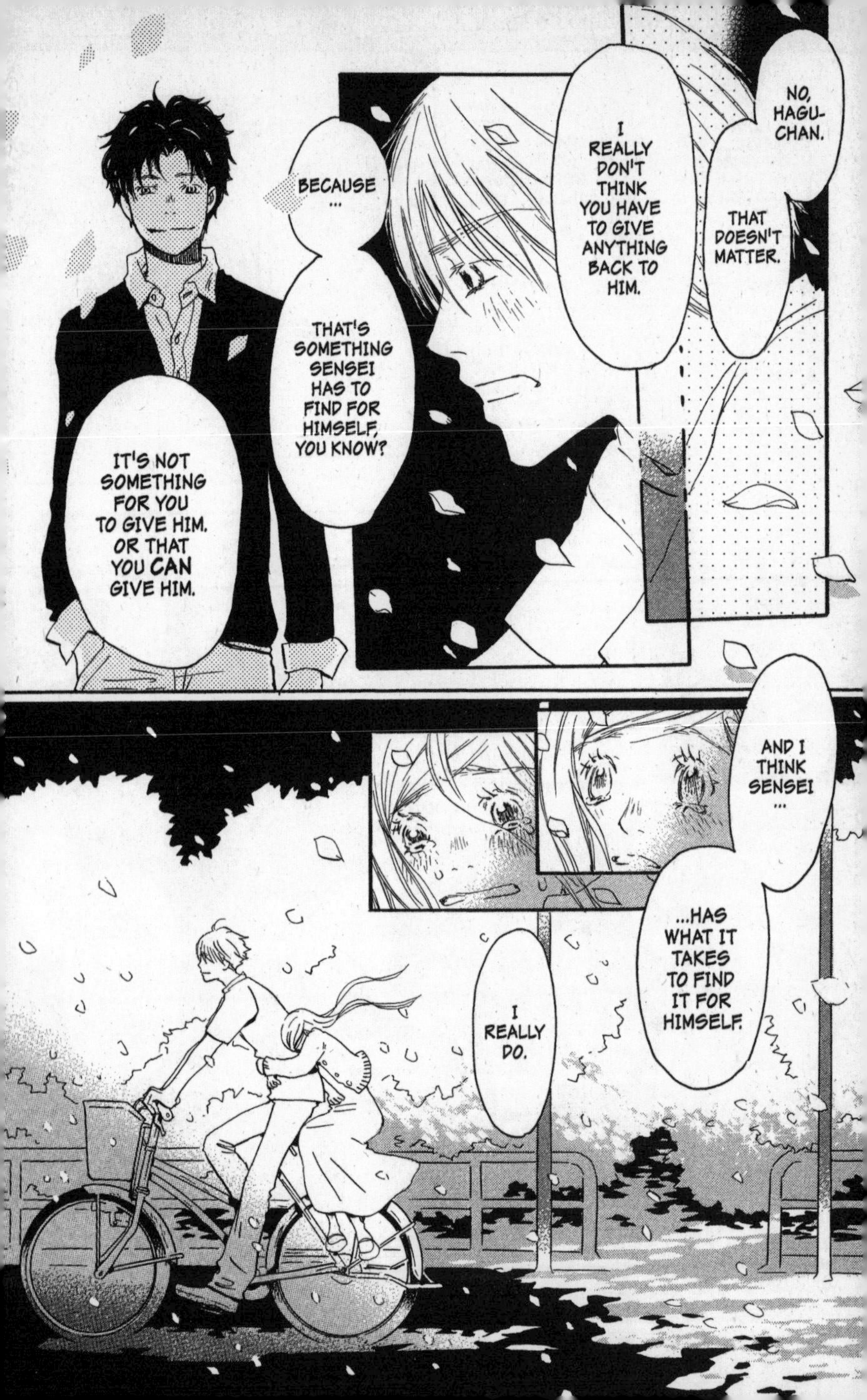
NO, HAGU-CHAN.
THAT DOESN'T MATTER.
I REALLY DON'T THINK YOU HAVE TO GIVE ANYTHING BACK TO HIM.
BECAUSE ...
THAT'S SOMETHING SENSEI HAS TO FIND FOR HIMSELF, YOU KNOW?
IT'S NOT SOMETHING FOR YOU TO GIVE HIM. OR THAT YOU CAN GIVE HIM.
AND I THINK SENSEI ...
...HAS WHAT IT TAKES TO FIND IT FOR HIMSELF.
I REALLY DO.

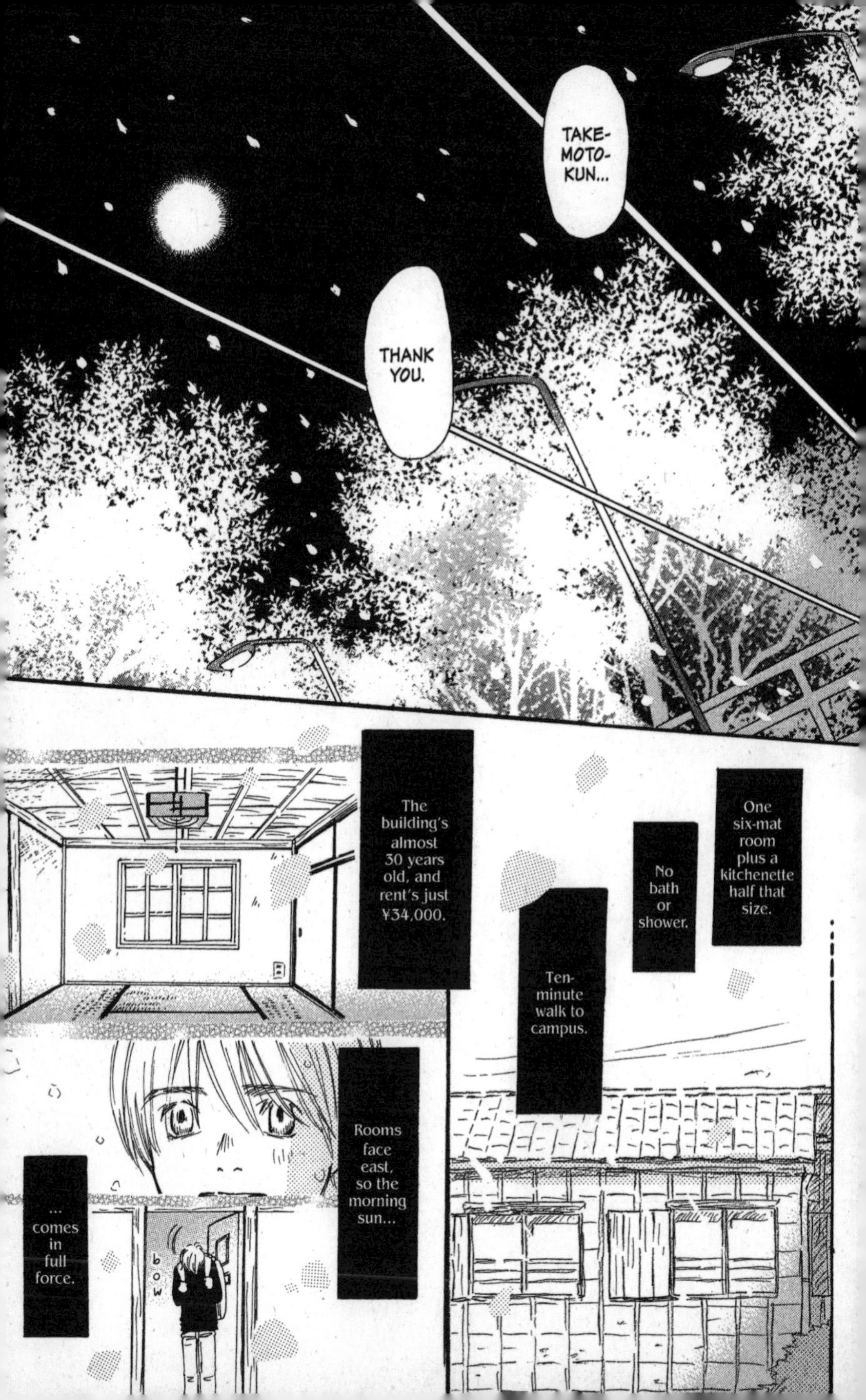
TAKE-MOTO-KUN...
THANK YOU.
One six-mat room plus a kitchenette half that size.
No bath or shower.
Ten-minute walk to campus.
The building's almost 30 years old, and rent's just ¥34,000.
Rooms face east, so the morning sun...
... comes in full force.
bow

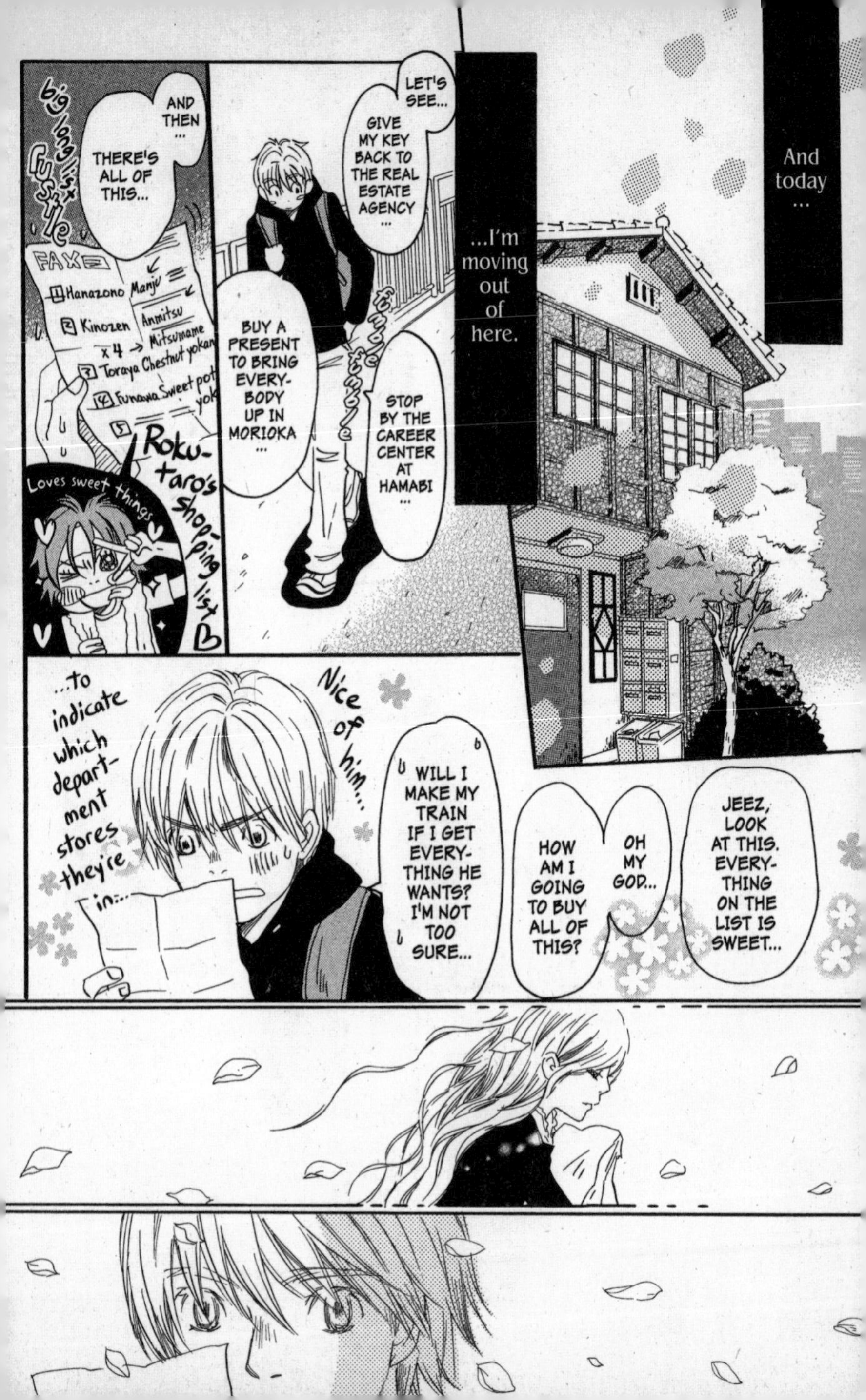

And today ...
...I'm moving out of here.
LET'S SEE... GIVE MY KEY BACK TO THE REAL ESTATE AGENCY ...
STOP BY THE CAREER CENTER AT HAMABI ...
BUY A PRESENT TO BRING EVERYBODY UP IN MORIOKA ...
fumble fumble
AND THEN ... THERE'S ALL OF THIS...
big long list
rustle
FAX
1 Hanazono Manju
2 Kinozen Anmitsu
x 4 → Mitsumame
3 Toraya Chestnut yokan
4 Funawa Sweet pot
yok
5
Roku-taro's shopping list
Loves sweet things
JEEZ, LOOK AT THIS. EVERYTHING ON THE LIST IS SWEET...
OH MY GOD...
HOW AM I GOING TO BUY ALL OF THIS?
WILL I MAKE MY TRAIN IF I GET EVERYTHING HE WANTS? I'M NOT TOO SURE...
Nice of him...
...to indicate which department stores they're in...

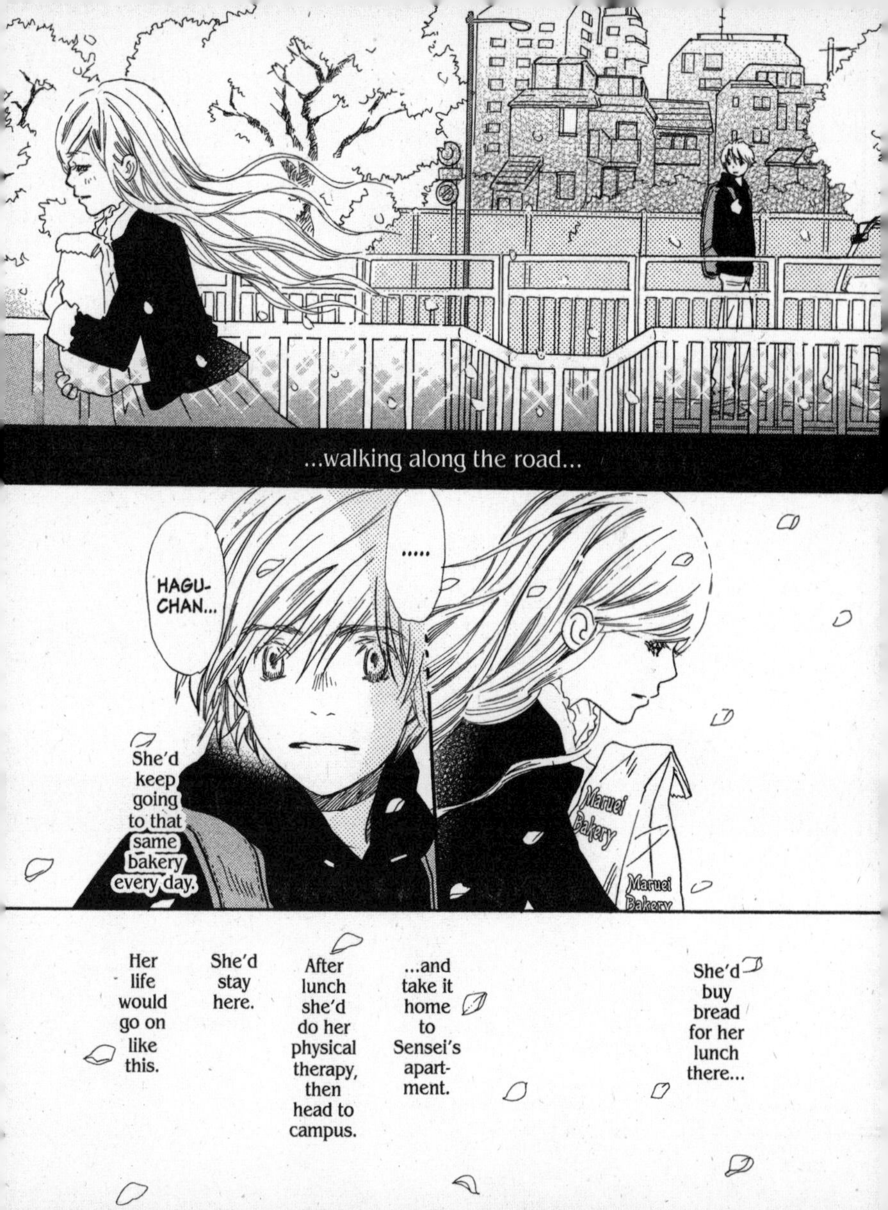

...walking along the road...
.....
HAGU-CHAN...
Maruei Bakery
Maruei Bakery
She'd keep going to that same bakery every day.
She'd buy bread for her lunch there...
...and take it home to Sensei's apartment.
After lunch she'd do her physical therapy, then head to campus.
She'd stay here.
Her life would go on like this.

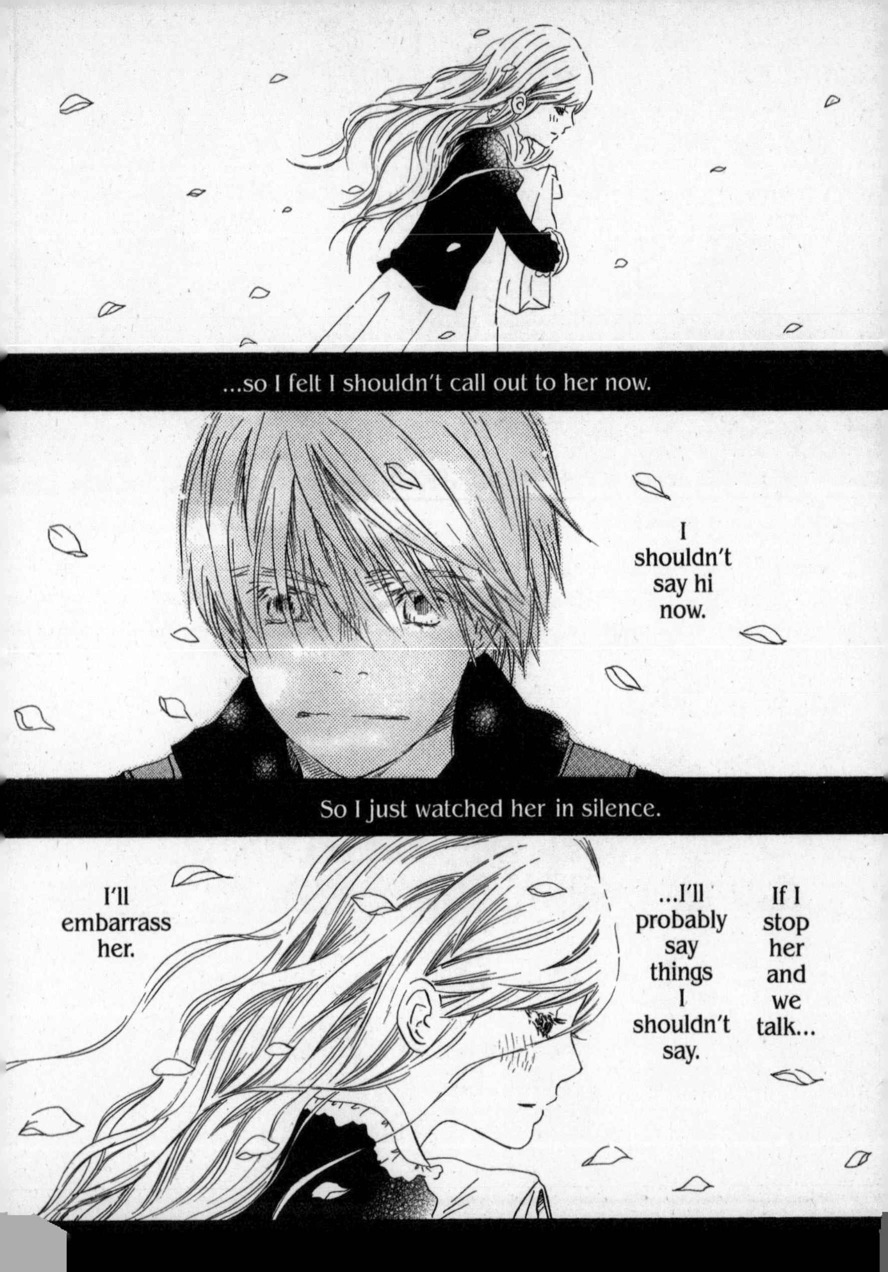
...so I felt I shouldn't call out to her now.
I shouldn't say hi now.
So I just watched her in silence.
If I stop her and we talk...
...I'll probably say things I shouldn't say.
I'll embarrass her.

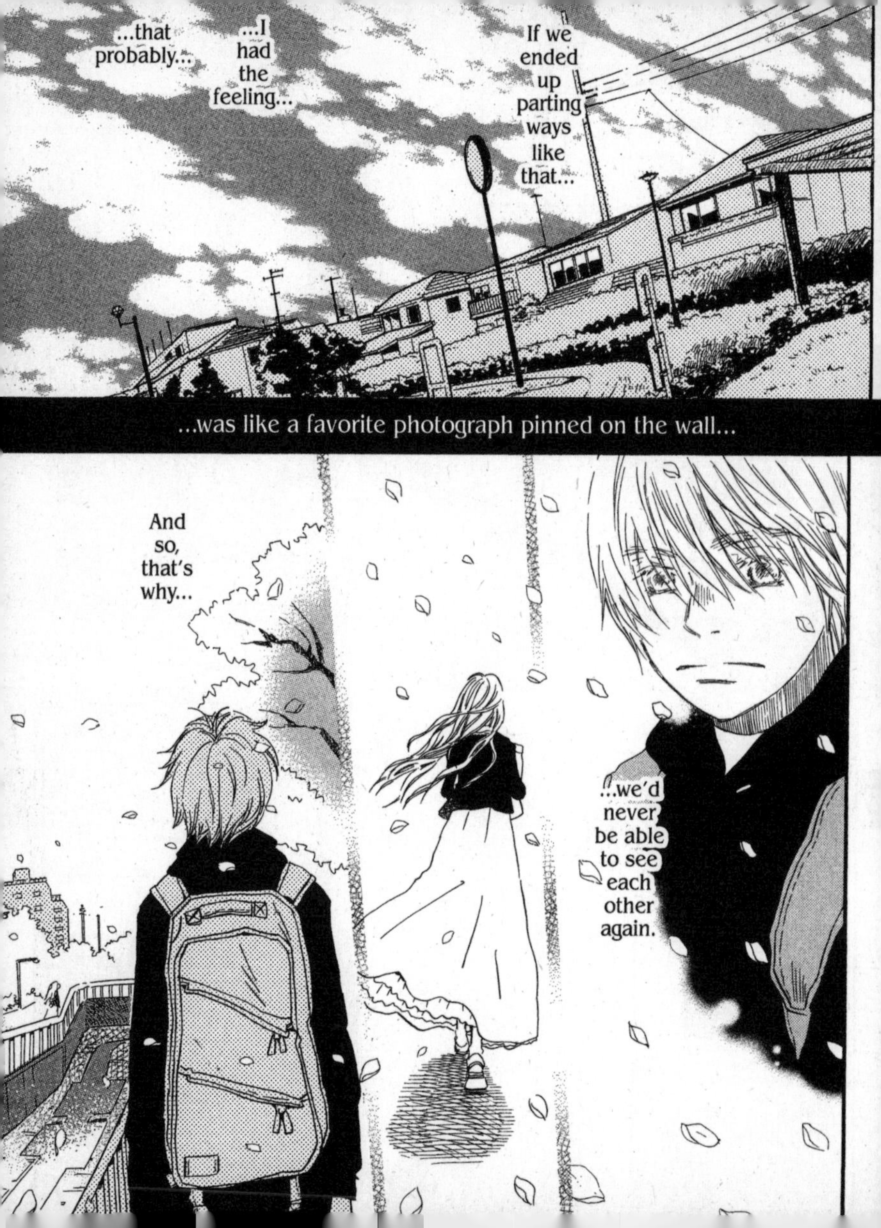
If we ended up parting ways like that...
...I had the feeling...
...that probably...
...was like a favorite photograph pinned on the wall...
...we'd never be able to see each other again.
And so, that's why...

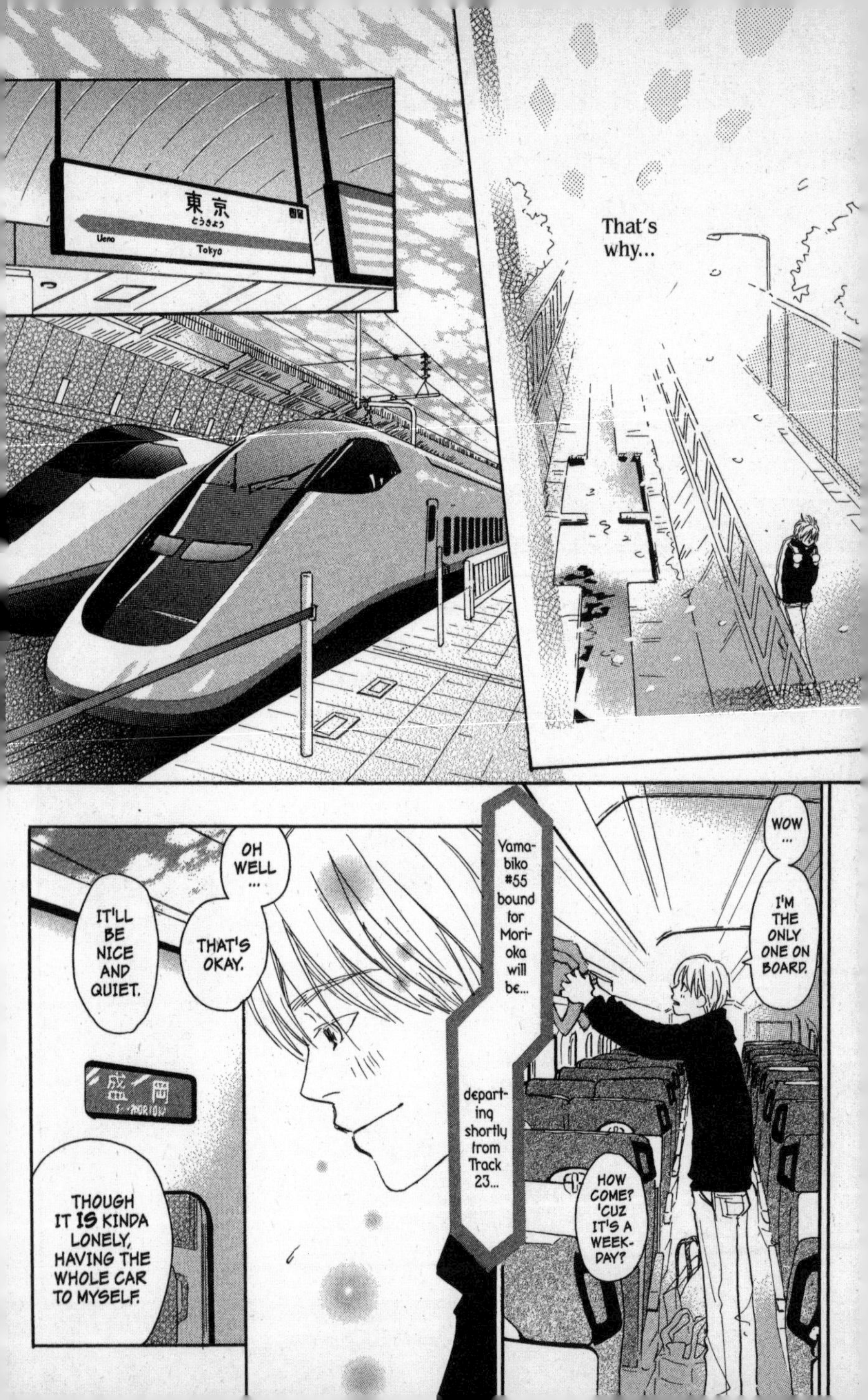
That's why...
東京
とうきょう
Ueno
Tokyo
WOW...
I'M THE ONLY ONE ON BOARD.
HOW COME? 'CUZ IT'S A WEEKDAY?
Yamabiko #55 bound for Morioka will be...
departing shortly from Track 23...
OH WELL...
THAT'S OKAY.
IT'LL BE NICE AND QUIET.
盛岡
THOUGH IT IS KINDA LONELY, HAVING THE WHOLE CAR TO MYSELF.

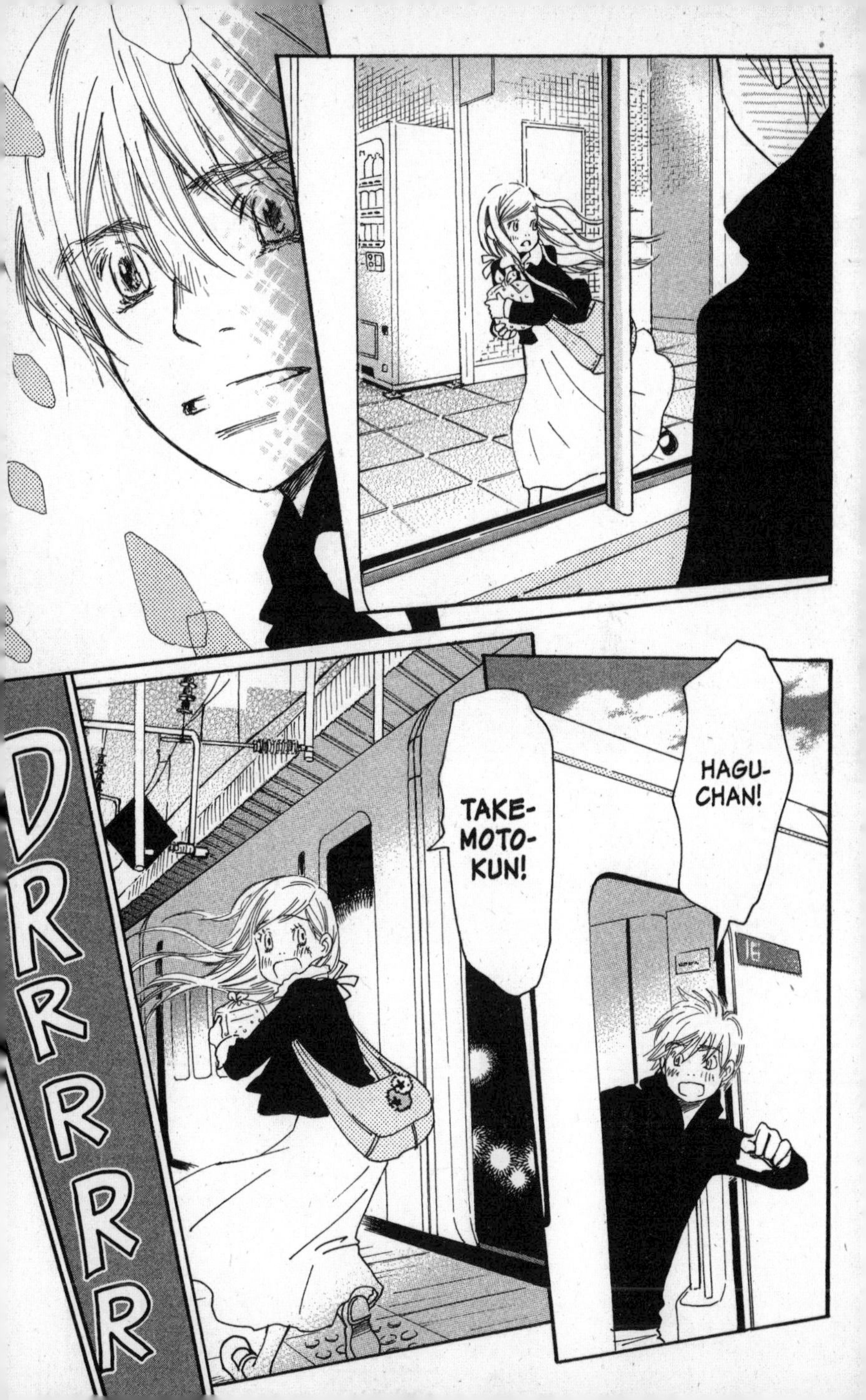
HAGU-CHAN!
TAKE-MOTO-KUN!
DRRRRR

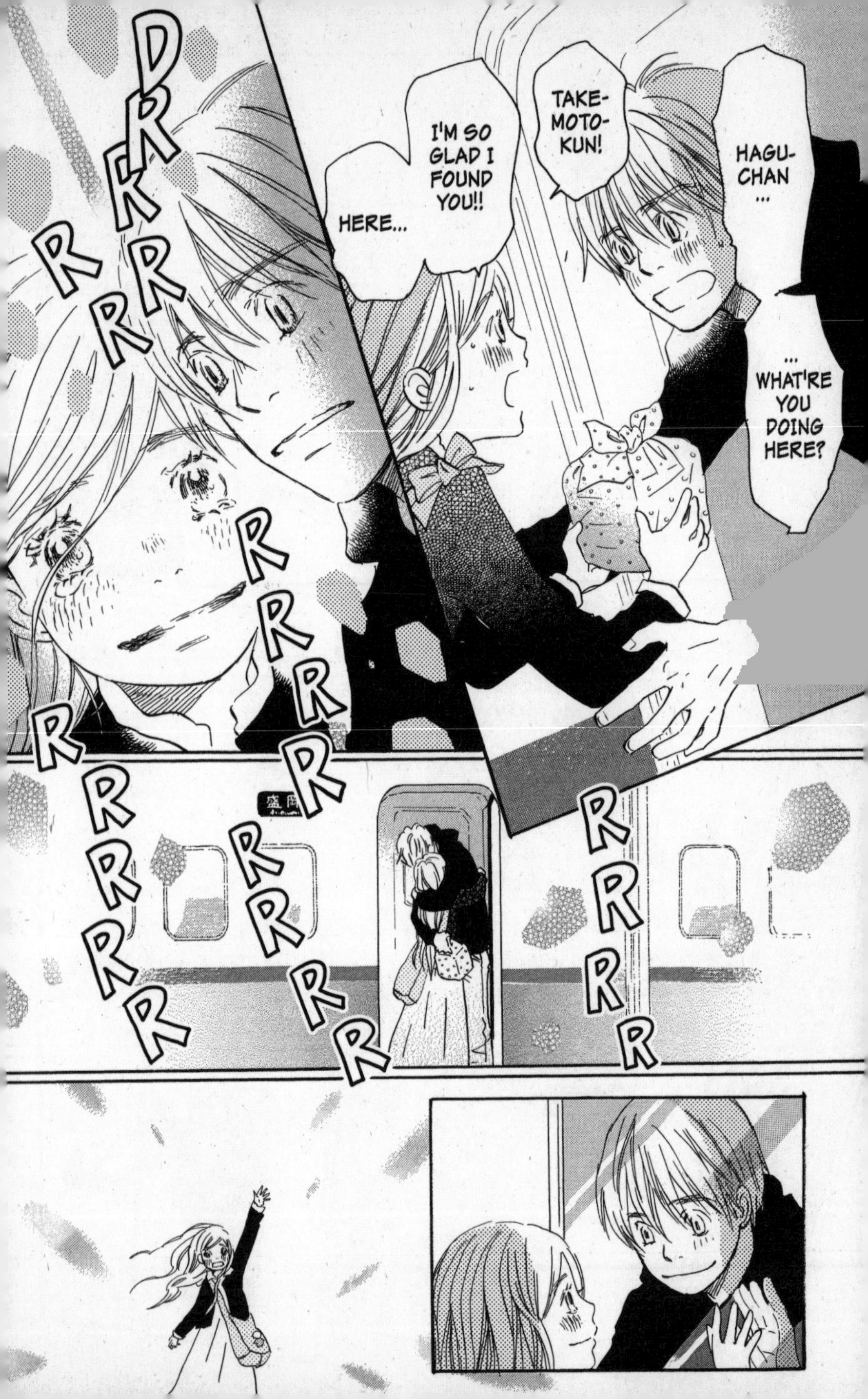
HAGU-CHAN ...
... WHAT'RE YOU DOING HERE?
TAKE-MOTO-KUN!
I'M SO GLAD I FOUND YOU!!
HERE...
DRRRRRR
RRRRRRRR
RRRRR
盛岡
RRRRR

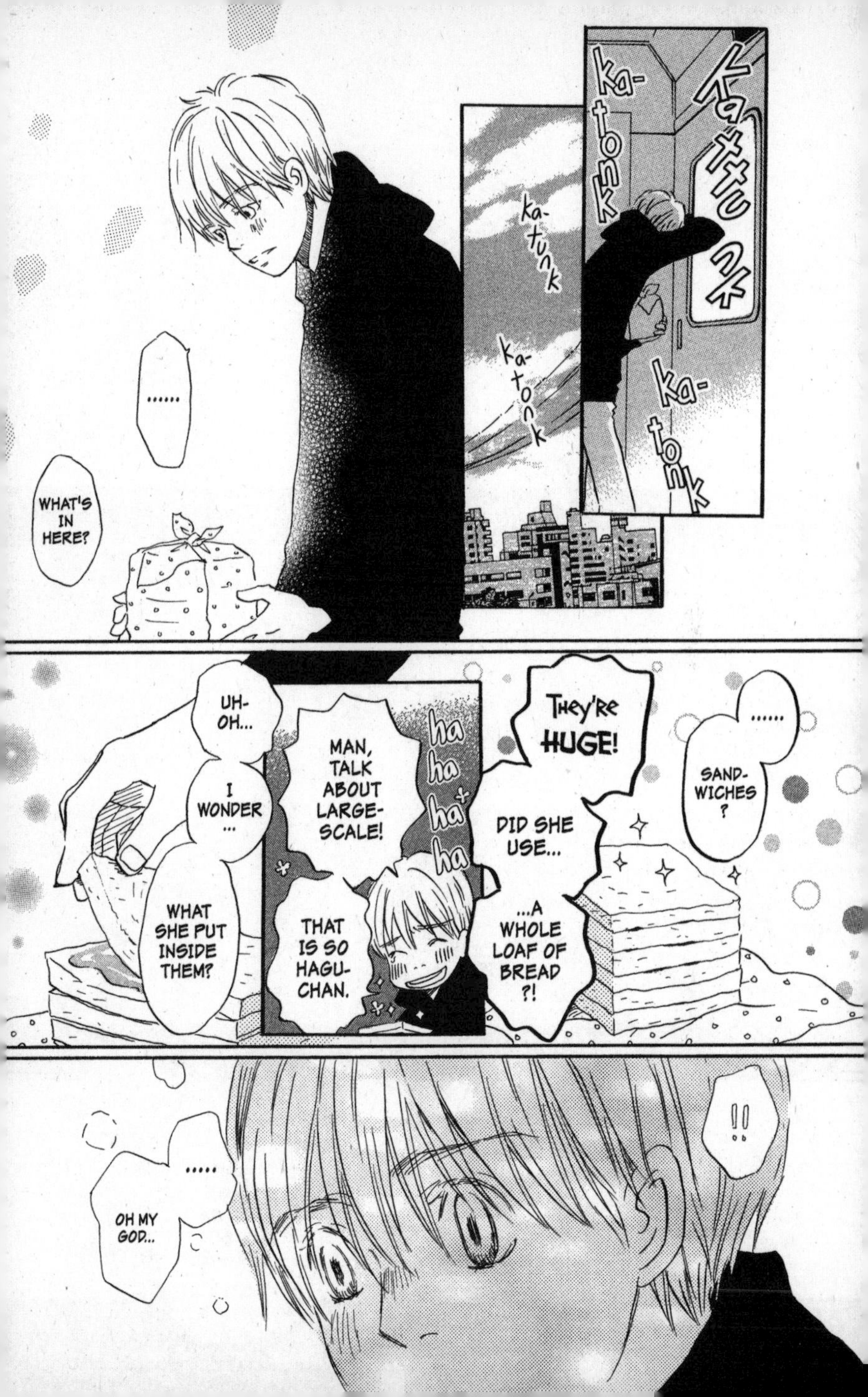
Kattunk
ka-tonk
ka-tonk
ka-tunk
ka-tonk
......
WHAT'S IN HERE?
......
SAND-WICHES?
They're HUGE!
DID SHE USE...
...A WHOLE LOAF OF BREAD?!
ha ha ha ha ha
MAN, TALK ABOUT LARGE-SCALE!
THAT IS SO HAGU-CHAN.
UH-OH...
I WONDER...
WHAT SHE PUT INSIDE THEM?
!!
......
OH MY GOD...

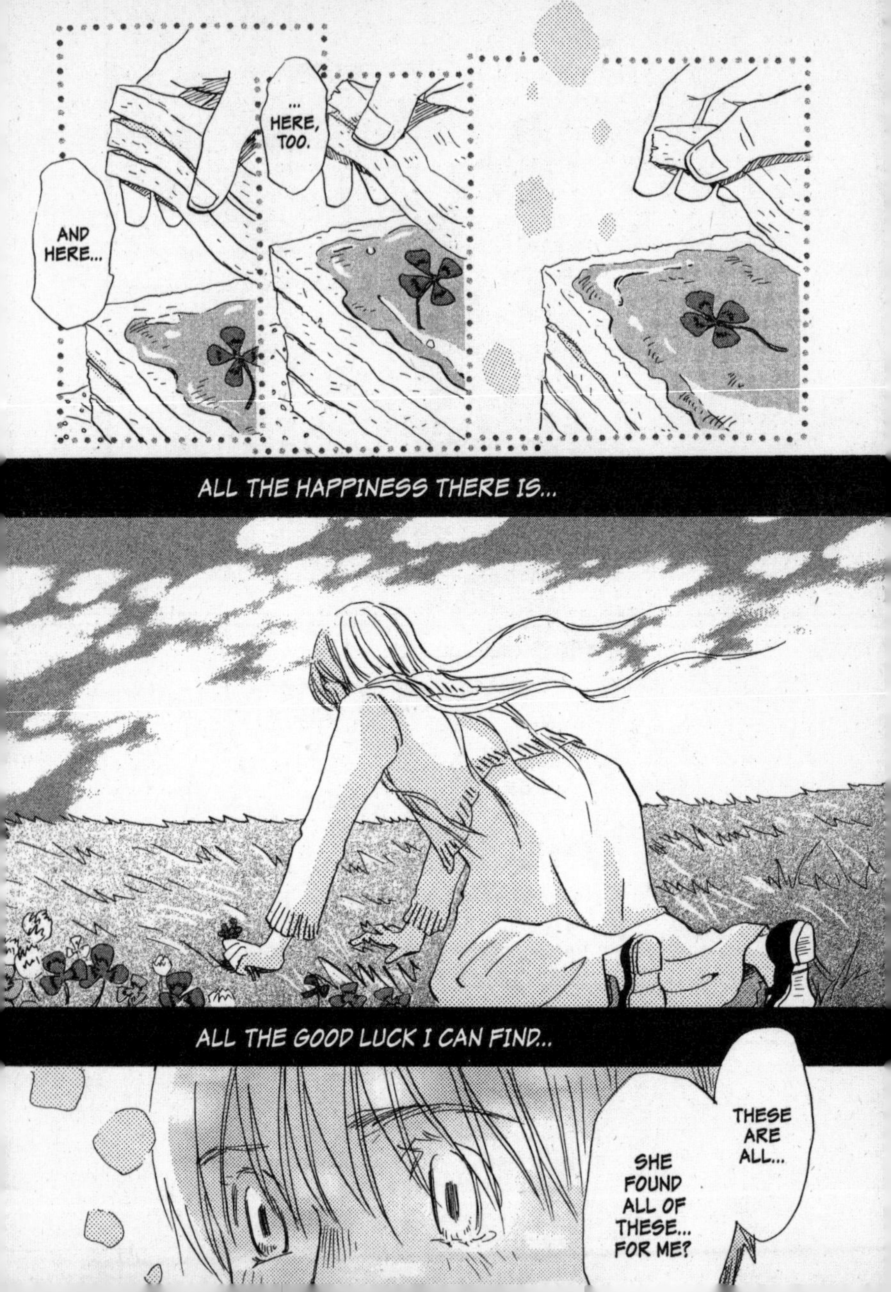
... HERE, TOO.
AND HERE...
ALL THE HAPPINESS THERE IS...
ALL THE GOOD LUCK I CAN FIND...
THESE ARE ALL...
SHE FOUND ALL OF THESE... FOR ME?

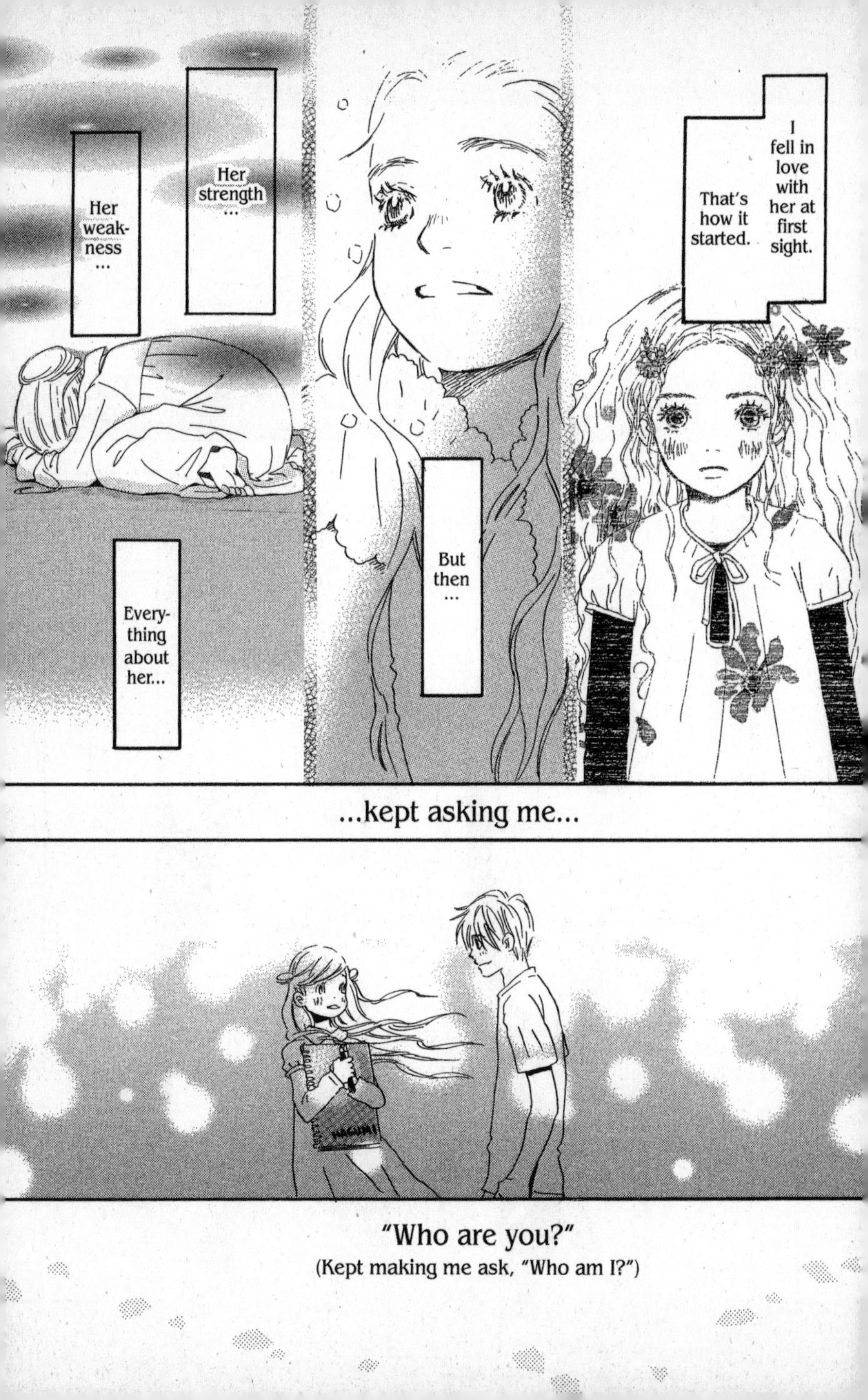
I fell in love with her at first sight.
That's how it started.
But then...
Her strength...
Her weakness...
Everything about her...
...kept asking me...
"Who are you?"
(Kept making me ask, "Who am I?")

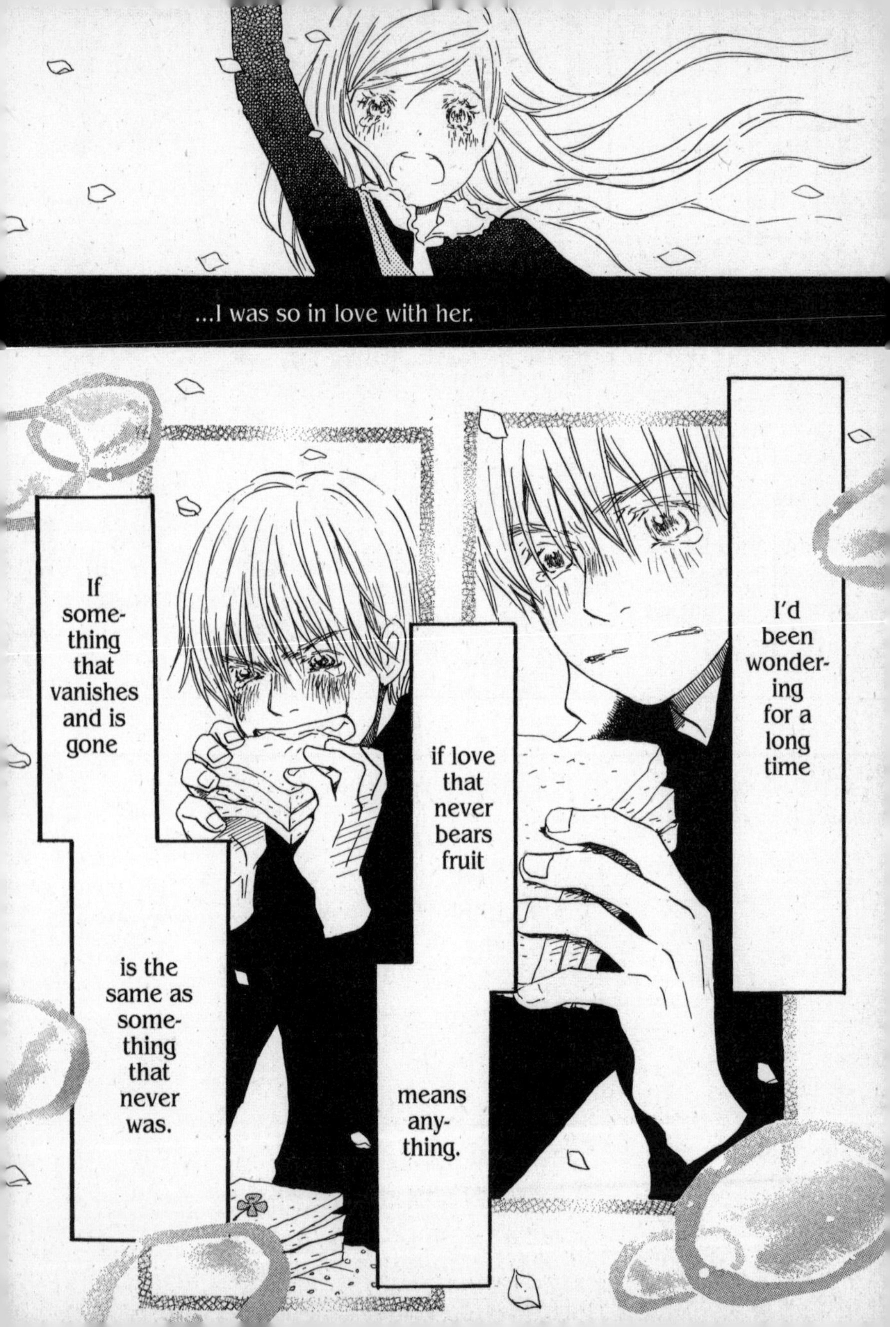
...I was so in love with her.
I'd been wonder-ing for a long time
if love that never bears fruit
means any-thing.
If some-thing that vanishes and is gone
is the same as some-thing that never was.

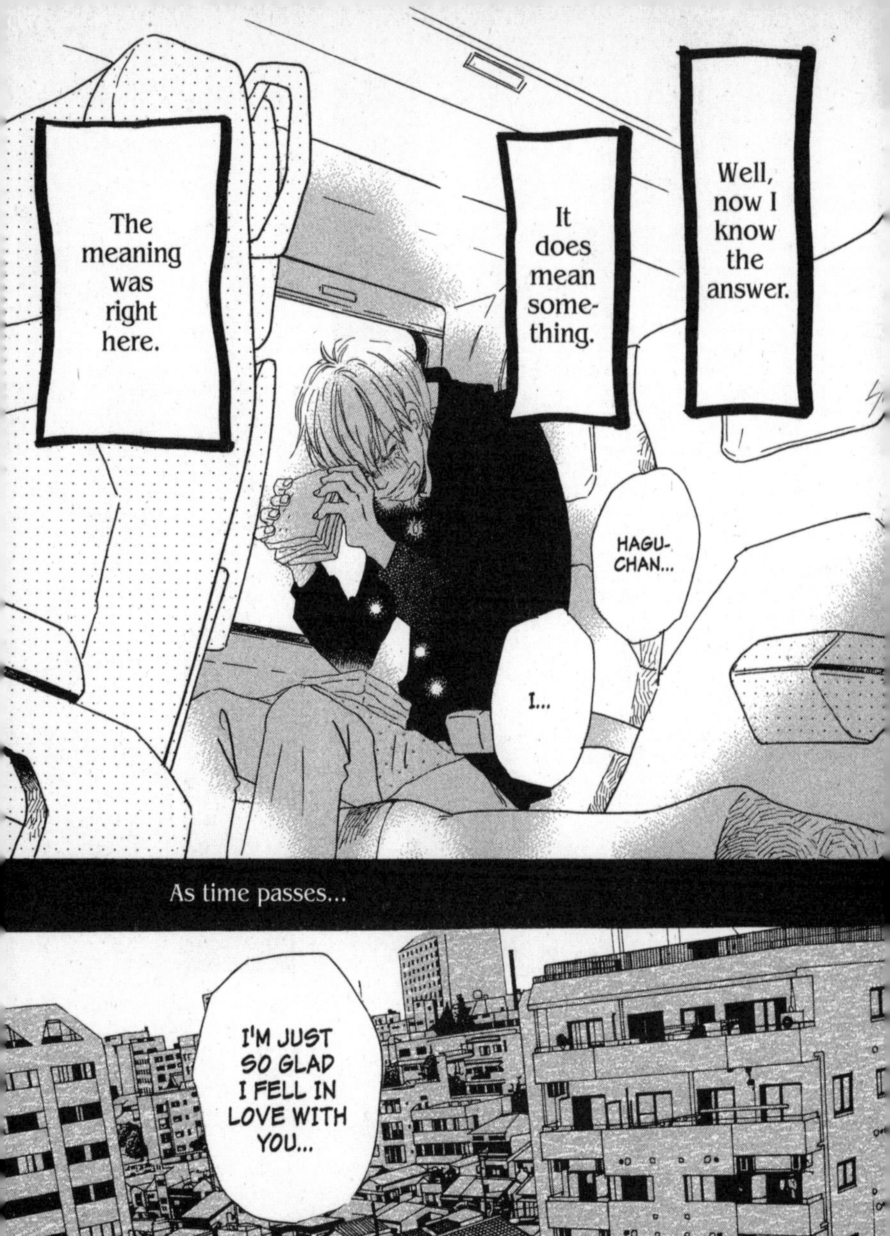
Well, now I know the answer.
It does mean something.
The meaning was right here.
HAGU-CHAN...
I...
As time passes...
I'M JUST SO GLAD I FELL IN LOVE WITH YOU...

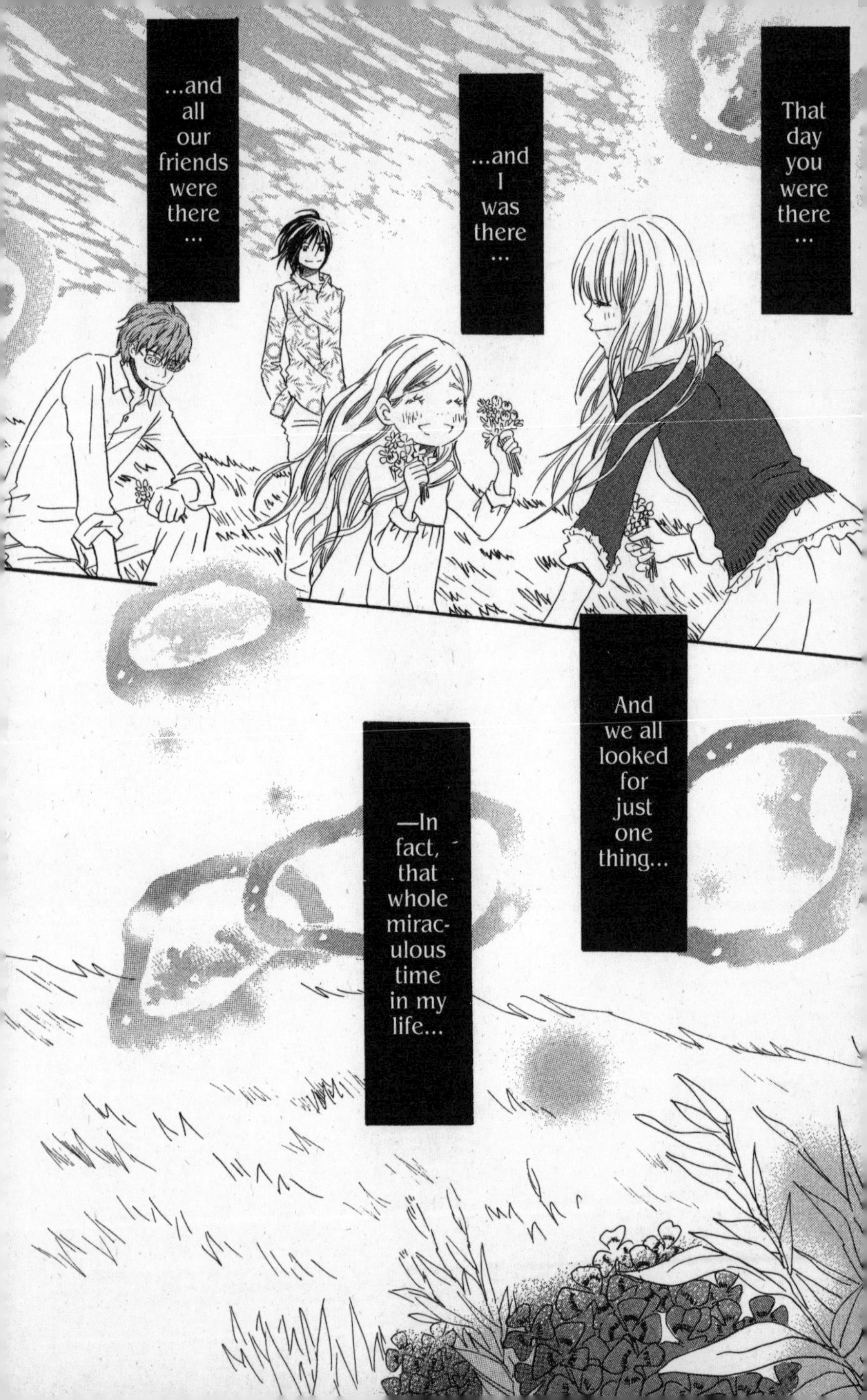
That day you were there...
...and I was there...
...and all our friends were there...
And we all looked for just one thing...
—In fact, that whole miraculous time in my life...

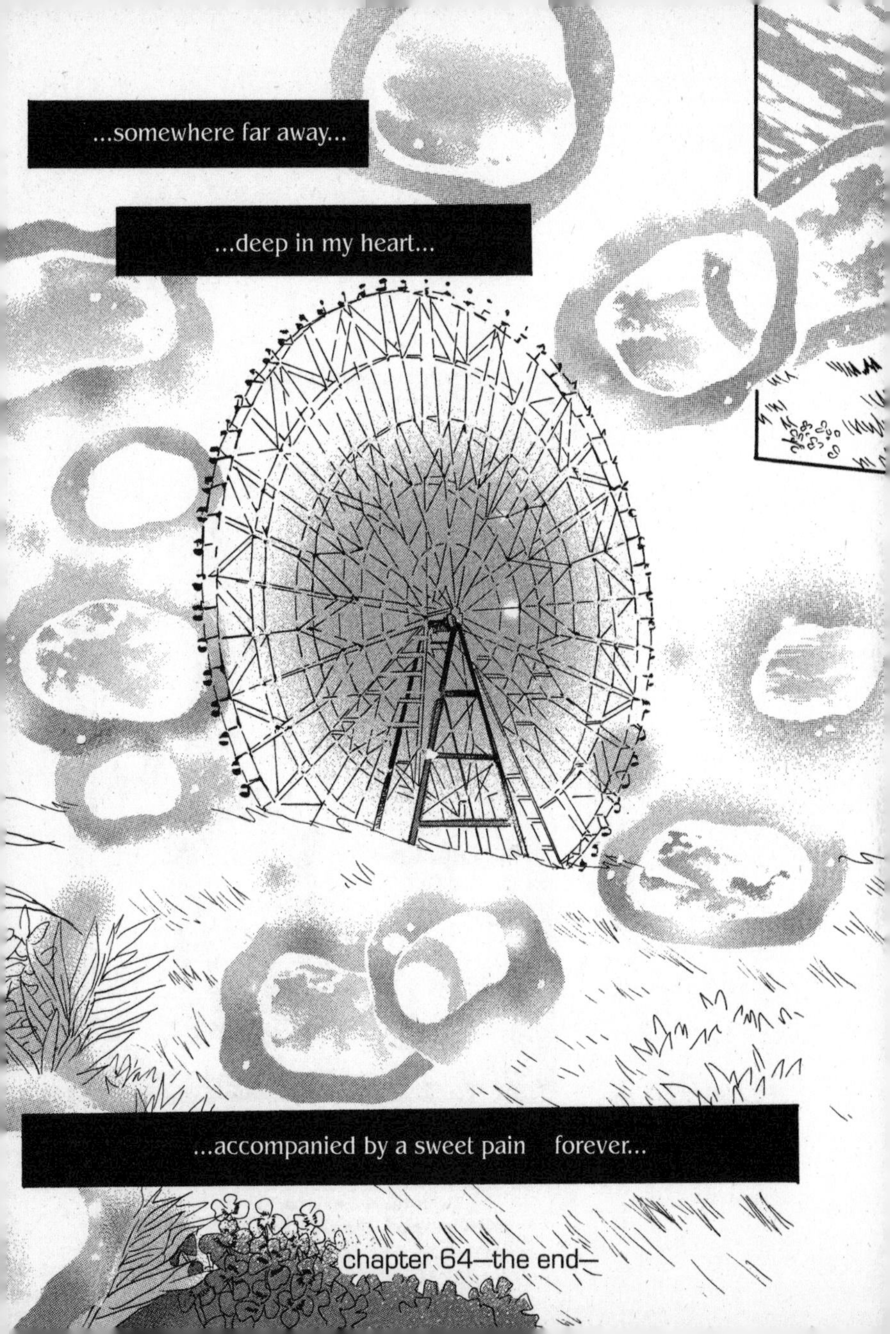
...somewhere far away...
...deep in my heart...
...accompanied by a sweet pain forever...
chapter 64—the end—

It was really hard work, but a lot of fun,
illustrating the packaging for the *HoneyClo* anime DVDs.
This is the rough sketch for Vol. 5.
I loved being able to use lots and lots of colors.

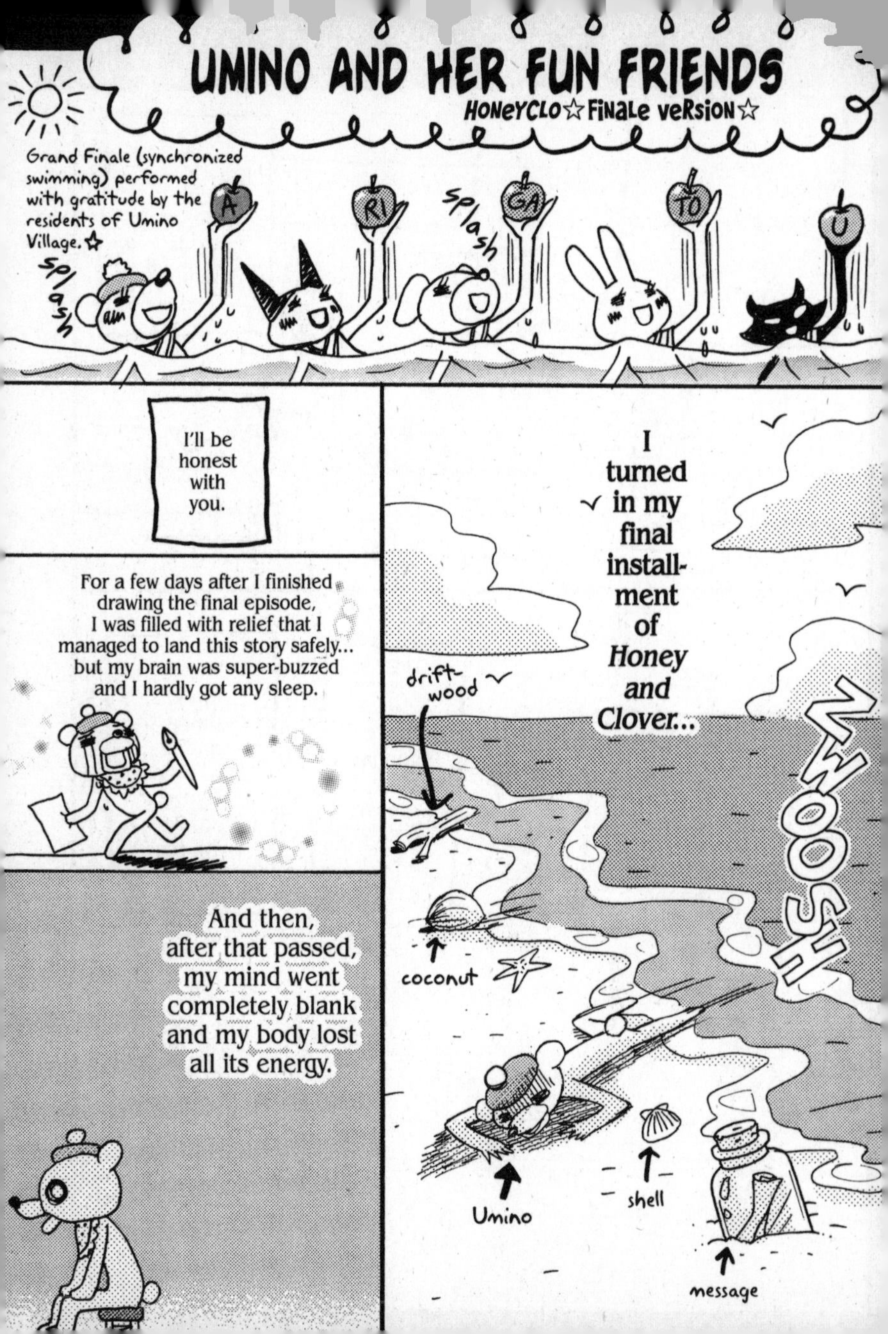
UMINO AND HER FUN FRIENDS
HONEYCLO☆FINALE VERSION☆
Grand Finale (synchronized swimming) performed with gratitude by the residents of Umino Village.✩
U
TO
splash
GA
RI
A
splash
I turned in my final installment of Honey and Clover...
WOOSH
drift-wood
coconut
message
shell
Umino
I'll be honest with you.
For a few days after I finished drawing the final episode, I was filled with relief that I managed to land this story safely... but my brain was super-buzzed and I hardly got any sleep.
And then, after that passed, my mind went completely blank and my body lost all its energy.

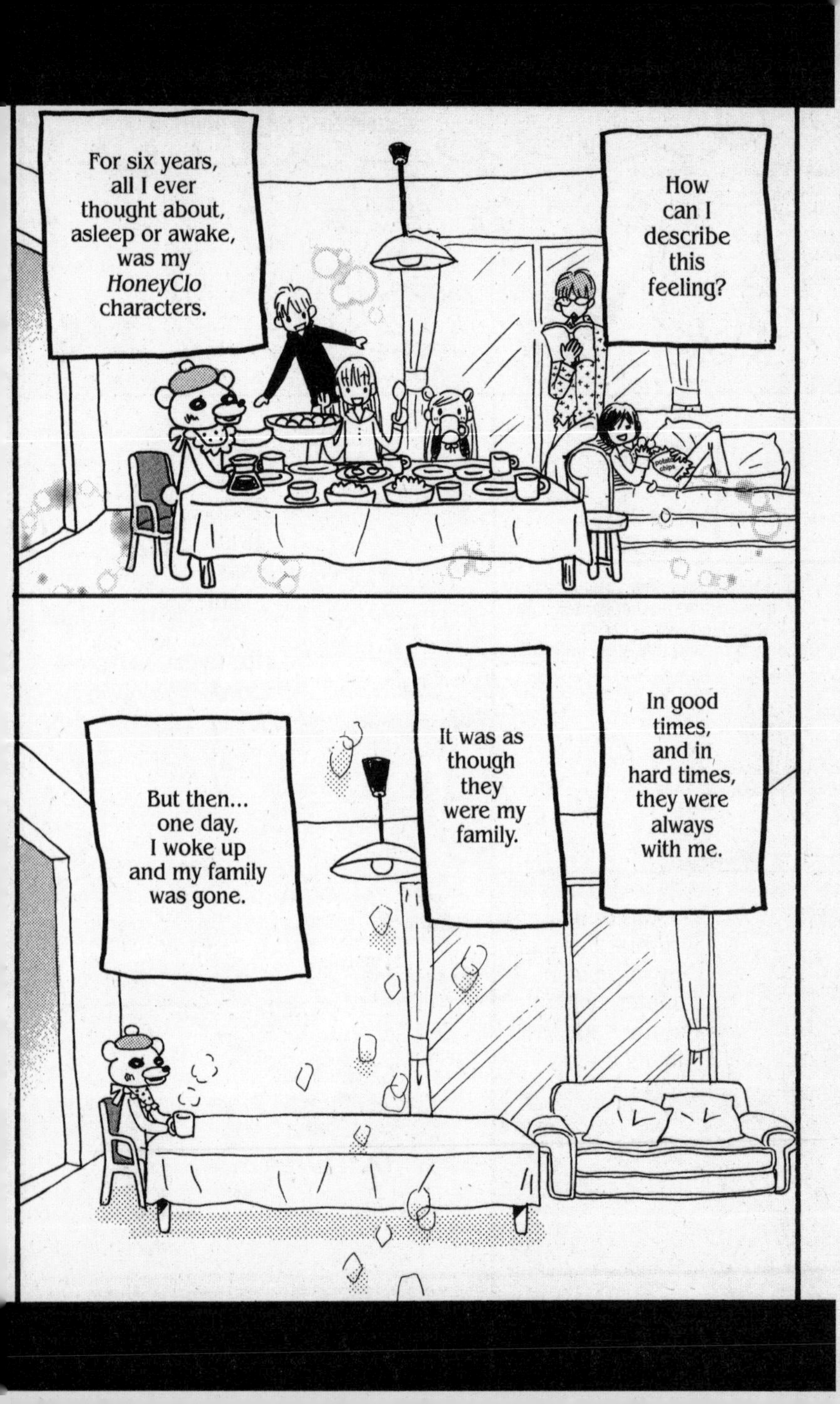
How can I describe this feeling?
For six years, all I ever thought about, asleep or awake, was my *HoneyClo* characters.
potato chips
In good times, and in hard times, they were always with me.
It was as though they were my family.
But then... one day, I woke up and my family was gone.

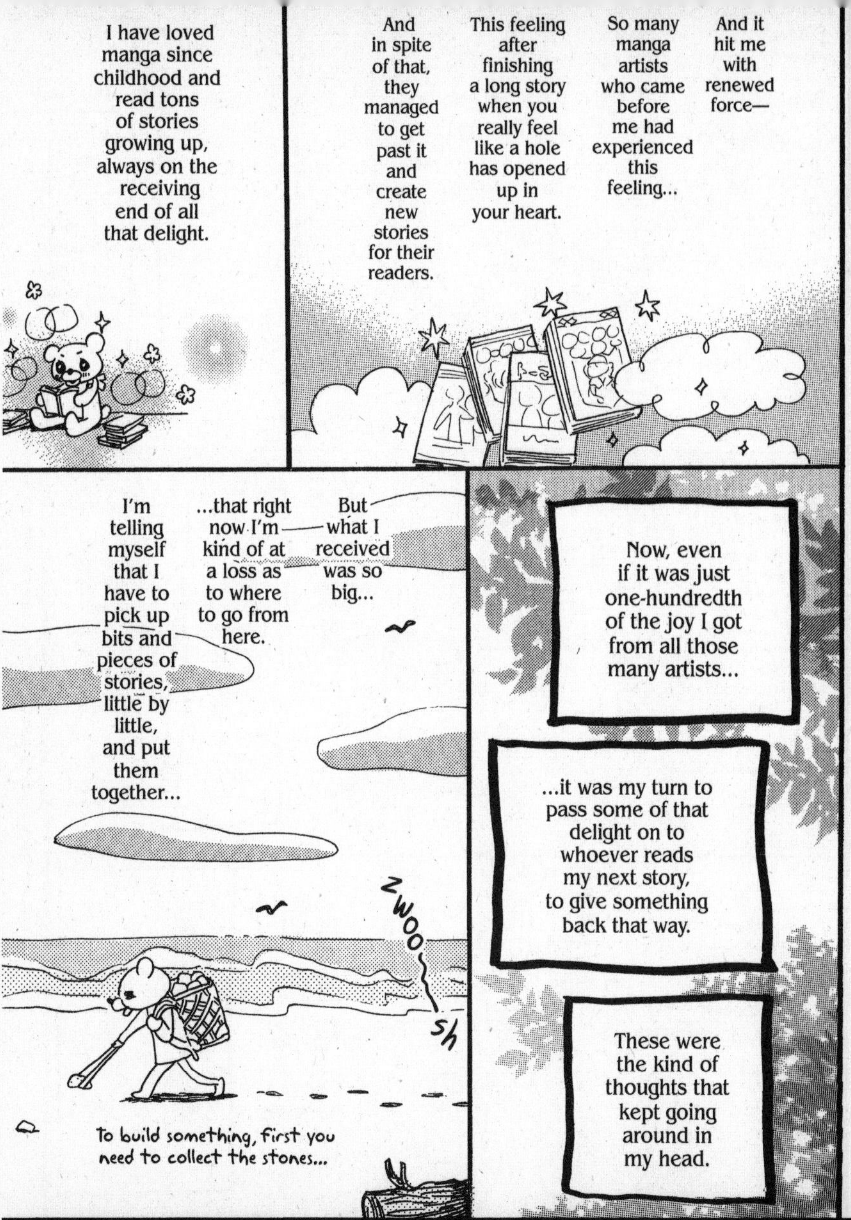
And it hit me with renewed force—
So many manga artists who came before me had experienced this feeling...
This feeling after finishing a long story when you really feel like a hole has opened up in your heart.
And in spite of that, they managed to get past it and create new stories for their readers.
I have loved manga since childhood and read tons of stories growing up, always on the receiving end of all that delight.
Now, even if it was just one-hundredth of the joy I got from all those many artists...
...it was my turn to pass some of that delight on to whoever reads my next story, to give something back that way.
These were the kind of thoughts that kept going around in my head.
But what I received was so big...
...that right now I'm kind of at a loss as to where to go from here.
I'm telling myself that I have to pick up bits and pieces of stories, little by little, and put them together...
ZWOO~SH
To build something, first you need to collect the stones...

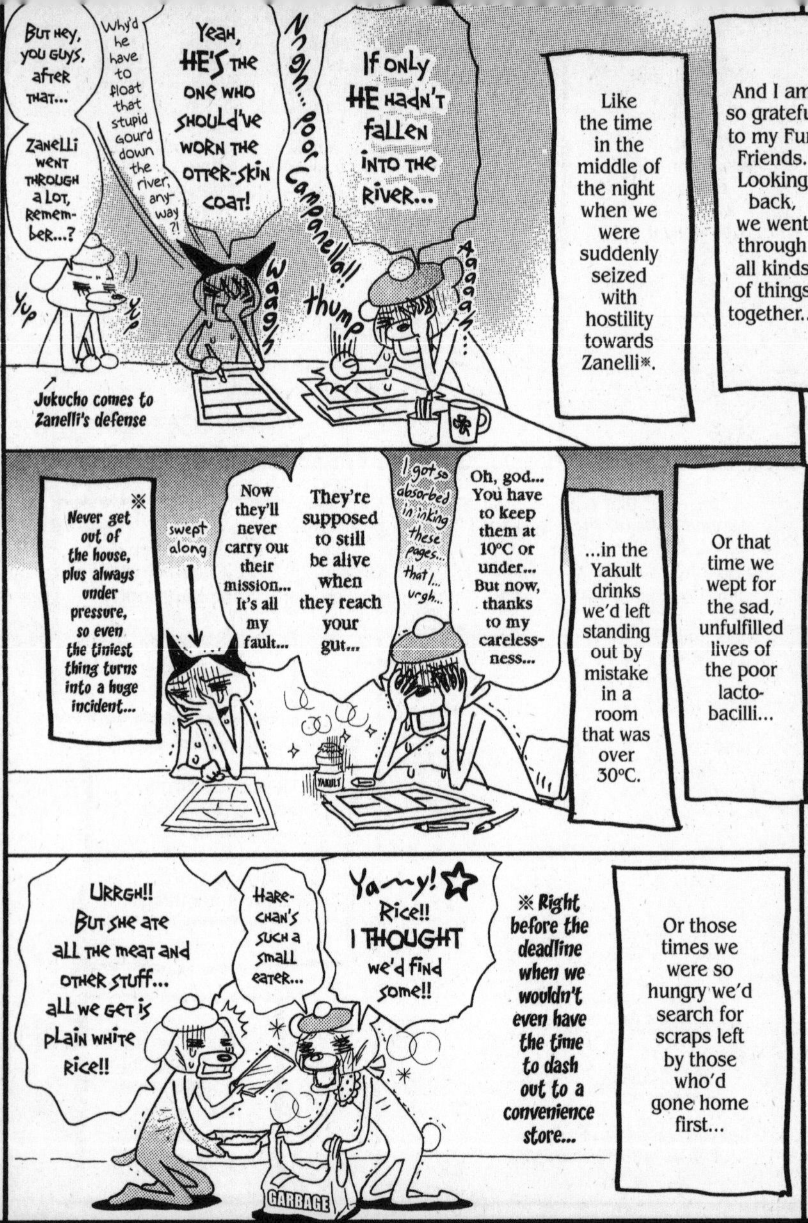
And I am so grateful to my Fun Friends. Looking back, we went through all kinds of things together...
Like the time in the middle of the night when we were suddenly seized with hostility towards Zanelli※.
If only HE hadn't fallen into the river...
Nngh... poor Campanella!!
Aggggh...
thump
Waagh
Yeah, HE'S the one who should've worn the otter-skin coat!
Why'd he have to float that stupid gourd down the river, anyway?!
But hey, you guys, after that...
Zanelli went through a lot, remember...?
Yup
Yup
Jukucho comes to Zanelli's defense
Or that time we wept for the sad, unfulfilled lives of the poor lacto-bacilli...
...in the Yakult drinks we'd left standing out by mistake in a room that was over 30°C.
Oh, god... You have to keep them at 10°C or under... But now, thanks to my careless-ness...
I got so absorbed in inking these pages... that I... urgh...
They're supposed to still be alive when they reach your gut...
Now they'll never carry out their mission... It's all my fault...
swept along
※ Never get out of the house, plus always under pressure, so even the tiniest thing turns into a huge incident...
YAKULT
Or those times we were so hungry we'd search for scraps left by those who'd gone home first...
※ Right before the deadline when we wouldn't even have the time to dash out to a convenience store...
Yamy! Rice!! I THOUGHT we'd find some!!
Hare-chan's such a small eater...
URRGH!! But she ate all the meat and other stuff... all we get is plain white rice!!
GARBAGE

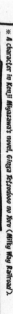

※ A character in Kenji Miyazawa's novel, *Ginga Tetsudooo no Yoru* (*Milky Way Railroad*).

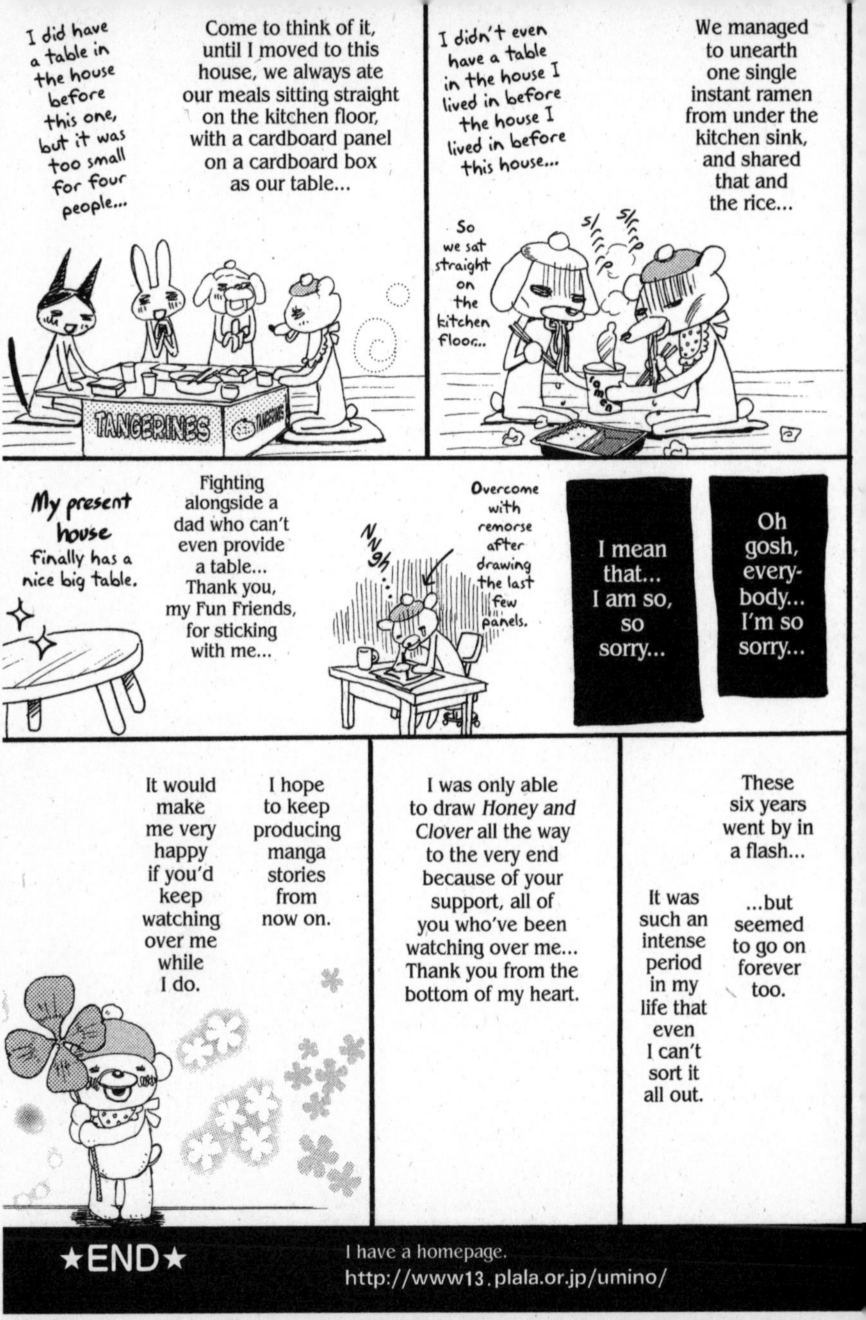
We managed to unearth one single instant ramen from under the kitchen sink, and shared that and the rice...
I didn't even have a table in the house I lived in before the house I lived in before this house...
Slrrp
Slrrp
So we sat straight on the kitchen floor...
ramen
Come to think of it, until I moved to this house, we always ate our meals sitting straight on the kitchen floor, with a cardboard panel on a cardboard box as our table...
I did have a table in the house before this one, but it was too small for four people...
TANGERINES
Oh gosh, everybody... I'm so sorry...
I mean that... I am so, so sorry...
Overcome with remorse after drawing the last few panels.
Nngh...
Fighting alongside a dad who can't even provide a table... Thank you, my Fun Friends, for sticking with me...
My present house finally has a nice big table.
These six years went by in a flash...
...but seemed to go on forever too.
It was such an intense period in my life that even I can't sort it all out.
I was only able to draw *Honey and Clover* all the way to the very end because of your support, all of you who've been watching over me... Thank you from the bottom of my heart.
I hope to keep producing manga stories from now on.
It would make me very happy if you'd keep watching over me while I do.
★END★
I have a homepage.
http://www13.plala.or.jp/umino/

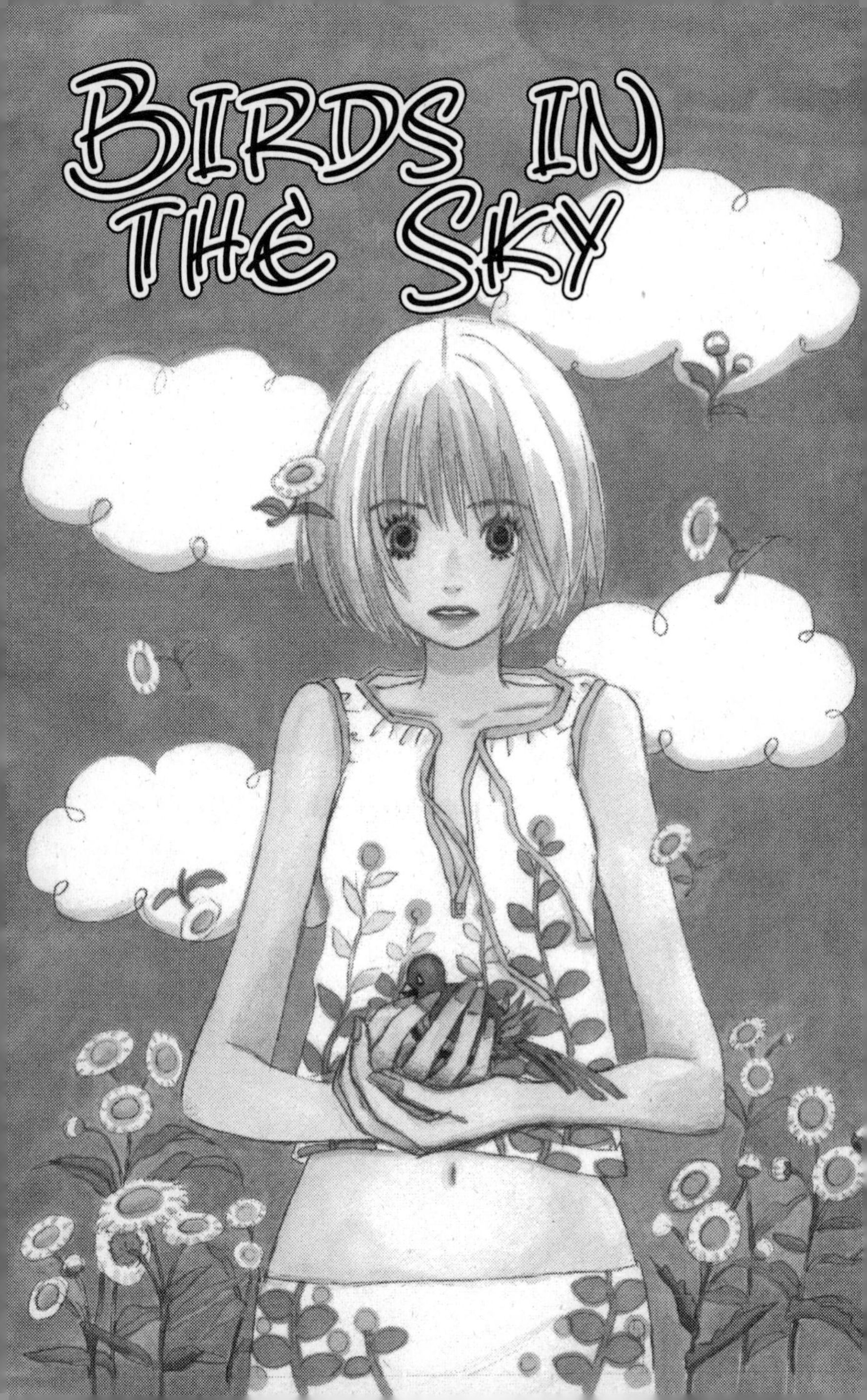
BIRDS IN THE SKY

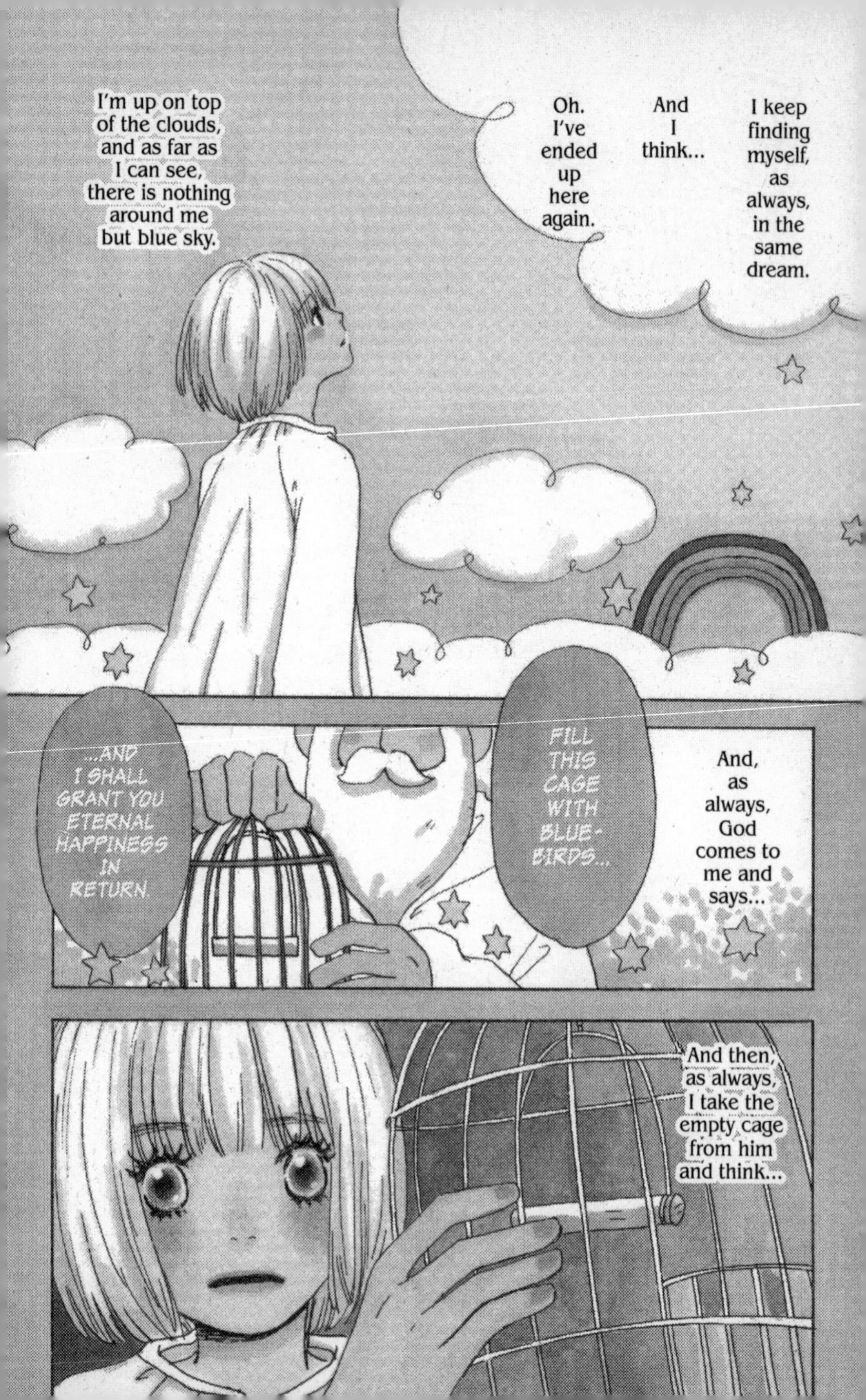
I keep finding myself, as always, in the same dream.
And I think...
Oh. I've ended up here again.
I'm up on top of the clouds, and as far as I can see, there is nothing around me but blue sky.
And, as always, God comes to me and says...
FILL THIS CAGE WITH BLUE-BIRDS...
...AND I SHALL GRANT YOU ETERNAL HAPPINESS IN RETURN.
And then, as always, I take the empty cage from him and think...

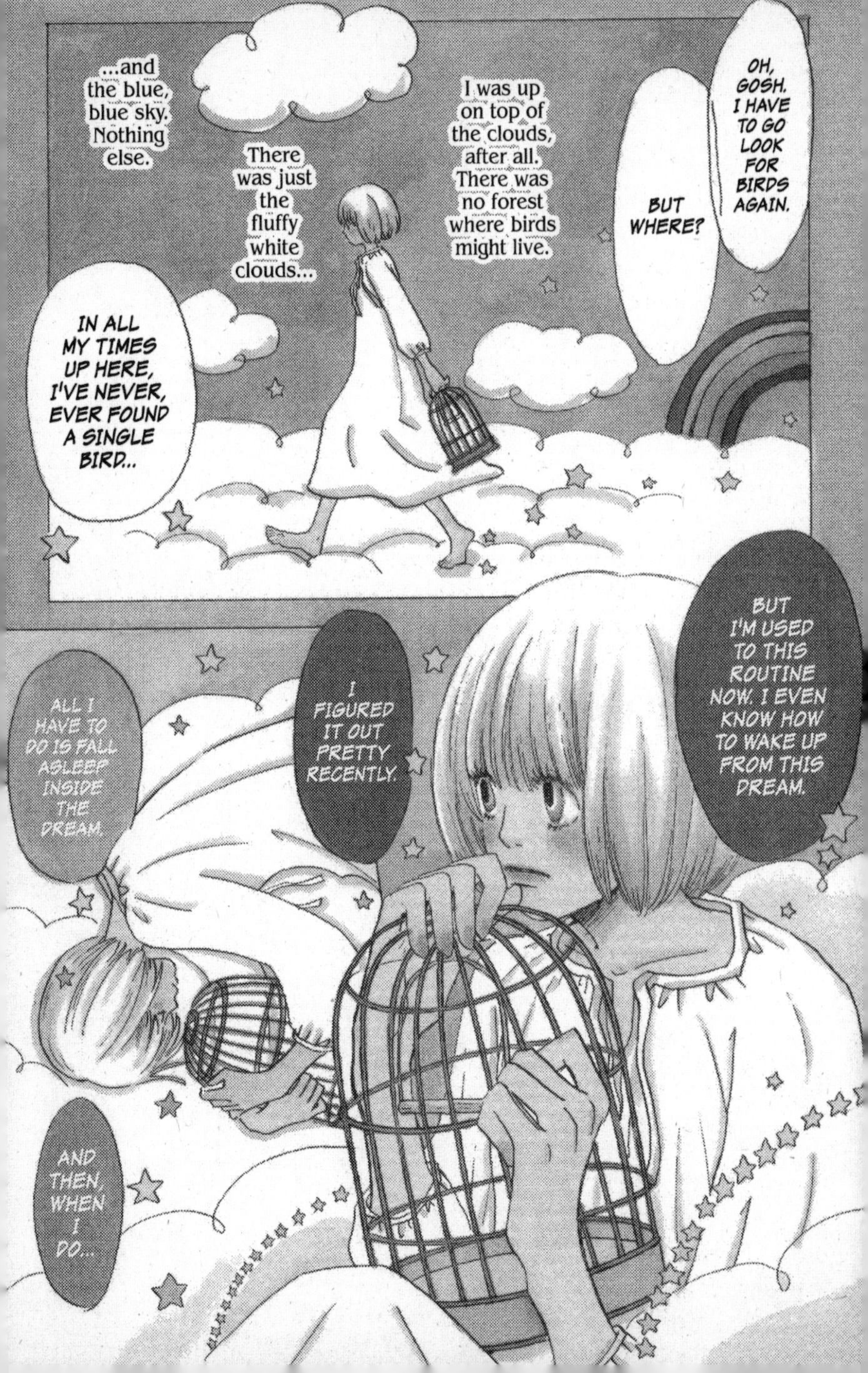
OH, GOSH. I HAVE TO GO LOOK FOR BIRDS AGAIN.
BUT WHERE?
I was up on top of the clouds, after all. There was no forest where birds might live.
There was just the fluffy white clouds...
...and the blue, blue sky. Nothing else.
IN ALL MY TIMES UP HERE, I'VE NEVER, EVER FOUND A SINGLE BIRD...
BUT I'M USED TO THIS ROUTINE NOW. I EVEN KNOW HOW TO WAKE UP FROM THIS DREAM.
I FIGURED IT OUT PRETTY RECENTLY.
ALL I HAVE TO DO IS FALL ASLEEP INSIDE THE DREAM.
AND THEN, WHEN I DO...

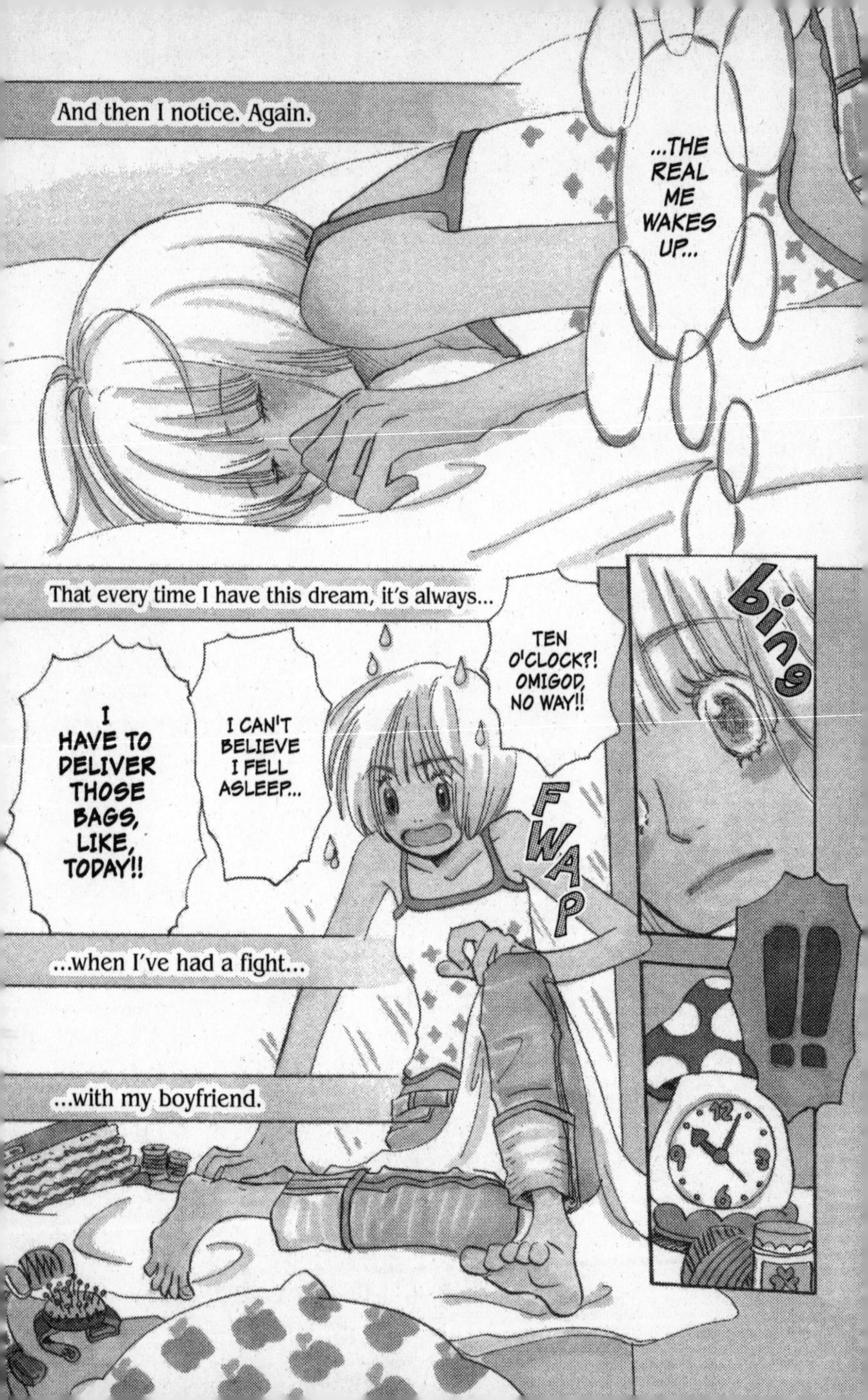
...THE REAL ME WAKES UP...
And then I notice. Again.
bing
!!
That every time I have this dream, it's always...
TEN O'CLOCK?! OMIGOD, NO WAY!!
FWAP
I CAN'T BELIEVE I FELL ASLEEP...
I HAVE TO DELIVER THOSE BAGS, LIKE, TODAY!!
...when I've had a fight...
...with my boyfriend.

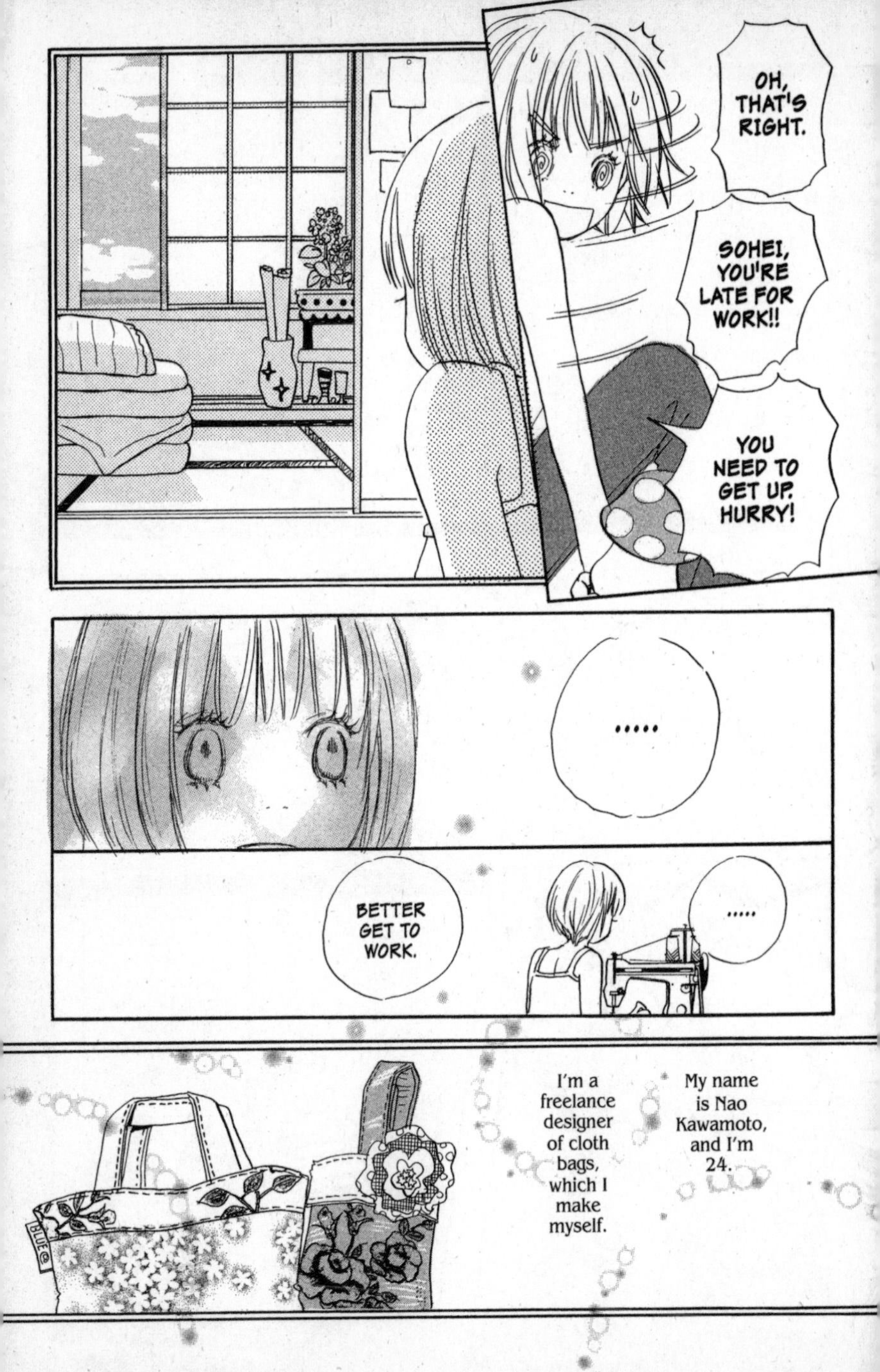
OH, THAT'S RIGHT.
SOHEI, YOU'RE LATE FOR WORK!!
YOU NEED TO GET UP. HURRY!
.....
.....
BETTER GET TO WORK.
My name is Nao Kawamoto, and I'm 24.
I'm a freelance designer of cloth bags, which I make myself.

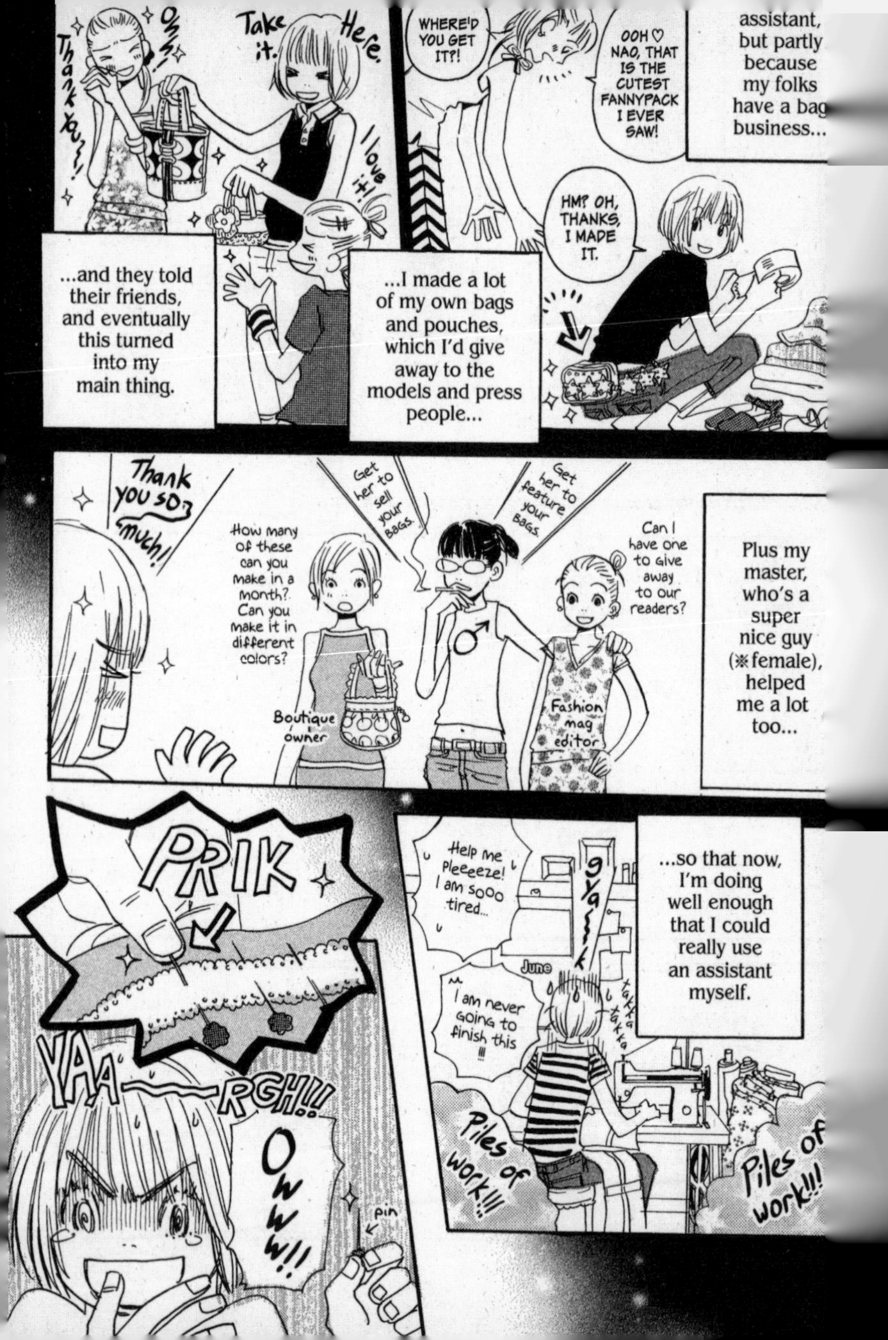
assistant, but partly because my folks have a bag business...
OOH ♡ NAO, THAT IS THE CUTEST FANNYPACK I EVER SAW!
WHERE'D YOU GET IT?!
HM? OH, THANKS, I MADE IT.
...I made a lot of my own bags and pouches, which I'd give away to the models and press people...
Here.
Take it.
Oh
Thank you~!
I love it!
...and they told their friends, and eventually this turned into my main thing.
Plus my master, who's a super nice guy (※female), helped me a lot too...
Can I have one to give away to our readers?
Get her to feature your bags.
Fashion mag editor
Get her to sell your bags.
How many of these can you make in a month? Can you make it in different colors?
Boutique owner
Thank you so much!
...so that now, I'm doing well enough that I could really use an assistant myself.
Help me Pleeeeze! I am sooo tired...
gyaak
June
I am never going to finish this!!!
takka takka
Piles of work!!!
Piles of work!!!
PRIK
YAA—RGH!!
Owww!!
pin

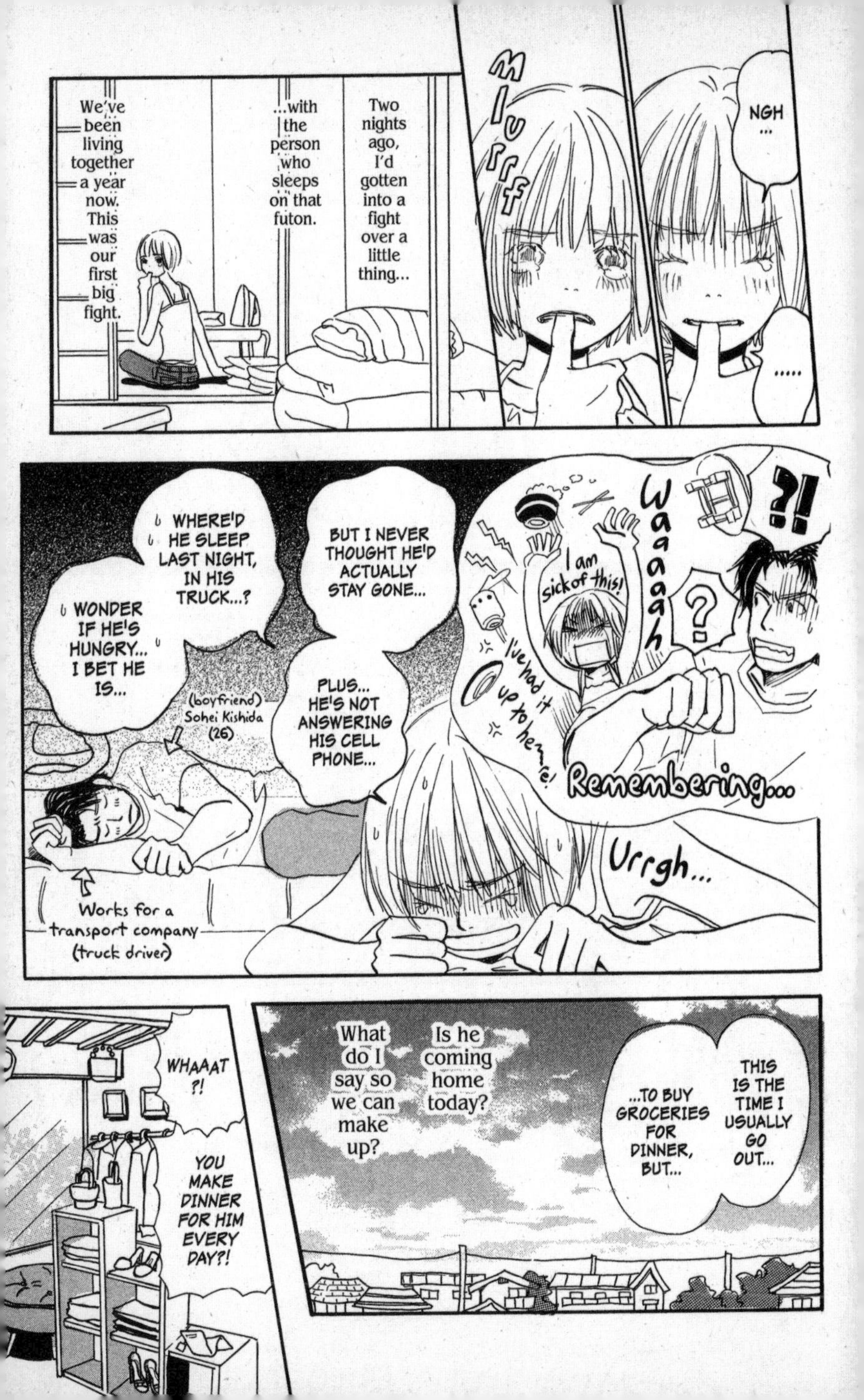
NGH...
.....
Mlurrff
Two nights ago, I'd gotten into a fight over a little thing...
...with the person who sleeps on that futon.
We've been living together a year now. This was our first big fight.
?!
Waaaaah
I am sick of this!
?
I've had it up to here!
Remembering...
Urrgh...
BUT I NEVER THOUGHT HE'D ACTUALLY STAY GONE...
PLUS... HE'S NOT ANSWERING HIS CELL PHONE...
WHERE'D HE SLEEP LAST NIGHT, IN HIS TRUCK...?
WONDER IF HE'S HUNGRY... I BET HE IS...
(boyfriend) Sohei Kishida (26)
Works for a transport company (truck driver)
THIS IS THE TIME I USUALLY GO OUT...
...TO BUY GROCERIES FOR DINNER, BUT...
Is he coming home today?
What do I say so we can make up?
WHAAAT ?!
YOU MAKE DINNER FOR HIM EVERY DAY?!

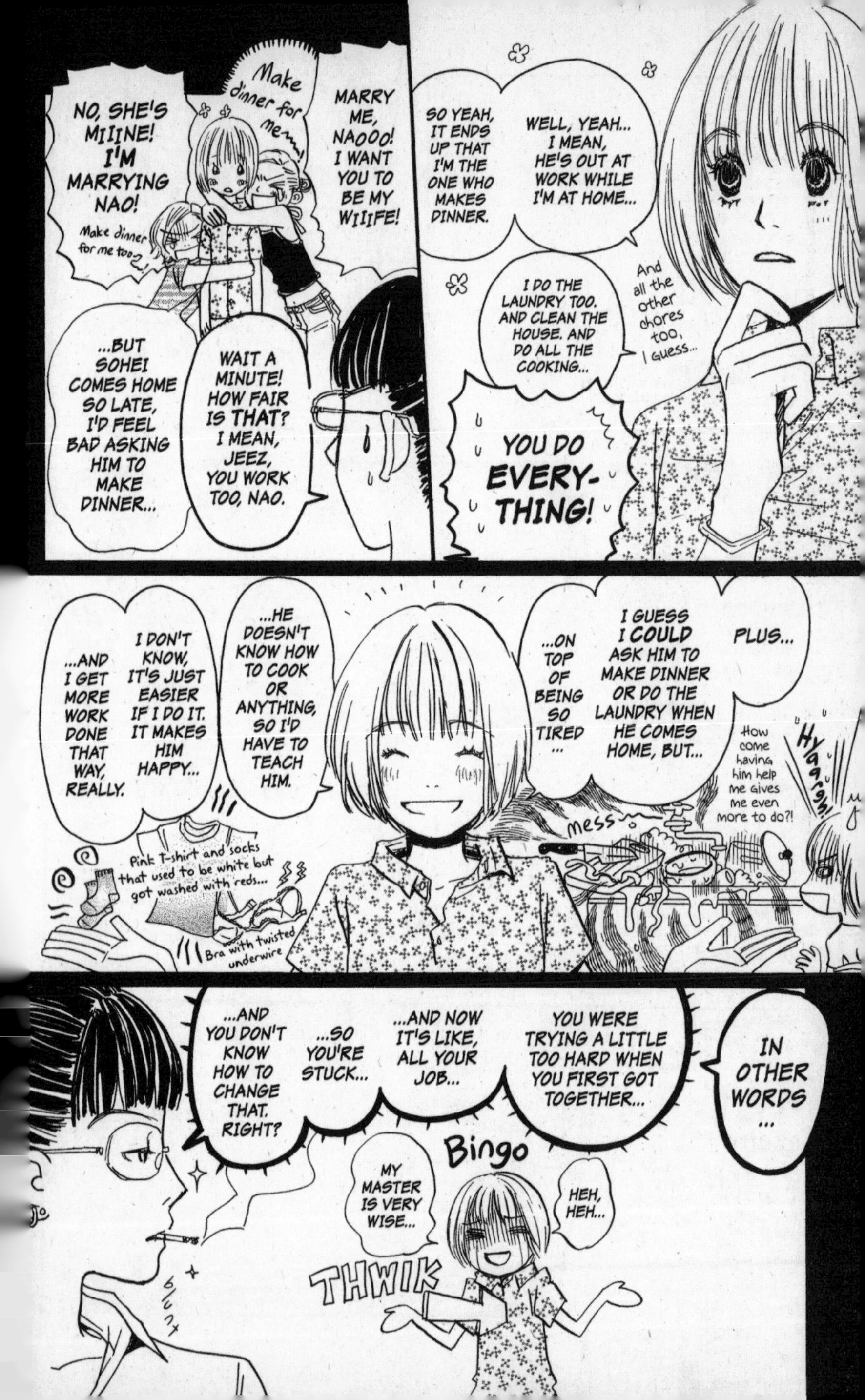
WELL, YEAH... I MEAN, HE'S OUT AT WORK WHILE I'M AT HOME...
SO YEAH, IT ENDS UP THAT I'M THE ONE WHO MAKES DINNER.
And all the other chores too, I guess...
I DO THE LAUNDRY TOO. AND CLEAN THE HOUSE. AND DO ALL THE COOKING...
YOU DO EVERYTHING!
MARRY ME, NAOOO! I WANT YOU TO BE MY WIIIFE!
Make dinner for me~!
NO, SHE'S MIIINE! I'M MARRYING NAO!
Make dinner for me too~!
WAIT A MINUTE! HOW FAIR IS THAT? I MEAN, JEEZ, YOU WORK TOO, NAO.
...BUT SOHEI COMES HOME SO LATE, I'D FEEL BAD ASKING HIM TO MAKE DINNER...
PLUS...
I GUESS I COULD ASK HIM TO MAKE DINNER OR DO THE LAUNDRY WHEN HE COMES HOME, BUT...
...ON TOP OF BEING SO TIRED...
Hyaargh!
How come having him help me gives me even more to do?!
mess
...HE DOESN'T KNOW HOW TO COOK OR ANYTHING, SO I'D HAVE TO TEACH HIM.
I DON'T KNOW, IT'S JUST EASIER IF I DO IT. IT MAKES HIM HAPPY...
...AND I GET MORE WORK DONE THAT WAY, REALLY.
Pink T-shirt and socks that used to be white but got washed with reds...
Bra with twisted underwire
IN OTHER WORDS...
YOU WERE TRYING A LITTLE TOO HARD WHEN YOU FIRST GOT TOGETHER...
...AND NOW IT'S LIKE, ALL YOUR JOB...
...SO YOU'RE STUCK...
...AND YOU DON'T KNOW HOW TO CHANGE THAT. RIGHT?
Bingo
HEH, HEH...
MY MASTER IS VERY WISE...
THWIK

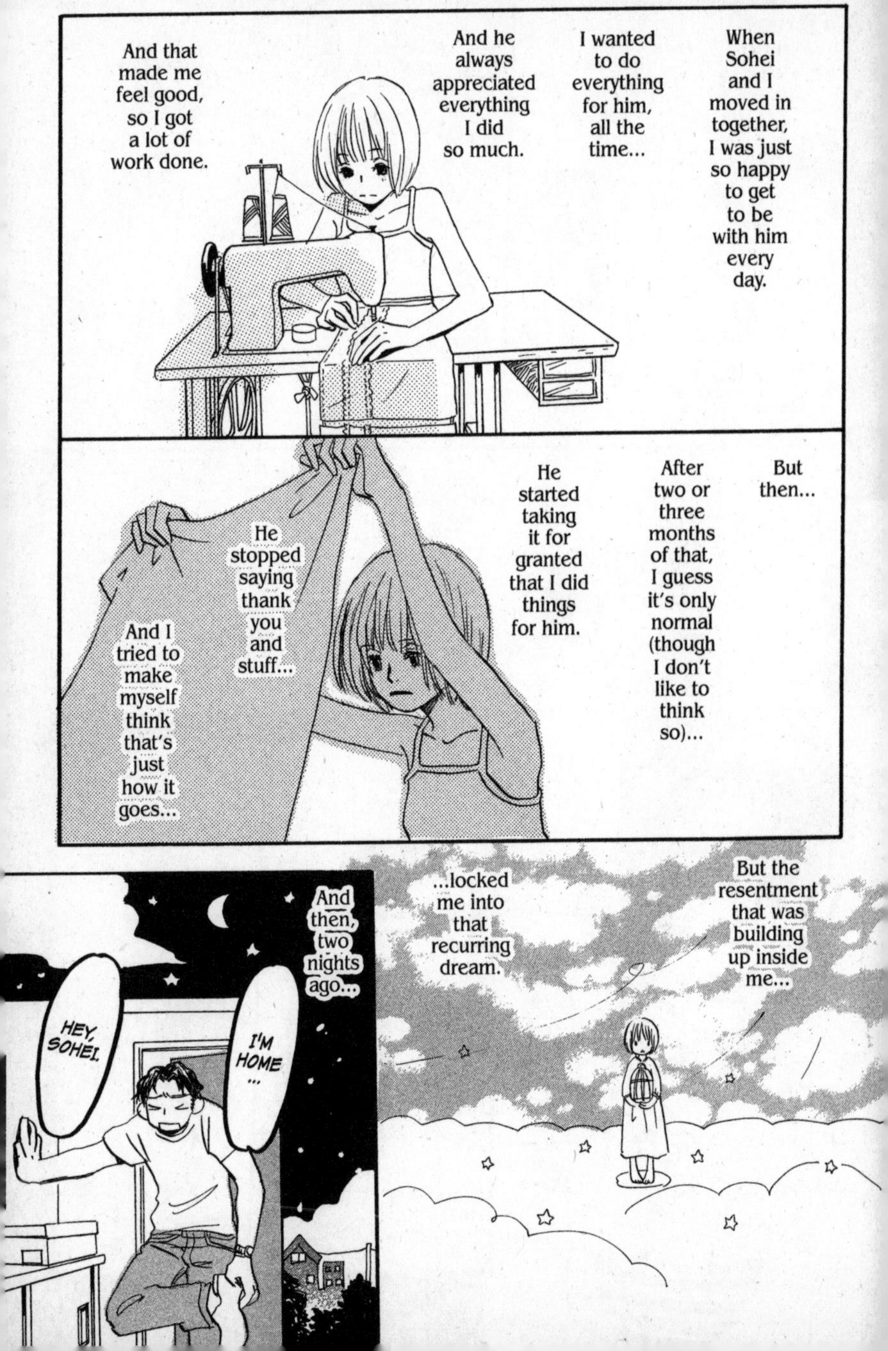
When Sohei and I moved in together, I was just so happy to get to be with him every day.
I wanted to do everything for him, all the time...
And he always appreciated everything I did so much.
And that made me feel good, so I got a lot of work done.
But then...
After two or three months of that, I guess it's only normal (though I don't like to think so)...
He started taking it for granted that I did things for him.
He stopped saying thank you and stuff...
And I tried to make myself think that's just how it goes...
But the resentment that was building up inside me...
...locked me into that recurring dream.
And then, two nights ago...
I'M HOME...
HEY, SOHEI.

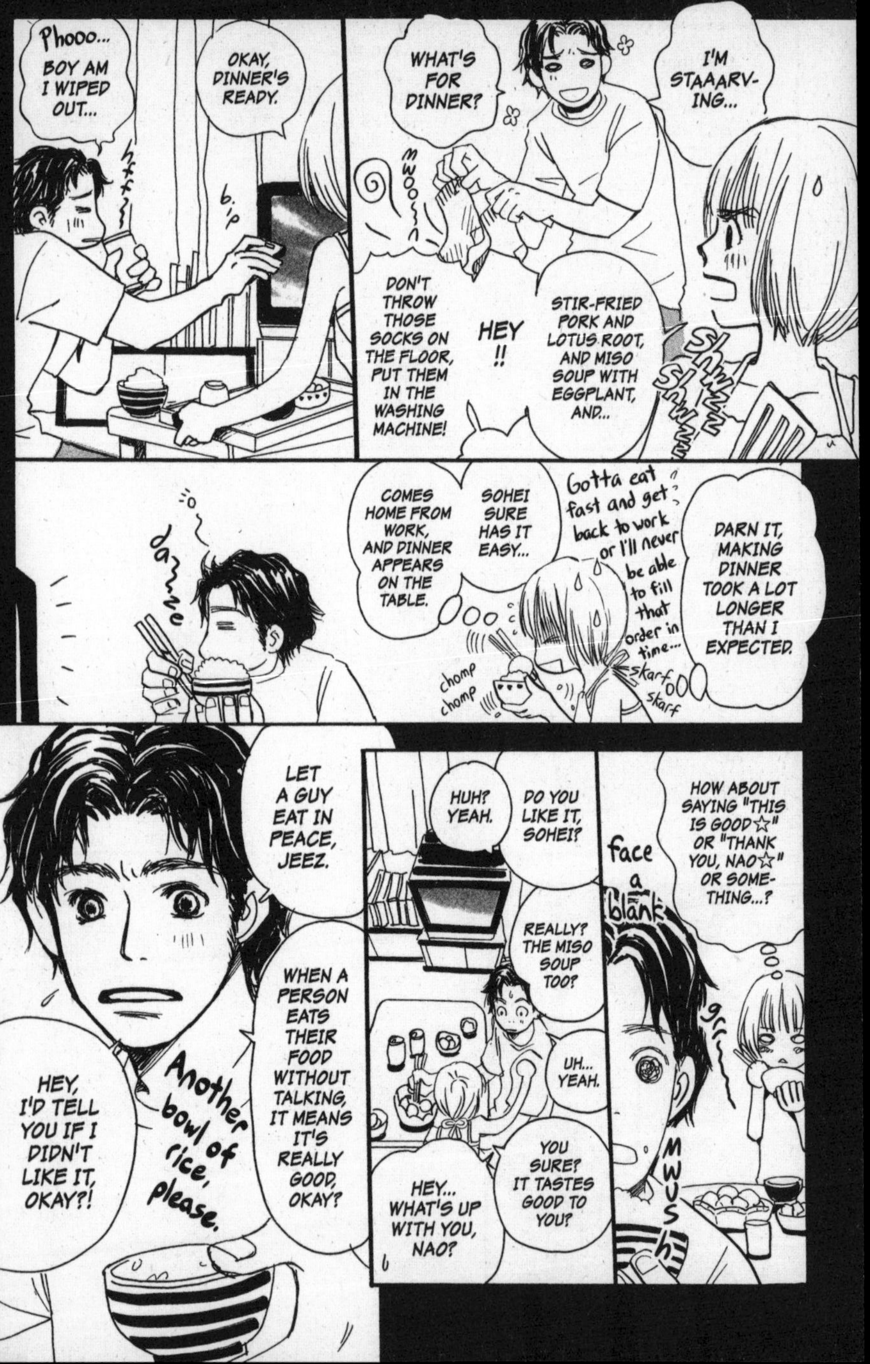
I'M STAAARV-ING...
WHAT'S FOR DINNER?
MWOO~N
STIR-FRIED PORK AND LOTUS ROOT, AND MISO SOUP WITH EGGPLANT, AND...
HEY !!
DON'T THROW THOSE SOCKS ON THE FLOOR, PUT THEM IN THE WASHING MACHINE!
Shwww Shwww
OKAY, DINNER'S READY.
Phooo... BOY AM I WIPED OUT...
bip
DARN IT, MAKING DINNER TOOK A LOT LONGER THAN I EXPECTED.
Gotta eat fast and get back to work or I'll never be able to fill that order in time...
SOHEI SURE HAS IT EASY...
COMES HOME FROM WORK, AND DINNER APPEARS ON THE TABLE.
skarf skarf
chomp chomp
daze
HOW ABOUT SAYING "THIS IS GOOD☆" OR "THANK YOU, NAO☆" OR SOME-THING...?
face a blank
grr
MWUSH
DO YOU LIKE IT, SOHEI?
HUH? YEAH.
REALLY? THE MISO SOUP TOO?
UH... YEAH.
YOU SURE? IT TASTES GOOD TO YOU?
HEY... WHAT'S UP WITH YOU, NAO?
LET A GUY EAT IN PEACE, JEEZ.
WHEN A PERSON EATS THEIR FOOD WITHOUT TALKING, IT MEANS IT'S REALLY GOOD, OKAY?
Another bowl of rice, please.
HEY, I'D TELL YOU IF I DIDN'T LIKE IT, OKAY?!

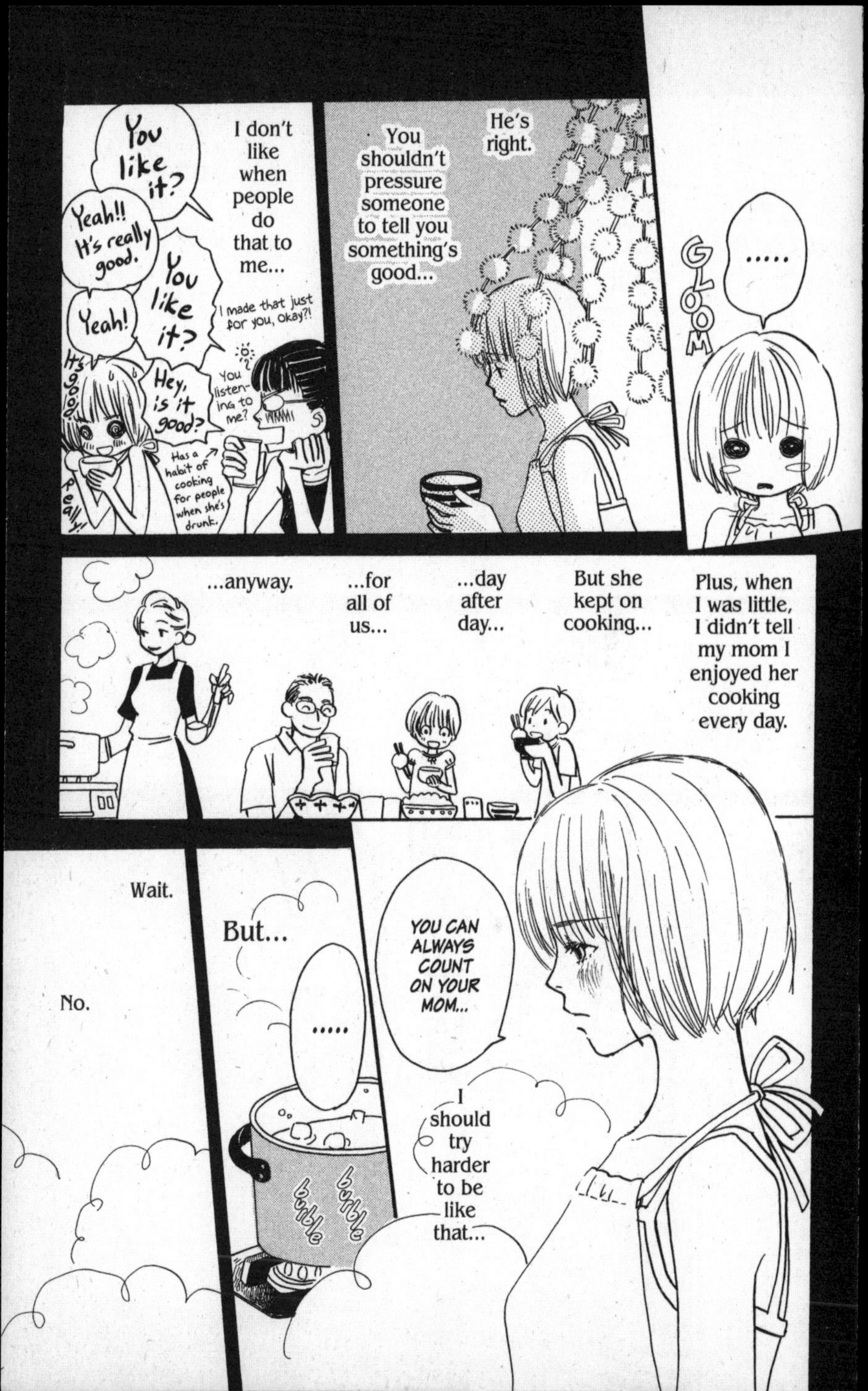
GLOOM
.....
He's right.
You shouldn't pressure someone to tell you something's good...
I don't like when people do that to me...
You like it?
Yeah!! It's really good.
You like it?
Yeah!
I made that just for you, okay?!
It's good.
Hey, is it good?
You listening to me?
Has a habit of cooking for people when she's drunk.
Really!
Plus, when I was little, I didn't tell my mom I enjoyed her cooking every day.
But she kept on cooking...
...day after day...
...for all of us...
...anyway.
YOU CAN ALWAYS COUNT ON YOUR MOM...
I should try harder to be like that...
But...
.....
bubble bubble
Wait.
No.

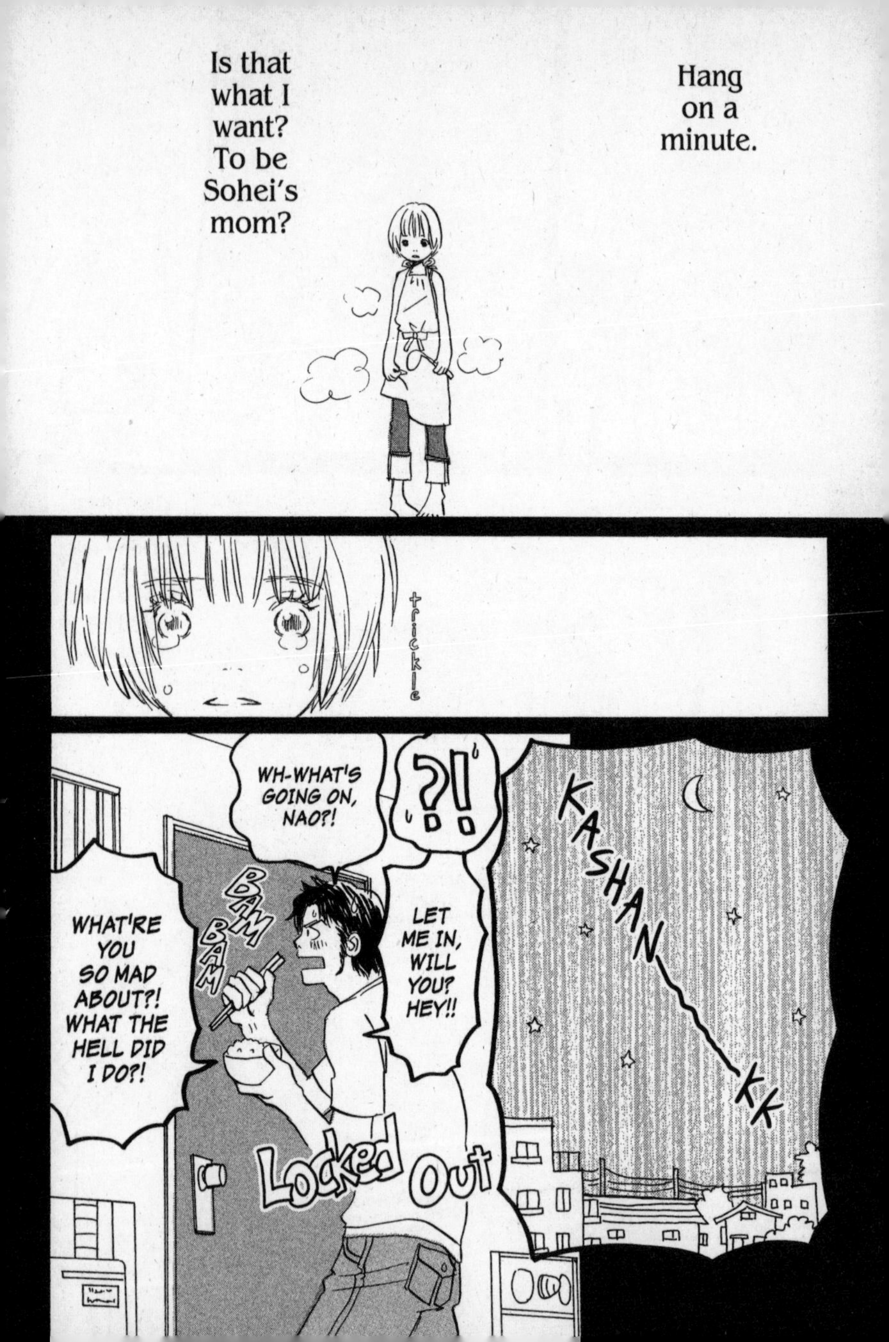
Hang on a minute.
Is that what I want? To be Sohei's mom?
trickle
KASHAN-KK
?!
WH-WHAT'S GOING ON, NAO?!
LET ME IN, WILL YOU? HEY!!
BAM BAM
WHAT'RE YOU SO MAD ABOUT?! WHAT THE HELL DID I DO?!
Locked Out

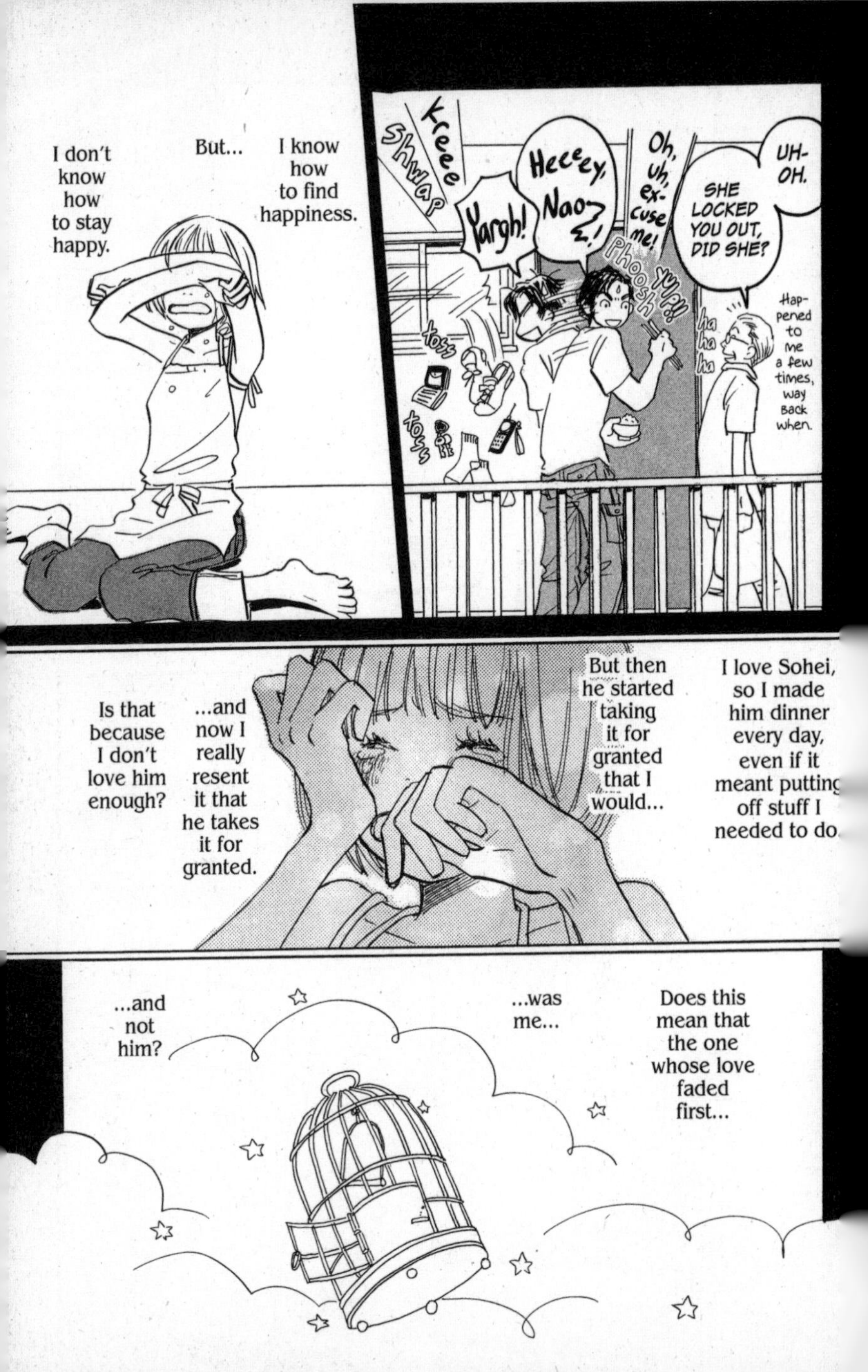
UH-OH.
SHE LOCKED YOU OUT, DID SHE?
Happened to me a few times, way back when.
ha ha ha
Oh, uh, excuse me!
Yup!!
Phoosh
Heeeey, Nao~!
Yargh!
Kreee
Shwap
toss
toss
I know how to find happiness.
But...
I don't know how to stay happy.
I love Sohei, so I made him dinner every day, even if it meant putting off stuff I needed to do.
But then he started taking it for granted that I would...
...and now I really resent it that he takes it for granted.
Is that because I don't love him enough?
Does this mean that the one whose love faded first...
...was me...
...and not him?

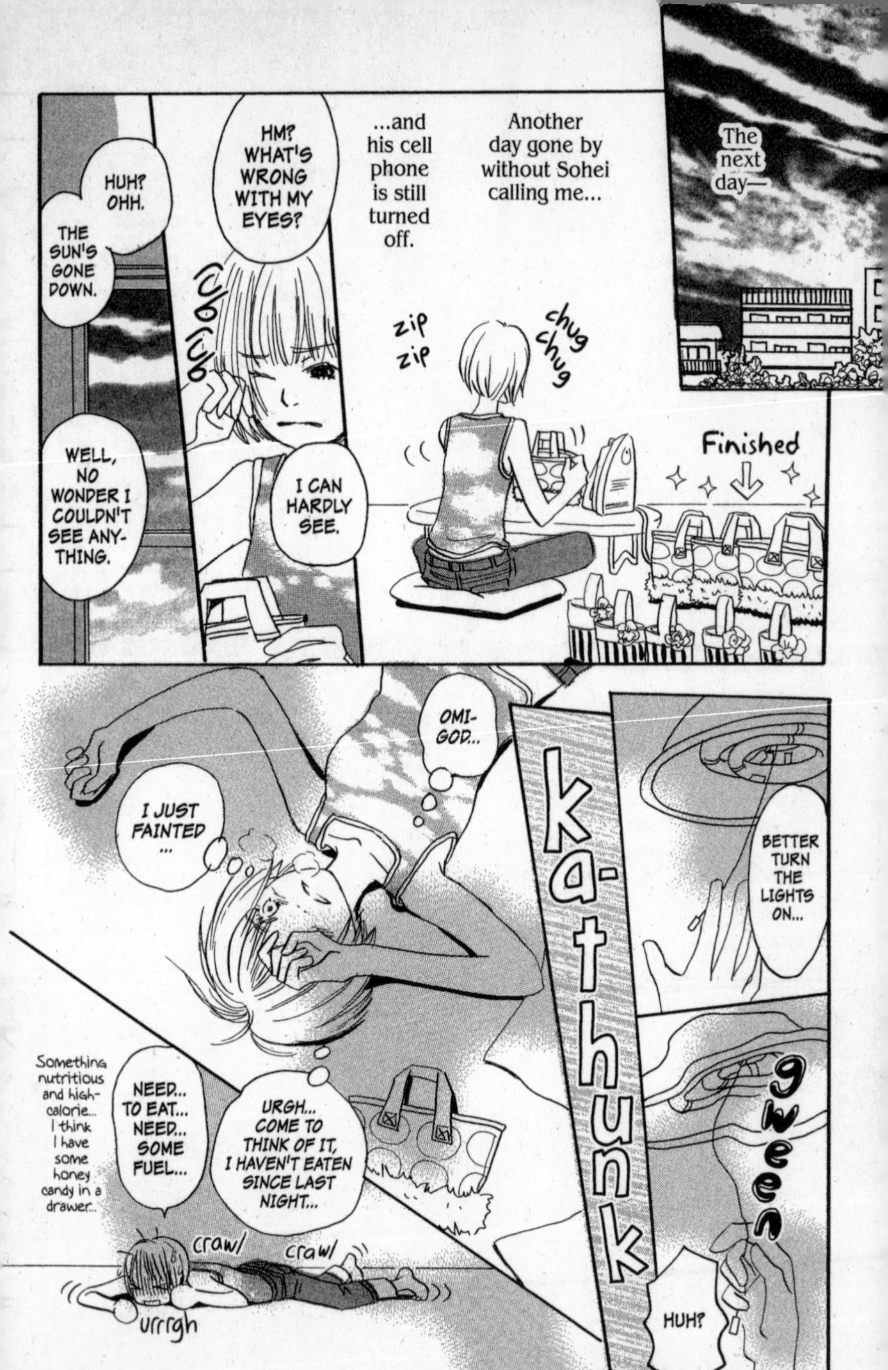
The next day—
Another day gone by without Sohei calling me...
...and his cell phone is still turned off.
zip zip
chug chug
Finished
HM? WHAT'S WRONG WITH MY EYES?
rub rub
HUH? OHH.
THE SUN'S GONE DOWN.
I CAN HARDLY SEE.
WELL, NO WONDER I COULDN'T SEE ANYTHING.
BETTER TURN THE LIGHTS ON...
ka-thunk
gween
HUH?
OMI-GOD...
I JUST FAINTED...
URGH... COME TO THINK OF IT, I HAVEN'T EATEN SINCE LAST NIGHT...
NEED... TO EAT... NEED... SOME FUEL...
Something nutritious and high-calorie... I think I have some honey candy in a drawer...
crawl
crawl
urrrgh

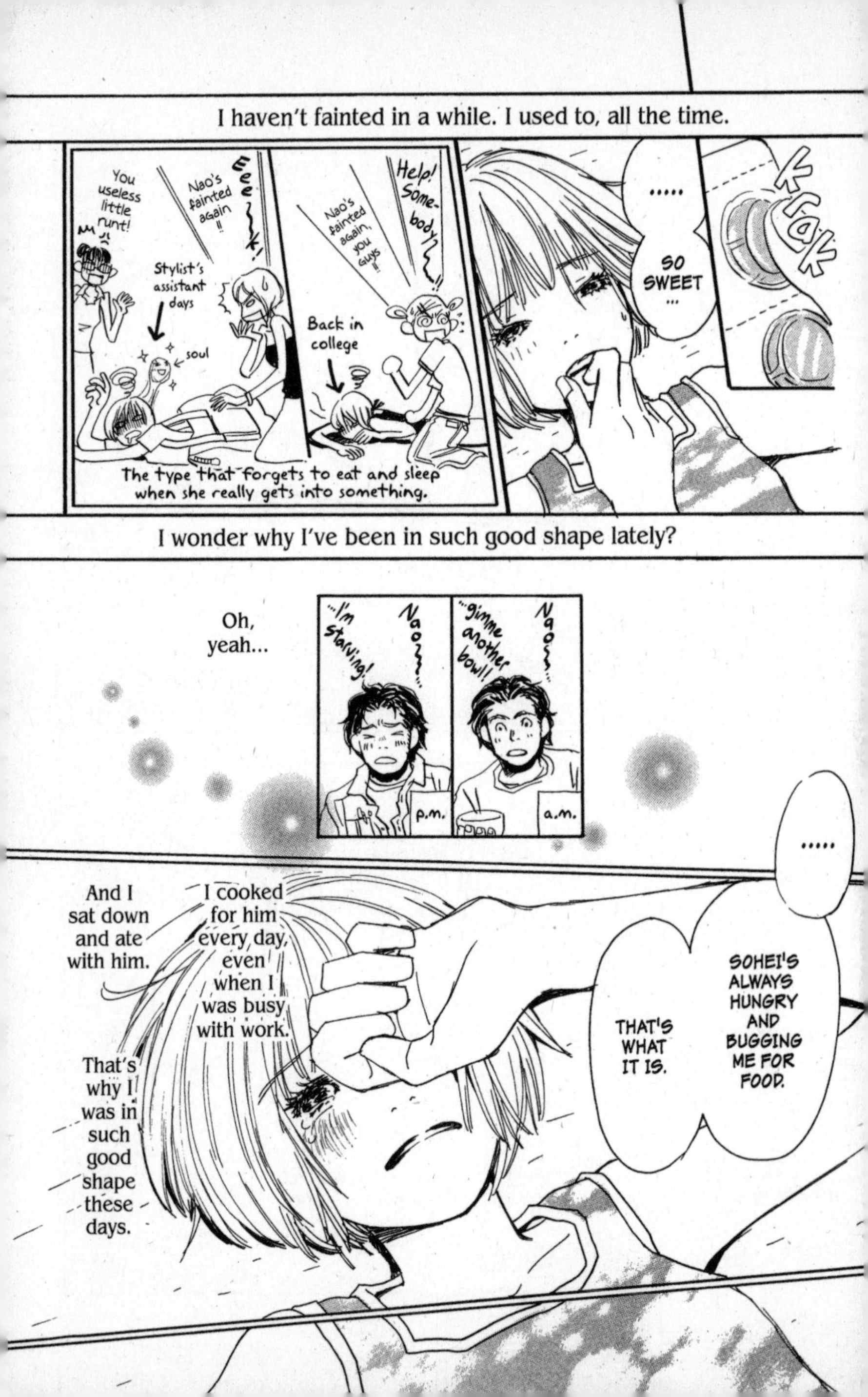
I haven't fainted in a while. I used to, all the time.
KRAK
.....
SO SWEET ...
Help! Somebody!!
Nao's fainted again, you guys!!
Back in college
Eeeek!
Nao's fainted again!!
You useless little runt!
Stylist's assistant days
soul
The type that forgets to eat and sleep when she really gets into something.
I wonder why I've been in such good shape lately?
Naooo...
...gimme another bowl!!
a.m.
Naooo...
...I'm starving!
p.m.
Oh, yeah...
.....
SOHEI'S ALWAYS HUNGRY AND BUGGING ME FOR FOOD.
THAT'S WHAT IT IS.
I cooked for him every day, even when I was busy with work.
And I sat down and ate with him.
That's why I was in such good shape these days.

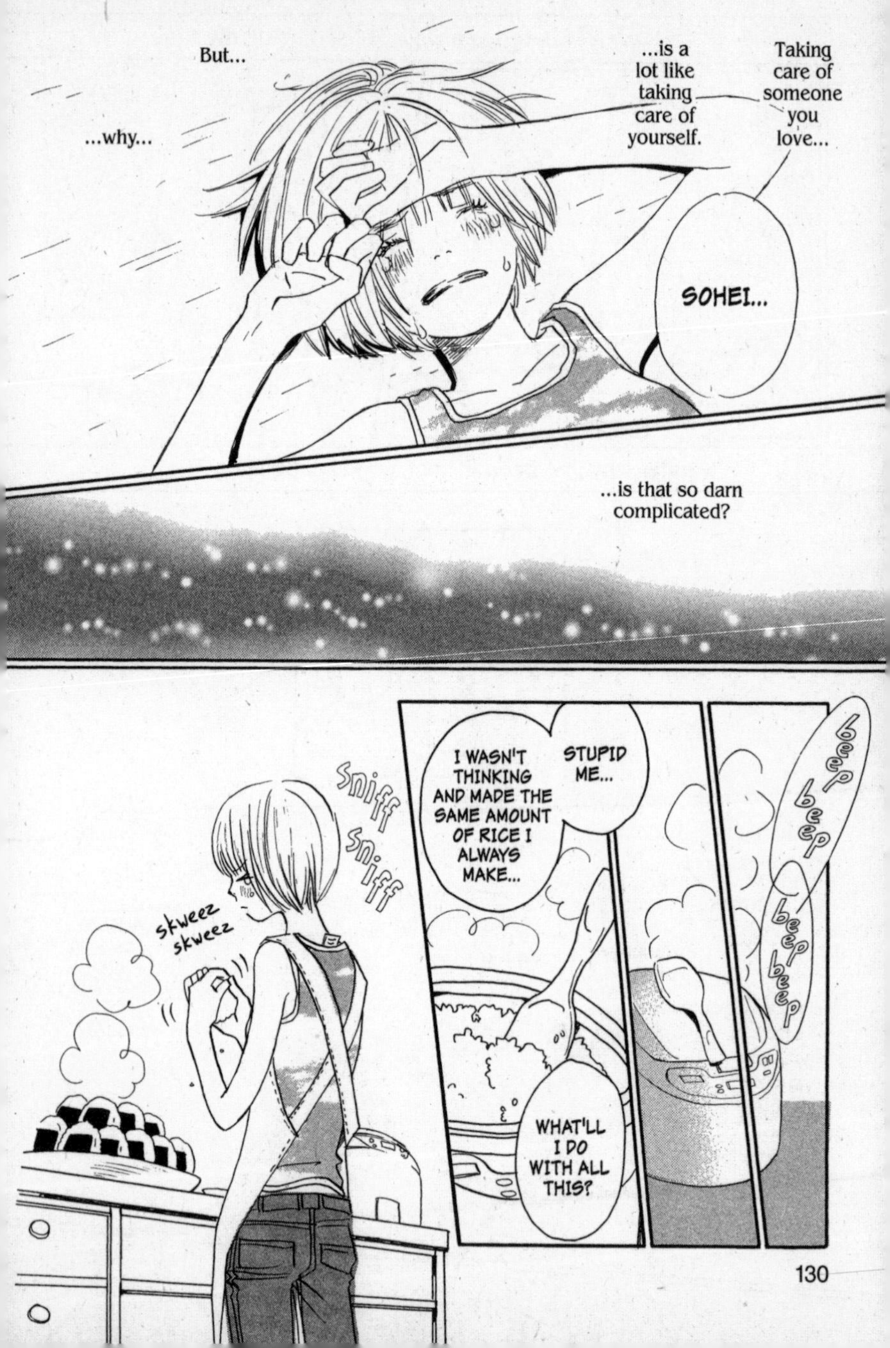
Taking care of someone you love...
...is a lot like taking care of yourself.
SOHEI...
But...
...why...
...is that so darn complicated?
beep beep beep beep
STUPID ME...
I WASN'T THINKING AND MADE THE SAME AMOUNT OF RICE I ALWAYS MAKE...
WHAT'LL I DO WITH ALL THIS?
Sniff Sniff
skweez skweez

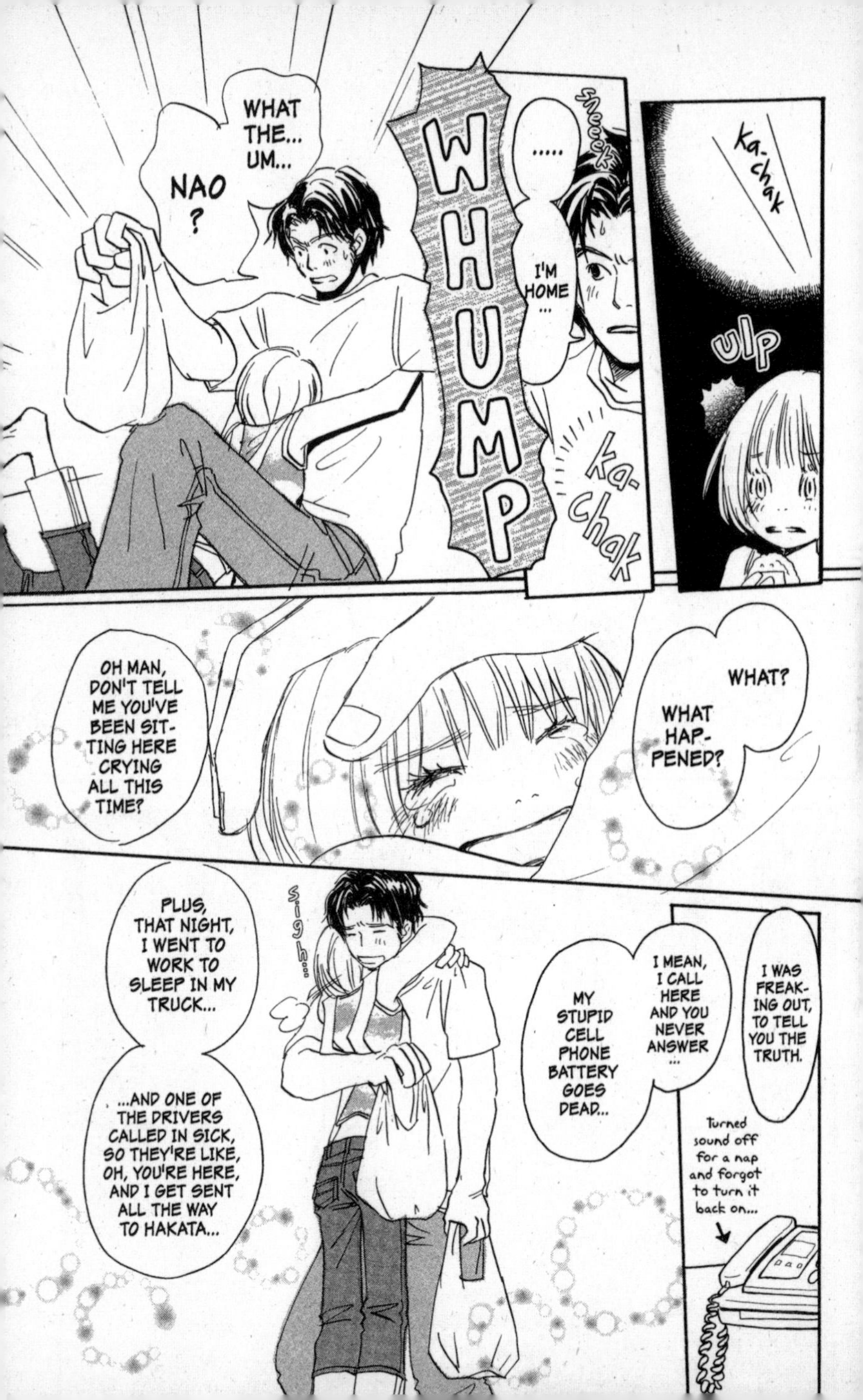
ka-chak
ulp
sneek
.....
I'M HOME...
ka-chak
WHUMP
WHAT THE... UM...
NAO?
WHAT?
WHAT HAPPENED?
OH MAN, DON'T TELL ME YOU'VE BEEN SITTING HERE CRYING ALL THIS TIME?
I WAS FREAKING OUT, TO TELL YOU THE TRUTH.
I MEAN, I CALL HERE AND YOU NEVER ANSWER...
MY STUPID CELL PHONE BATTERY GOES DEAD...
Turned sound off for a nap and forgot to turn it back on...
sigh...
PLUS, THAT NIGHT, I WENT TO WORK TO SLEEP IN MY TRUCK...
...AND ONE OF THE DRIVERS CALLED IN SICK, SO THEY'RE LIKE, OH, YOU'RE HERE, AND I GET SENT ALL THE WAY TO HAKATA...

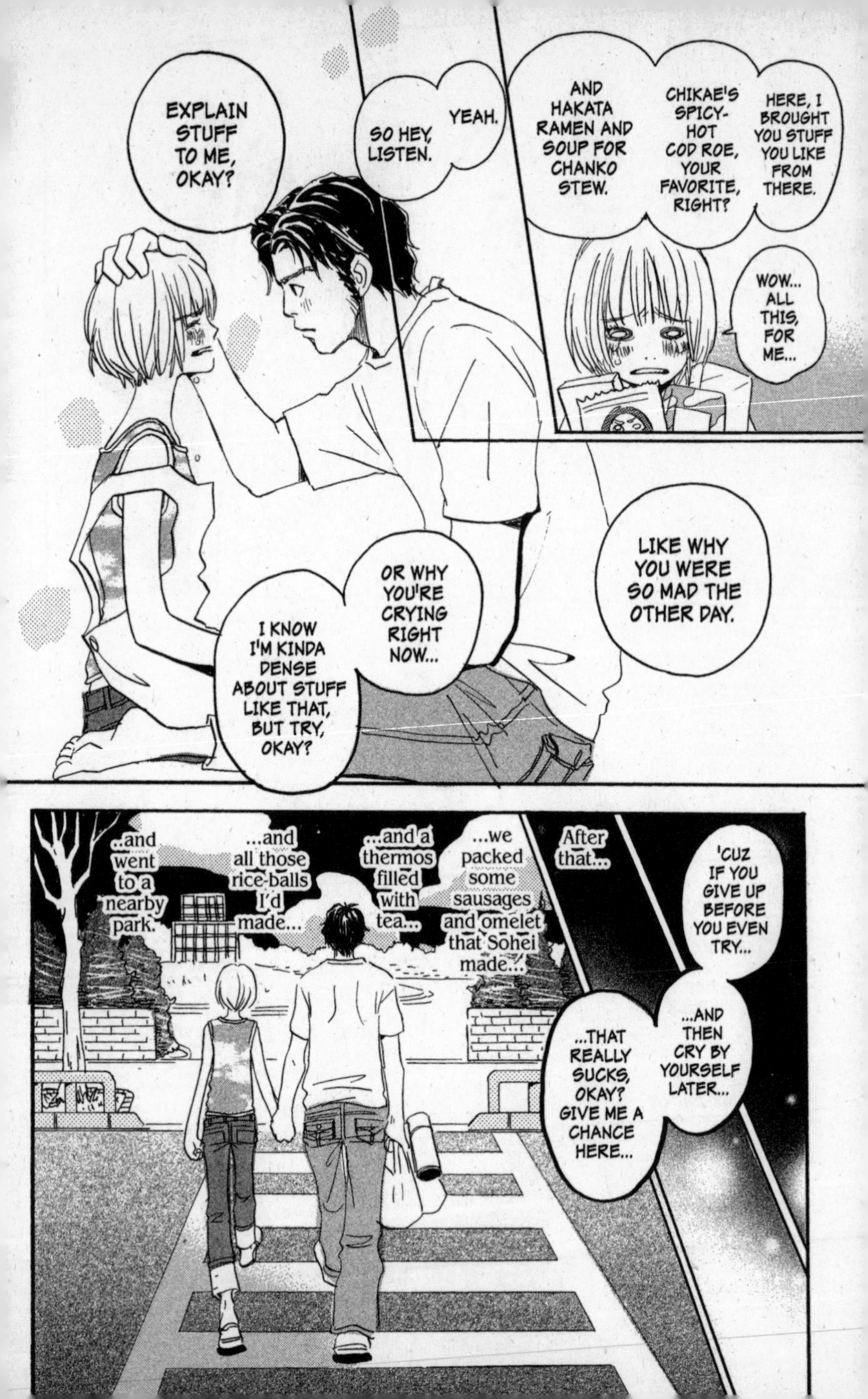
HERE, I BROUGHT YOU STUFF YOU LIKE FROM THERE.
CHIKAE'S SPICY-HOT COD ROE, YOUR FAVORITE, RIGHT?
AND HAKATA RAMEN AND SOUP FOR CHANKO STEW.
WOW... ALL THIS, FOR ME...
YEAH.
SO HEY, LISTEN.
EXPLAIN STUFF TO ME, OKAY?
LIKE WHY YOU WERE SO MAD THE OTHER DAY.
OR WHY YOU'RE CRYING RIGHT NOW...
I KNOW I'M KINDA DENSE ABOUT STUFF LIKE THAT, BUT TRY, OKAY?
'CUZ IF YOU GIVE UP BEFORE YOU EVEN TRY...
...AND THEN CRY BY YOURSELF LATER...
...THAT REALLY SUCKS, OKAY? GIVE ME A CHANCE HERE...
After that...
...we packed some sausages and omelet that Sohei made...
...and a thermos filled with tea...
...and all those rice-balls I'd made...
..and went to a nearby park.

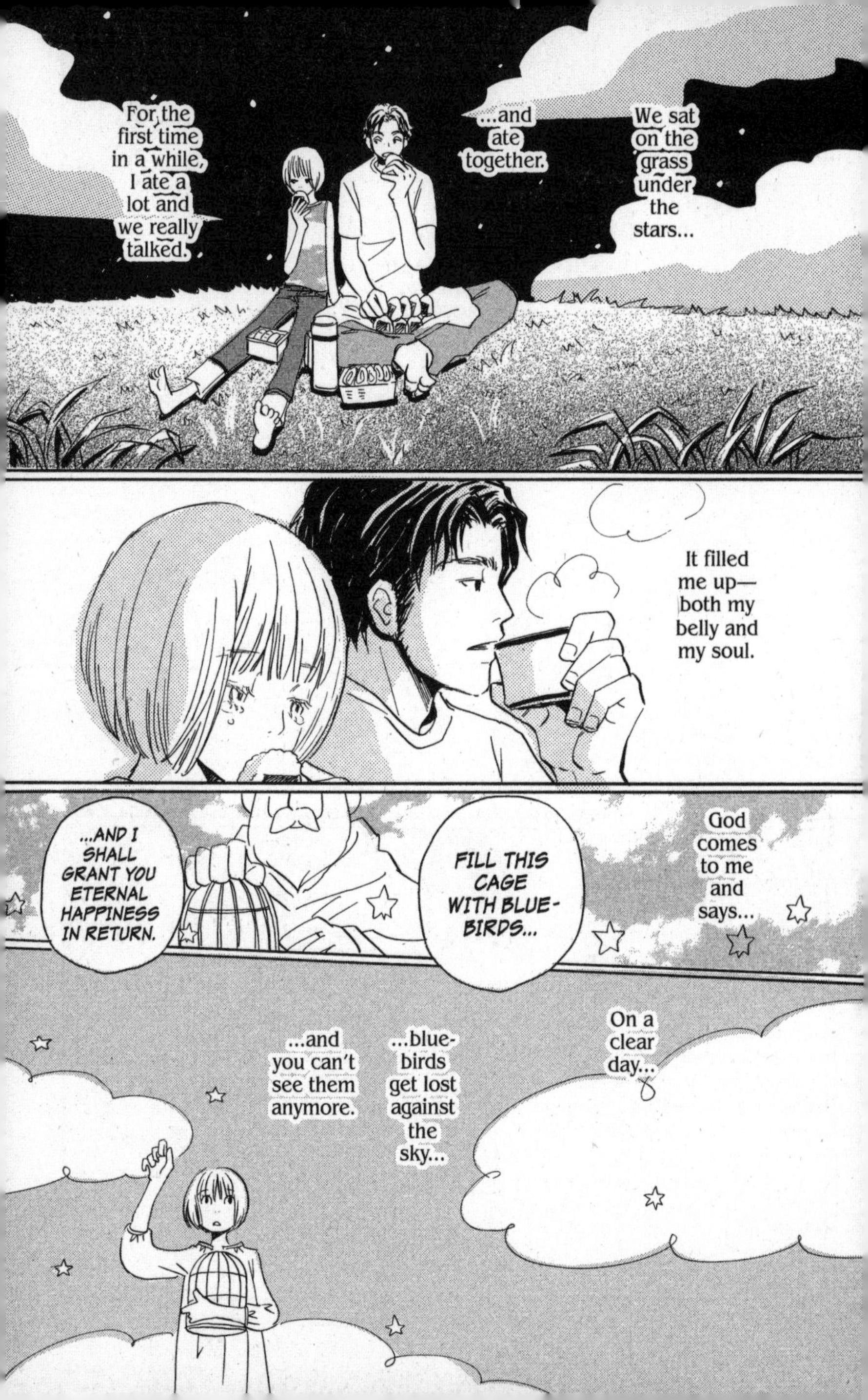
We sat on the grass under the stars...
...and ate together.
For the first time in a while, I ate a lot and we really talked.
It filled me up—both my belly and my soul.
God comes to me and says...
FILL THIS CAGE WITH BLUE-BIRDS...
...AND I SHALL GRANT YOU ETERNAL HAPPINESS IN RETURN.
On a clear day...
...blue-birds get lost against the sky...
...and you can't see them anymore.

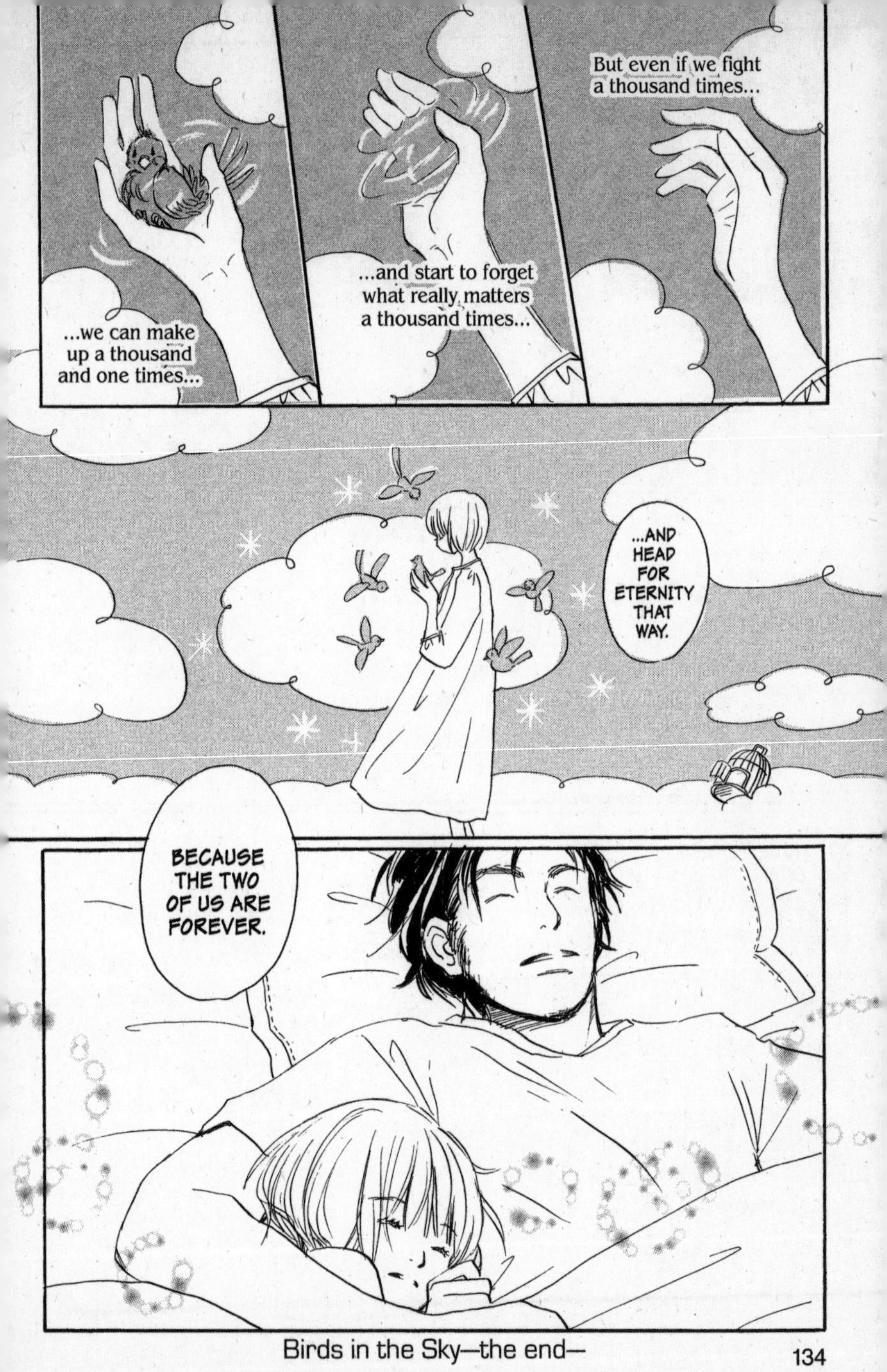
But even if we fight a thousand times...
...and start to forget what really matters a thousand times...
...we can make up a thousand and one times...
...AND HEAD FOR ETERNITY THAT WAY.
BECAUSE THE TWO OF US ARE FOREVER.

Birds in the Sky—the end—

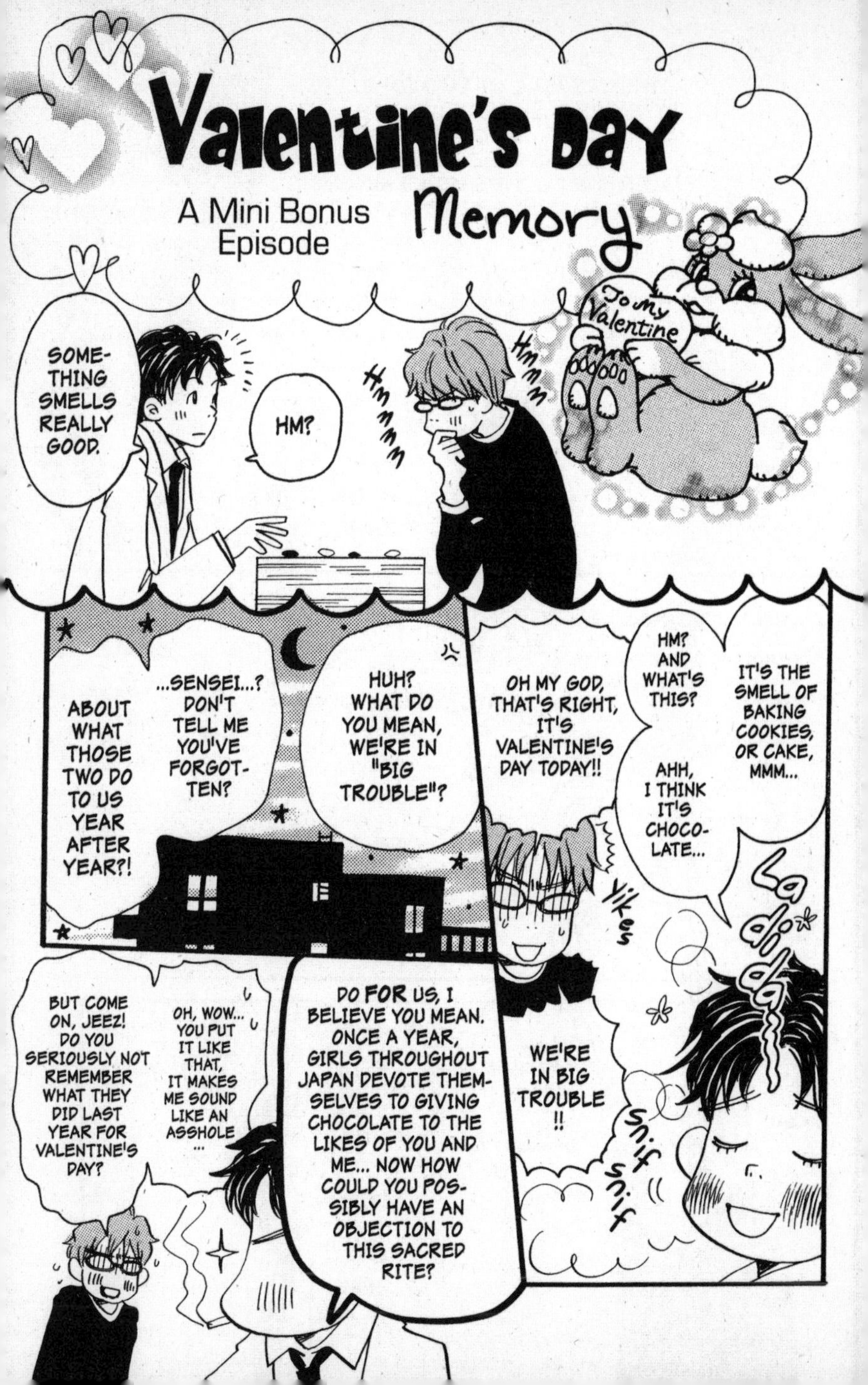
Valentine's Day Memory
A Mini Bonus Episode
To my Valentine
Hmmm
Hmmmm
HM?
SOME-THING SMELLS REALLY GOOD.
IT'S THE SMELL OF BAKING COOKIES, OR CAKE, MMM...
HM? AND WHAT'S THIS?
AHH, I THINK IT'S CHOCO-LATE...
La di da
Snif snif
OH MY GOD, THAT'S RIGHT, IT'S VALENTINE'S DAY TODAY!!
Yikes
WE'RE IN BIG TROUBLE !!
HUH? WHAT DO YOU MEAN, WE'RE IN "BIG TROUBLE"?
...SENSEI...? DON'T TELL ME YOU'VE FORGOT-TEN?
ABOUT WHAT THOSE TWO DO TO US YEAR AFTER YEAR?!
DO FOR US, I BELIEVE YOU MEAN. ONCE A YEAR, GIRLS THROUGHOUT JAPAN DEVOTE THEM-SELVES TO GIVING CHOCOLATE TO THE LIKES OF YOU AND ME... NOW HOW COULD YOU POS-SIBLY HAVE AN OBJECTION TO THIS SACRED RITE?
OH, WOW... YOU PUT IT LIKE THAT, IT MAKES ME SOUND LIKE AN ASSHOLE ...
BUT COME ON, JEEZ! DO YOU SERIOUSLY NOT REMEMBER WHAT THEY DID LAST YEAR FOR VALENTINE'S DAY?

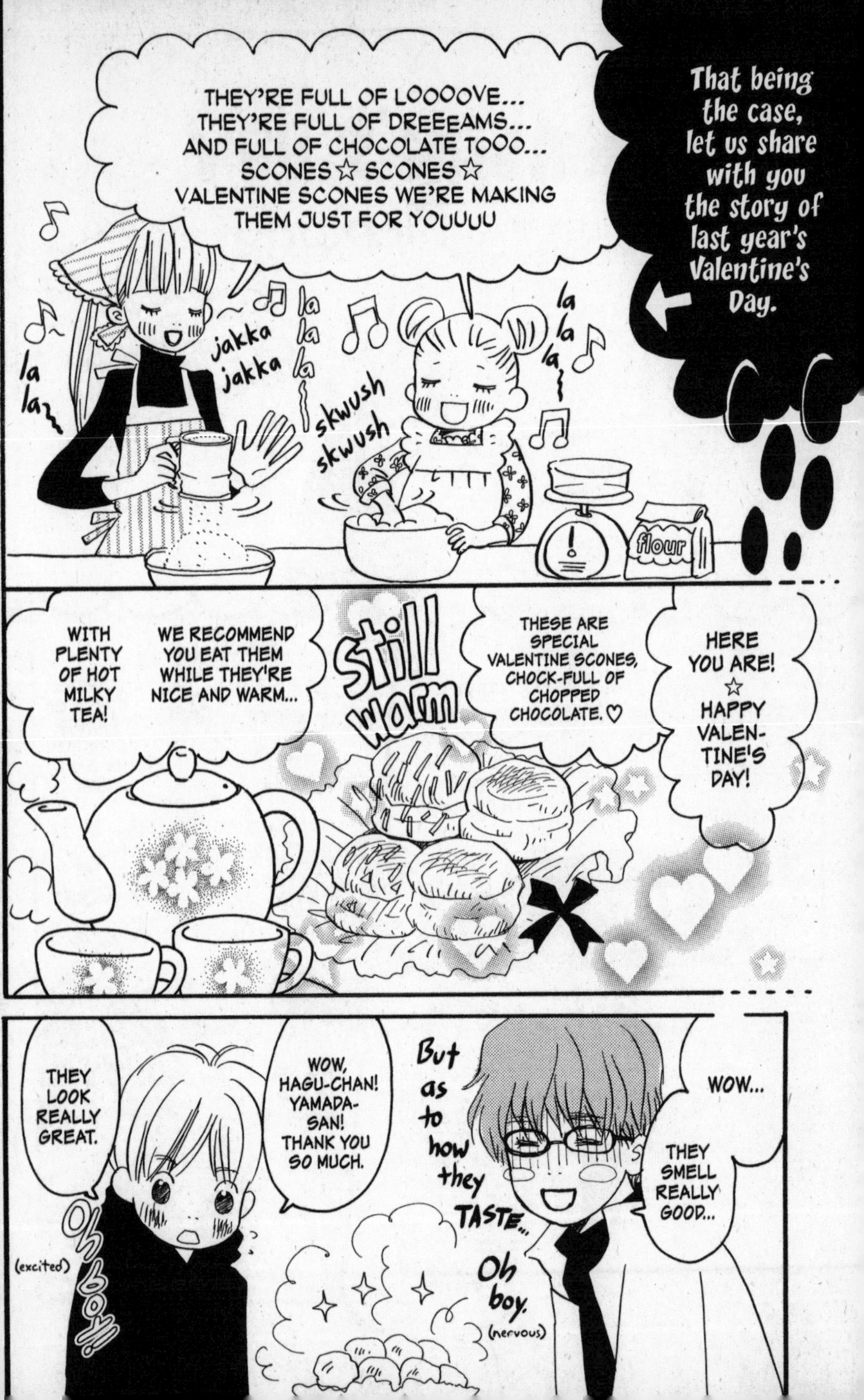
That being the case, let us share with you the story of last year's Valentine's Day.
THEY'RE FULL OF LOOOOVE... THEY'RE FULL OF DREEEAMS... AND FULL OF CHOCOLATE TOOO... SCONES☆ SCONES☆ VALENTINE SCONES WE'RE MAKING THEM JUST FOR YOUUUU
la la la
skwush skwush
la la la
jakka jakka
la la
HERE YOU ARE! ☆ HAPPY VALEN-TINE'S DAY!
THESE ARE SPECIAL VALENTINE SCONES, CHOCK-FULL OF CHOPPED CHOCOLATE.♡
still warm
WE RECOMMEND YOU EAT THEM WHILE THEY'RE NICE AND WARM...
WITH PLENTY OF HOT MILKY TEA!
WOW...
THEY SMELL REALLY GOOD...
But as to how they TASTE..
Oh boy. (nervous)
WOW, HAGU-CHAN! YAMADA-SAN! THANK YOU SO MUCH.
THEY LOOK REALLY GREAT.
Oh boy!! (excited)

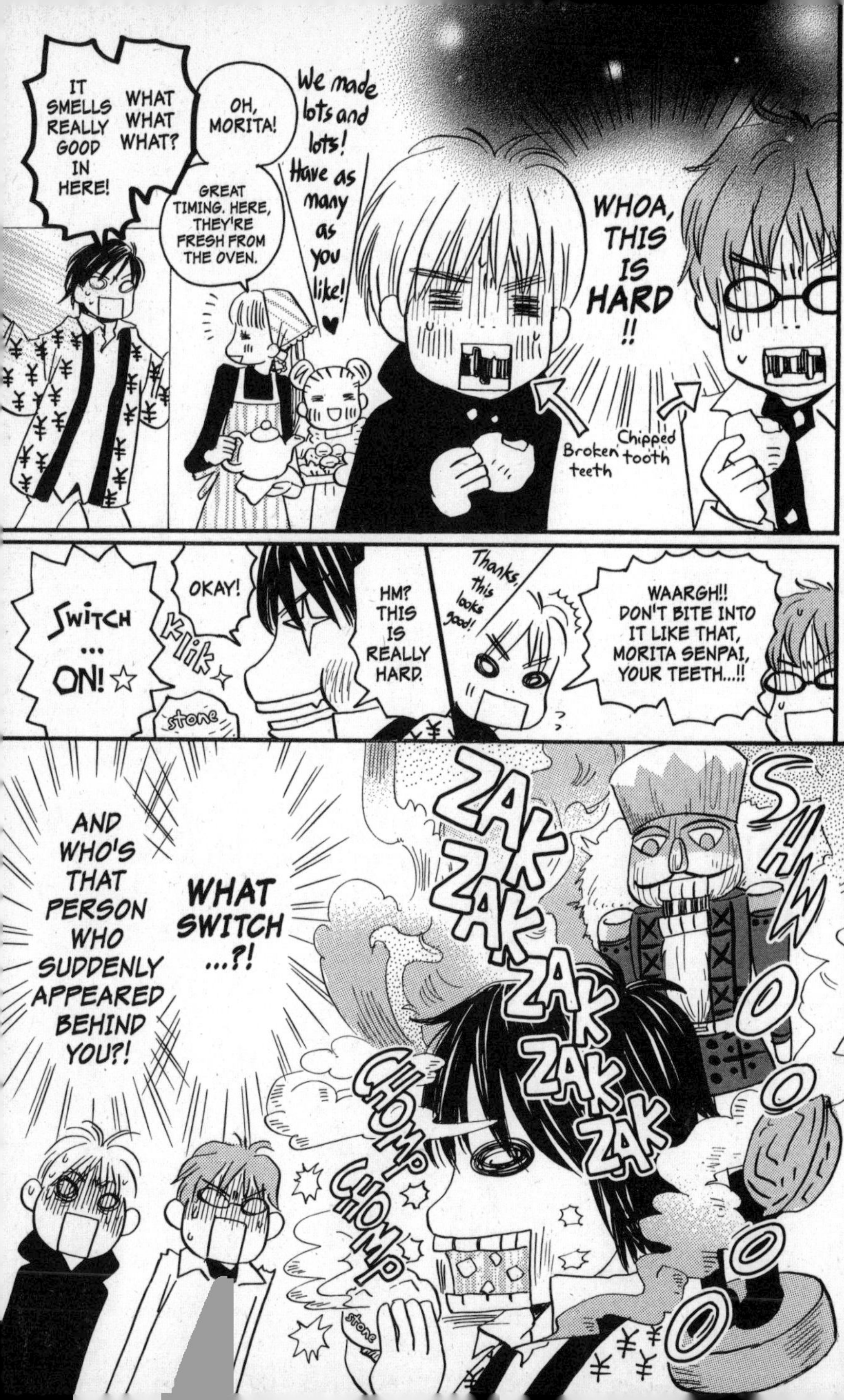
WHOA, THIS IS HARD!!
Chipped tooth
Broken teeth
We made lots and lots! Have as many as you like! ♥
OH, MORITA!
GREAT TIMING. HERE, THEY'RE FRESH FROM THE OVEN.
WHAT WHAT WHAT?
IT SMELLS REALLY GOOD IN HERE!
WAARGH!! DON'T BITE INTO IT LIKE THAT, MORITA SENPAI, YOUR TEETH...!!
Thanks, this looks good!
HM? THIS IS REALLY HARD.
OKAY!
klik
SWITCH ... ON! ☆
stone
SHWOOOOO
ZAK ZAK ZAK ZAK ZAK
CHOMP CHOMP
stone
WHAT SWITCH ...?!
AND WHO'S THAT PERSON WHO SUDDENLY APPEARED BEHIND YOU?!

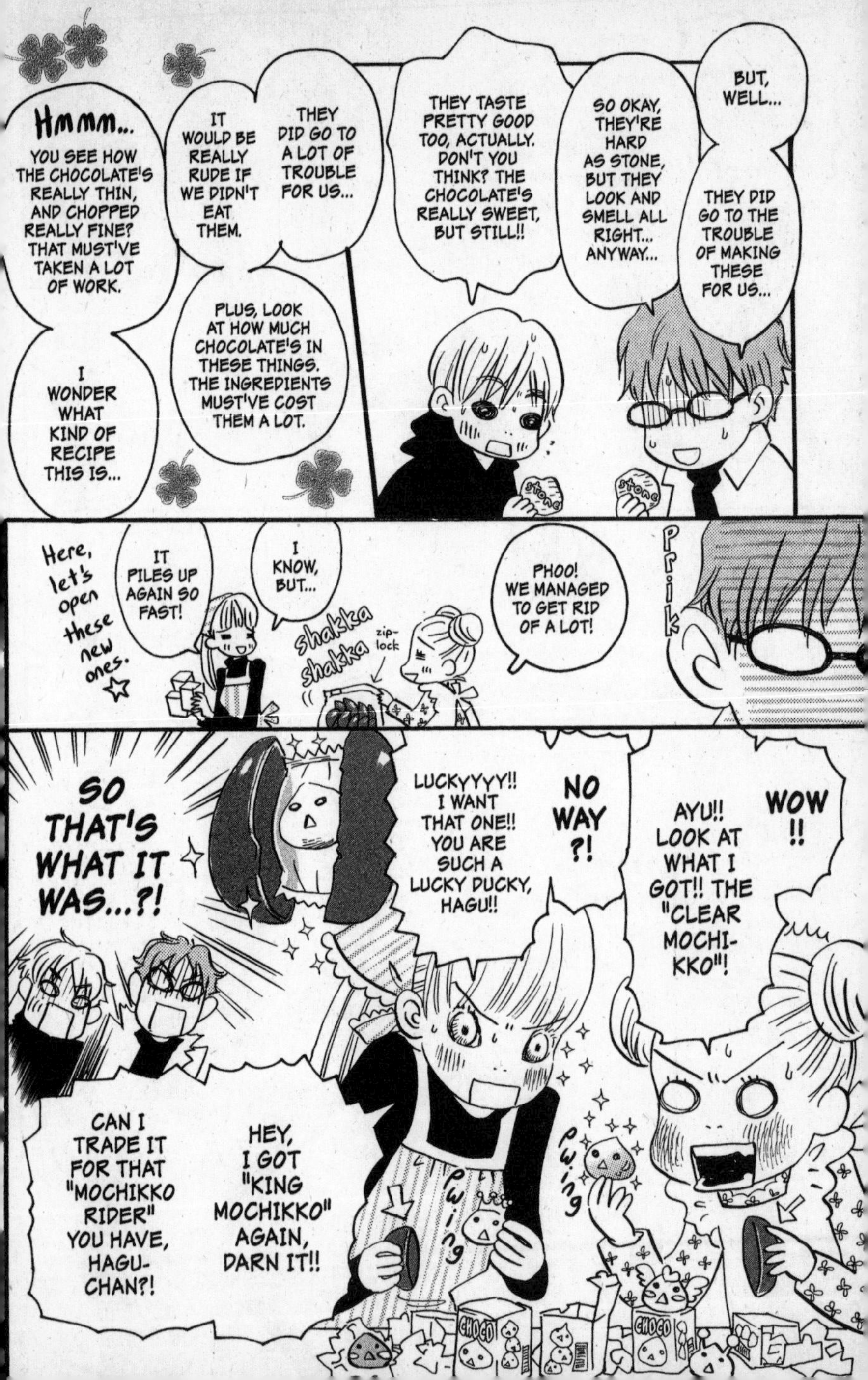
BUT, WELL...
THEY DID GO TO THE TROUBLE OF MAKING THESE FOR US...
SO OKAY, THEY'RE HARD AS STONE, BUT THEY LOOK AND SMELL ALL RIGHT... ANYWAY...
THEY TASTE PRETTY GOOD TOO, ACTUALLY. DON'T YOU THINK? THE CHOCOLATE'S REALLY SWEET, BUT STILL!!
stone
stone
THEY DID GO TO A LOT OF TROUBLE FOR US...
IT WOULD BE REALLY RUDE IF WE DIDN'T EAT THEM.
PLUS, LOOK AT HOW MUCH CHOCOLATE'S IN THESE THINGS. THE INGREDIENTS MUST'VE COST THEM A LOT.
Hmmm... YOU SEE HOW THE CHOCOLATE'S REALLY THIN, AND CHOPPED REALLY FINE? THAT MUST'VE TAKEN A LOT OF WORK.
I WONDER WHAT KIND OF RECIPE THIS IS...
prik
PHOO! WE MANAGED TO GET RID OF A LOT!
zip-lock
shakka shakka
I KNOW, BUT...
IT PILES UP AGAIN SO FAST!
Here, let's open these new ones.
WOW!!
AYU!! LOOK AT WHAT I GOT!! THE "CLEAR MOCHIKKO"!
NO WAY?!
LUCKYYYY!! I WANT THAT ONE!! YOU ARE SUCH A LUCKY DUCKY, HAGU!!
SO THAT'S WHAT IT WAS...?!
pwing
pwing
HEY, I GOT "KING MOCHIKKO" AGAIN, DARN IT!!
CAN I TRADE IT FOR THAT "MOCHIKKO RIDER" YOU HAVE, HAGU-CHAN?!
CHOCO
CHOCO

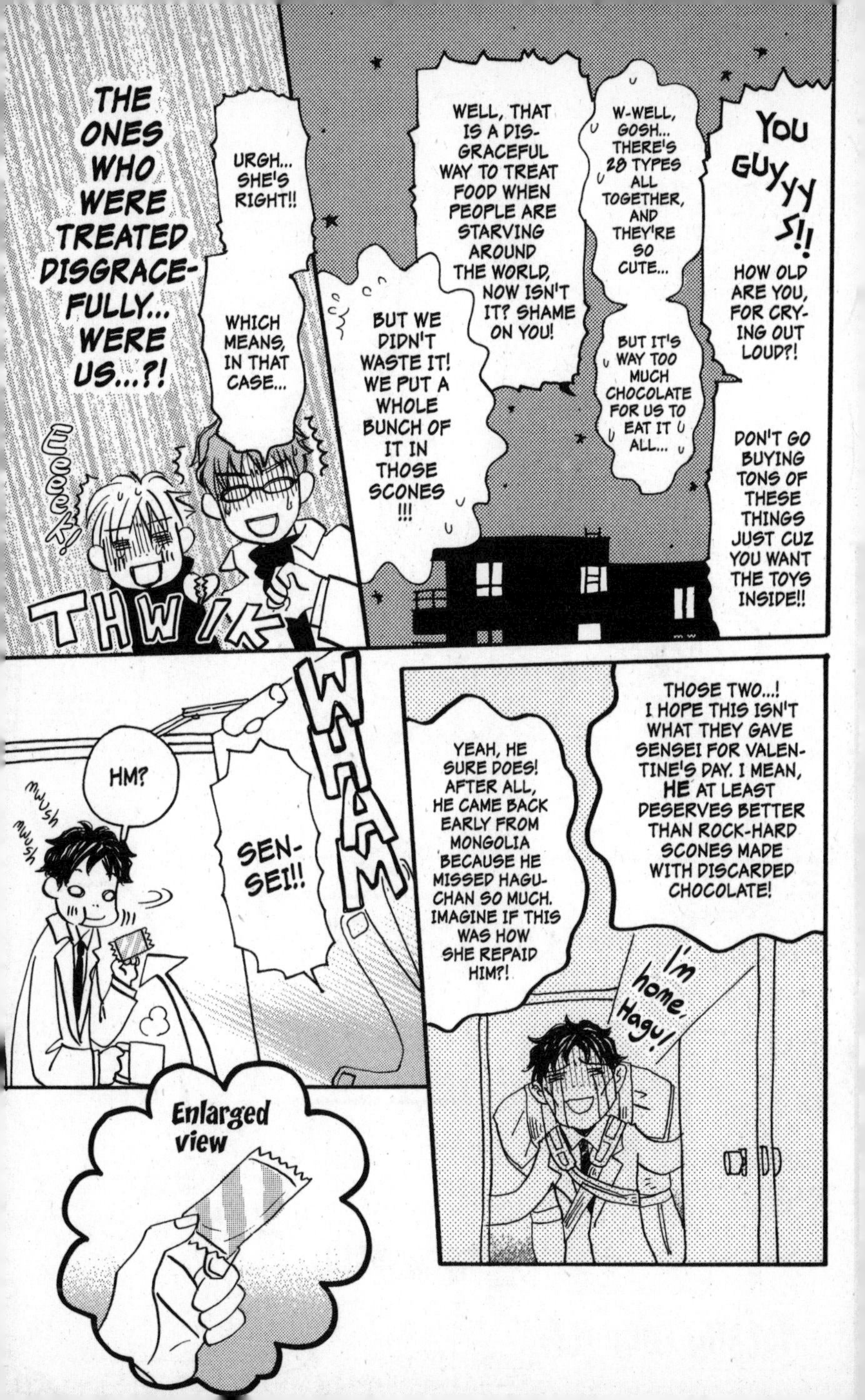
YOU GUYYYS!!
HOW OLD ARE YOU, FOR CRYING OUT LOUD?!
DON'T GO BUYING TONS OF THESE THINGS JUST CUZ YOU WANT THE TOYS INSIDE!!
W-WELL, GOSH... THERE'S 28 TYPES ALL TOGETHER, AND THEY'RE SO CUTE...
BUT IT'S WAY TOO MUCH CHOCOLATE FOR US TO EAT IT ALL...
WELL, THAT IS A DISGRACEFUL WAY TO TREAT FOOD WHEN PEOPLE ARE STARVING AROUND THE WORLD, NOW ISN'T IT? SHAME ON YOU!
BUT WE DIDN'T WASTE IT! WE PUT A WHOLE BUNCH OF IT IN THOSE SCONES!!!
URGH... SHE'S RIGHT!!
WHICH MEANS, IN THAT CASE...
THE ONES WHO WERE TREATED DISGRACEFULLY... WERE US...?!
Eeeek!
THWIK
THOSE TWO...! I HOPE THIS ISN'T WHAT THEY GAVE SENSEI FOR VALENTINE'S DAY. I MEAN, HE AT LEAST DESERVES BETTER THAN ROCK-HARD SCONES MADE WITH DISCARDED CHOCOLATE!
YEAH, HE SURE DOES! AFTER ALL, HE CAME BACK EARLY FROM MONGOLIA BECAUSE HE MISSED HAGU-CHAN SO MUCH. IMAGINE IF THIS WAS HOW SHE REPAID HIM?!
I'm home, Hagu!
WHAM
SEN-SEI!!
HM?
mwush
mwush
Enlarged view

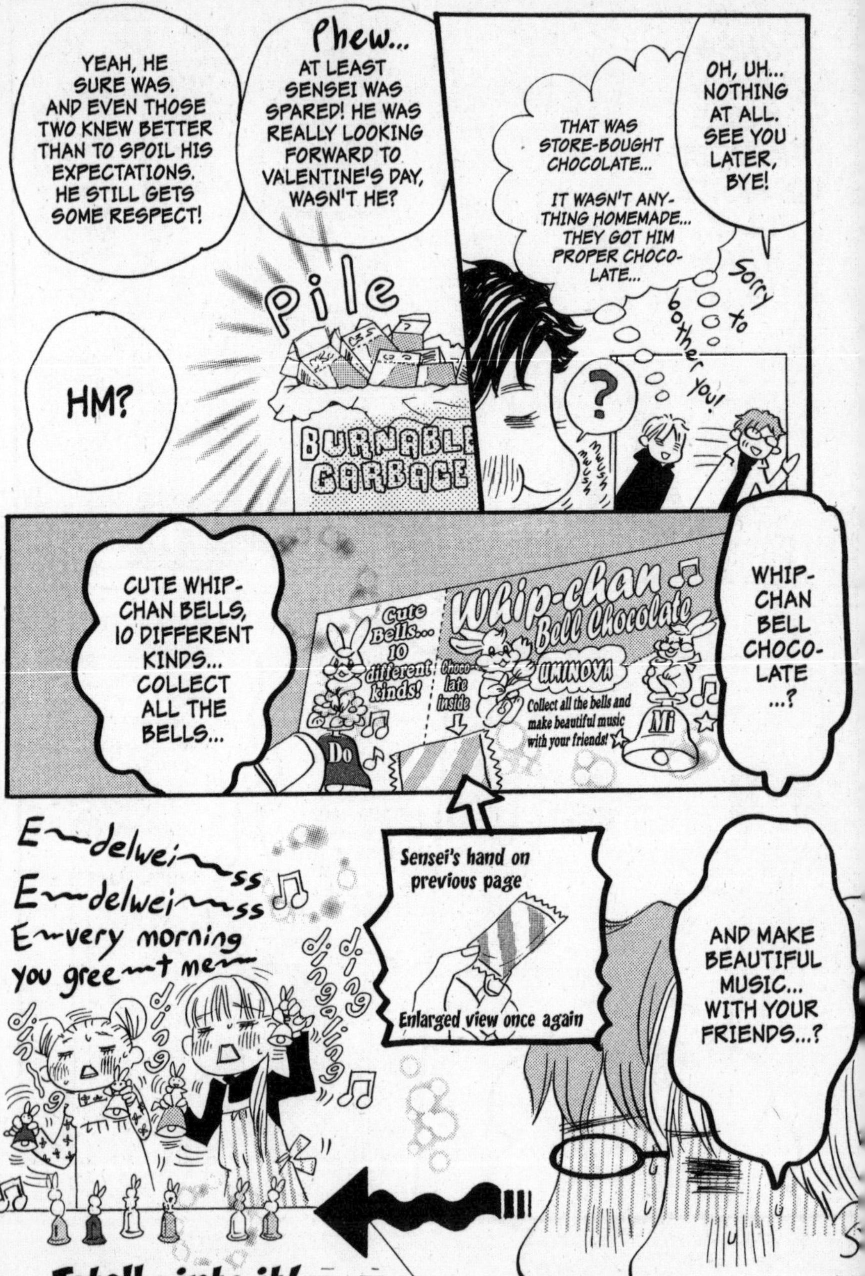
OH, UH... NOTHING AT ALL. SEE YOU LATER, BYE!
THAT WAS STORE-BOUGHT CHOCOLATE...
IT WASN'T ANYTHING HOMEMADE... THEY GOT HIM PROPER CHOCOLATE...
Sorry to bother you!
?
MUSH MUSH
Phew...
AT LEAST SENSEI WAS SPARED! HE WAS REALLY LOOKING FORWARD TO VALENTINE'S DAY, WASN'T HE?
YEAH, HE SURE WAS. AND EVEN THOSE TWO KNEW BETTER THAN TO SPOIL HIS EXPECTATIONS. HE STILL GETS SOME RESPECT!
pile
HM?
BURNABLE GARBAGE
WHIP-CHAN BELL CHOCOLATE ...?
CUTE WHIP-CHAN BELLS, 10 DIFFERENT KINDS... COLLECT ALL THE BELLS...
Whip-chan Bell Chocolate
Cute Bells... 10 different kinds!
Chocolate inside
UMINOYA
Collect all the bells and make beautiful music with your friends!
Do
Mi
AND MAKE BEAUTIFUL MUSIC... WITH YOUR FRIENDS...?
Sensei's hand on previous page
Enlarged view once again
E~delwei~ss
E~delwei~ss
E~very morning you gree~t me~
dingaling
dingaling
Totally into it!

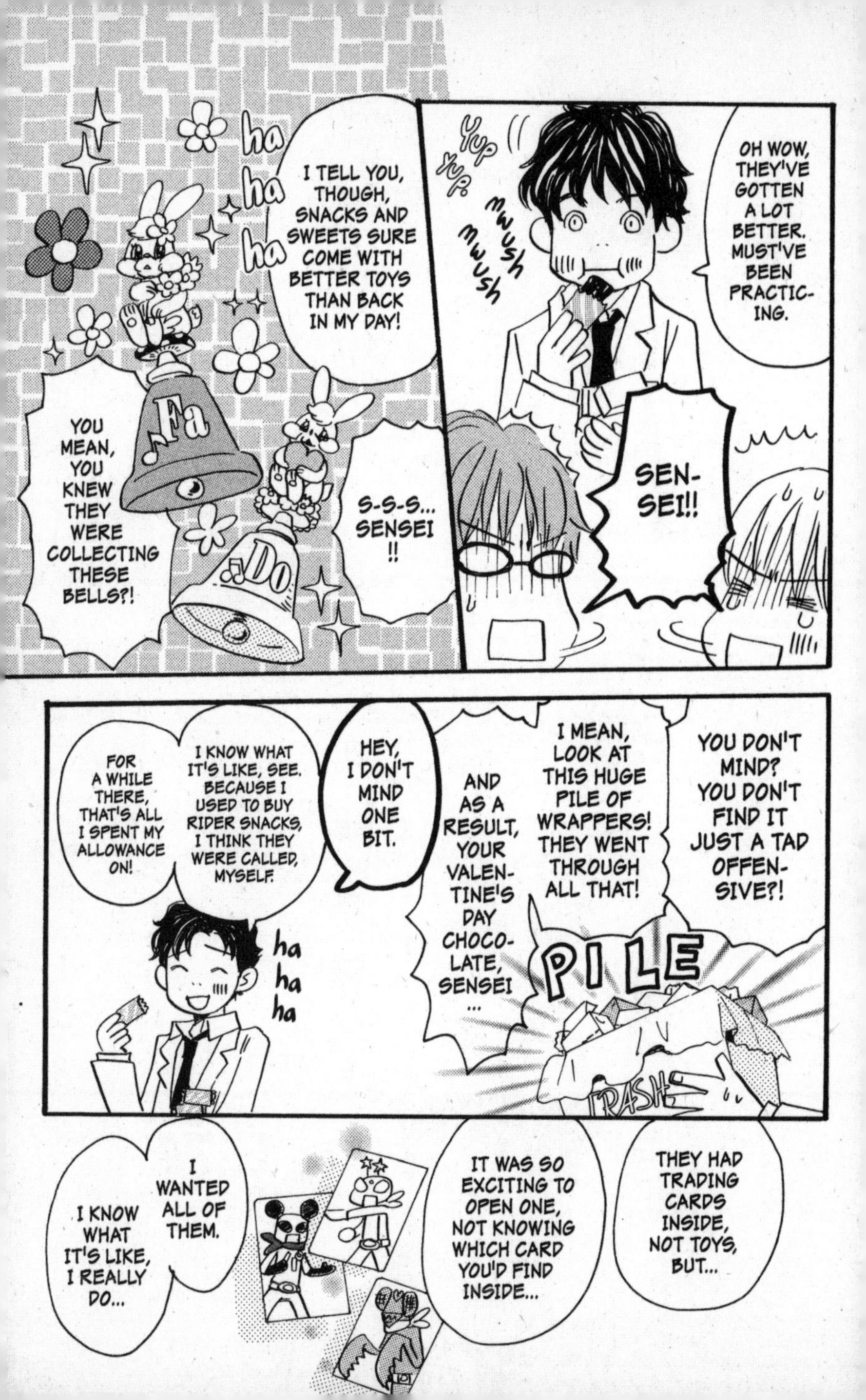
OH WOW, THEY'VE GOTTEN A LOT BETTER. MUST'VE BEEN PRACTIC-ING.
YUP YUP
MWUSH MWUSH
SEN-SEI!!
I TELL YOU, THOUGH, SNACKS AND SWEETS SURE COME WITH BETTER TOYS THAN BACK IN MY DAY!
ha ha ha
S-S-S... SENSEI!!
YOU MEAN, YOU KNEW THEY WERE COLLECTING THESE BELLS?!
Fa
Do
YOU DON'T MIND? YOU DON'T FIND IT JUST A TAD OFFEN-SIVE?!
I MEAN, LOOK AT THIS HUGE PILE OF WRAPPERS! THEY WENT THROUGH ALL THAT!
AND AS A RESULT, YOUR VALEN-TINE'S DAY CHOCO-LATE, SENSEI...
PILE
TRASH
HEY, I DON'T MIND ONE BIT.
I KNOW WHAT IT'S LIKE, SEE. BECAUSE I USED TO BUY RIDER SNACKS, I THINK THEY WERE CALLED, MYSELF.
FOR A WHILE THERE, THAT'S ALL I SPENT MY ALLOWANCE ON!
ha ha ha
THEY HAD TRADING CARDS INSIDE, NOT TOYS, BUT...
IT WAS SO EXCITING TO OPEN ONE, NOT KNOWING WHICH CARD YOU'D FIND INSIDE...
I WANTED ALL OF THEM.
I KNOW WHAT IT'S LIKE, I REALLY DO...

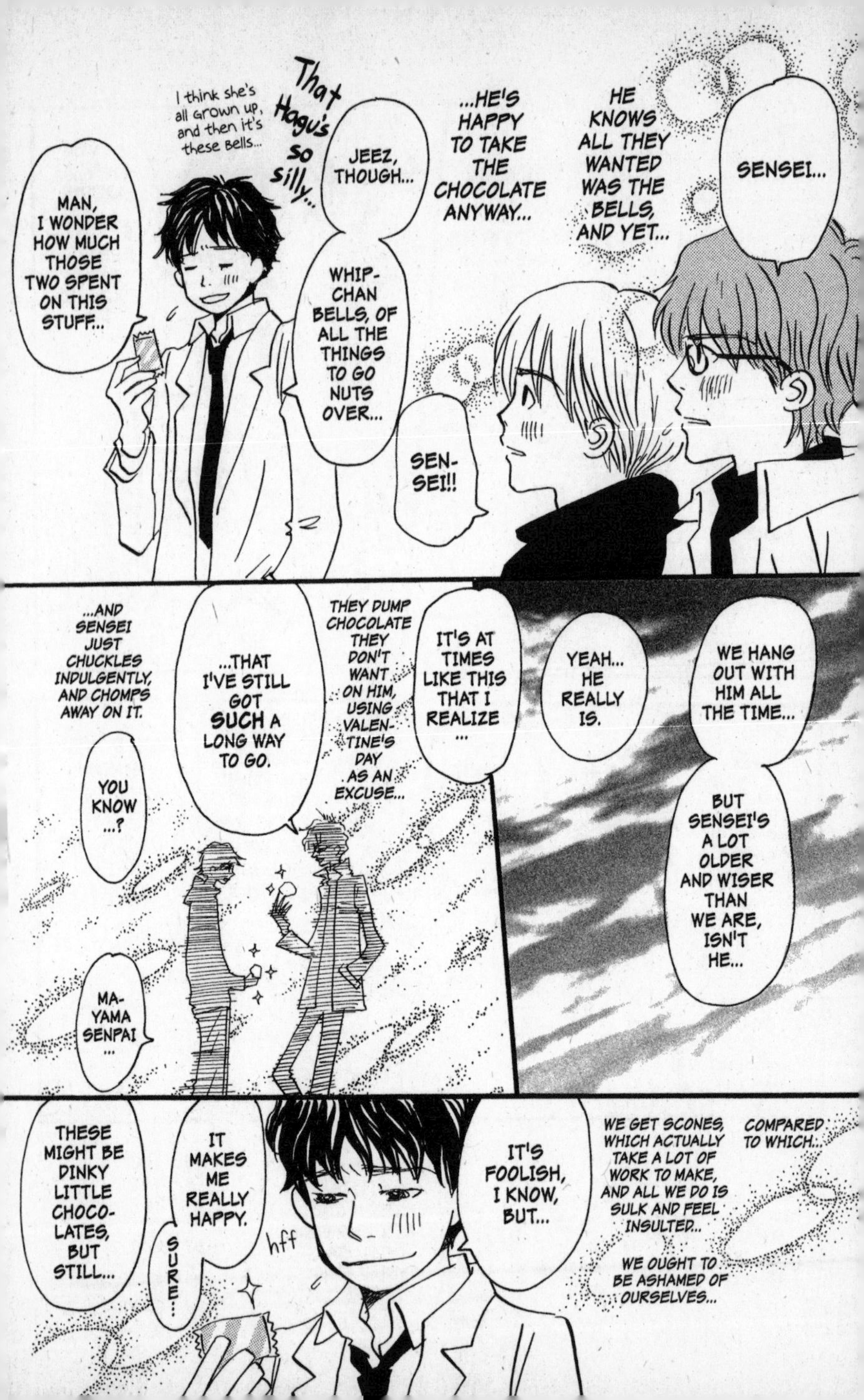
SENSEI...
HE KNOWS ALL THEY WANTED WAS THE BELLS, AND YET...
...HE'S HAPPY TO TAKE THE CHOCOLATE ANYWAY...
SEN-SEI!!
JEEZ, THOUGH...
WHIP-CHAN BELLS, OF ALL THE THINGS TO GO NUTS OVER...
That Hagu's so silly...
I think she's all grown up, and then it's these Bells...
MAN, I WONDER HOW MUCH THOSE TWO SPENT ON THIS STUFF...
WE HANG OUT WITH HIM ALL THE TIME...
BUT SENSEI'S A LOT OLDER AND WISER THAN WE ARE, ISN'T HE...
YEAH... HE REALLY IS.
IT'S AT TIMES LIKE THIS THAT I REALIZE...
THEY DUMP CHOCOLATE THEY DON'T WANT ON HIM, USING VALENTINE'S DAY AS AN EXCUSE...
...THAT I'VE STILL GOT SUCH A LONG WAY TO GO.
...AND SENSEI JUST CHUCKLES INDULGENTLY, AND CHOMPS AWAY ON IT.
YOU KNOW...?
MA-YAMA SENPAI...
COMPARED TO WHICH...
WE GET SCONES, WHICH ACTUALLY TAKE A LOT OF WORK TO MAKE, AND ALL WE DO IS SULK AND FEEL INSULTED...
WE OUGHT TO BE ASHAMED OF OURSELVES...
IT'S FOOLISH, I KNOW, BUT...
hff
IT MAKES ME REALLY HAPPY.
SURE...
THESE MIGHT BE DINKY LITTLE CHOCOLATES, BUT STILL...

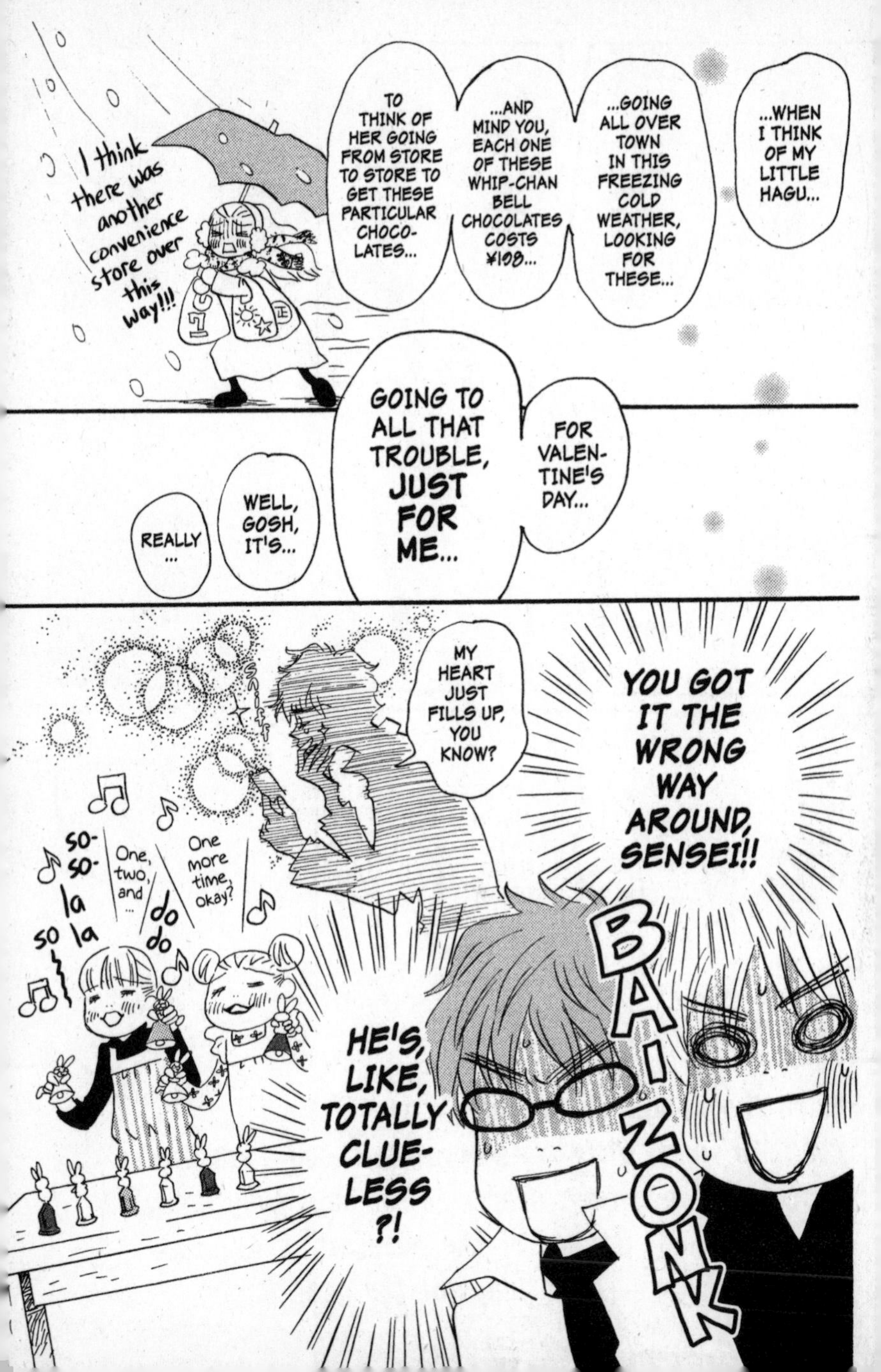
...WHEN I THINK OF MY LITTLE HAGU...
...GOING ALL OVER TOWN IN THIS FREEZING COLD WEATHER, LOOKING FOR THESE...
...AND MIND YOU, EACH ONE OF THESE WHIP-CHAN BELL CHOCOLATES COSTS ¥108...
TO THINK OF HER GOING FROM STORE TO STORE TO GET THESE PARTICULAR CHOCOLATES...
I think there was another convenience store over this way!!!
FOR VALENTINE'S DAY...
GOING TO ALL THAT TROUBLE, JUST FOR ME...
WELL, GOSH, IT'S...
REALLY...
YOU GOT IT THE WRONG WAY AROUND, SENSEI!!
MY HEART JUST FILLS UP, YOU KNOW?
sniff
BA-I-ZONK
HE'S, LIKE, TOTALLY CLUELESS?!
One more time, okay?
One, two, and...
do do
so-so-la so la

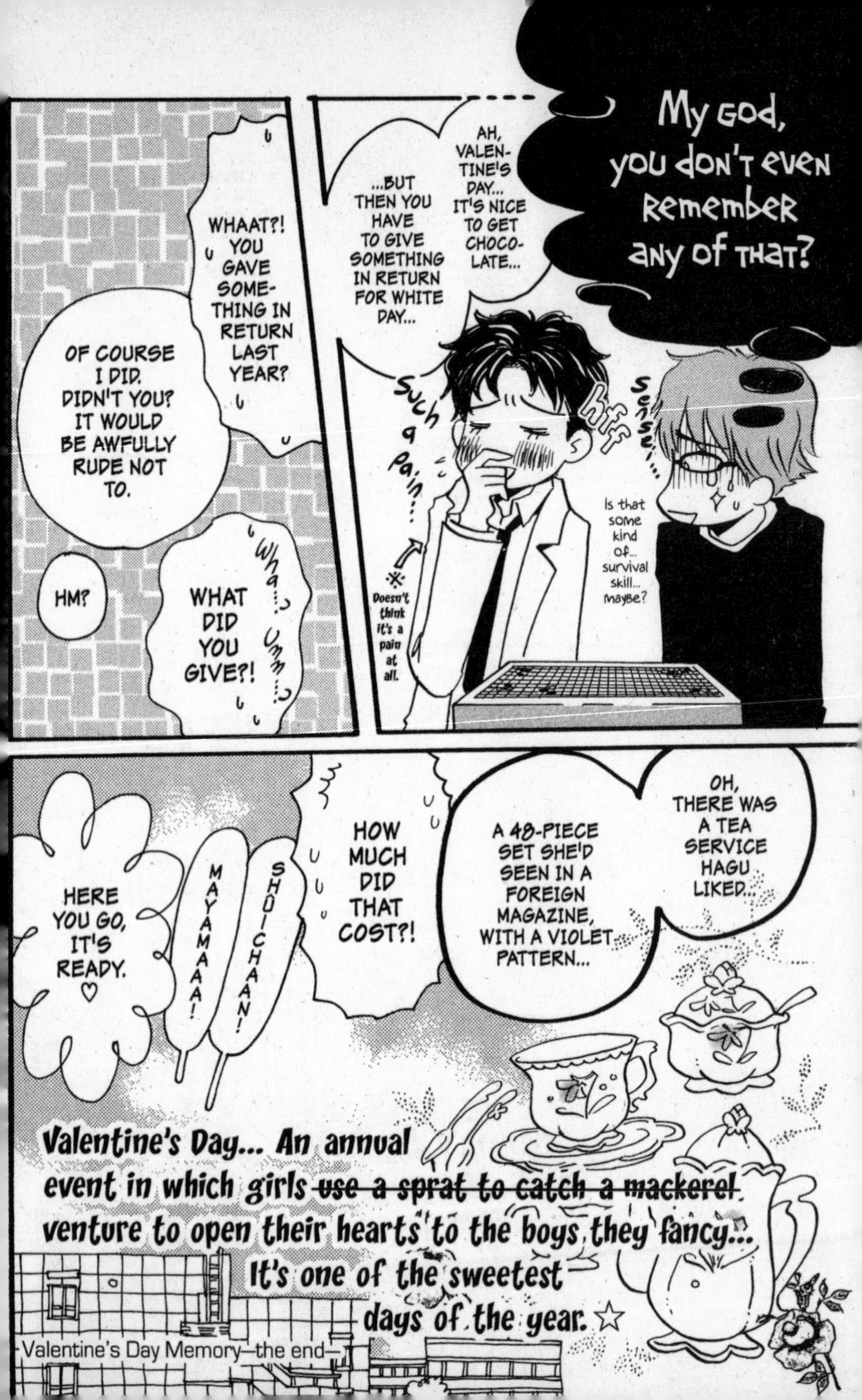

My god, you don't even remember any of that?
AH, VALENTINE'S DAY... IT'S NICE TO GET CHOCOLATE...
...BUT THEN YOU HAVE TO GIVE SOMETHING IN RETURN FOR WHITE DAY...
Sensei...
hff
Is that some kind of... survival skill... maybe?
Such a pain...
※Doesn't think it's a pain at all.
WHAAT?! YOU GAVE SOMETHING IN RETURN LAST YEAR?
OF COURSE I DID. DIDN'T YOU? IT WOULD BE AWFULLY RUDE NOT TO.
WHAT DID YOU GIVE?!
Wha...? Umm...?
HM?
OH, THERE WAS A TEA SERVICE HAGU LIKED...
A 48-PIECE SET SHE'D SEEN IN A FOREIGN MAGAZINE, WITH A VIOLET PATTERN...
HOW MUCH DID THAT COST?!
SHUICHAAN!
MAYAMAAA!
HERE YOU GO, IT'S READY. ♡
Valentine's Day... An annual event in which girls ~~use a sprat to catch a mackerel~~ venture to open their hearts to the boys they fancy... It's one of the sweetest days of the year. ☆
-Valentine's Day Memory—the end-

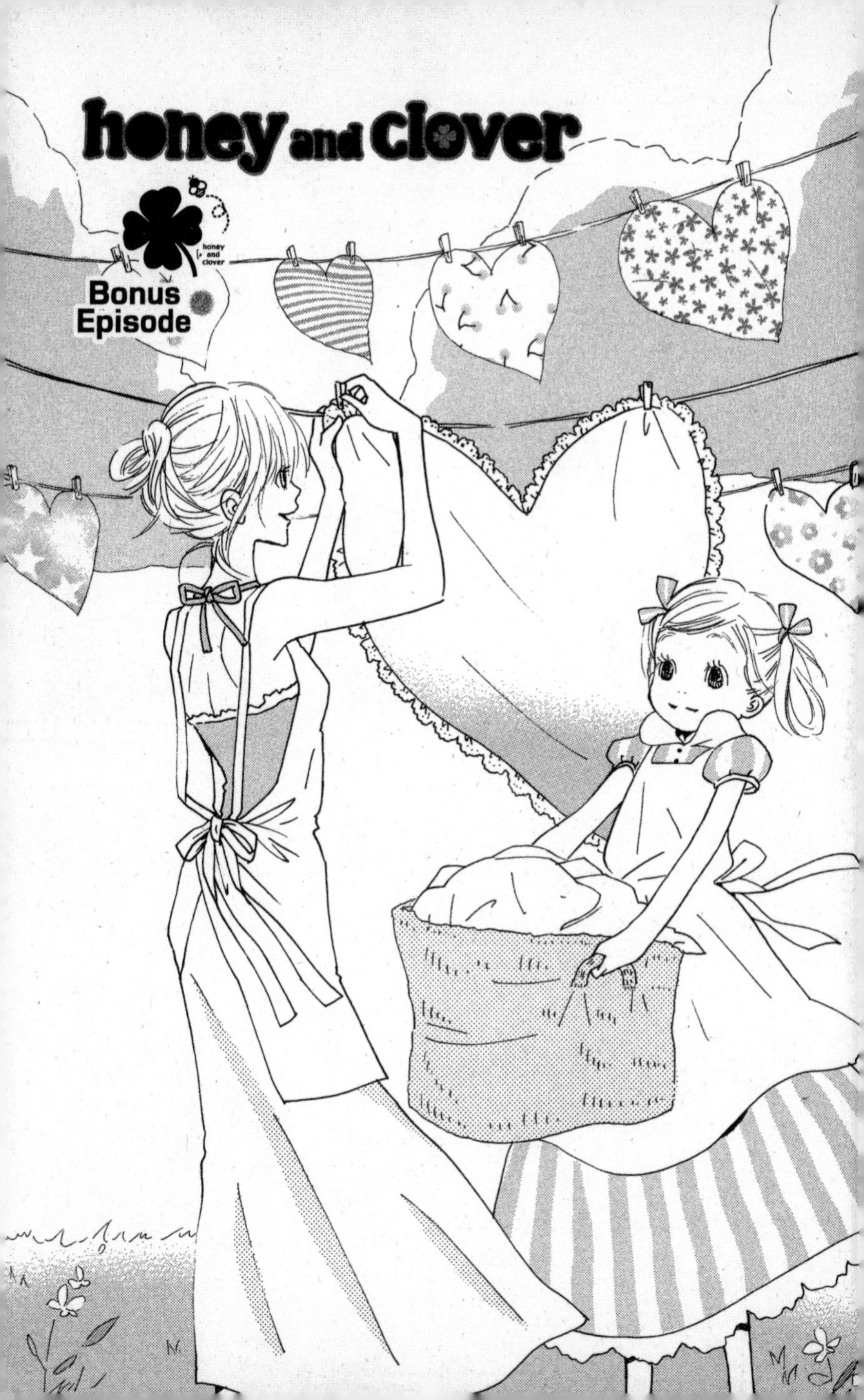
honey and clover
honey and clover
Bonus Episode

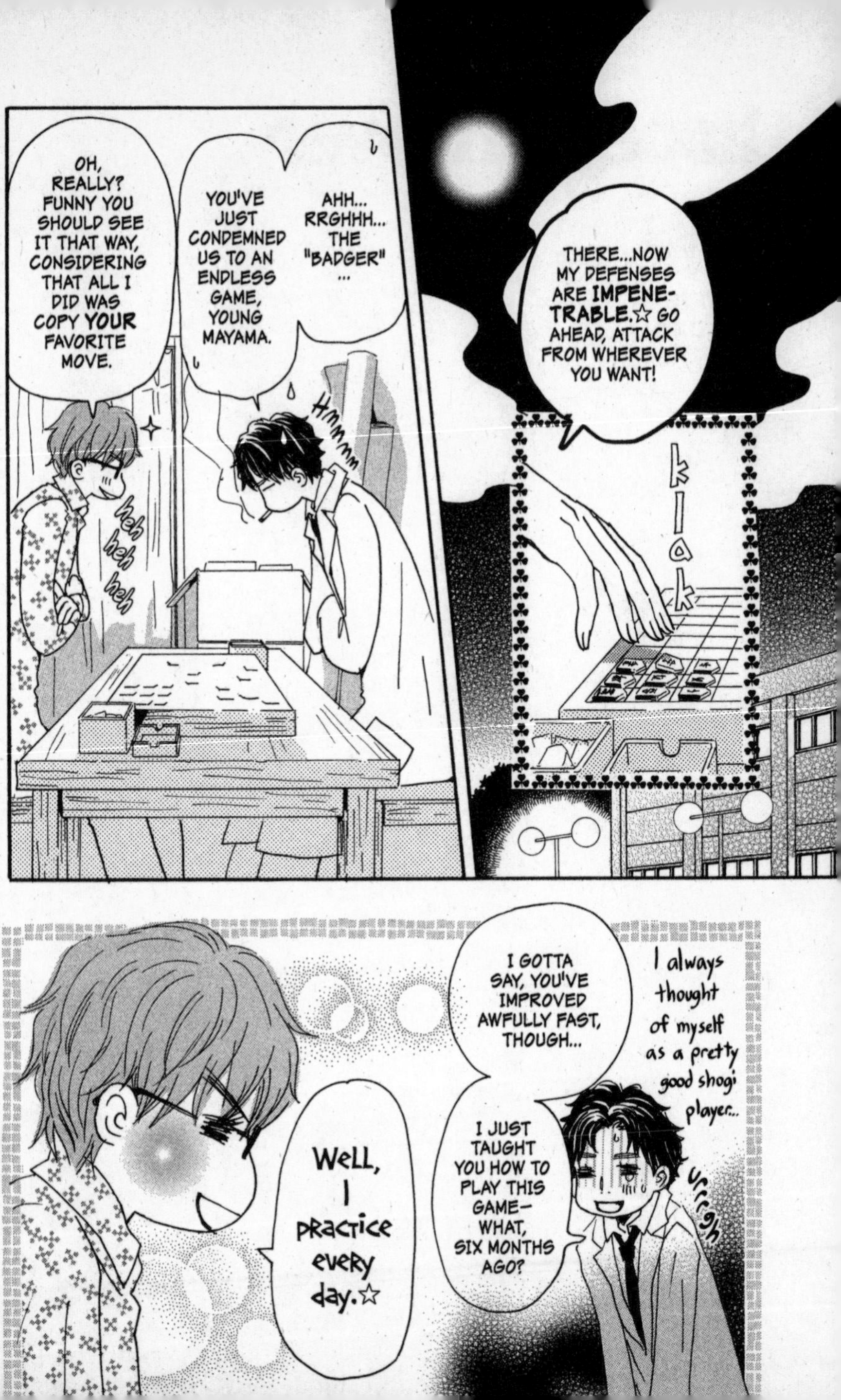
THERE...NOW MY DEFENSES ARE IMPENETRABLE.☆ GO AHEAD, ATTACK FROM WHEREVER YOU WANT!
klak
AHH... RRGHHH... THE "BADGER"...
YOU'VE JUST CONDEMNED US TO AN ENDLESS GAME, YOUNG MAYAMA.
Hmmmm
OH, REALLY? FUNNY YOU SHOULD SEE IT THAT WAY, CONSIDERING THAT ALL I DID WAS COPY YOUR FAVORITE MOVE.
heh heh heh
I always thought of myself as a pretty good shogi player...
I GOTTA SAY, YOU'VE IMPROVED AWFULLY FAST, THOUGH...
I JUST TAUGHT YOU HOW TO PLAY THIS GAME—WHAT, SIX MONTHS AGO?
urrgh
Well, I practice every day.☆

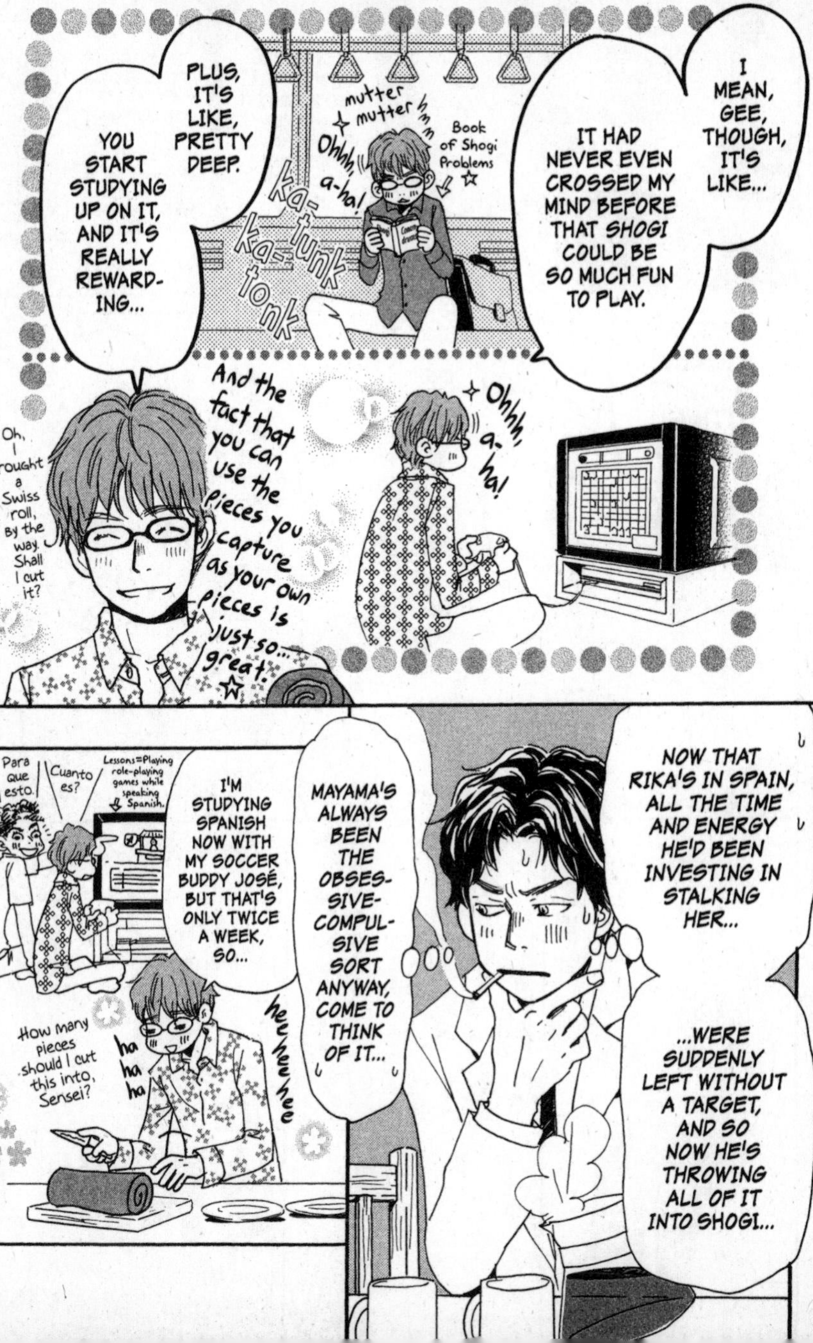
I MEAN, GEE, THOUGH, IT'S LIKE...
IT HAD NEVER EVEN CROSSED MY MIND BEFORE THAT SHOGI COULD BE SO MUCH FUN TO PLAY.
mutter mutter hmm
Book of Shogi Problems
Ohhh, a-ha!
ka-tunk ka-tonk
PLUS, IT'S LIKE, PRETTY DEEP.
YOU START STUDYING UP ON IT, AND IT'S REALLY REWARDING...
Ohhh, a-ha!
And the fact that you can use the pieces you capture as your own pieces is just so... great.
Oh, I brought a Swiss roll, by the way. Shall I cut it?
NOW THAT RIKA'S IN SPAIN, ALL THE TIME AND ENERGY HE'D BEEN INVESTING IN STALKING HER...
...WERE SUDDENLY LEFT WITHOUT A TARGET, AND SO NOW HE'S THROWING ALL OF IT INTO SHOGI...
MAYAMA'S ALWAYS BEEN THE OBSESSIVE-COMPULSIVE SORT ANYWAY, COME TO THINK OF IT...
I'M STUDYING SPANISH NOW WITH MY SOCCER BUDDY JOSÉ, BUT THAT'S ONLY TWICE A WEEK, SO...
Lessons=Playing role-playing games while speaking Spanish.
Cuanto es?
Para que esto.
hee hee hee
ha ha ha
How many pieces should I cut this into, Sensei?

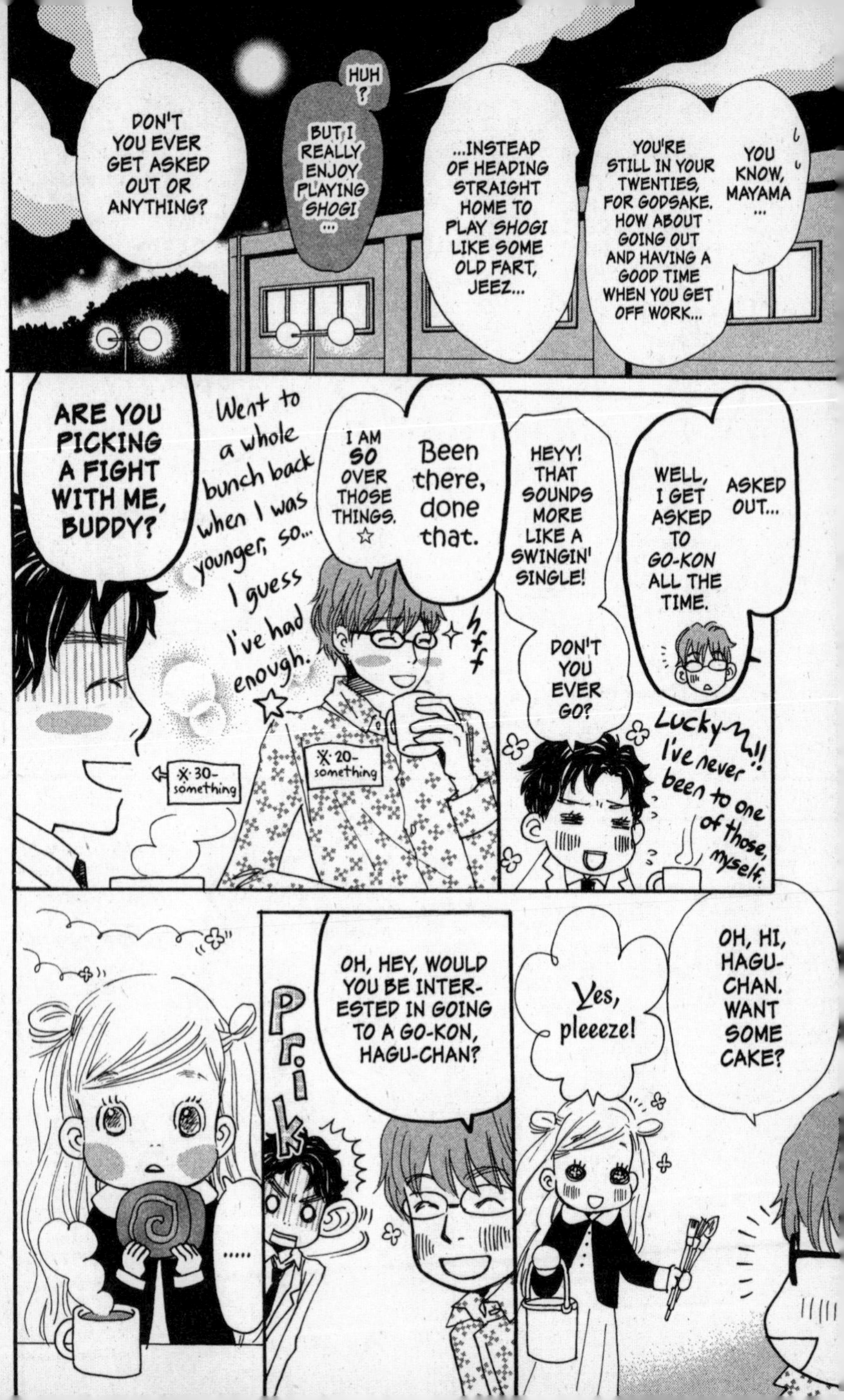
YOU KNOW, MAYAMA...
YOU'RE STILL IN YOUR TWENTIES, FOR GODSAKE. HOW ABOUT GOING OUT AND HAVING A GOOD TIME WHEN YOU GET OFF WORK...
...INSTEAD OF HEADING STRAIGHT HOME TO PLAY SHOGI LIKE SOME OLD FART, JEEZ...
HUH?
BUT I REALLY ENJOY PLAYING SHOGI...
DON'T YOU EVER GET ASKED OUT OR ANYTHING?
ASKED OUT...
WELL, I GET ASKED TO GO-KON ALL THE TIME.
HEYY! THAT SOUNDS MORE LIKE A SWINGIN' SINGLE!
DON'T YOU EVER GO?
Lucky!! I've never been to one of those, myself.
Been there, done that.
I AM SO OVER THOSE THINGS. ☆
Went to a whole bunch back when I was younger, so... I guess I've had enough. ☆
hff
※ 20-something
※ 30-something
ARE YOU PICKING A FIGHT WITH ME, BUDDY?
OH, HI, HAGU-CHAN. WANT SOME CAKE?
Yes, pleeeze!
OH, HEY, WOULD YOU BE INTERESTED IN GOING TO A GO-KON, HAGU-CHAN?
Prik
.....

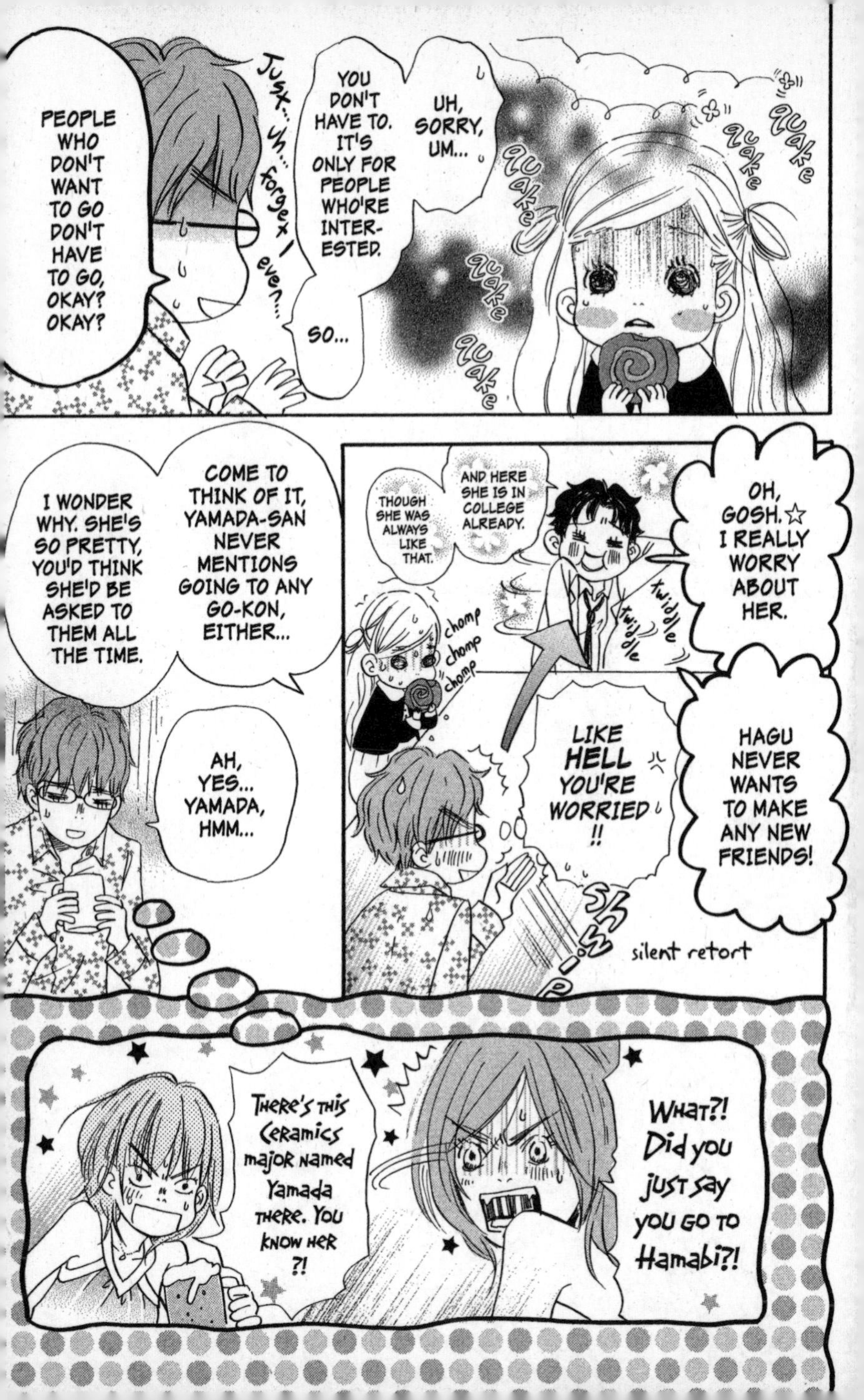
quake quake
quake quake
UH, SORRY, UM...
YOU DON'T HAVE TO. IT'S ONLY FOR PEOPLE WHO'RE INTERESTED.
SO...
Just... uh... forget I even...
PEOPLE WHO DON'T WANT TO GO DON'T HAVE TO GO, OKAY? OKAY?
OH, GOSH.☆ I REALLY WORRY ABOUT HER.
AND HERE SHE IS IN COLLEGE ALREADY.
THOUGH SHE WAS ALWAYS LIKE THAT.
twiddle twiddle
chomp chomp chomp
HAGU NEVER WANTS TO MAKE ANY NEW FRIENDS!
LIKE HELL YOU'RE WORRIED!!
silent retort
COME TO THINK OF IT, YAMADA-SAN NEVER MENTIONS GOING TO ANY GO-KON, EITHER...
I WONDER WHY. SHE'S SO PRETTY, YOU'D THINK SHE'D BE ASKED TO THEM ALL THE TIME.
AH, YES... YAMADA, HMM...
WHAT?! Did you just say you go to Hamabi?!
There's this Ceramics major named Yamada there. You know her?!

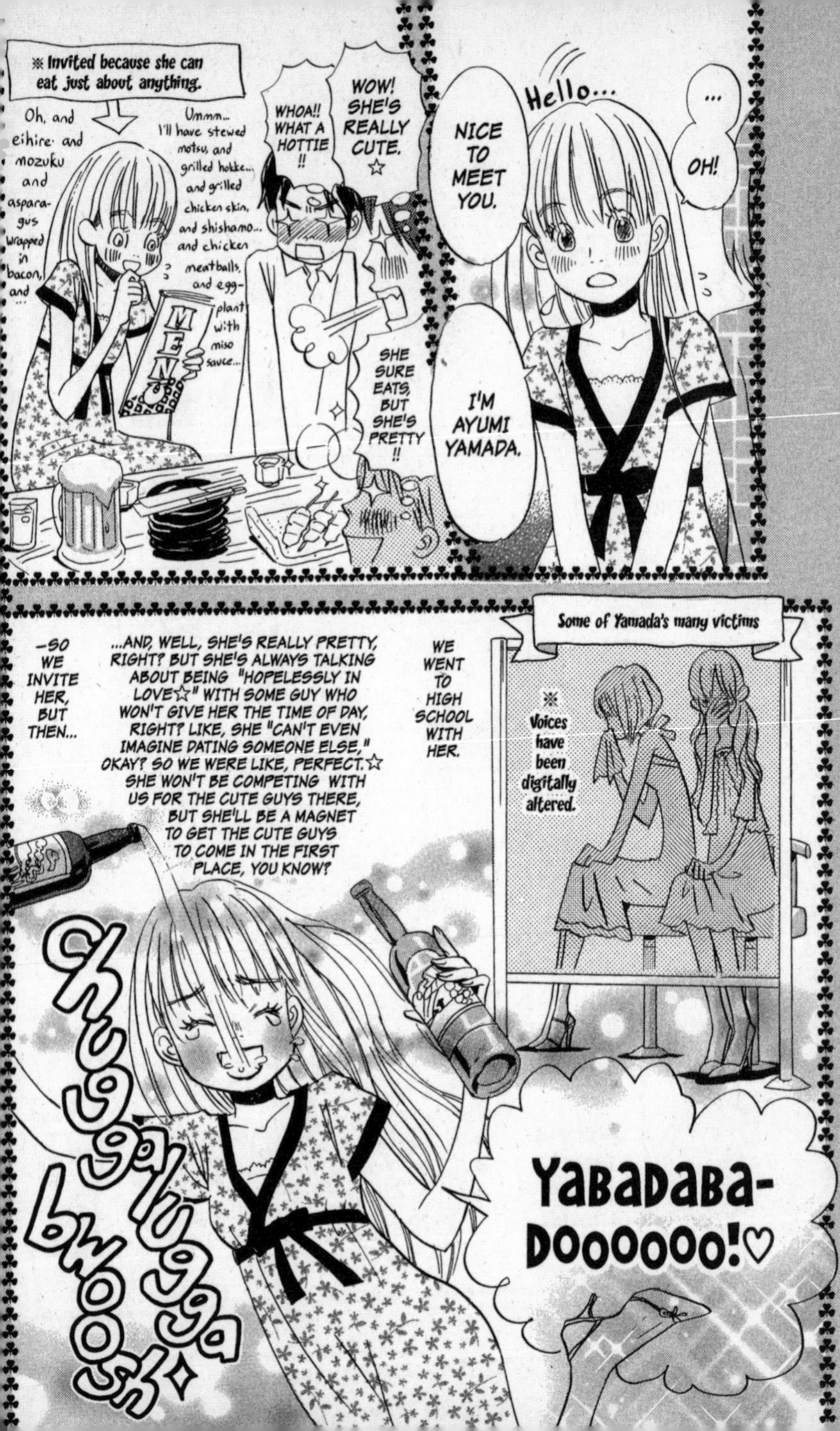
...
OH!
Hello...
NICE TO MEET YOU.
I'M AYUMI YAMADA.
WOW! SHE'S REALLY CUTE. ☆
WHOA!! WHAT A HOTTIE!!
Ummm... I'll have stewed motsu, and grilled hokke... and grilled chicken skin, and shishamo... and chicken meatballs, and egg-plant with miso sauce...
※ Invited because she can eat just about anything.
Oh, and eihire and mozuku and asparagus wrapped in bacon, and ...
MENU
SHE SURE EATS, BUT SHE'S PRETTY!!
Some of Yamada's many victims
※ Voices have been digitally altered.
WE WENT TO HIGH SCHOOL WITH HER.
...AND, WELL, SHE'S REALLY PRETTY, RIGHT? BUT SHE'S ALWAYS TALKING ABOUT BEING "HOPELESSLY IN LOVE☆" WITH SOME GUY WHO WON'T GIVE HER THE TIME OF DAY, RIGHT? LIKE, SHE "CAN'T EVEN IMAGINE DATING SOMEONE ELSE," OKAY? SO WE WERE LIKE, PERFECT.☆ SHE WON'T BE COMPETING WITH US FOR THE CUTE GUYS THERE, BUT SHE'LL BE A MAGNET TO GET THE CUTE GUYS TO COME IN THE FIRST PLACE, YOU KNOW?
—SO WE INVITE HER, BUT THEN...
Yabadaba-DOOOOOO!♡
chuggalugga bwoosh

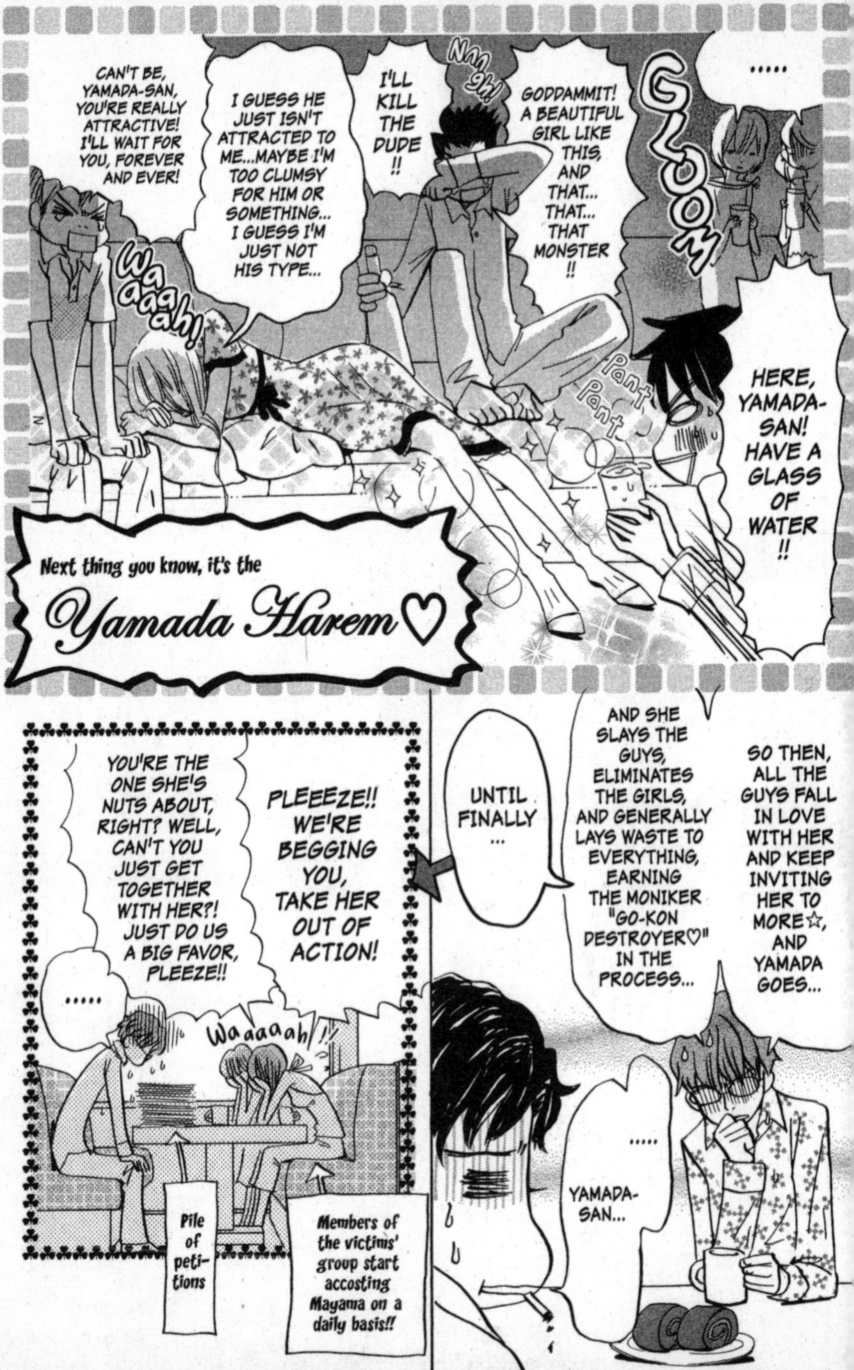

.....
GLOOM
GODDAMMIT! A BEAUTIFUL GIRL LIKE THIS, AND THAT... THAT... THAT MONSTER !!
Nngh!
I'LL KILL THE DUDE !!
I GUESS HE JUST ISN'T ATTRACTED TO ME...MAYBE I'M TOO CLUMSY FOR HIM OR SOMETHING... I GUESS I'M JUST NOT HIS TYPE...
CAN'T BE, YAMADA-SAN, YOU'RE REALLY ATTRACTIVE! I'LL WAIT FOR YOU, FOREVER AND EVER!
Waaaah!
HERE, YAMADA-SAN! HAVE A GLASS OF WATER !!
Pant Pant
Next thing you know, it's the
Yamada Harem♡
SO THEN, ALL THE GUYS FALL IN LOVE WITH HER AND KEEP INVITING HER TO MORE☆, AND YAMADA GOES...
AND SHE SLAYS THE GUYS, ELIMINATES THE GIRLS, AND GENERALLY LAYS WASTE TO EVERYTHING, EARNING THE MONIKER "GO-KON DESTROYER♡" IN THE PROCESS...
UNTIL FINALLY ...
.....
YAMADA-SAN...
PLEEEZE!! WE'RE BEGGING YOU, TAKE HER OUT OF ACTION!
YOU'RE THE ONE SHE'S NUTS ABOUT, RIGHT? WELL, CAN'T YOU JUST GET TOGETHER WITH HER?! JUST DO US A BIG FAVOR, PLEEZE!!
.....
Waaaaah!!
Members of the victims' group start accosting Mayama on a daily basis!!
Pile of peti-tions

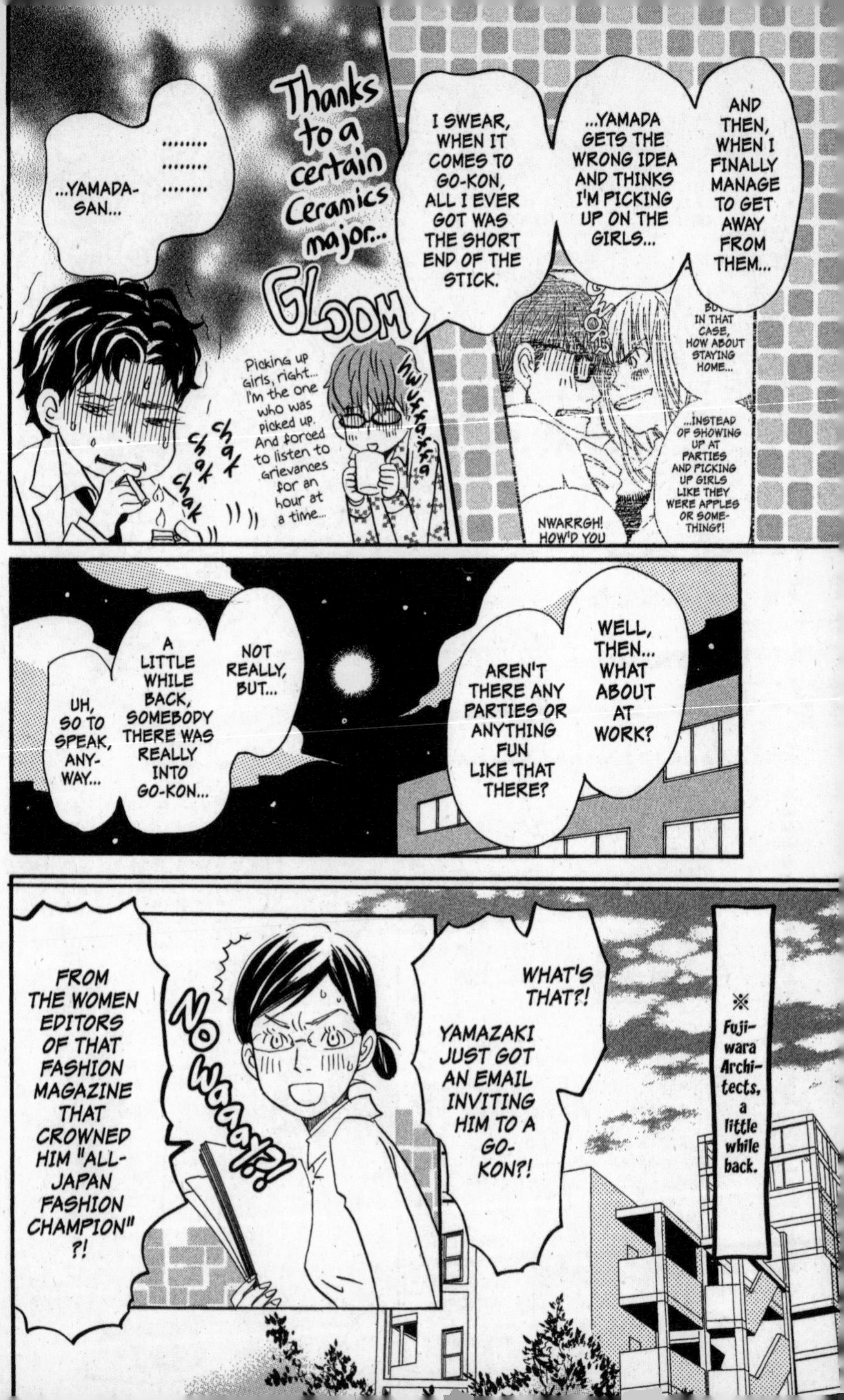
AND THEN, WHEN I FINALLY MANAGE TO GET AWAY FROM THEM...
...YAMADA GETS THE WRONG IDEA AND THINKS I'M PICKING UP ON THE GIRLS...
BUT IN THAT CASE, HOW ABOUT STAYING HOME...
...INSTEAD OF SHOWING UP AT PARTIES AND PICKING UP GIRLS LIKE THEY WERE APPLES OR SOMETHING?!
NWARRGH! HOW'D YOU
I SWEAR, WHEN IT COMES TO GO-KON, ALL I EVER GOT WAS THE SHORT END OF THE STICK.
Thanks to a certain Ceramics major...
GLOOM
Picking up girls, right... I'm the one who was picked up. And forced to listen to grievances for an hour at a time...
chak chak chak
....
....
....
...YAMADA-SAN...
WELL, THEN... WHAT ABOUT AT WORK?
AREN'T THERE ANY PARTIES OR ANYTHING FUN LIKE THAT THERE?
NOT REALLY, BUT...
A LITTLE WHILE BACK, SOMEBODY THERE WAS REALLY INTO GO-KON...
UH, SO TO SPEAK, ANYWAY...
※ Fujiwara Architects, a little while back.
WHAT'S THAT?!
YAMAZAKI JUST GOT AN EMAIL INVITING HIM TO A GO-KON?!
No waaay?!
FROM THE WOMEN EDITORS OF THAT FASHION MAGAZINE THAT CROWNED HIM "ALL-JAPAN FASHION CHAMPION"?!

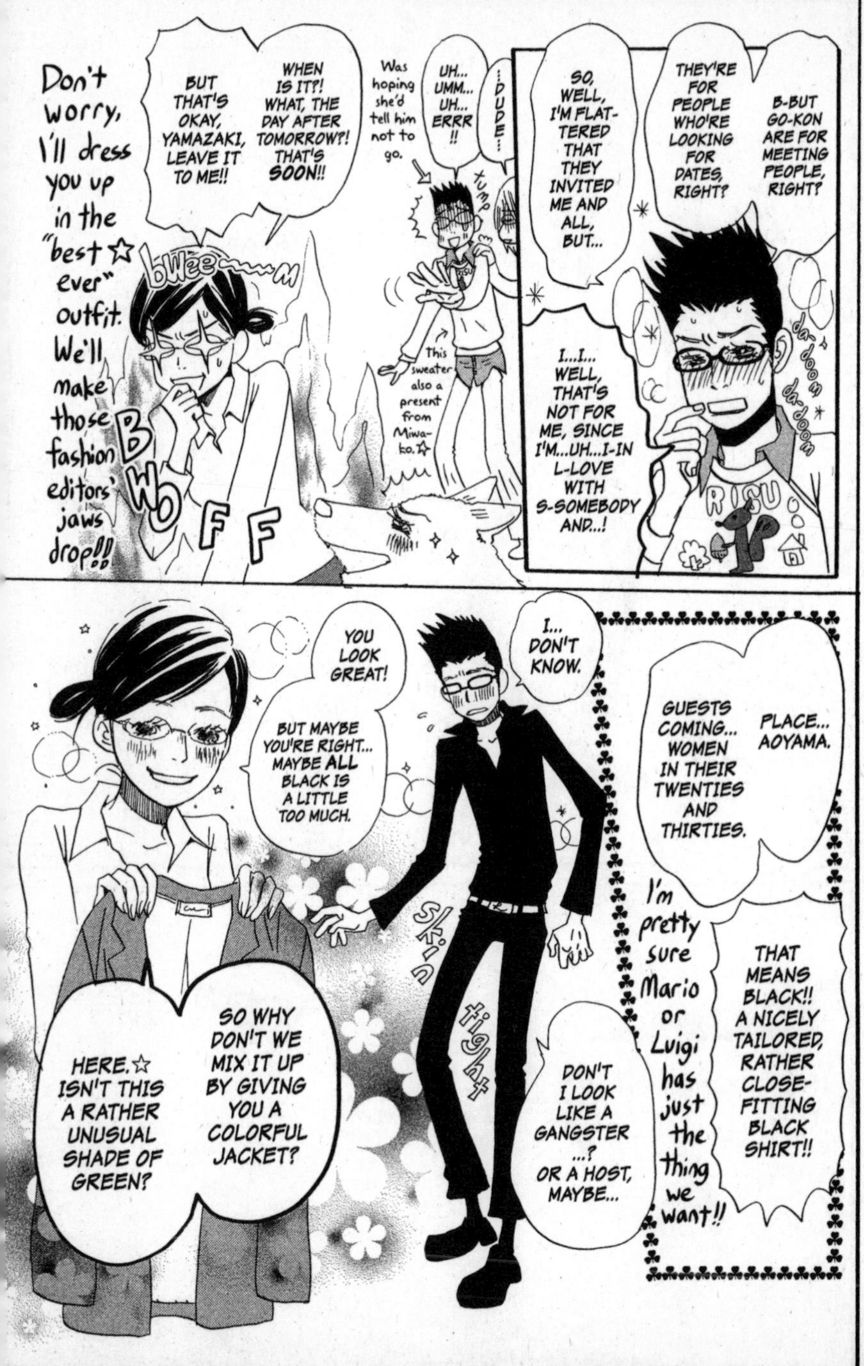
B-BUT GO-KON ARE FOR MEETING PEOPLE, RIGHT?
THEY'RE FOR PEOPLE WHO'RE LOOKING FOR DATES, RIGHT?
SO, WELL, I'M FLATTERED THAT THEY INVITED ME AND ALL, BUT...
I...I... WELL, THAT'S NOT FOR ME, SINCE I'M...UH...I-IN L-LOVE WITH S-SOMEBODY AND...!
da-doom da-doom
...DUDE...
UH... UMM... UH... ERRR!!
Was hoping she'd tell him not to go.
This sweater also a present from Miwako.☆
WHEN IS IT?! WHAT, THE DAY AFTER TOMORROW?! THAT'S SOON!!
BUT THAT'S OKAY, YAMAZAKI, LEAVE IT TO ME!!
Don't worry, I'll dress you up in the "best☆ ever" outfit. We'll make those fashion editors' jaws drop!!
bwee~~m
BWOFF
PLACE... AOYAMA.
GUESTS COMING... WOMEN IN THEIR TWENTIES AND THIRTIES.
THAT MEANS BLACK!! A NICELY TAILORED, RATHER CLOSE-FITTING BLACK SHIRT!!
I'm pretty sure Mario or Luigi has just the thing we want!!
DON'T I LOOK LIKE A GANGSTER ...? OR A HOST, MAYBE...
I... DON'T KNOW.
YOU LOOK GREAT!
BUT MAYBE YOU'RE RIGHT... MAYBE ALL BLACK IS A LITTLE TOO MUCH.
skin tight
SO WHY DON'T WE MIX IT UP BY GIVING YOU A COLORFUL JACKET?
HERE.☆ ISN'T THIS A RATHER UNUSUAL SHADE OF GREEN?

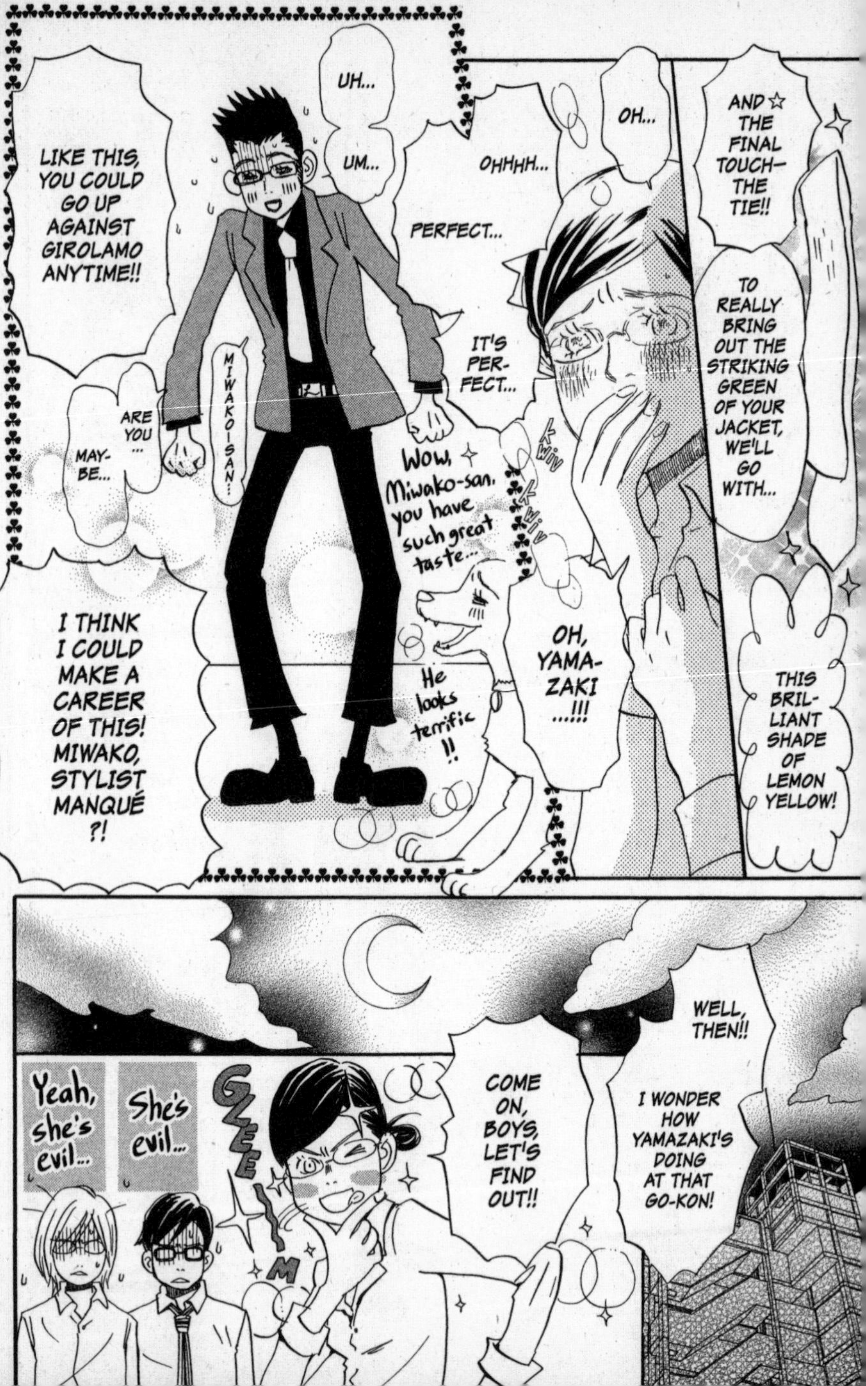
AND☆ THE FINAL TOUCH—THE TIE!!
TO REALLY BRING OUT THE STRIKING GREEN OF YOUR JACKET, WE'LL GO WITH...
THIS BRILLIANT SHADE OF LEMON YELLOW!
OH...
OHHHH...
PERFECT...
IT'S PERFECT...
KWIV KWIV
OH, YAMAZAKI...!!!
UH...
UM...
LIKE THIS, YOU COULD GO UP AGAINST GIROLAMO ANYTIME!!
MIWAKO-SAN...!
ARE YOU...
MAYBE...
Wow, Miwako-san, you have such great taste...
He looks terrific!!
I THINK I COULD MAKE A CAREER OF THIS! MIWAKO, STYLIST MANQUÉ?!
WELL, THEN!!
I WONDER HOW YAMAZAKI'S DOING AT THAT GO-KON!
COME ON, BOYS, LET'S FIND OUT!!
GZEEM
She's evil...
Yeah, she's evil...

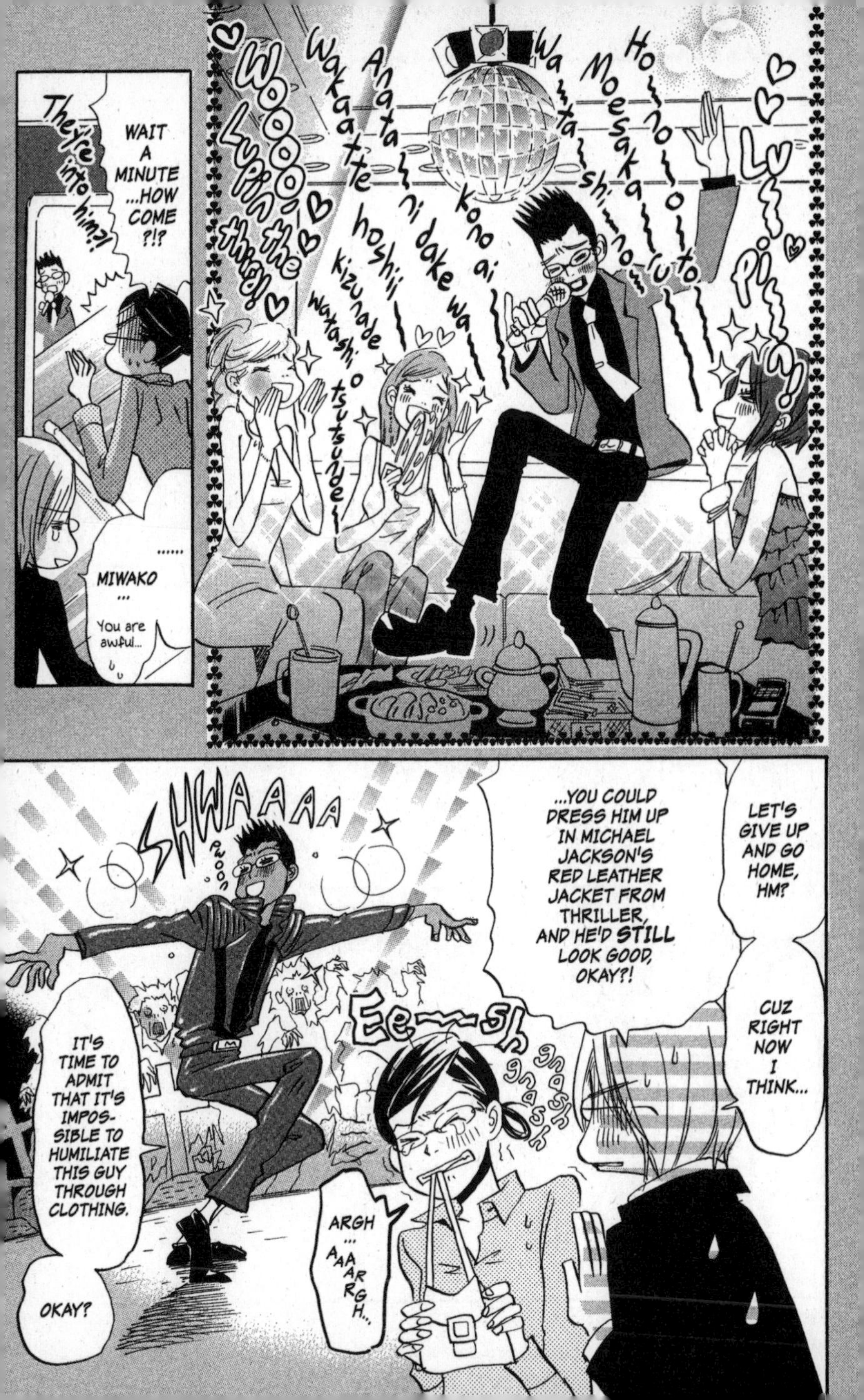
Lu~pi~n!
Ho~no~o~to~
Moesakaru~
Wa~ta~shi~no~
kono ai
Anata~ni dake wa~
Wakaatte hoshii~
kizunade
watashi o tsutsunde~
Woooo~ the Lupin thing! ♡
WAIT A MINUTE ...HOW COME ?!?
They're into him?!
......
MIWAKO ...
You are awful...
LET'S GIVE UP AND GO HOME, HM?
CUZ RIGHT NOW I THINK...
...YOU COULD DRESS HIM UP IN MICHAEL JACKSON'S RED LEATHER JACKET FROM THRILLER, AND HE'D STILL LOOK GOOD, OKAY?!
Ee—sh
gnash gnash
SHWAAAAA
PWOON
IT'S TIME TO ADMIT THAT IT'S IMPOSSIBLE TO HUMILIATE THIS GUY THROUGH CLOTHING.
OKAY?
ARGH ... AAAARRGH...

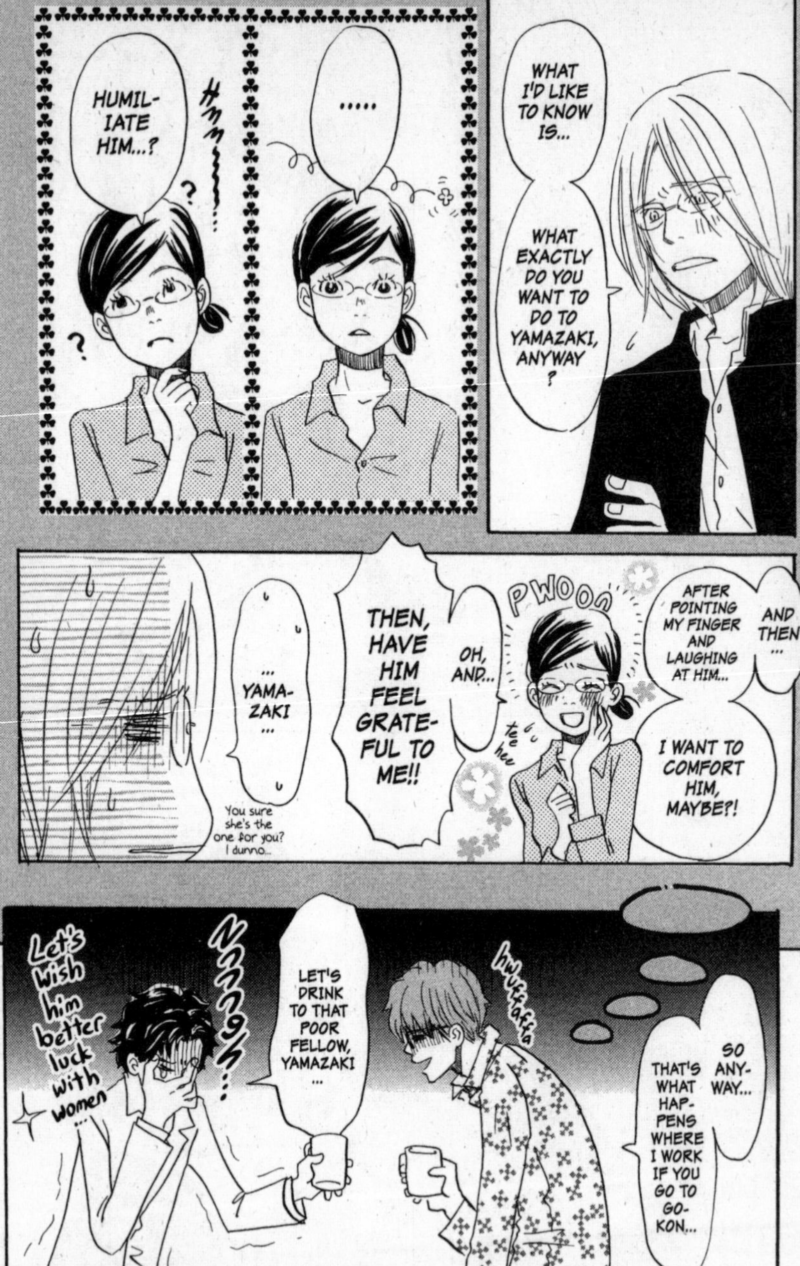
WHAT I'D LIKE TO KNOW IS...
WHAT EXACTLY DO YOU WANT TO DO TO YAMAZAKI, ANYWAY?
.....
HUMILIATE HIM...?
Hmmm...
AND THEN...
AFTER POINTING MY FINGER AND LAUGHING AT HIM...
I WANT TO COMFORT HIM, MAYBE?!
PWOOO
tee hee
OH, AND...
THEN, HAVE HIM FEEL GRATEFUL TO ME!!
...YAMAZAKI...
You sure she's the one for you? I dunno...
SO ANYWAY...
THAT'S WHAT HAPPENS WHERE I WORK IF YOU GO TO GO-KON...
hwuffaffa
LET'S DRINK TO THAT POOR FELLOW, YAMAZAKI...
Nnnngh...
Let's wish him better luck with women...

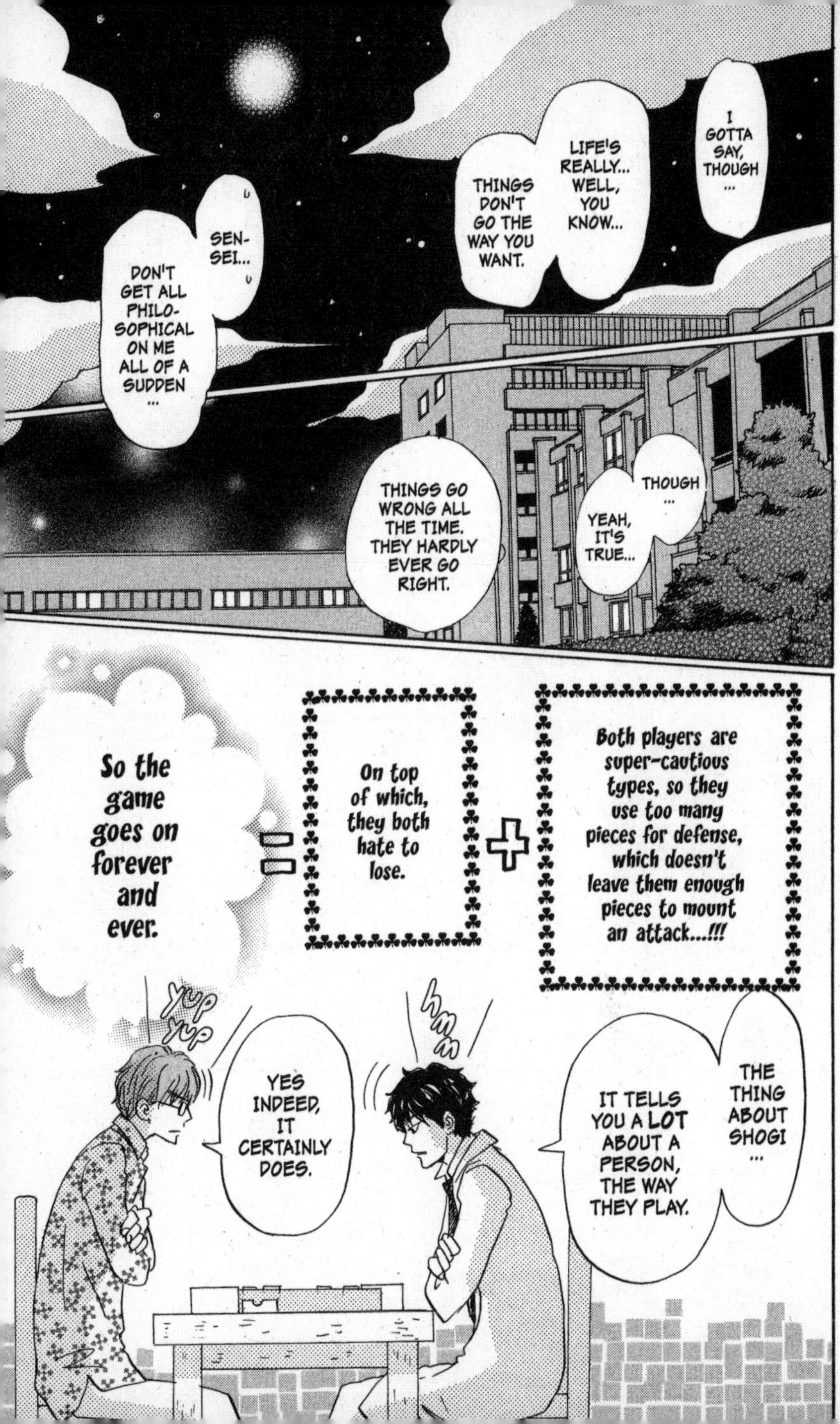
I GOTTA SAY, THOUGH...
LIFE'S REALLY... WELL, YOU KNOW...
THINGS DON'T GO THE WAY YOU WANT.
SEN-SEI...
DON'T GET ALL PHILO-SOPHICAL ON ME ALL OF A SUDDEN...
YEAH, IT'S TRUE...
THOUGH...
THINGS GO WRONG ALL THE TIME. THEY HARDLY EVER GO RIGHT.
Both players are super-cautious types, so they use too many pieces for defense, which doesn't leave them enough pieces to mount an attack...!!!
+
On top of which, they both hate to lose.
=
So the game goes on forever and ever.
THE THING ABOUT SHOGI...
IT TELLS YOU A LOT ABOUT A PERSON, THE WAY THEY PLAY.
hmm
YES INDEED, IT CERTAINLY DOES.
yup yup

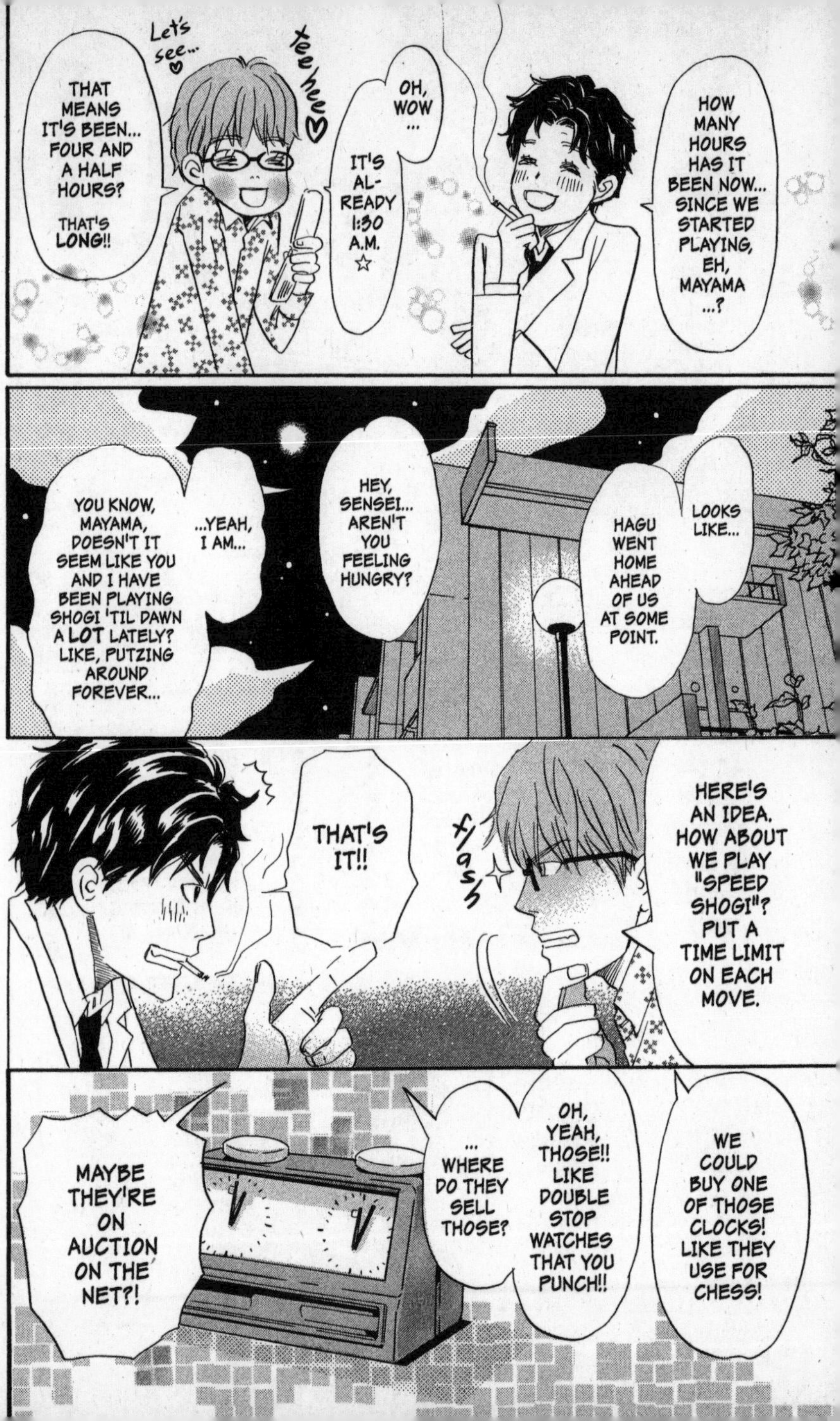
HOW MANY HOURS HAS IT BEEN NOW... SINCE WE STARTED PLAYING, EH, MAYAMA ...?
OH, WOW ... IT'S AL-READY 1:30 A.M. ☆
tee hee ♥
Let's see... ♥
THAT MEANS IT'S BEEN... FOUR AND A HALF HOURS? THAT'S LONG!!
LOOKS LIKE... HAGU WENT HOME AHEAD OF US AT SOME POINT.
HEY, SENSEI... AREN'T YOU FEELING HUNGRY?
...YEAH, I AM...
YOU KNOW, MAYAMA, DOESN'T IT SEEM LIKE YOU AND I HAVE BEEN PLAYING SHOGI 'TIL DAWN A LOT LATELY? LIKE, PUTZING AROUND FOREVER...
HERE'S AN IDEA. HOW ABOUT WE PLAY "SPEED SHOGI"? PUT A TIME LIMIT ON EACH MOVE.
flash
THAT'S IT!!
WE COULD BUY ONE OF THOSE CLOCKS! LIKE THEY USE FOR CHESS!
OH, YEAH, THOSE!! LIKE DOUBLE STOP WATCHES THAT YOU PUNCH!!
... WHERE DO THEY SELL THOSE?
MAYBE THEY'RE ON AUCTION ON THE NET?!

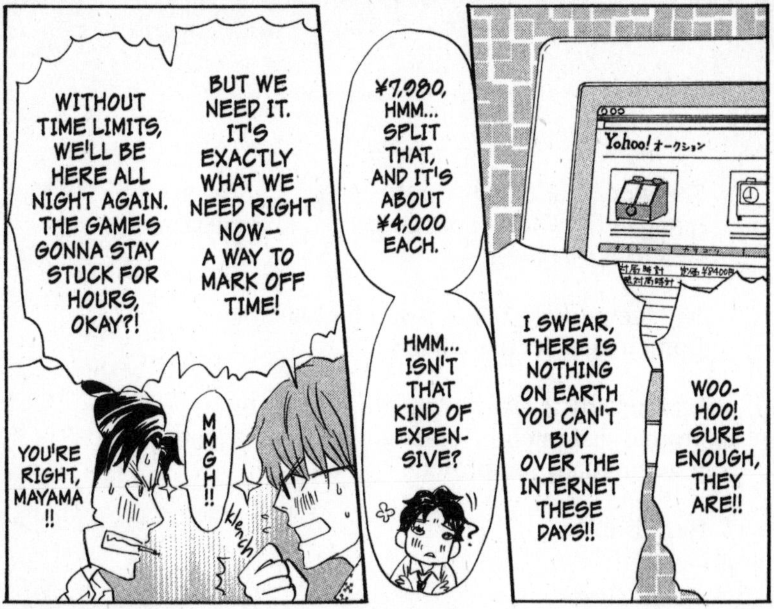
Yohoo! オークション
WOO-HOO! SURE ENOUGH, THEY ARE!!
I SWEAR, THERE IS NOTHING ON EARTH YOU CAN'T BUY OVER THE INTERNET THESE DAYS!!
¥7,980, HMM... SPLIT THAT, AND IT'S ABOUT ¥4,000 EACH.
HMM... ISN'T THAT KIND OF EXPENSIVE?
BUT WE NEED IT. IT'S EXACTLY WHAT WE NEED RIGHT NOW— A WAY TO MARK OFF TIME!
WITHOUT TIME LIMITS, WE'LL BE HERE ALL NIGHT AGAIN. THE GAME'S GONNA STAY STUCK FOR HOURS, OKAY?!
MMGH!!
klench
YOU'RE RIGHT, MAYAMA!!

Wait a minute!!

Hey...

Is the issue really whether or not to set time limits, or to buy a chess clock?

Isn't it more whether or not it's a good thing for two grown men to be spending almost every evening together, playing a game until morning and forgetting to eat dinner?

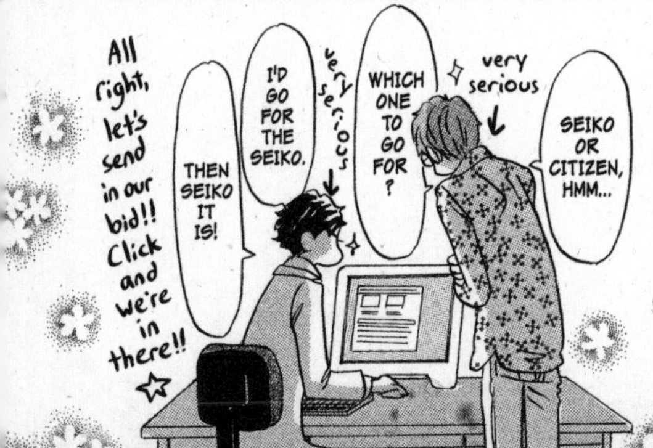
very serious
SEIKO OR CITIZEN, HMM...
WHICH ONE TO GO FOR?
very serious
I'D GO FOR THE SEIKO.
THEN SEIKO IT IS!
All right, let's send in our bid!! Click and we're in there!!

Friendship is beautiful, they say...

But there are cases where it is not necessarily beautiful, per se.

This is what we would like to communicate somehow to these two gentlemen here...

Bonus Episode—the end—

The story that begins on the next page was a
manga I drew for a special feature in a magazine
called Comic Cue.

The theme was, "What if you had one of
Doraemon's secret gadgets?"

Various artists were invited to create stories
around just one of Doraemon's many gadgets.
It was a really fun project.

Here is mine.

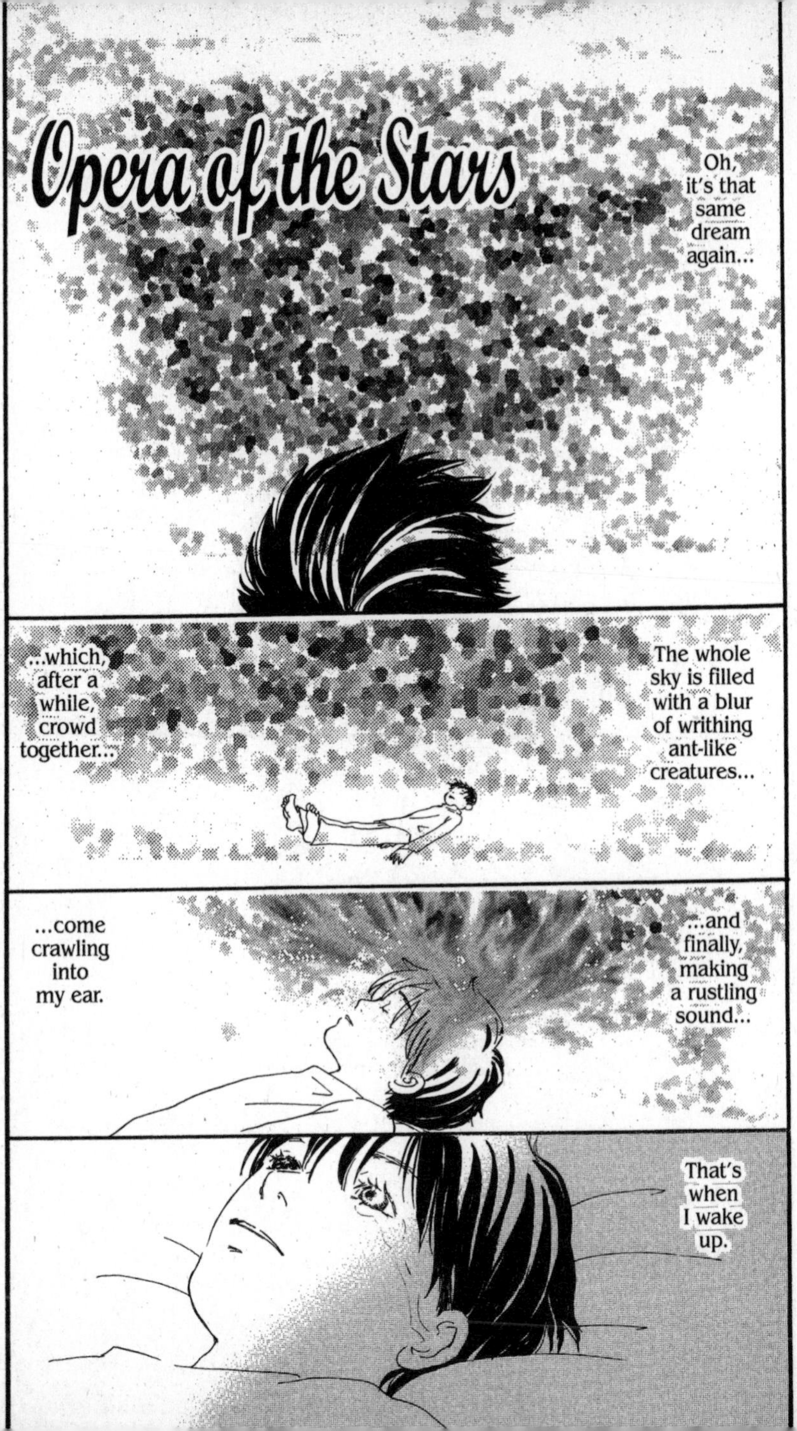
Opera of the Stars
Oh, it's that same dream again...
The whole sky is filled with a blur of writhing ant-like creatures...
...which, after a while, crowd together...
...and finally, making a rustling sound...
...come crawling into my ear.
That's when I wake up.

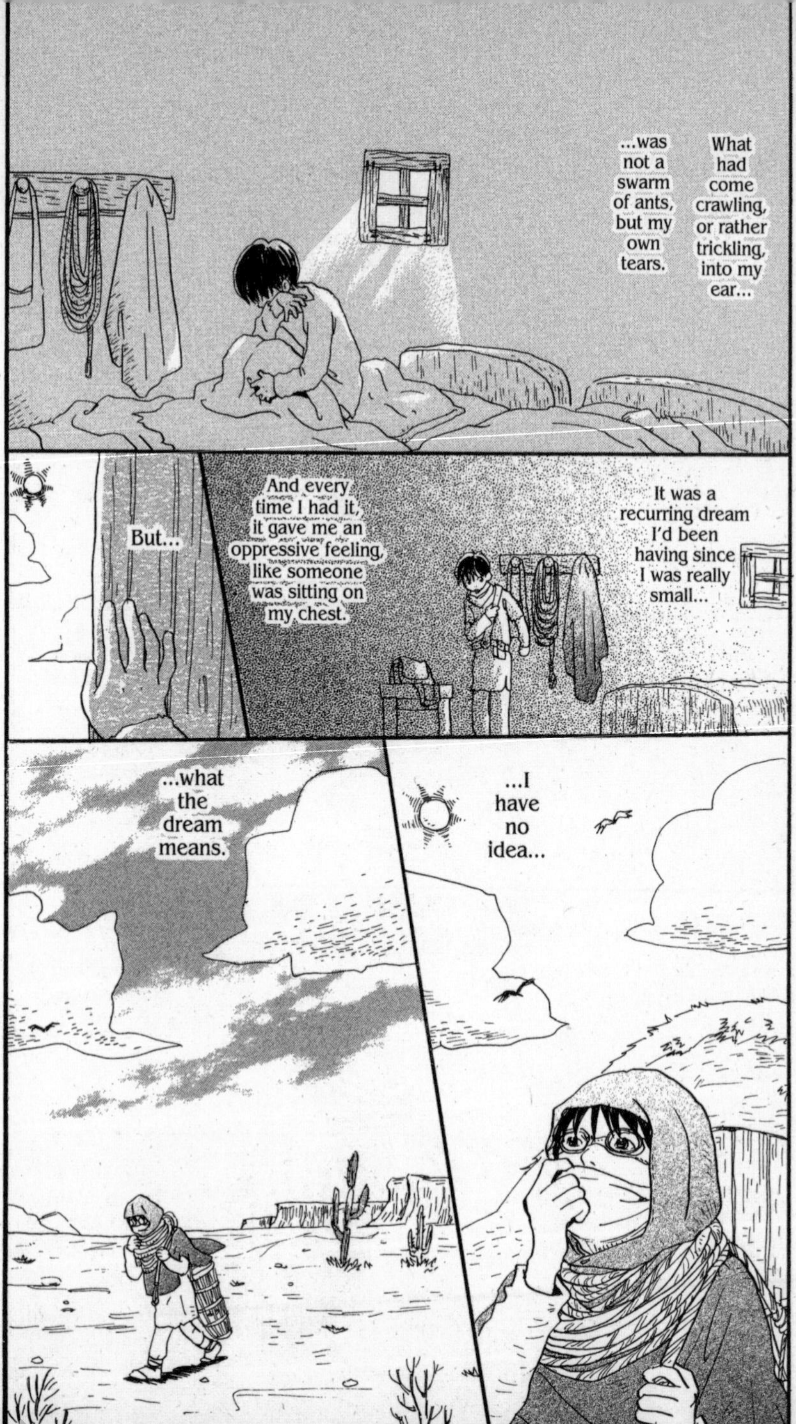
What had come crawling, or rather trickling, into my ear...
...was not a swarm of ants, but my own tears.
It was a recurring dream I'd been having since I was really small...
And every time I had it, it gave me an oppressive feeling, like someone was sitting on my chest.
But...
...I have no idea...
...what the dream means.

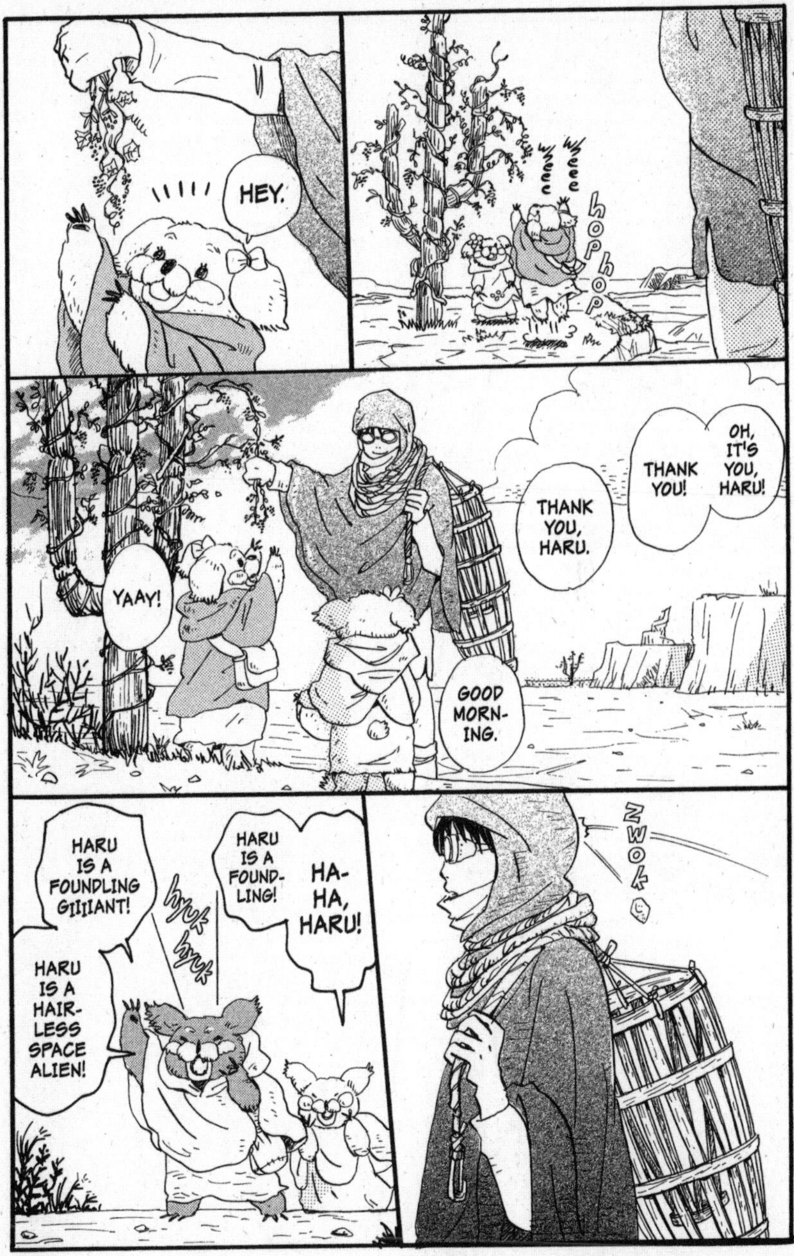
wheee
wheee
hop hop hop
HEY.
OH, IT'S YOU, HARU!
THANK YOU!
THANK YOU, HARU.
GOOD MORNING.
YAAY!
ZWOK
HA-HA, HARU!
HARU IS A FOUNDLING!
HARU IS A FOUNDLING GIIIIANT!
hyuk hyuk
HARU IS A HAIRLESS SPACE ALIEN!

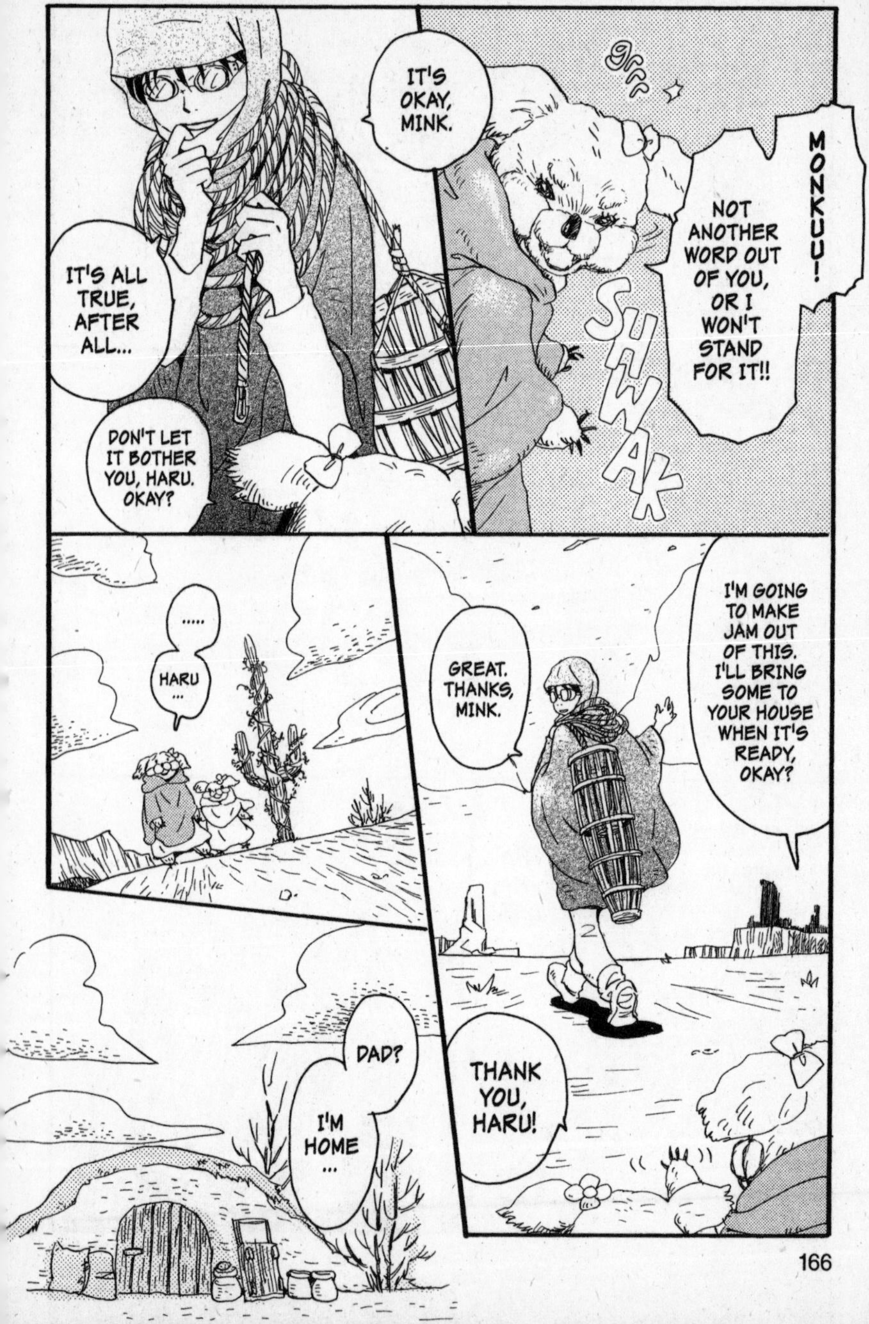
grrr
MONKUU!
NOT ANOTHER WORD OUT OF YOU, OR I WON'T STAND FOR IT!!
SHWAK
IT'S OKAY, MINK.
IT'S ALL TRUE, AFTER ALL...
DON'T LET IT BOTHER YOU, HARU. OKAY?
I'M GOING TO MAKE JAM OUT OF THIS. I'LL BRING SOME TO YOUR HOUSE WHEN IT'S READY, OKAY?
GREAT. THANKS, MINK.
THANK YOU, HARU!
.....
HARU...
DAD?
I'M HOME...

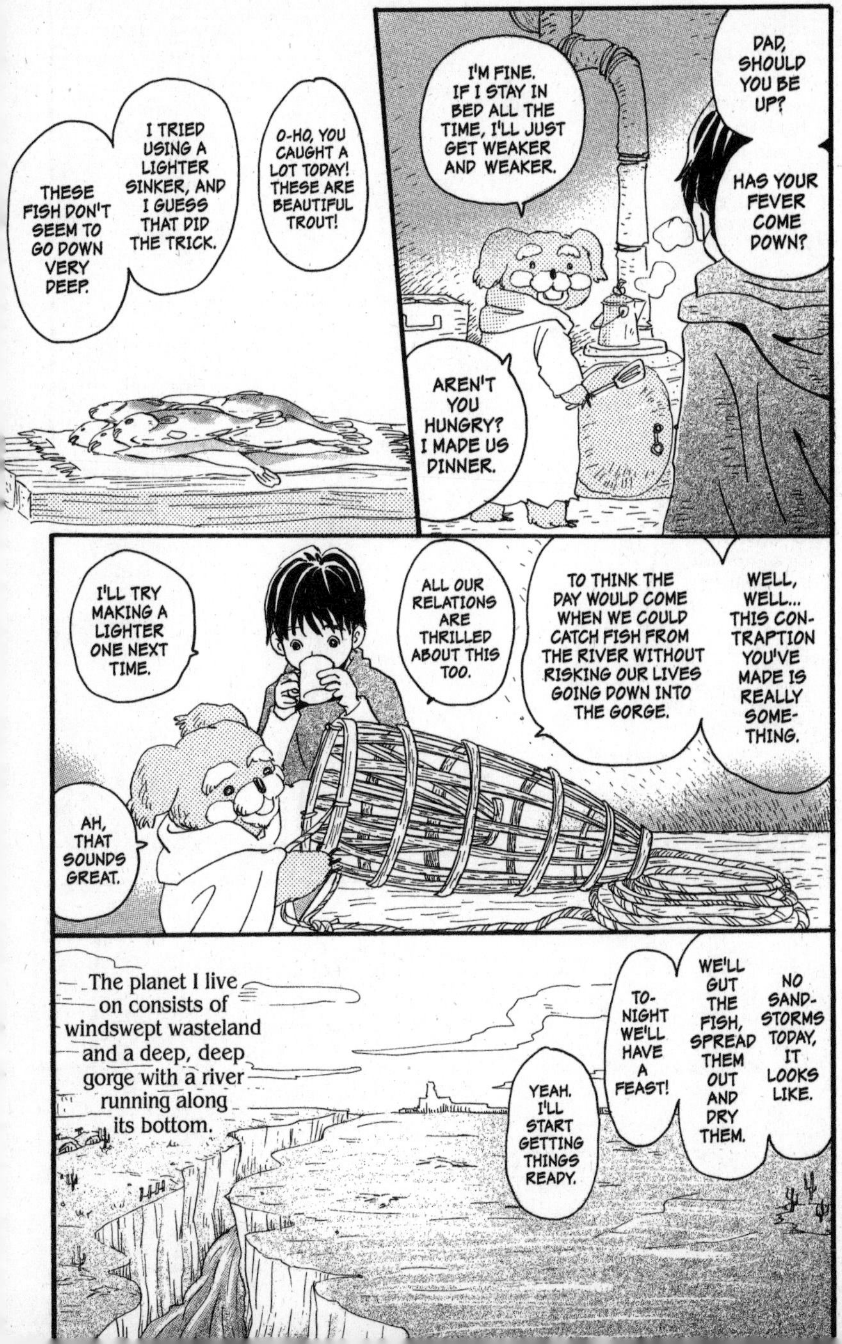
DAD, SHOULD YOU BE UP?
HAS YOUR FEVER COME DOWN?
I'M FINE. IF I STAY IN BED ALL THE TIME, I'LL JUST GET WEAKER AND WEAKER.
AREN'T YOU HUNGRY? I MADE US DINNER.
O-HO, YOU CAUGHT A LOT TODAY! THESE ARE BEAUTIFUL TROUT!
I TRIED USING A LIGHTER SINKER, AND I GUESS THAT DID THE TRICK.
THESE FISH DON'T SEEM TO GO DOWN VERY DEEP.
WELL, WELL... THIS CON-TRAPTION YOU'VE MADE IS REALLY SOME-THING.
TO THINK THE DAY WOULD COME WHEN WE COULD CATCH FISH FROM THE RIVER WITHOUT RISKING OUR LIVES GOING DOWN INTO THE GORGE.
ALL OUR RELATIONS ARE THRILLED ABOUT THIS TOO.
I'LL TRY MAKING A LIGHTER ONE NEXT TIME.
AH, THAT SOUNDS GREAT.
NO SAND-STORMS TODAY, IT LOOKS LIKE.
WE'LL GUT THE FISH, SPREAD THEM OUT AND DRY THEM.
TO-NIGHT WE'LL HAVE A FEAST!
YEAH. I'LL START GETTING THINGS READY.
The planet I live on consists of windswept wasteland and a deep, deep gorge with a river running along its bottom.

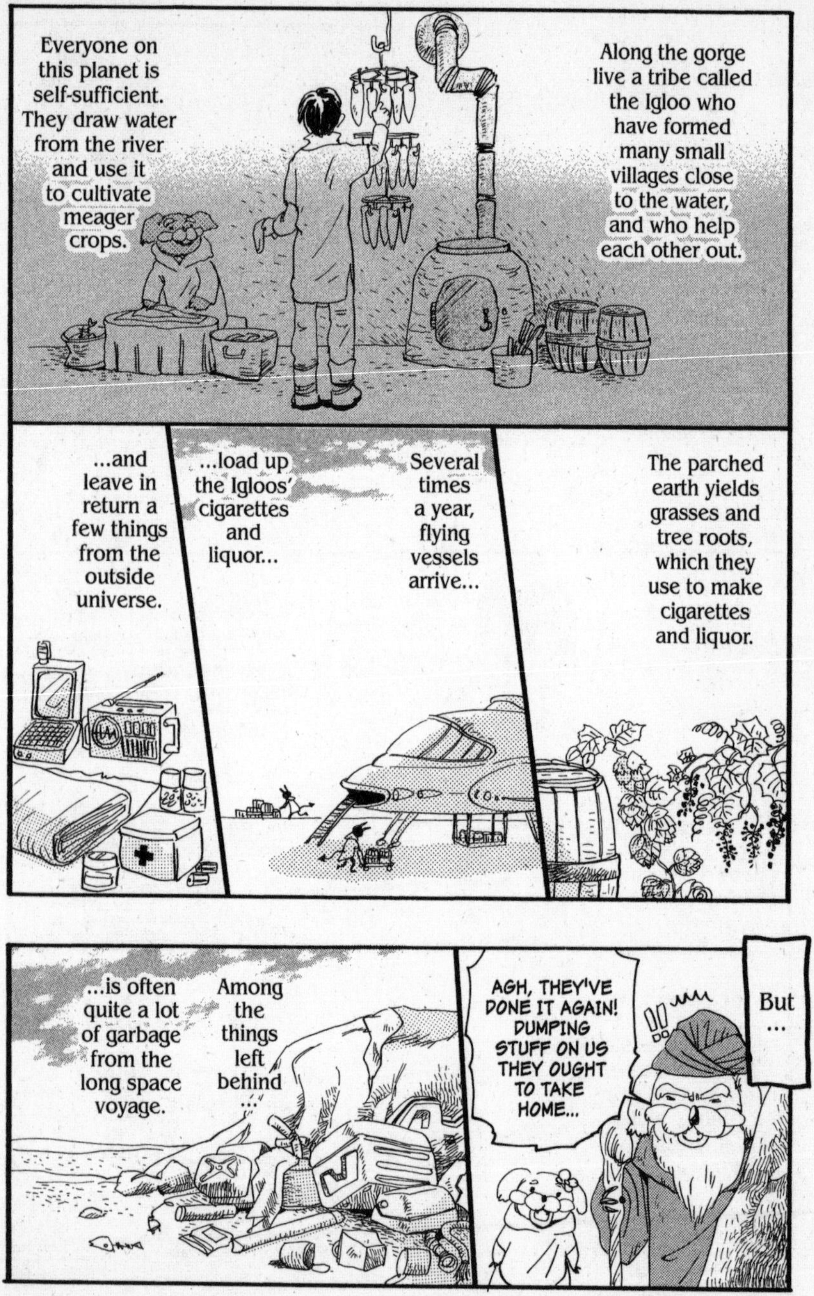
Along the gorge live a tribe called the Igloo who have formed many small villages close to the water, and who help each other out.
Everyone on this planet is self-sufficient. They draw water from the river and use it to cultivate meager crops.
The parched earth yields grasses and tree roots, which they use to make cigarettes and liquor.
Several times a year, flying vessels arrive...
...load up the Igloos' cigarettes and liquor...
...and leave in return a few things from the outside universe.
But ...
AGH, THEY'VE DONE IT AGAIN! DUMPING STUFF ON US THEY OUGHT TO TAKE HOME...
Among the things left behind ...
...is often quite a lot of garbage from the long space voyage.

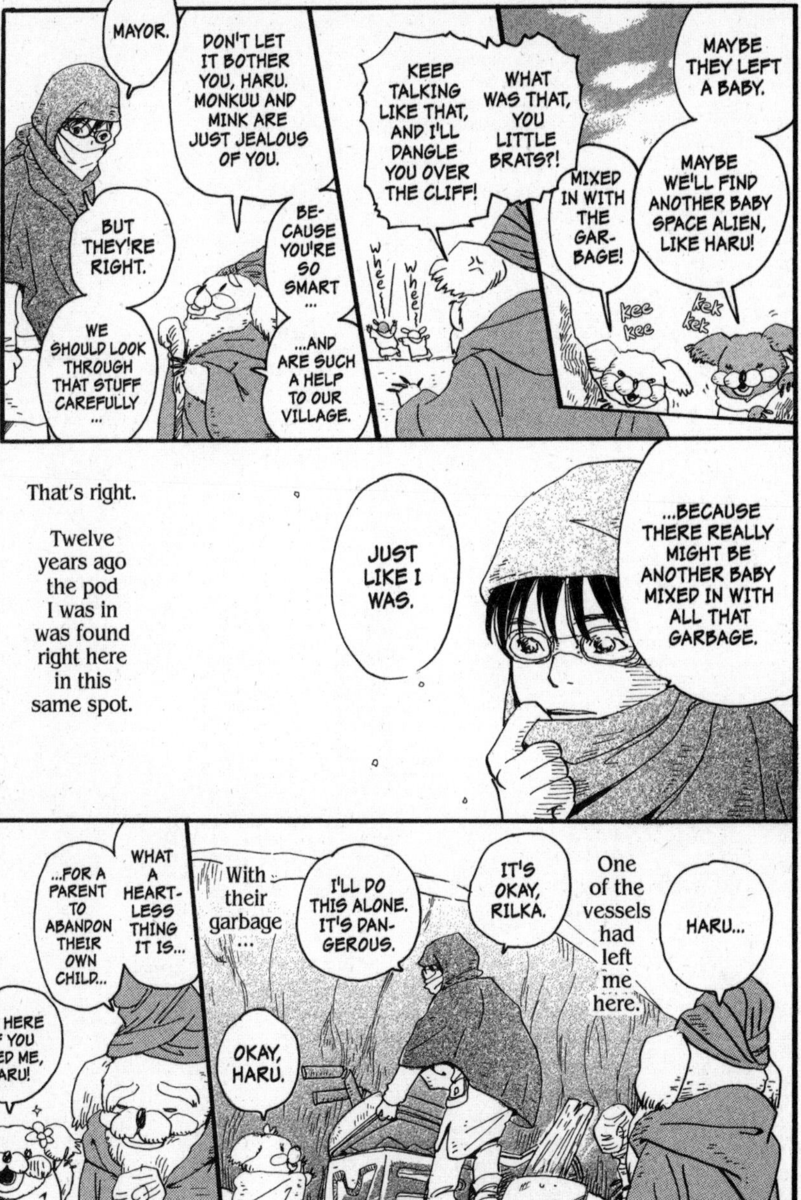
MAYBE THEY LEFT A BABY.
MAYBE WE'LL FIND ANOTHER BABY SPACE ALIEN, LIKE HARU!
MIXED IN WITH THE GARBAGE!
kek kek
kee kee
WHAT WAS THAT, YOU LITTLE BRATS?!
KEEP TALKING LIKE THAT, AND I'LL DANGLE YOU OVER THE CLIFF!
whee
whee
DON'T LET IT BOTHER YOU, HARU. MONKUU AND MINK ARE JUST JEALOUS OF YOU.
MAYOR.
BE-CAUSE YOU'RE SO SMART...
...AND ARE SUCH A HELP TO OUR VILLAGE.
BUT THEY'RE RIGHT.
WE SHOULD LOOK THROUGH THAT STUFF CAREFULLY...
...BECAUSE THERE REALLY MIGHT BE ANOTHER BABY MIXED IN WITH ALL THAT GARBAGE.
JUST LIKE I WAS.
That's right.
Twelve years ago the pod I was in was found right here in this same spot.
HARU...
One of the vessels had left me here.
IT'S OKAY, RILKA.
I'LL DO THIS ALONE. IT'S DAN-GEROUS.
With their garbage...
OKAY, HARU.
WHAT A HEART-LESS THING IT IS...
...FOR A PARENT TO ABANDON THEIR OWN CHILD...
I'M HERE IF YOU NEED ME, HARU!

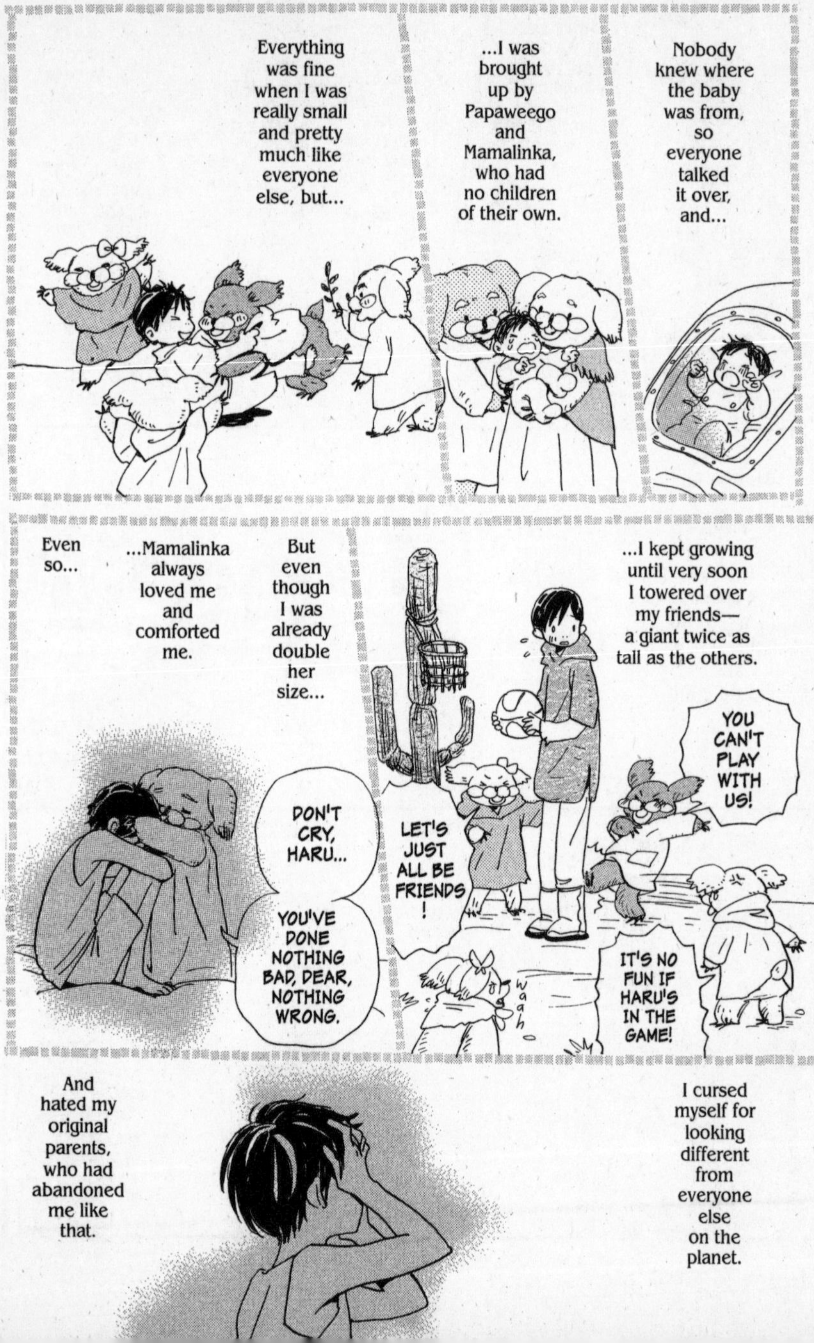
Nobody knew where the baby was from, so everyone talked it over, and...
...I was brought up by Papaweego and Mamalinka, who had no children of their own.
Everything was fine when I was really small and pretty much like everyone else, but...
...I kept growing until very soon I towered over my friends— a giant twice as tall as the others.
YOU CAN'T PLAY WITH US!
LET'S JUST ALL BE FRIENDS!
IT'S NO FUN IF HARU'S IN THE GAME!
Waah
But even though I was already double her size...
...Mamalinka always loved me and comforted me.
Even so...
DON'T CRY, HARU...
YOU'VE DONE NOTHING BAD, DEAR, NOTHING WRONG.
I cursed myself for looking different from everyone else on the planet.
And hated my original parents, who had abandoned me like that.

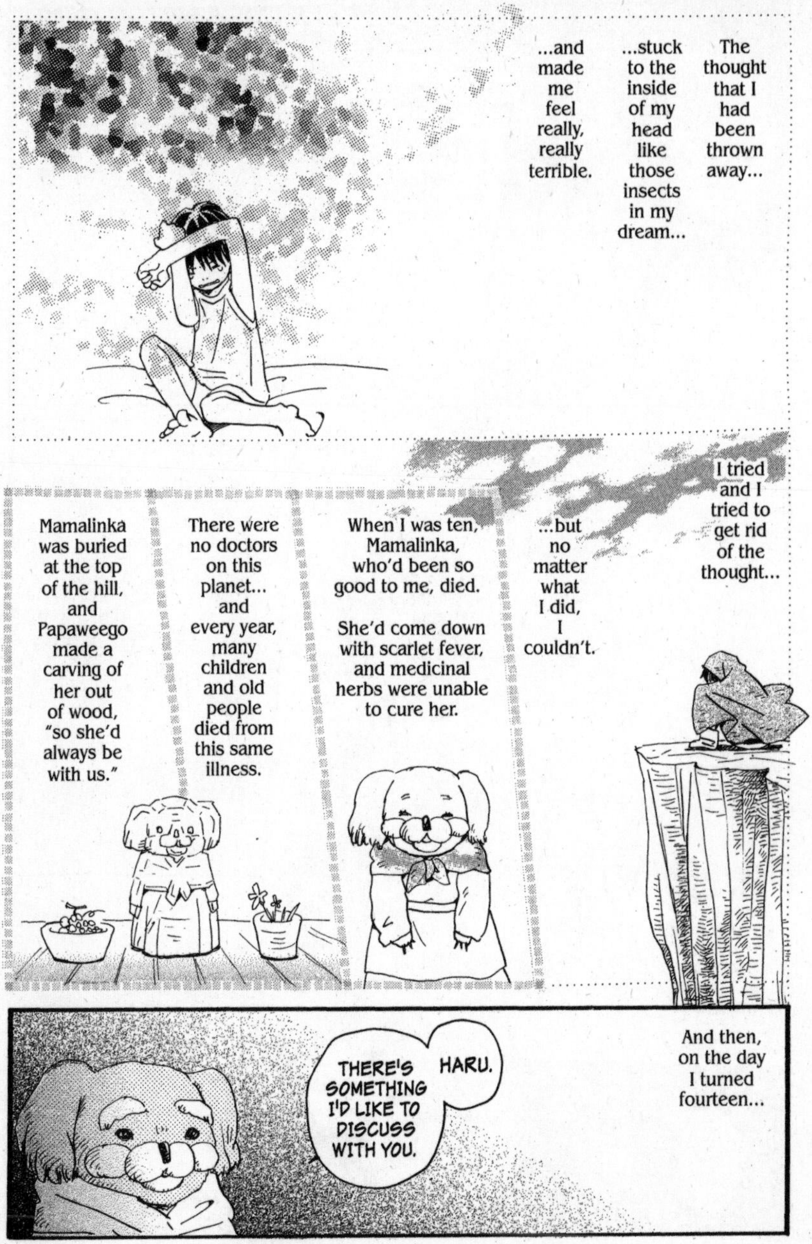
The thought that I had been thrown away...
...stuck to the inside of my head like those insects in my dream...
...and made me feel really, really terrible.
I tried and I tried to get rid of the thought...
...but no matter what I did, I couldn't.
When I was ten, Mamalinka, who'd been so good to me, died.
She'd come down with scarlet fever, and medicinal herbs were unable to cure her.
There were no doctors on this planet... and every year, many children and old people died from this same illness.
Mamalinka was buried at the top of the hill, and Papaweego made a carving of her out of wood, "so she'd always be with us."
And then, on the day I turned fourteen...
HARU.
THERE'S SOMETHING I'D LIKE TO DISCUSS WITH YOU.

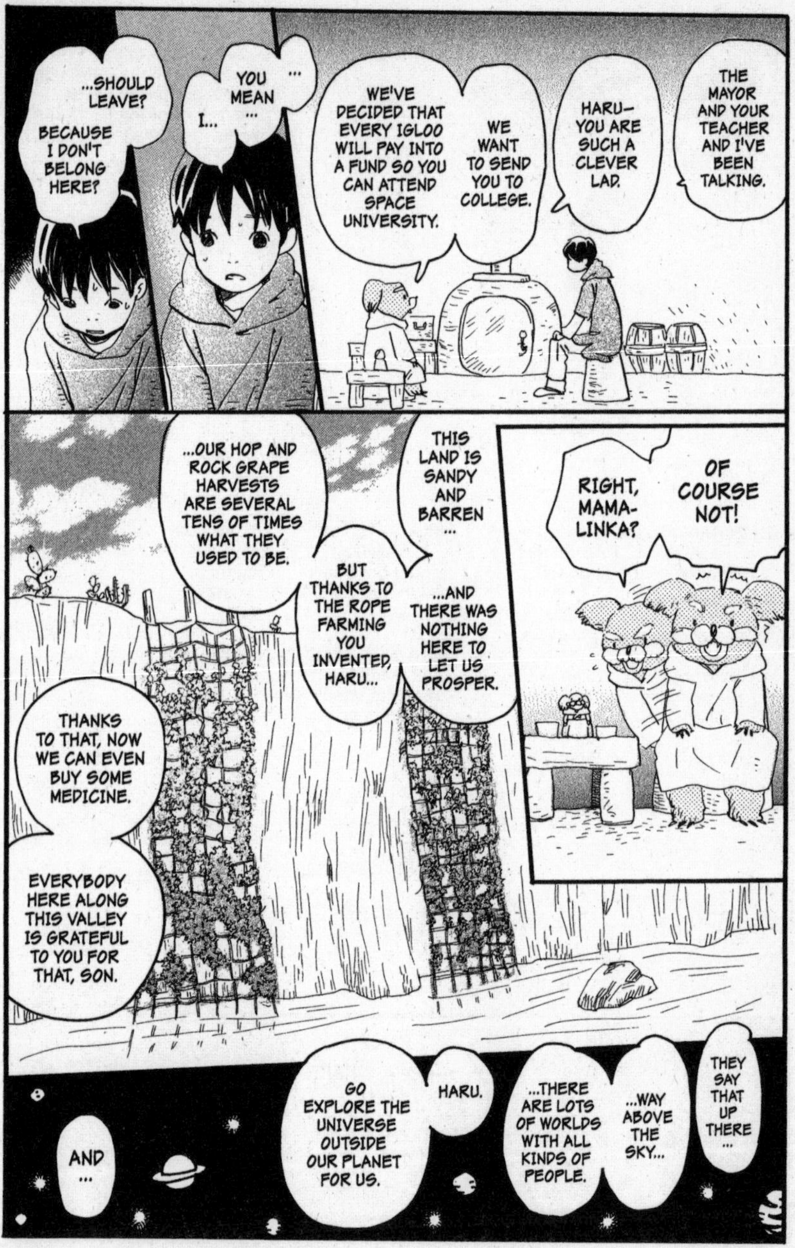
THE MAYOR AND YOUR TEACHER AND I'VE BEEN TALKING.
HARU— YOU ARE SUCH A CLEVER LAD.
WE WANT TO SEND YOU TO COLLEGE.
WE'VE DECIDED THAT EVERY IGLOO WILL PAY INTO A FUND SO YOU CAN ATTEND SPACE UNIVERSITY.
...
YOU MEAN ...
I...
...SHOULD LEAVE?
BECAUSE I DON'T BELONG HERE?
OF COURSE NOT!
RIGHT, MAMA-LINKA?
THIS LAND IS SANDY AND BARREN ...
...AND THERE WAS NOTHING HERE TO LET US PROSPER.
BUT THANKS TO THE ROPE FARMING YOU INVENTED, HARU...
...OUR HOP AND ROCK GRAPE HARVESTS ARE SEVERAL TENS OF TIMES WHAT THEY USED TO BE.
THANKS TO THAT, NOW WE CAN EVEN BUY SOME MEDICINE.
EVERYBODY HERE ALONG THIS VALLEY IS GRATEFUL TO YOU FOR THAT, SON.
THEY SAY THAT UP THERE ...
...WAY ABOVE THE SKY...
...THERE ARE LOTS OF WORLDS WITH ALL KINDS OF PEOPLE.
HARU.
GO EXPLORE THE UNIVERSE OUTSIDE OUR PLANET FOR US.
AND ...

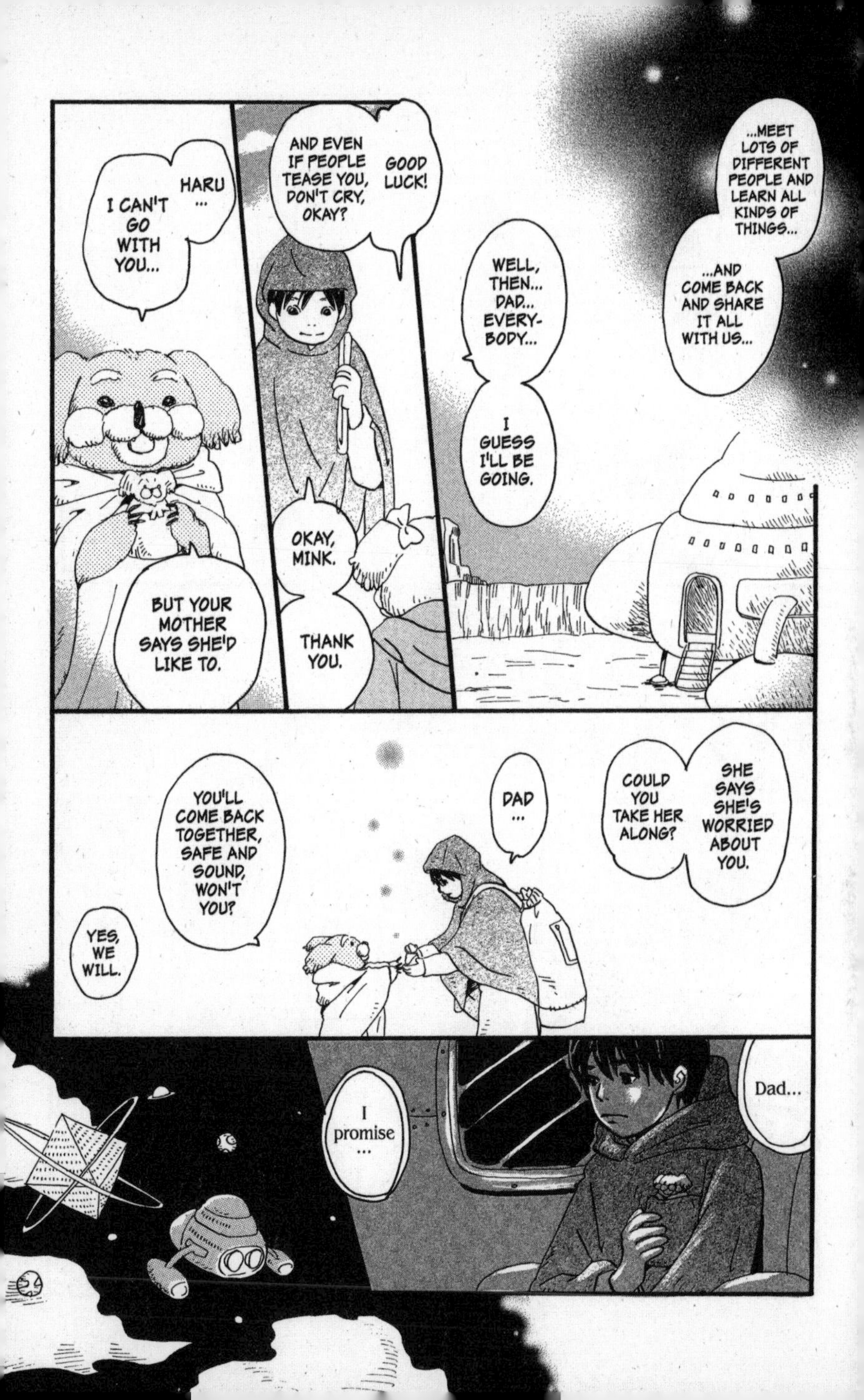
...MEET LOTS OF DIFFERENT PEOPLE AND LEARN ALL KINDS OF THINGS...
...AND COME BACK AND SHARE IT ALL WITH US...
WELL, THEN... DAD... EVERY-BODY...
I GUESS I'LL BE GOING.
GOOD LUCK!
AND EVEN IF PEOPLE TEASE YOU, DON'T CRY, OKAY?
OKAY, MINK.
THANK YOU.
HARU...
I CAN'T GO WITH YOU...
BUT YOUR MOTHER SAYS SHE'D LIKE TO.
SHE SAYS SHE'S WORRIED ABOUT YOU.
COULD YOU TAKE HER ALONG?
DAD...
YOU'LL COME BACK TOGETHER, SAFE AND SOUND, WON'T YOU?
YES, WE WILL.
Dad...
I promise...

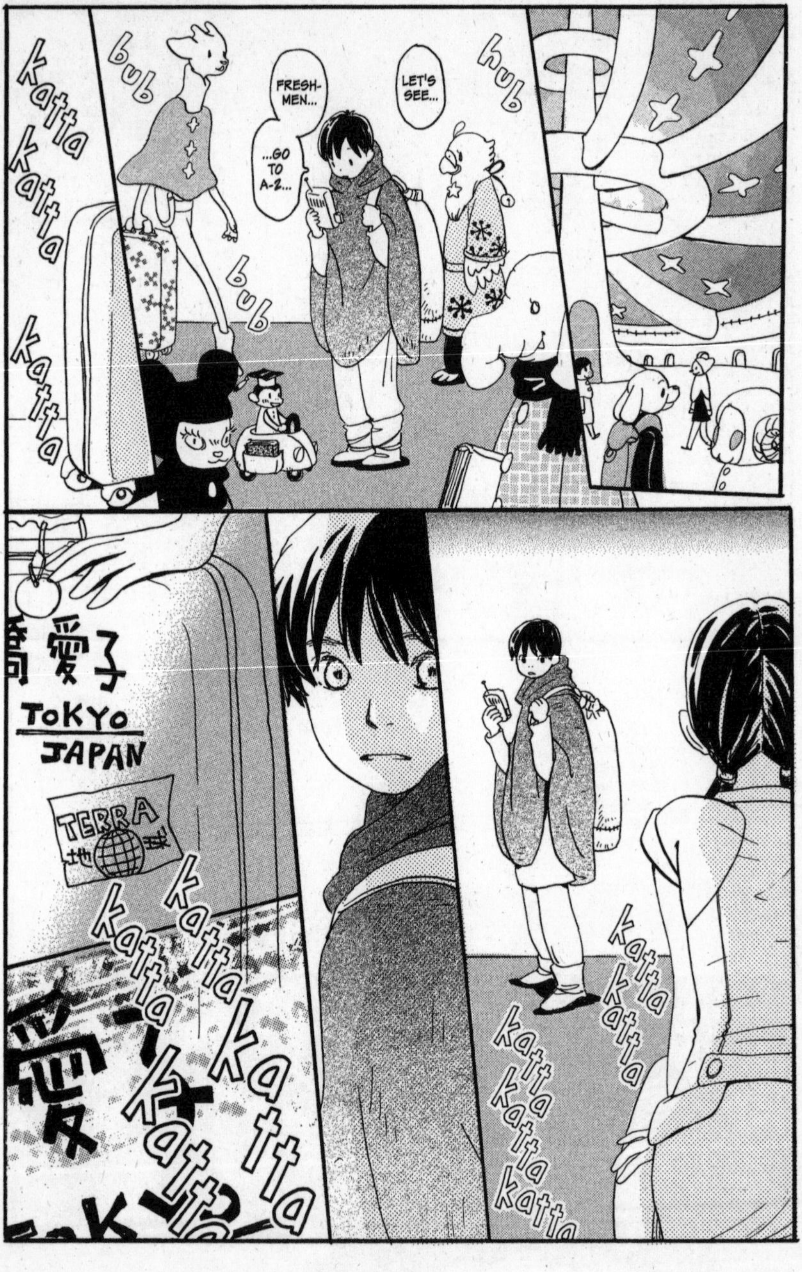
huh
LET'S SEE...
FRESH-MEN...
...GO TO A-2...
bub
bub
katta katta
katta
katta katta
katta katta
katta
katta
愛子
TOKYO
JAPAN
TERRA
地球
katta
katta
katta
ka tta

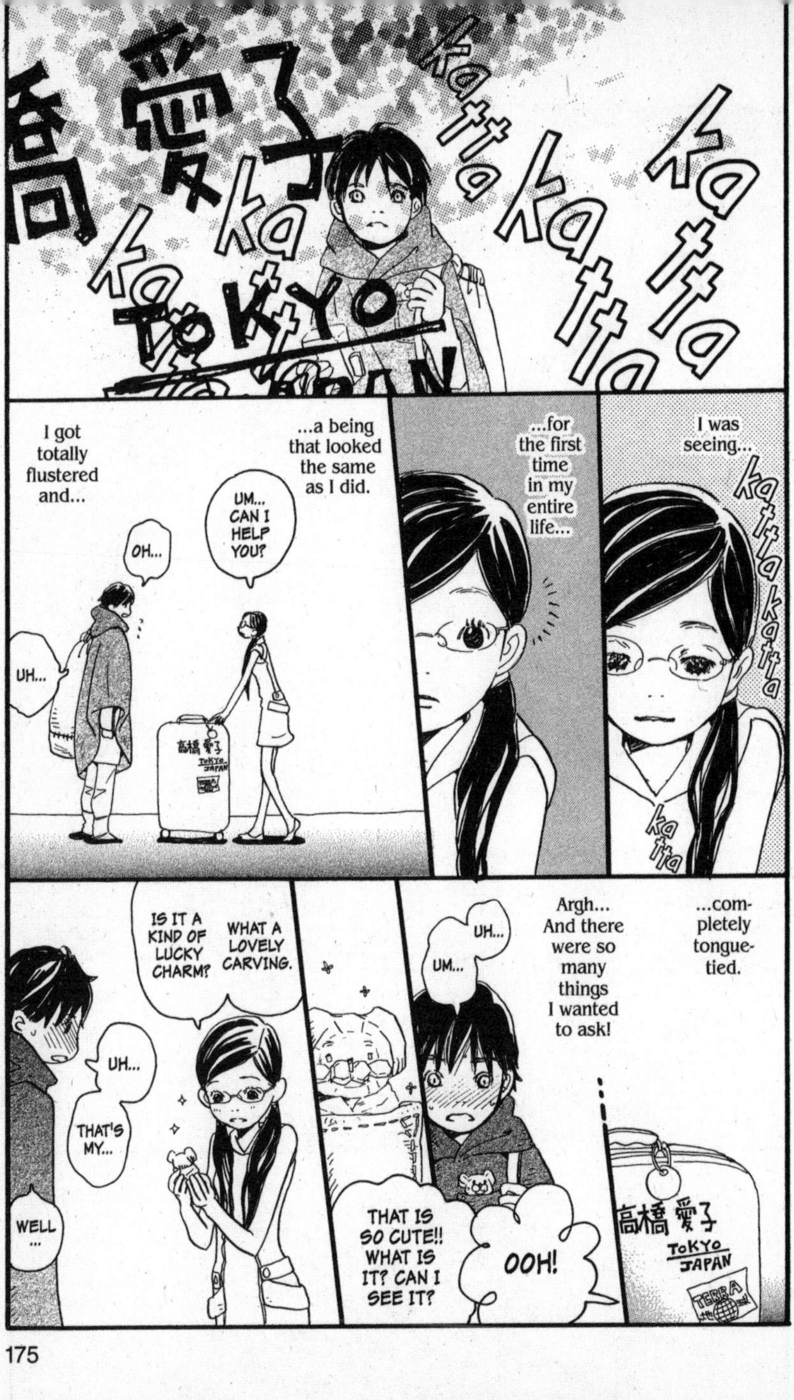
ka tta ka tta
ka tta ka tta
I was seeing...
ka tta ka tta ka tta
ka tta
...for the first time in my entire life...
...a being that looked the same as I did.
UM... CAN I HELP YOU?
OH...
I got totally flustered and...
UH...
高橋 愛子
TOKYO JAPAN
...completely tongue-tied.
高橋 愛子
TOKYO JAPAN
TERRA
Argh... And there were so many things I wanted to ask!
UH...
UM...
OOH!
THAT IS SO CUTE!! WHAT IS IT? CAN I SEE IT?
WHAT A LOVELY CARVING.
IS IT A KIND OF LUCKY CHARM?
UH...
THAT'S MY...
WELL...

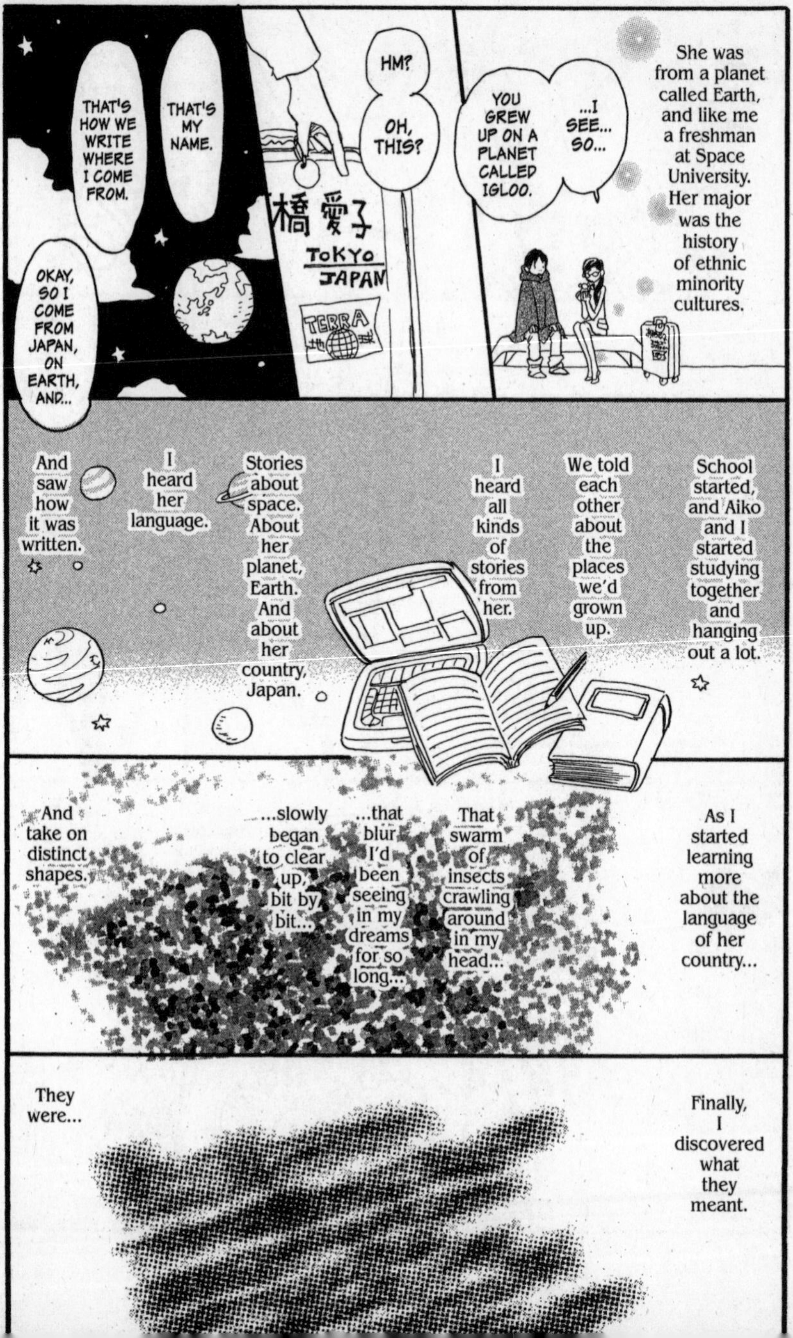
She was from a planet called Earth, and like me a freshman at Space University. Her major was the history of ethnic minority cultures.
...I SEE... SO...
YOU GREW UP ON A PLANET CALLED IGLOO.
HM?
OH, THIS?
橋愛子
TOKYO JAPAN
TERRA
地球
THAT'S MY NAME.
THAT'S HOW WE WRITE WHERE I COME FROM.
OKAY, SO I COME FROM JAPAN, ON EARTH, AND...
School started, and Aiko and I started studying together and hanging out a lot.
We told each other about the places we'd grown up.
I heard all kinds of stories from her.
Stories about space. About her planet, Earth. And about her country, Japan.
I heard her language.
And saw how it was written.
As I started learning more about the language of her country...
That swarm of insects crawling around in my head...
...that blur I'd been seeing in my dreams for so long...
...slowly began to clear up, bit by bit...
And take on distinct shapes.
Finally, I discovered what they meant.
They were...

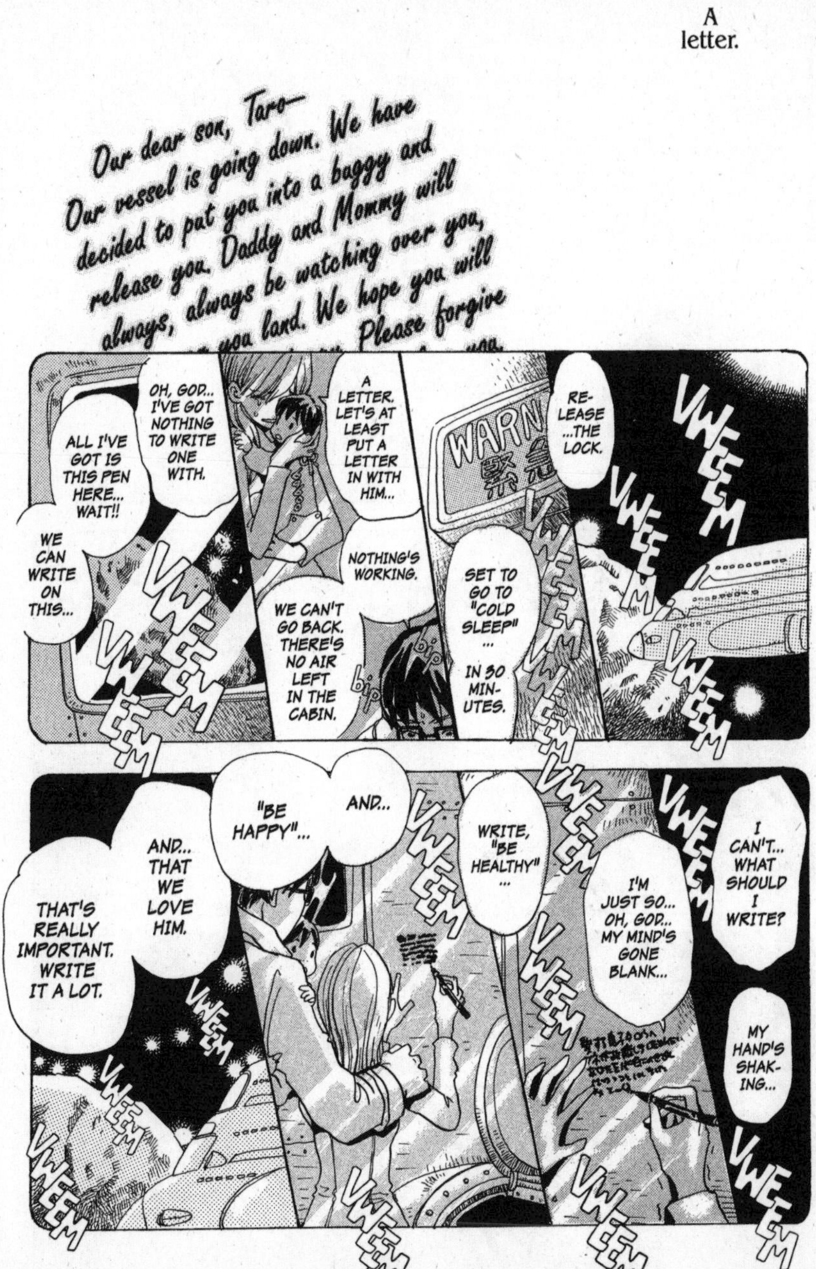

A letter.
Our dear son, Taro—
Our vessel is going down. We have
decided to put you into a baggy and
release you. Daddy and Mommy will
always, always be watching over you,
you land. We hope you will
Please forgive
RE-LEASE ...THE LOCK.
VWEEEM
VWEEM
VWEEM
SET TO GO TO "COLD SLEEP" ...
IN 30 MINUTES.
VWEEM
A LETTER. LET'S AT LEAST PUT A LETTER IN WITH HIM...
NOTHING'S WORKING.
WE CAN'T GO BACK. THERE'S NO AIR LEFT IN THE CABIN.
bip
bip
OH, GOD... I'VE GOT NOTHING TO WRITE ONE WITH.
ALL I'VE GOT IS THIS PEN HERE... WAIT!!
WE CAN WRITE ON THIS...
VWEEM
VWEEM
VWEEM
I CAN'T... WHAT SHOULD I WRITE?
MY HAND'S SHAKING...
VWEEM
I'M JUST SO... OH, GOD... MY MIND'S GONE BLANK...
VWEEM
VWEEM
VWEEM
WRITE, "BE HEALTHY" ...
AND...
"BE HAPPY"...
VWEEM
AND... THAT WE LOVE HIM.
THAT'S REALLY IMPORTANT. WRITE IT A LOT.
VWEEM
VWEEM
VWEEM
VWEEM

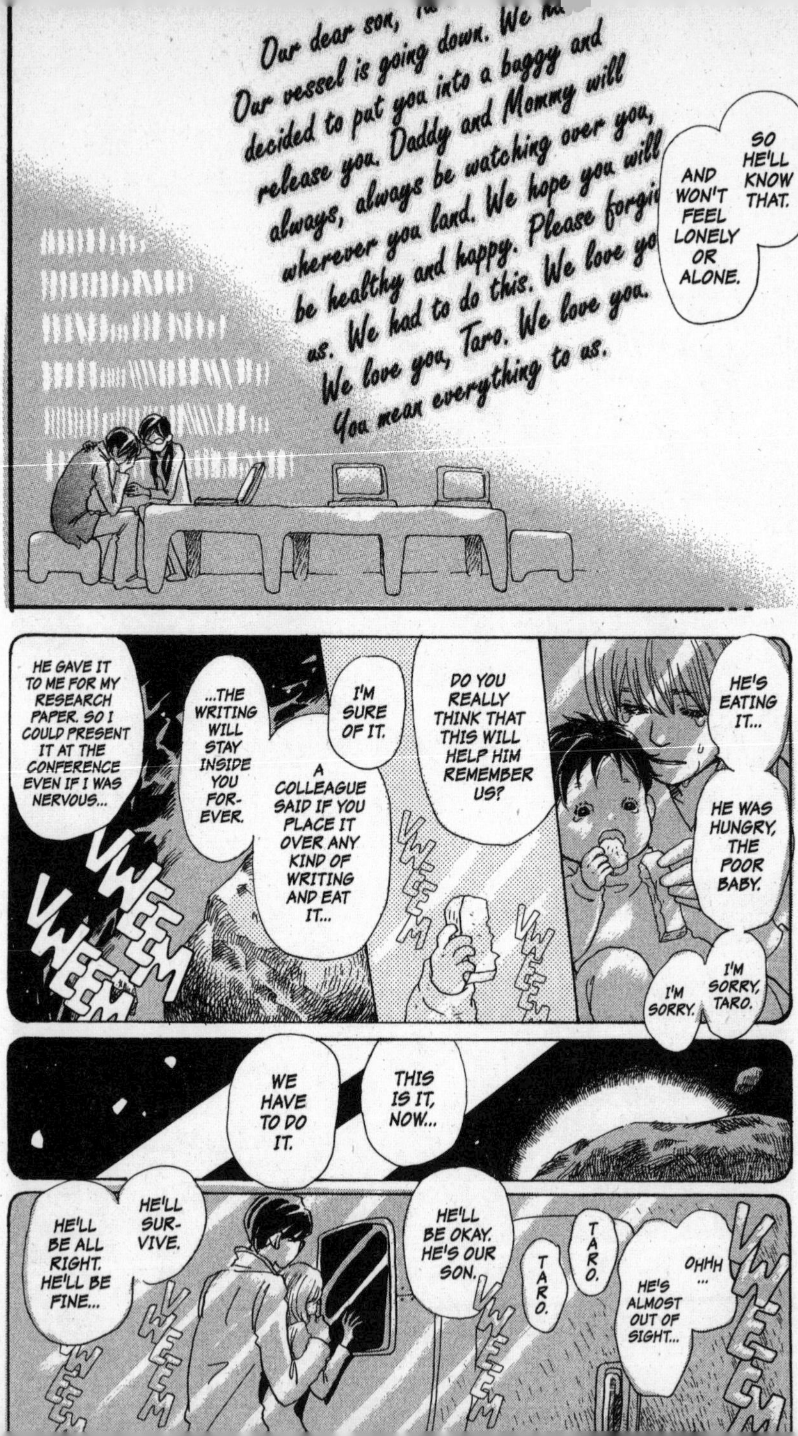
Our dear son,
Our vessel is going down. We
decided to put you into a baggy and
release you. Daddy and Mommy will
always, always be watching over you,
wherever you land. We hope you will
be healthy and happy. Please forgi
us. We had to do this. We love yo
We love you, Taro. We love you.
You mean everything to us.
SO HE'LL KNOW THAT.
AND WON'T FEEL LONELY OR ALONE.
HE'S EATING IT...
HE WAS HUNGRY, THE POOR BABY.
I'M SORRY, TARO.
I'M SORRY.
DO YOU REALLY THINK THAT THIS WILL HELP HIM REMEMBER US?
VWEEM
VWEEM
I'M SURE OF IT.
A COLLEAGUE SAID IF YOU PLACE IT OVER ANY KIND OF WRITING AND EAT IT...
...THE WRITING WILL STAY INSIDE YOU FOR-EVER.
HE GAVE IT TO ME FOR MY RESEARCH PAPER. SO I COULD PRESENT IT AT THE CONFERENCE EVEN IF I WAS NERVOUS...
VWEEM
VWEEM
VWEEM
THIS IS IT, NOW...
WE HAVE TO DO IT.
VWEEM
OHHH...
HE'S ALMOST OUT OF SIGHT...
TARO.
TARO.
HE'LL BE OKAY. HE'S OUR SON.
VWEEM
HE'LL SUR-VIVE.
HE'LL BE ALL RIGHT. HE'LL BE FINE...
VWEEM
VWEEM

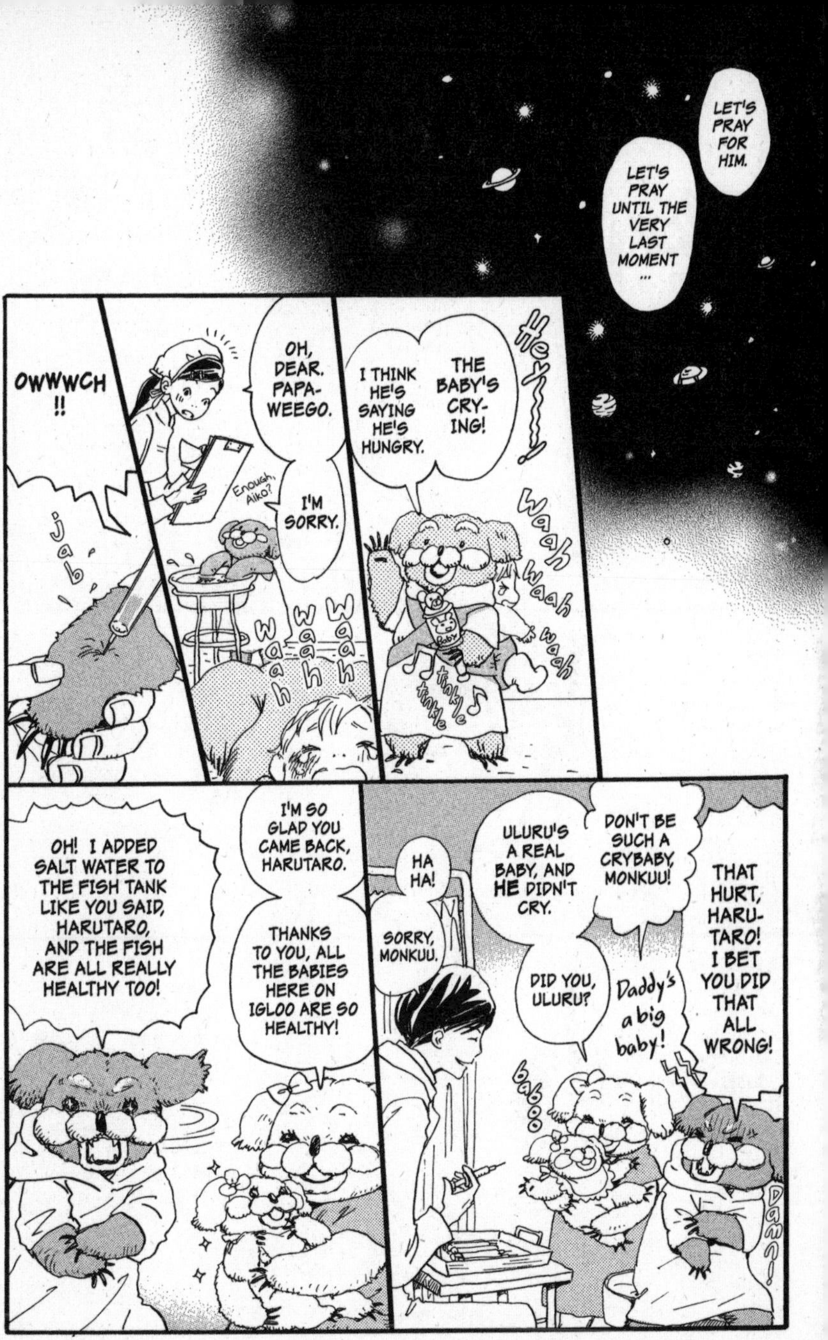
LET'S PRAY FOR HIM.
LET'S PRAY UNTIL THE VERY LAST MOMENT ...
Hey~!
THE BABY'S CRY-ING!
I THINK HE'S SAYING HE'S HUNGRY.
Waah waah waah
tinkle tinkle
OH, DEAR. PAPA-WEEGO.
I'M SORRY.
Enough, Aiko?
Waah Waah Waah
OWWWCH !!
jab
THAT HURT, HARU-TARO! I BET YOU DID THAT ALL WRONG!
DON'T BE SUCH A CRYBABY, MONKUU!
ULURU'S A REAL BABY, AND HE DIDN'T CRY.
DID YOU, ULURU?
Daddy's a big baby!
baboo
HA HA!
SORRY, MONKUU.
Damn!
I'M SO GLAD YOU CAME BACK, HARUTARO.
THANKS TO YOU, ALL THE BABIES HERE ON IGLOO ARE SO HEALTHY!
OH! I ADDED SALT WATER TO THE FISH TANK LIKE YOU SAID, HARUTARO, AND THE FISH ARE ALL REALLY HEALTHY TOO!

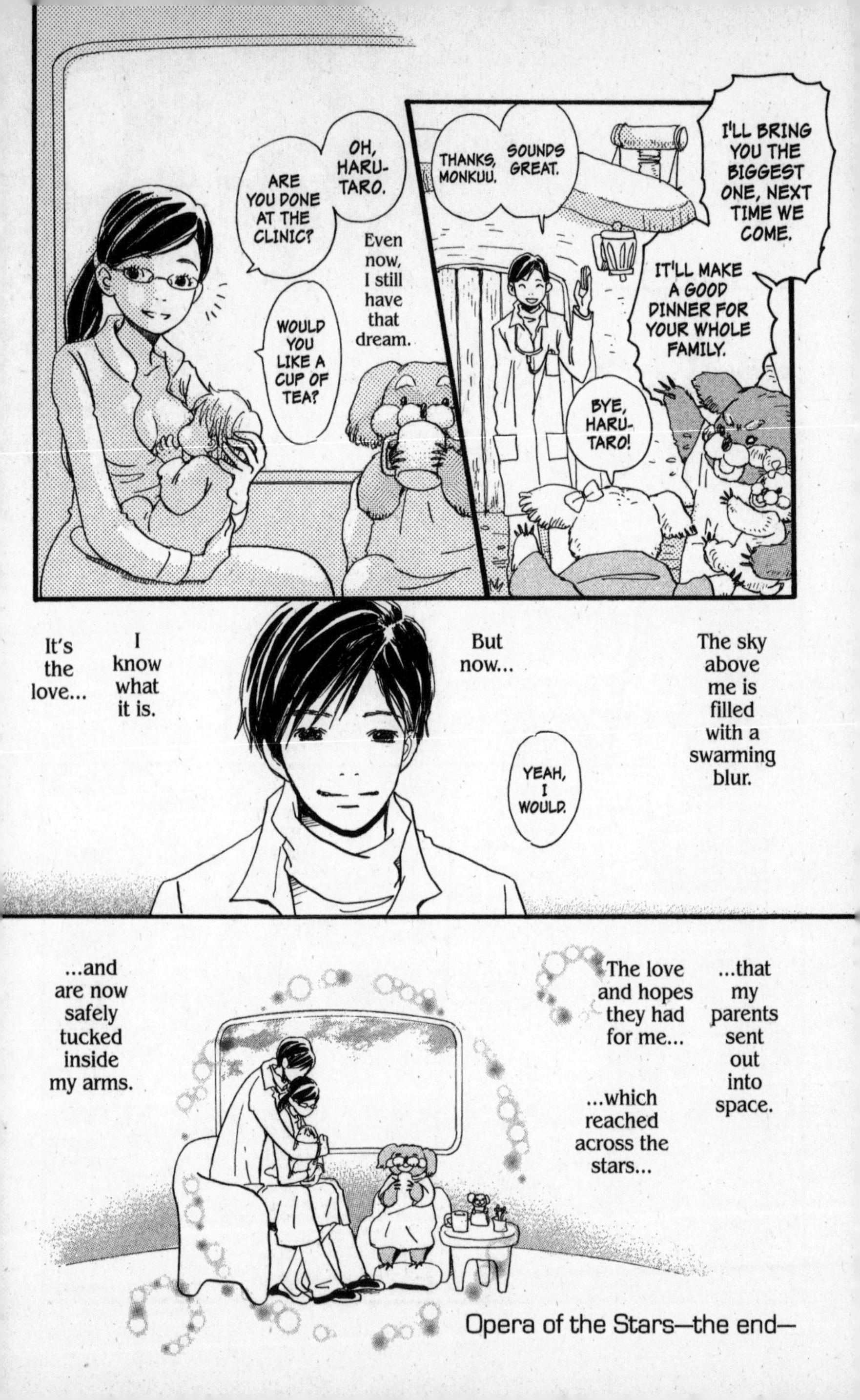
I'LL BRING YOU THE BIGGEST ONE, NEXT TIME WE COME.
IT'LL MAKE A GOOD DINNER FOR YOUR WHOLE FAMILY.
SOUNDS GREAT.
THANKS, MONKUU.
BYE, HARU-TARO!
OH, HARU-TARO.
ARE YOU DONE AT THE CLINIC?
Even now, I still have that dream.
WOULD YOU LIKE A CUP OF TEA?
The sky above me is filled with a swarming blur.
YEAH, I WOULD.
But now...
I know what it is.
It's the love...
...that my parents sent out into space.
The love and hopes they had for me...
...which reached across the stars...
...and are now safely tucked inside my arms.
Opera of the Stars—the end—

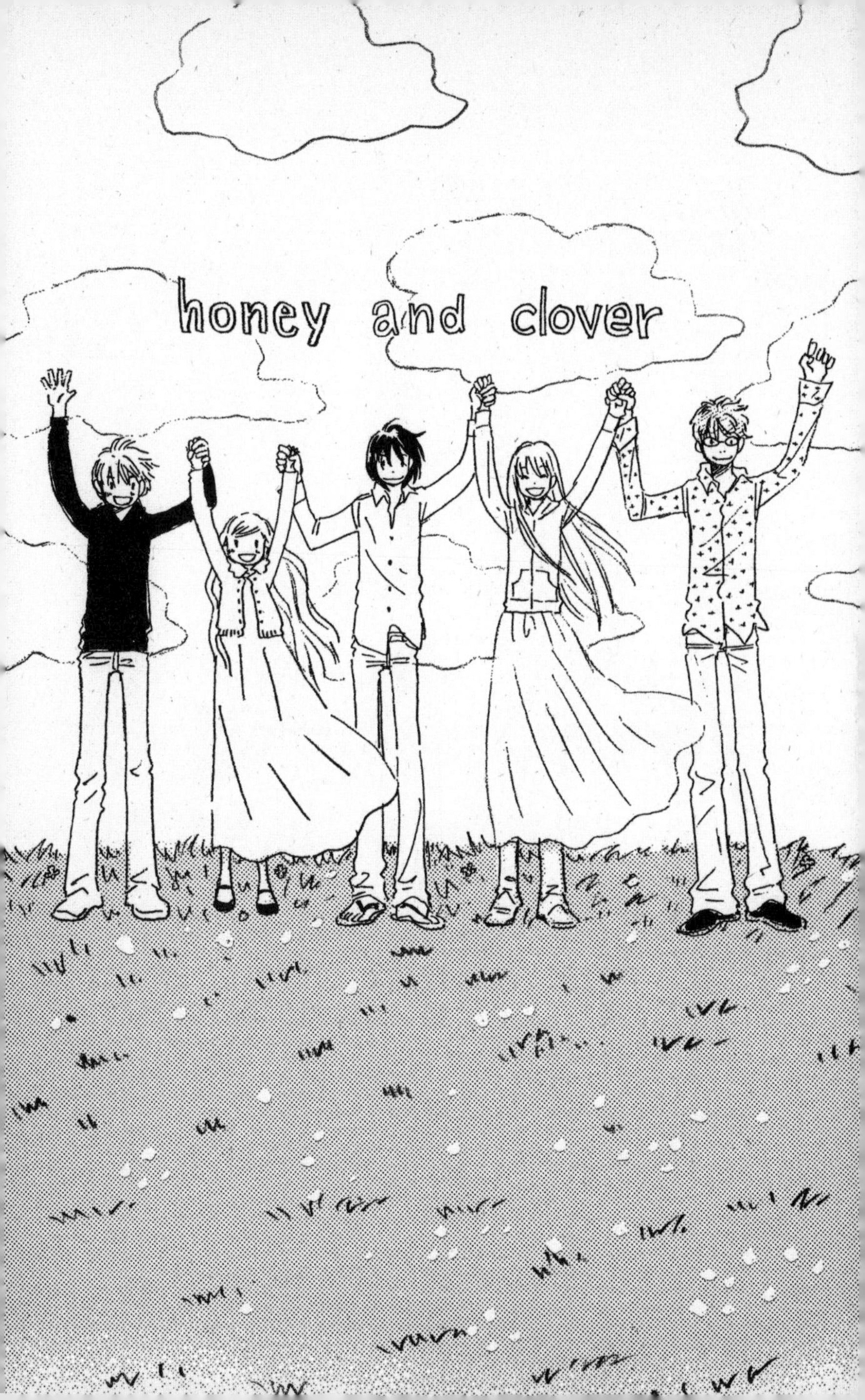
honey and clover

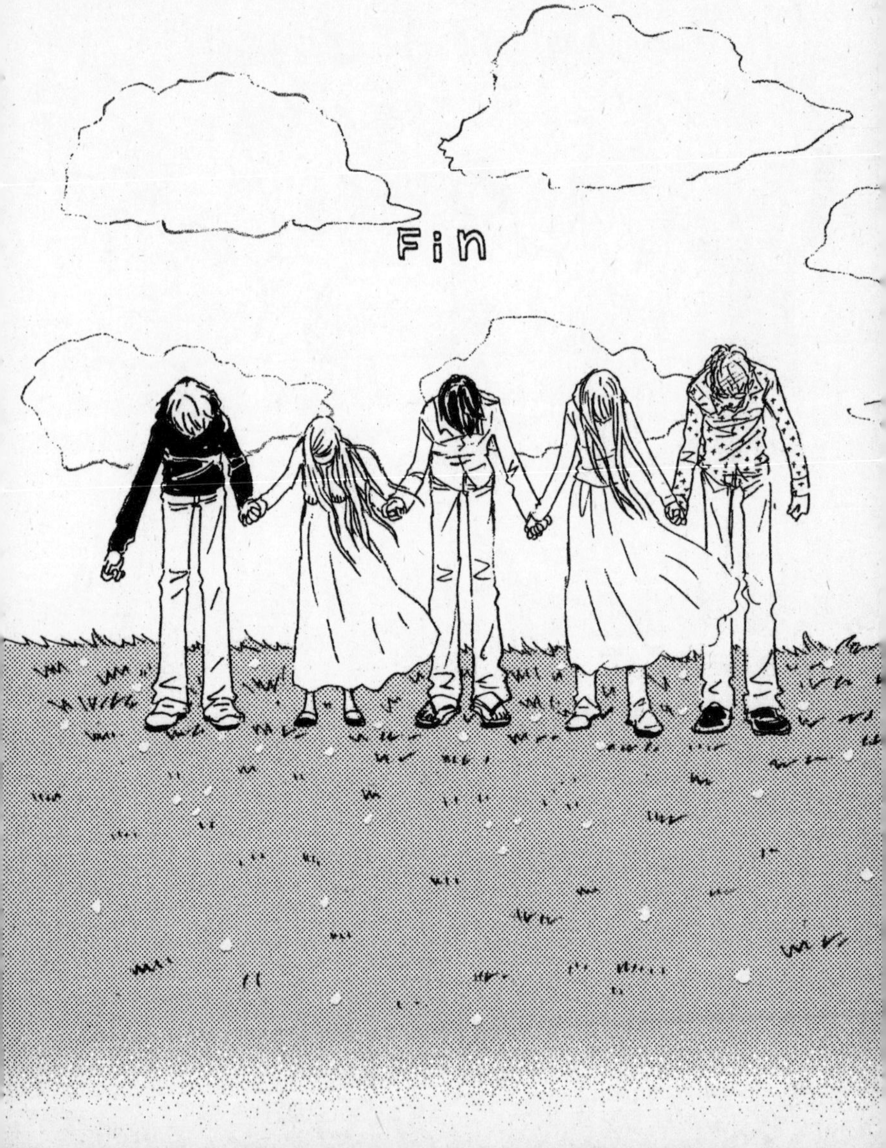
Fin

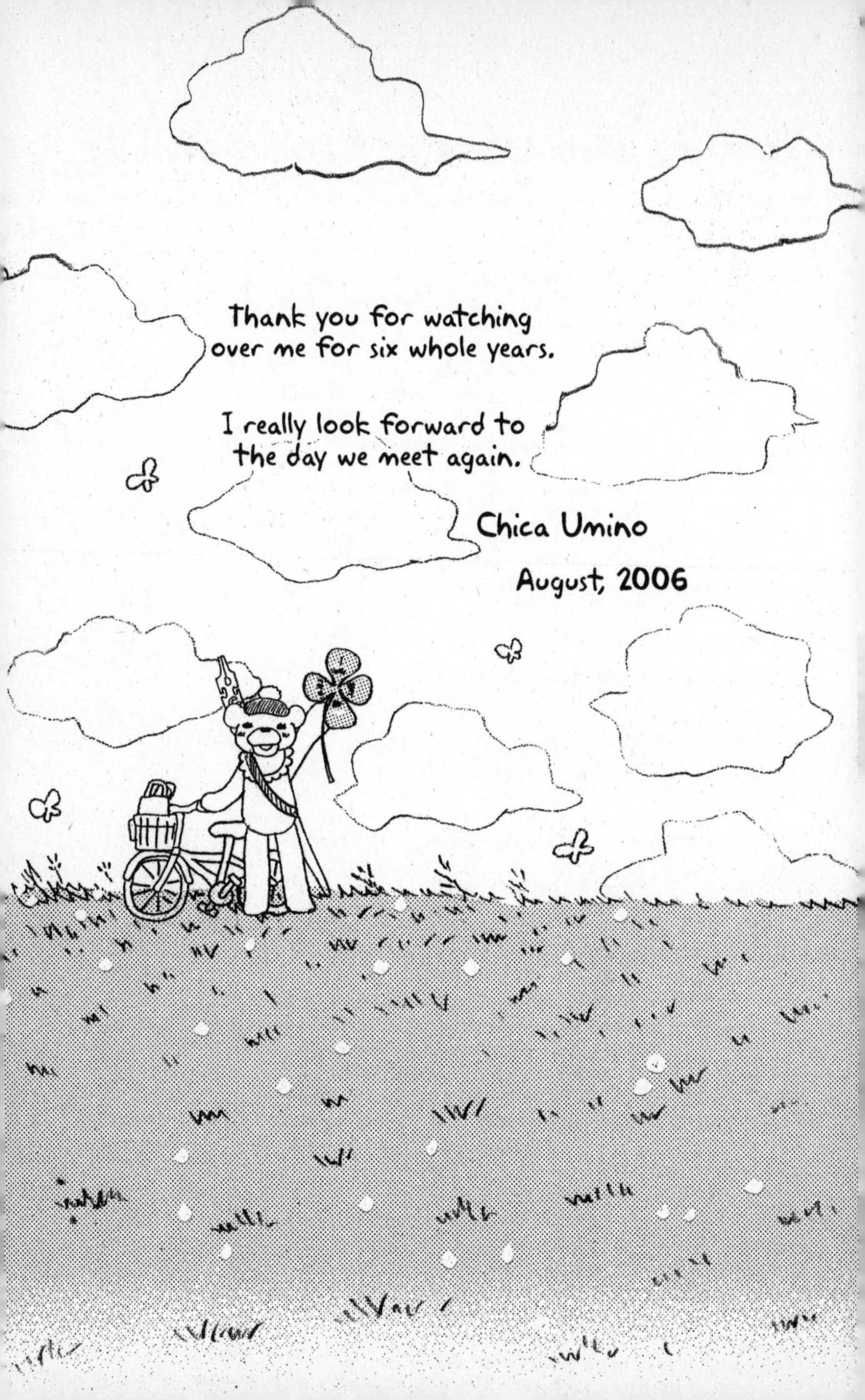
Thank you for watching
over me for six whole years.
I really look forward to
the day we meet again.
Chica Umino
August, 2006

Honey and Clover Study Guide

Page 60, panel 2: Seal
A signature seal is a stamp used to sign official documents.

Page 88, panel 4: Morioka
A city in Iwate Prefecture, in Northern Honshu.

Page 94, panel 3: Manju, anmitsu, mitsumame, yokan
Manju are sweet bean-filled buns; *anmitsu* is a dessert made with sweetened cubes of agar jelly and topped with sweet syrup, sweet red bean paste, and fruit; *mitsumame* is similar to anmitsu but without the bean paste; *yokan* is a firm jellied dessert made from agar, sugar, and a flavoring such as red bean paste, chestnut, or sweet potato.

Page 109, panel 1: Arigatou
Japanese for "thanks." Also rendered as *arigato*.

Page 112, panel 1: Kenji Miyazawa
Kenji Miyazawa was beloved Japanese children's author and poet from the early 20th century (1896–1933). His novel *Milky Way Railroad*, among other titles, has been translated into English.

Page 131, panel 6: Hakata
A major district in Fukuoka City, which is the capital of Fukuoka Prefecture, located on the northwestern coast of Kyushu.

Page 132, panel 1: Chikae, Hakata, Chanko
Chikae is a restaurant and shop famous for its spicy-hot cod roe (*mentaiko*), a Fukuoka specialty. The Nagahama area of the Hakata district is renowned nationwide for its tonkotsu ramen. *Chanko-nabe* is a stew eaten by sumo wrestlers.

Page 150, panel 2: Gokon
Something like a group blind date.

Page 152, panel 2: Motsu, hokke, shishamo, eihire, mozuku
Motsu are innards; *hokke* and *shishamo* are types of fish; *eihire* is the dried fin of a ray; and *mozuku* is a type of seaweed served in vinegar.

Page 156, panel 3: Girolamo Panzetta
An Italian who started out on Japanese television on an educational Italian language show. He is now a well-known celebrity considered to be very stylish in a sharp, Italian way.

Page 161, panel 5: Friendship is beautiful
A line of poetry by Saneatsu Mushanokoji, a poet, novelist, artist, playwright and philosopher (1885–1976).

Page 162, panel 1: Doraemon
The titular character of a beloved manga series by Fujiko F Fujio. Doraemon is a robot cat that travels back in time to help young Nobita Nobi. Doraemon's pouch is actually a four-dimensional pocket from which he can produce all kinds of useful and interesting gadgets.

Page 178, panel 2: Memory bread
The original Dorameon gadget was called *anki pan* in Japanese. When the bread is placed over a page of writing the text is imprinted onto the bread. When you eat the bread, the words enter your brain.

Umino Bear, made for me by Yûji Ueda, who played Morita in the anime!! Too, too wonderful!!

I'd like to express my heartfelt gratitude to all the dear friends I made through *Honey and Clover*, and also to all the people who watched over us during this series. I was only able to finish drawing this story to the very end because of all my readers. Thank you so much for sticking with me over six long years. I'll keep working as a manga artist, and I hope you'll continue to look out for me.

-Chica Umino

Chica Umino was born in Tokyo and started out as a product designer and illustrator. Her beloved *Honey and Clover* debuted in 2000 and received the Kodansha Manga Award in 2003. *Honey and Clover* was also nominated for the Tezuka Culture Prize and an award from the Japan Media Arts Festival. The *Honey and Clover* movie is available in the U.S. from VIZ Pictures, and the anime is available in the U.S. from VIZ Media.

HONEY AND CLOVER
VOL. 10
Shojo Beat Edition

STORY AND ART BY CHICA UMINO

English Translation & Adaptation/Akemi Wegmuller
Touch-up Art & Lettering/Sabrina Heep
Design/Yukiko Whitley
Editor/Pancha Diaz

VP, Production/Alvin Lu
VP, Sales & Product Marketing/Gonzalo Ferreyra
VP, Creative/Linda Espinosa
Publisher/Hyoe Narita

Printed in Canada

Published by VIZ Media, LLC
P.O. Box 77010
San Francisco, CA 94107

10 9 8 7 6 5 4 3 2 1
First printing, May 2010

www.viz.com

www.shojobeat.com

RATED T+ FOR OLDER TEEN

PARENTAL ADVISORY
HONEY AND CLOVER is rated T+ for Older Teen and is recommended for ages 16 and up. This volume contains adult situations.

ratings.viz.com